METHODS FOR THE STUDY OF
MARINE BENTHOS

Methods for the Study of Marine Benthos

Edited by
N. A. HOLME
and
A. D. McINTYRE

RXTSA

INTERNATIONAL BIOLOGICAL PROGRAMME

7 MARYLEBONE ROAD, LONDON NW1

BLACKWELL SCIENTIFIC PUBLICATIONS

OXFORD AND EDINBURGH

ISBN 0 632 06420 X

First Edition 1971

Distributed in the U.S.A. by
F. A. DAVIS COMPANY,
1915 ARCH STREET,
PHILADELPHIA, PENNSYLVANIA

Printed in Great Britain by
BURGESS AND SON (ABINGDON) LIMITED
ABINGDON, BERKS
and bound by
THE KEMP HALL BINDERY, OXFORD

Contents

Appendix

Contributors

Leon Birkett Fisheries Laboratory, Lowestoft, Suffolk, England

John B. Buchanan Dove Marine Laboratory, University of Newcastle-upon-Tyne, England

Dennis J. Crisp Marine Science Laboratories, Menai Bridge, Anglesey, North Wales

Michael Hickman Department of Botany, University of Alberta, Edmonton, Alberta, Canada

Norman A. Holme Marine Biological Laboratory, Plymouth, England

Norman S. Jones Marine Biological Station, Port Erin, Isle of Man

Joanna M. Kain (Mrs. N. S. Jones) Marine Biological Station, Port Erin, Isle of Man

Alasdair D. McIntyre Marine Laboratory, Victoria Road, Torry, Aberdeen, Scotland

E. Ivor S. Rees Marine Science Laboratories, Menai Bridge, Anglesey, North Wales

Frank E. Round Department of Botany, The University, Bristol 8, England

Foreword

The International Biological Programme is a world-wide plan of co-ordinated research concerned with "the biological basis of productivity and human welfare". It was started in 1964 and is designed to come to a close in 1972 or soon afterwards. The handbook series of IBP consists of volumes which are needed by biologists who are participating in the programme around the world.

With these facts in mind, it may seem odd that, of the twenty or so handbooks already published or in preparation, this is the only one which has emerged from the section on Productivity of Marine Communities (PM), one of the seven sections into which IBP is divided. The need for guidance in the methodology of research, in order to achieve comparability of results all over the world, is certainly no less in marine biology than in terrestrial ecology or limnology, but this need is being largely met through the activities of organizations other than IBP. Thus there is a series of UNESCO monographs on oceanographic methodology of which the first two deal with the "determination of photosynthetic pigments in sea water" and "zooplankton sampling". FAO has been active particularly in the methodology of fishery research, while the Special Committee on Oceanographic Research (SCOR) of ICSU has been collaborating with IBP/PM and other bodies on such matters as the "estimation of primary production in the sea", "continuous monitoring of biological oceanography", and "phytoplankton methods", on each of which a publication is planned. The only major branch of importance in IBP studies which was not already provided for was one of the most difficult, namely the benthos.

The process of designing and preparing this handbook has been similar to that of a number of others in the series. In 1965 the IBP/PM section, after consultation with SCOR, set up a working group on methods for the study of marine benthos under the chairmanship of Professor D. J. Crisp (UK) with Dr. Z. A. Filatova (USSR), Professor G. Thorson (Denmark) and Dr. K. Banse (USA) as members. It reported late in 1965 and delegated the preparation of a draft handbook to Professor Crisp and a group of workers in the British Isles. The draft was discussed at special meetings held by courtesy of Professor Weill at Arcachon in France in September 1968, following the III European Marine Biological Symposium. Later Professor Crisp had to relinquish the general editorship owing to pressure of other duties and this important function passed to Mr. N. A. Holme of Plymouth and Mr. A. D. McIntyre of Aberdeen to whom we are greatly indebted for bringing the task to finality. The book remains, however, the co-operative production of a considerable number of specialists.

At Arcachon it was decided that a substantial bibliography concerning the marine benthos, which had meantime been compiled in connection with work on the handbook, would be issued separately, thereby reducing the literature references in the handbook itself to those which are particularly relevant to the advised methods of research. The fishery division of FAO in Rome kindly took over the benthos bibliography and have now reproduced it for world-wide distribution.

Independently from this work on the benthos handbook and bibliography, but related thereto, *A Manual for the Study of Meiofauna,* edited by Dr. N. C. Hulings and Dr. J. S. Gray (Smithsonian Contribution to Zoology; Number 78) has been prepared following an international conference in Tunis during July 1969. This manual, which is in some measure complementary to the handbook, will be published in 1971.

July 1970   E. B. WORTHINGTON

Preface

This Handbook has been written to meet the needs of three kinds of worker: the newcomer to the field, the isolated worker without access to large libraries or the advice of colleagues, and those in related disciplines who may for some reason require to collect or study biological samples from the sea bed. Because of the very varied nature of the sea bed in different regions and because of the differing requirements of individual workers, we have from the first avoided laying down definite rules and procedures to be adopted. However, there is a right and a wrong way to set about things, and the Handbook had to contain more than a set of platitudes. The best general advice that can be given is for a preliminary survey to be made to see the range of possibilities for study. Before a large scale survey at sea is made, for example, some preliminary sampling, perhaps by dredge, should be made to show the types and size-range of the animals and plants to be studied, the nature of the deposits, and the topography of the sea bed. Only then will it be possible to decide what techniques to adopt in the main survey.

This is an International Handbook, but at the same time it is an English-language edition written by workers in one part of the world. We appreciate that we may not have been able to give adequate coverage to some techniques which may have been successfully adopted in other countries, and similarly the list of gear suppliers in the Appendix may seem to be somewhat restricted geographically. Such limitations may be remedied in a later edition, should this appear, and meanwhile it may be possible to have French and Spanish translations of this Handbook produced through the assistance of FAO.

Acknowledgements to those who have kindly given permission for reproduction of figures are given in the text. Our thanks are due to the staff of the

Drawing Offices at Plymouth and Aberdeen for redrawing some of the figures, and to Mr. A. Eleftheriou of Aberdeen who provided the cover drawing. Helpful discussions with colleagues in our different laboratories, and with other workers at the Arcachon meetings, have contributed much to this Handbook, and special mention must be made of the assistance given by Library staff at our Laboratories and at the National Institute of Oceanography, Wormley, Surrey, both in the preparation of this Handbook and of the Bibliography. We would also like to thank Mrs. W. D. S. Kennedy and Mrs. H. Readings for assistance in the editing of the Handbook, and Mr. A. Varley for compiling the index.

Marine Biological Laboratory,   *Norman A. Holme*
Plymouth, England

Marine Laboratory,   *Alasdair D. McIntyre*
Victoria Road,
Torry, Aberdeen,
Scotland

July 1970

1

Introduction:
Design of Sampling Programmes

A. D. McIntyre

The object of this handbook is to indicate and evaluate the equipment and techniques which are at present in general use for studying marine benthos, and to provide a comprehensive reference list to relevant publications. While it is primarily intended as an aid to those approaching the field for the first time, it is hoped that some sections will be of use to established workers, and that the existence of this volume may help to produce a degree of uniformity in the collection and treatment of material, and in the presentation of results, which will make data from laboratories in different parts of the world more readily comparable.

Perhaps because of the inherent difficulties of benthos sampling—the necessity for heavy gear, ship facilities, labour for sorting—knowledge of benthic infauna has been slow to build up in spite of the early lead given by C.G.J. Petersen and his Danish colleagues. While the epifauna both of rocks and of soft sediments has been more intensively studied in recent years by new techniques such as SCUBA diving, underwater photography, and television, there has been by contrast a lack of any dramatic advance in techniques for collecting the burrowing infauna, except perhaps through recently developed suction devices. But many sedentary members of the epifauna have protective devices such as external shells or skeletons which make them unpalatable or unavailable to predators, while infauna species tend to be soft and succulent and form an important source of food for bottom-feeding fish which can either extract them from the sediment or snap off portions which may be extended above the surface. The bottom fauna and in particular the infauna is therefore of considerable importance in marine food chains.

Information on the benthos is required for studies on productivity, fisheries, and, in recent years particularly, on pollution, a field in which long-term work on marine benthic communities and on possible indicator species may make a valuable contribution.

This handbook deals primarily with the sampling of sediments and their fauna, from the intertidal region to the deep sea. The division into macro-fauna and meiofauna has been used as a convenient way of separating the fauna into two size groups which for the most part require different sampling and processing techniques, the division being made between those animals passing, and those retained on, a sieve of about 0·5 mm mesh.

Macrofauna here comprises mainly the infauna of uncompacted sediments. The epifauna of hard bottoms and the active epifauna, including bottom fish, are less fully treated. Meiofauna is taken to include mainly the smaller metazoans: protozoans and organisms of bacterial size comprising the micro-fauna are referred to only briefly. Study of the phytobenthos requires special techniques, which are dealt with in Chapter 11, where the sampling of different habitats and measurements of primary production by benthic plants are considered.

Various parts of the field covered by this handbook have been dealt with by previous reviews. Those of Thorson (1957a), Holme (1964), and Hopkins (1964) as well as the publication of the International Commission for Scientific Exploration of the Mediterranean Sea (C.I.E.S.M.M., 1965) deal mainly with gear and techniques for macrofauna investigations, while the volume edited by Schlieper (1968) covers a wide range of methods for marine studies. A review by McIntyre (1969) refers briefly to problems of sampling the meiofauna, and the Manual for the Study of Meiofauna produced after the International Conference on Meiofauna in Tunis in 1969 (Hulings & Gray, 1971) presents detailed procedures for each taxon.

The design of sampling programmes

In planning the collection of samples it is important to realise that several different types of gear will be required to deal adequately with a range of substrata and with all faunal elements. It is also important to be aware of the limitations of the sampling and processing techniques employed and of the extent to which they may miss some elements of the fauna.

For macrofauna the main difficulties probably arise at the sampling stage. The larger animals and in particular the more active ones are always difficult to sample quantitatively. If they live on the surface they may move out of the way of the sampler; if burrowers they may bury too deeply to be taken by most grabs; and in both cases they are often widely dispersed (singly or in aggregations) so that the area sampled proves inadequate.

Problems of collecting smaller organisms arise mainly at the processing stage, when the object is to separate animals of different sizes from one another and from the sediment, and the arbitrary divisions into macro, meio and microbenthos make sense largely because different techniques are required for each group.

Although different collecting devices or methods may be used it is obviously best, in building up a composite picture of the benthos and its environment, if the different samples are taken as close together as possible. In correlating the fauna and the sediment for example, the sediment sample should come from the same grab sample as the fauna, since two successive hauls can differ considerably in sediment type. Cameras attached to grabs have been used to photograph the bottom immediately before the grab bites (Fig. 4.3), and perhaps the ideal unit for sampling is such a grab-camera set-up with a bathythermograph attached, with subsamples taken from the grab for meiofauna and sediment analysis.

Pilot surveys. For qualitative work the dredges and trawls described on pp. 86–92 can be used, and rigorous planning of the sampling programme will not usually be required.

For quantitative surveys a standardised procedure is desirable, for which decisions must be made at an early stage on such matters as the layout of the stations; the type of sampler to be used; routine observations to be made at each station; the treatment of samples at sea and in the laboratory, and the presentation of results—decisions which can more easily be reached after preliminary observations have been made in the selected area. Some information on depths and deposits can be obtained from charts, but if possible, a small scale pilot survey should be carried out. This could include visual examination on beaches, and, in offshore areas, exploration by SCUBA divers, underwater photography and television. Preliminary qualitative sampling by dredge will give some idea of the types of animals and plants to be sampled and of the patchiness of organisms and sediment. Some limited measurements of physical and chemical factors such as temperature and salinity may give further help with decisions on the layout of stations. It is particularly important that such pilot surveys be carried out if little is known of the local flora, fauna and conditions, since time and thought expended at this stage will prove worthwhile in the avoidance of mistakes later.

Layout of stations. If there are no obvious environmental gradients, the sampling may be laid out in the form of a grid over the study area. By taking several samples at random in each square the whole area will be covered and a measure of variability obtained. If there is an obvious gradient of, for example, depth or salinity, then stratified sampling may be best, working on transects across the gradients with stations arranged to give equal coverage of the different zones. The final layout adopted will depend on the purpose of the sampling and on the methods of analysis to be used (see p. 10) but whenever possible each station should be sufficiently representative of a wider area to allow valid replicate hauls to be made.

When surveying a very large area, whether qualitatively or quantitatively, account should be taken of the economical use of ship's time. Some time must elapse between stations while a sample is being sieved or rough-sorted, preserved and labelled, and minor repairs to gear may have to be made, so that it is convenient if the ship can be steaming on to the next station meanwhile. Spacing of stations at intervals of about $\frac{3}{4}$ to 1 hour's steaming time apart allows the maximum amount of ground to be covered in a day. Unless deck lighting is adequate for sorting catches, sampling must be confined to daylight hours, so that even more careful planning of the programmes is required.

The importance of accurate position fixing, both for finding and maintaining station, must be emphasised, and this is dealt with in Chapter 2.

The number of samples required. It is generally agreed that for macrofauna sampling an instrument covering at least 0.1 m² is required, and most of the instruments available for fully quantitative work cover either 0.1 or 0.2 m². No absolute advantage has been demonstrated for one or other of these sample sizes. If time were short at the collecting stage, or if comparatively large animals were to be sampled, the larger size may be more appropriate, while the smaller has the advantage of providing additional information in terms of more replicate samples for the same surface area as the large one. Having selected the gear as discussed in Chapters 6 and 8, the important question is how many samples should be collected, given that the object of quantitative sampling is to enable valid statements to be made about the number of species present and about the distribution and density (number of individuals and/or biomass per unit area) of the fauna.

To test how many grab hauls are sufficient to collect a high proportion of the species, Holme (1953) examined the recruitment of species to the sample total from each successive haul by plotting on a cumulative basis the number of species against the number of hauls. He arranged his samples in random order before constructing the cumulative curve, but Ursin (1960) states if one sample contained all the species in the total set, then the slope of the curve would depend on the number this sample was given in the process of randomisation. Ursin therefore suggested that the number of species in one sample should be obtained by using the mean of all the samples in the set. The mean number in two samples is then got by taking the samples 2 by 2, and so on. The construction of a species/area cumulative curve will indicate for the ground in question, how many samples are required to sample a given proportion of the species. For a theoretical discussion of the species/ area problem see Williams (1964).

The next question is concerned with how many samples are required to give an acceptable estimate of population numbers, and this depends on the variability of the observations. Unfortunately, in sampling with a grab the variance of fauna counts tends to be very large. This variance is due partly to factors associated with the functioning of the grab as an instrument, and partly to the dispersal of the fauna. The first set of factors (which includes avoidance reactions of the animal) is discussed in Chapter 8, and the resulting variation can be reduced by selecting the most suitable grab and operating it carefully. Variation due to the dispersal of the fauna can be a more complex problem.

In studying dispersal of plants and terrestrial animals a common procedure has been to make the assumption of random distribution and test departure from the Poisson series using the chi-square test or some variance ratio statistic. These tests are discussed in statistical text-books, and their application to marine benthos sampling was first made by Holme (1950) who gives relevant references. The terms used to describe the patterns encountered have caused some confusion, but Cassie (1963) points out that ambiguity is avoided if 'dispersion' is regarded as a mathematical term indicating the spread of numbers about their mean, and 'dispersal' as an ecological term referring to the spread of individuals in space so that 'aggregation' could be kept for cases of interaction between organisms. Thus 'over-dispersion' of sample counts would correspond to 'under-dispersal' or aggregation of animals. The essential relationship is that the variance equals the mean for random distribution, is greater than the mean for overdispersion, and less for underdispersion.

A variety of dispersal patterns have been observed in marine benthos. Holme (1950) found even dispersion (variance less than mean) in the intertidal bivalve *Tellina tenuis*. This is not a common distribution for the benthos, and can perhaps be explained in terms of the searching activities of the mollusc's siphons on the sand surface. Most benthos workers have described mainly aggregated distribution (Buchanan, 1967; Kosler, 1968) or were unable to detect departure from random (Clark and Milne, 1955). For the epifauna, Fager (1968) found that in a community of 9 species living on sand in shallow water, 7 species were aggregated and two randomly distributed. However, patterns of dispersal tend to be complex, and their elucidation depends on a number of factors, including the area scale of the sampling, the size of sample, time of the year, and even the size of the sieve used in processing.

The importance of area scale is emphasised by Buchanan (1967) who studied echinoderms off the N.E. coast of England. He found that over a large area (about 200 square miles) the species were aggregated into communities bounded by the line of 20% silt in the sediment. Within the smaller areas of each community another type of aggregation, described as a faunal density trend, associated with various environmental parameters, was encountered. On an even smaller scale, when 150 samples were taken within 3 square miles, some species (such as *Echinocardium cordatum*) were found to show a third type of aggregation which was very unstable and probably associated with larval settlement. Finally, when sampling was reduced to a single station—a circle of 100 m radius, *E.cordatum* was aggregated only at the spawning season, and at other times the distribution was random.

The size of the sample unit is also important, since if counts drop to less than 1 per unit, it is difficult to detect significant departures from Poisson. Angel and Angel (1967) used divers to collect 256 contiguous core samples (each 7·62 cm diameter) and by variously grouping the samples together into blocks of different sizes, they were able to study the effect of sample size on the analysis of dispersion. They found that in three of the eleven species studied the distribution patterns varied according to the block size, and concluded that the microdistribution of these species could not be determined using conventional remote sampling methods. Again, the results may depend on the size of sieve used. Thus Jackson (1968) showed that while second-year individuals of a mollusc population which he studied were randomly distributed, the total population was aggregated because of ovoviviparous habit. Similar results are described by Gilbert (1968), who found juveniles of *Tellina agilis* aggregated, but adult dispersion not significantly different from random.

Given knowledge of the dispersion it is possible to set limits to the accuracy of the mean. Since the statistical techniques involved assume a normal distribution of the data, and the fauna counts have been shown usually to be random or aggregated, the data must be normalized by a transformation. For randomly distributed populations (when the variance is equal to the mean) a square root transformation of the form $Y = \sqrt{(x+c)}$ is appropriate, but for many aggregated populations (when the standard deviation is roughly proportional to the mean) a log transformation; $Y = \log_{10}(x+c)$ has been found satisfactory. 'c' represents a constant which depends on the exact form of the data, but is frequently 0·375 for the square root and 1 for the log transformation. The theory of these transformations is dealt with in most text-books of statistics, and their use in marine biology is discussed by Barnes (1952).

Given the appropriate transformation, statistical limits can be set to the means, and the number of samples required to give a satisfactory population estimate can be determined. As an example of what may be expected from a grab survey, data collected off the east coast of Scotland on a ground of medium sand have been used. The small echinoderm, *Echinocyamus pusillus*, was selected for study since it lives near the sand surface, is comparatively inactive, and is conspicuous in the samples because of its colour. It can thus be adequately collected and sorted. Over a three-month period three separate surveys were made each usually consisting of 12 stations with 3 hauls with a 0·1 m² grab at each station. The area sampled could be regarded as homogeneous with respect to the ecology of *Echinocyamus*, and the mean of all hauls on a survey gives the estimate of population density per unit area. The accuracy of this estimate is provided by its standard error, and when working from a logarithmic scale (the standard deviation had been found to increase with the mean) it is convenient to express this as a percentage of the mean. It was found that to achieve a coefficient of variation in the mean, on the untransformed scale, of 10 per cent with 3 hauls at each station, 47 stations must be worked—a total of 141 hauls. If wider coefficients are acceptable, then for 20 per cent 11 stations (33 hauls), for 30 per cent 5 stations (15 hauls) and for 40 per cent 3 stations (9 hauls) are adequate. Thus if any great precision is required for the mean, a large number of samples are required, and if this is necessary for each different ground or for each seasonal survey, then the effort involved may be much too great.

As well as enquiring how accurately a mean estimates a population density, we may wish to know how sensitive the mean is in detecting differences in densities between surveys on perhaps two different grounds or at two seasons. Returning to the *Echinocyamus* surveys described above, it was found that the number of stations (with 3 hauls at each) which would need to be visited in order to detect a 50 per cent difference between two means, are as shown below (calculated for three probabilities of detection):

Probability of detection	0·25	0·50	0·75
Number of 3-haul stations	10	21	37

In other words, to attain a 3 out of 4 probability of detecting a 50 per cent difference, 111 hauls would be required. Again, a discouragingly large volume of laboratory work.

If groups of animals are dealt with rather than single species the results may be less variable. In a survey of benthos off the Scottish west coast the fauna was divided into molluscs, polychaetes and crustaceans, and the 95 per cent confidence limits of the mean counts ($\bar{x}$) for different numbers of grab hauls were found to be:

	5 hauls	10 hauls	15 hauls	20 hauls
Polychaeta	$0·78(\bar{x})$–$1·28(\bar{x})$	$0·84(\bar{x})$–$1·19(\bar{x})$	$0·87(\bar{x})$–$1·15(\bar{x})$	$0·88(\bar{x})$–$1·13(\bar{x})$
Crustacea	$0·67(\bar{x})$–$1·49(\bar{x})$	$0·76(\bar{x})$–$1·32(\bar{x})$	$0·79(\bar{x})$–$1·26(\bar{x})$	$0·82(\bar{x})$–$1·22(\bar{x})$
Mollusca	$0·64(\bar{x})$–$1·56(\bar{x})$	$0·73(\bar{x})$–$1·37(\bar{x})$	$0·78(\bar{x})$–$1·29(\bar{x})$	$0·80(\bar{x})$–$1·25(\bar{x})$

This shows, for example, that for a true mean of 100 polychaetes the limits from 5 hauls are 78 to 128, while for 20 hauls the narrower limits are 88 to 113, an increase in accuracy which may well not be considered worthwhile at the price of multiplying the sampling effort by four.

Taking this a stage further, Longhurst (1959) has pointed out that there is usually less variation between hauls for the gross faunal indices of total biomass or total number of individuals than there is between numbers of individuals of each species, and suggests that such faunal indices may be a useful quick overall measure of the density on particular grounds. As a result of surveys of different sediment types off West Africa he considers that a standard 5-haul station covering 0·5 m² will adequately estimate the faunal indices.

In conclusion it appears that a high degree of accuracy would require a very large number of samples, and that moderate increases in sampling effort might not repay the extra time involved in processing. It is suggested that for statistical study a standard 5-haul station with a 0·1 m² grab should be regarded as a minimum requirement, and that even if data are not sub-jected to detailed analyses, the presentation of means should always be accompanied by an estimate of their accuracy. If, for example, a log transformation is found necessary, then at least a plot of the means with ± 2 standard errors all on a log scale should be regarded as the minimum presentation, giving at a glance both the limits of each mean and an indication of the significance of the differences between them. The advantage of using transformed values to compare sample means is that this avoids the complications which arise on converting back to the original scale (Bagenal, 1955).

The above discussion deals with macrofauna, but the problems for meiofauna are in general similar. In comparing meiofauna populations from widely separated sites and in several seasons off the Scottish coast (McIntyre, 1964) the means and variances were found to show a tendency to increase together, and in the statistical analysis a logarithmic transformation was used for the nematodes, and a square root transformation for the copepods. Vitiello (1968) made counts of the meiofauna at a single restricted station and found that his data on the more numerous groups fitted a negative binomial distribution. Studies of meiofauna distribution are perhaps more complex because of the difficulties of recognising microhabitats, because of a wider range of sample size and because subsampling is frequently done. Again, however, replicates should always be collected, and standard errors indicated.

General considerations. While the overall design of the programme will obviously depend on the objectives, in practice the details of the sampling will, as suggested above, be controlled to a considerable extent by the facilities available—gear, ships, staff and time—so that the result will be a compromise between the desirable and the practicable.

In particular before any large survey is initiated the very large amount of time required for subsequent sorting of samples should be taken into account. Estimates of the time taken to sort the fauna from a sample vary from an hour or so to several days, or even weeks in the case of deep-sea material, indicating not only the variability in samples but also the diverse interests of individual scientists. However, it would be unwise for a single worker to undertake the sorting and identifying of the full range of species to be found in the course of a general survey. If the help of specialists is not readily accessible it is better to concentrate on a single class or phylum, or on some restricted problem appropriate to the expertise available.

In coastal waters where the collection of extra samples at each station may involve little extra effort in the field, it may be useful to collect more than it is initially intended to work up, to provide for the loss or damage of main samples, or for the later desire for additional replicates. In the deep sea, however, samples are difficult and expensive to obtain, and because replicate sampling may not be practicable, and because of the lower density of deep sea fauna, each lowering of the gear should aim at collecting the biggest sample which can be handled. The difficulty of collecting the sample influences subsequent treatment, which should be carefully organised to make maximum use of the material. It should, for example, be ensured that no material is lost in initial sieving that could later be utilised for meiofauna extraction or soil analysis. Also, it should be remembered that most animals brought up from deep sea will not survive the temperature shock of normal washing on deck. They may reach the surface alive but if they are to be kept alive, or even fixed from the living state, arrangements must be made to wash the sample in refrigerated water, or to transfer it immediately to an appropriate constant temperature room.

The seasonal element may be of considerable importance in shallow water work and this also should be recognised at the planning stage. If the survey consists of a single sampling series, due allowance must be made for biological (e.g. spawning, migration, etc.) and environmental factors (e.g. monsoons) which might lead to non-representative sampling.

Analysis of results

As already indicated, knowledge of frequency distribution of the data is helpful in determining the dispersal of animals and is a necessary prerequisite for the application of many standard statistical techniques. But there are other approaches to the analyses of data from benthos surveys. The classical concepts of marine benthic communities tended to be applied on the assumption that communities could often be clearly discerned from large collections of samples by an experienced researcher. The subjective element in this has been criticised, and Thorson (1957a) put forward a number of recommendations for standardisation of the procedures, involving the definition of 1st, 2nd and 3rd order 'characterisıng species' and 'associated animals', and including the use of suggested standard sampling units— 0.1 m² for depths of 0–200 m; 0.2 m² for 200–2000 m; and 1 m² for the abyssal zone. Ellis (1970) recognised the difficulties of delimiting ecosystems, and used indices of dispersion, density, biomass and respiration rate to suggest objectively which species in his samples were sufficiently important to merit autecological study. Emphasis has not always been placed primarily on the animals, and Jones (1950) puts forward a scheme of classification of animal associations based on environmental factors—depth, salinity and the nature of the substratum.

Another approach involves the use of some form of similarity index, based on occurrence or abundance of the species (Jaccard, 1912; Sørensen, 1948; Webb, 1950; Wieser, 1960 and Fager, 1963). These indices can be arranged in a matrix or trellis diagram (MacFadyen, 1963) to indicate patterns. Recent developments in numerical taxonomy (Sokal and Sneath, 1963) have suggested techniques for the further examination of these patterns, with the use of cluster analysis, and the results displayed in the form of dendrograms. Detailed discussion of these techniques is beyond the scope of this handbook, but they are reviewed by Fager (1963) and applied to specific marine situations by Sanders (1960), Wieser (1960), Valentine (1966), O'Gower and Wacasey (1967), Field and McFarlane (1968), and Popham and Ellis (1970).

For the calculations involved in dealing with the indices referred to above, and in the application to benthos work of such statistical techniques as multivariate analysis, computers have frequently been used and are essential if even moderately large numbers of samples are available. Computers have also been used in the study of gross faunal indices (Ellis, 1968, Popham and Ellis, 1970) and computer programes for sediment analysis can readily be written, which eliminates much of the vast amount of work normally involved in statistical analysis of grain size data in computing modes, medians, arithmetic means, standard deviation, skewness and kurtosis (Schlee and Webster, 1967).

2

Position Fixing

N. A. HOLME

Navigation aids

It is important to determine accurately the positions at which samples are taken, as this will enable comparable samples to be taken at a later date if required. While the accuracy obtainable at sea will depend upon the navigation aids carried by the ship and the presence or absence of electronic navigation systems in the area, the degree of accuracy required will depend upon the patchiness of bottom fauna and substratum. In some places it will not be possible, even with the ship anchored, to obtain replicate samples, while in others, perhaps farther offshore, the sediments and their fauna may not vary significantly over several miles*, so requiring a lesser degree of accuracy in position fixing. A pilot survey is therefore desirable to assess the characteristics and distribution of both sediments and fauna before the main survey is started. As repeatability of samples is the criterion, a small error in an electronic navigation system is of little importance provided it is constant, and it may be better to express positions initially in terms of, for example, Decca co-ordinates. In published reports, however, permanency of position data is best assured by quoting in terms of latitude and longitude.

Position fixing will in general follow the normal navigation procedures used on the ship. The methods will depend on the location of the ship: (a) close to, and in sight of land, (b) in coastal waters, not normally within sight of land, (c) in areas requiring deep-sea navigation procedures. Methods of surveying on the shore are referred to in Chapter 6, and the special problems of position fixing by divers in Chapter 5.

For inshore waters the normal methods of position fixing by compass bearings (usually the least accurate method), range-finder, transits (the lining up of points on the shore), horizontal sextant angles between landmarks,

* See Appendix p. 293 for units used in measurements at sea.

and vertical sextant angles ('danger' angles) on landmarks of known height are applicable.

Transits are the most accurate means of returning to the same place, but if the landmarks used are not marked on the chart it may not be easy to determine latitude and longitude precisely. Transits are also useful for *approaching* a spot the position of which is determined by Decca Navigator or other means. For surveys in harbours and land-locked bays, two horizontal sextant angles taken simultaneously between pairs of suitably placed landmarks are an accurate means of position-fixing. Murray (1966) shows how a chart may be prepared for rapid plotting of positions from sextant angles.

For coastal waters where shore or other marks may not be visible, Radar and Decca Navigator can provide accurate fixes. When within a mile or so of the shore, Radar may be preferable, since in such circumstances the small errors inherent in the Decca system (sometimes magnified close to steep shore-lines) may cause significant navigation errors. Offshore, Decca has a range of 240 miles from the 'Master' shore station, the error at 100 miles range being claimed to be as little as 30 m under ideal conditions. The Decca Navigator system now covers many of the coastal areas of the world frequented by high density shipping, and should be considered the standard method for position fixing in coastal waters, except when very close to land.

In the deep sea, or where the above aids to navigation cannot be employed the time-honoured methods of Dead Reckoning (calculating position by course and speed made good from a previous fix), radio-direction finding (RDF), and sextant sights of the sun and stars are still of prime importance. Longer-range electronic navigation systems such as Consol, Loran and Omega (a comparatively new VLF system) are also of value, as is navigation by artificial satellite for ships carrying the necessary equipment.

When positions must be fixed with the greatest degree of accuracy, the Decca Hi-Fix system can be employed. This system depends on small transmitting stations on shore especially set up for the purpose in hand. The range of operation is from 25–200 miles from these stations, according to power of the transmitters, and latitude. This system is likely to be used only for special purposes such as harbour surveys or for the manoeuvring of dredgers and oil rigs.

Descriptions of traditional navigation methods are given in the *Admiralty Manual of Navigation* (Admiralty, Vol. 1, 1967; Vol. 2, 1966; Vol. 3, 1954), the *American Practical Navigator* (U.S. Navy Hydrographic Office, 1962),

Chapter 2

or equivalent works in other languages. Electronic navigation systems are described in the above, and by Bigelow (1964). However, up-to-date information should be sought from the manufacturers, or from articles in current journals such as *Hydrospace, Ocean Engineering, Oceanology International, Undersea Technology, Fishing News International* and *World Fishing*. The subject has recently been reviewed by Freiesleben (1969).

Depth-finding

Wire sounding. Sounding with the hand lead, although now largely superseded by echo sounding, is still required for checking the latter in shallow water and for obtaining a sample of the bottom, which is picked up by tallow placed in a hollow at the lower end of the lead. Soundings should be recorded in metres, and for inshore work should be corrected for tidal height.

For deep-sea work, soundings are made with 0·7 mm diameter galvanised piano wire, single strand, to the end of which a lead weight is attached. In depths of less than about 2000 m a simple sounding tube with flap valve, weighted to about 12 kg, may be used. By this means a sample of the bottom can be obtained under favourable circumstances. In deeper water a rather heavier weight or sounding tube is used, so designed that weights are released on striking bottom. This avoids the extra strains involved when hauling up from very deep water on a thin wire. For deep-sea sounding a special winch, the Lucas Deep-Sea Sounding Machine or its equivalent, is used. Descriptions of the gear and techniques for deep-sea sounding are given by Sigsbee (1880), Murray and Hjort (1912), Fowler and Allen (1928), and Hopkins (1964). Piano-wire soundings are now seldom made except by survey ships, where they are used for checking echo soundings and for further investigation of anomalous depth records obtained by the sounder.

Echo sounding. Depths are usually measured by the echo sounder, a device for measuring the time interval between the emission of a sound signal from a transducer in the ship's hull and the returning echo from the sea bed. For deep-sea sounding, frequencies of 10 or 12 kHz (10,000 or 12,000 cycles/sec) are used, but higher frequencies of 15, 30 or 50 kHz are used for recording on the continental shelf and for fish-detection. Some small echo sounders employ frequencies as high as 200 kHz. Low frequencies are needed in deeper water but require relatively large transducers which may require modification of the ship's frames for their insertion. Higher frequency transducers are smaller and less expensive, but the sound is absorbed more quickly by the water and they therefore have limited depth capability.

Most echo sounders record depths graphically, so that a profile is traced of the bottom over which the ship is passing. The more irregular contours of rocky reefs contrast with the smooth or gently undulating contours of sand or mud bottoms, and the density of the trace at any one place is also some guide as to the nature of the bottom (see p. 27).

The accuracy of an echo sounder is dependent on a constant speed of movement of the recording stylus. Ordinary echo sounders have a stabilising mechanism or may depend on manual adjustment of a governor to attain the correct timing. It is in any case important to make frequent checks on the speed of rotation, using a stop-watch. It is also necessary to allow for the depth of transmitting and receiving transducers below water level.

On the continental slope and in the deep sea the returning echo is often weak, and ship's noise may interfere with satisfactory reception of the signal. This, and a requirement for more accurate timing of the recording stylus, led to the development of the Precision Depth Recorder for research and survey purposes, particularly in the deep sea. A Precision Depth Recorder usually has high-quality ceramic or crystal transducers, mounted in a streamlined torpedo-shaped 'fish' suspended from a cable attached to a boom projecting clear of the ship's side. The 'fish' is towed a few metres below the sea surface, giving it increased stability, freedom from aeration, and a decrease in interference from ship's noise. The signals are recorded on a graphic chart recorder (Figs. 2.1; 2.2), often a modified facsimile recorder used for the radio transmission of photographs and weather maps, for example the Mufax, which has a helical rotating stylus traversing the chart once per second. The speed of rotation is governed by a tuning-fork within the instrument, and so is independent of fluctuations in the electricity supply. At one revolution per second the full width of the chart corresponds to about 400 fathoms or 750 m, so that in deep water the returning echo will arrive after several traverses of the chart have been made. Some confusion may therefore arise as to the actual depth. This is overcome by a 'gating' procedure by which at certain intervals of time transmission signals are stopped for a short time so that the correspondence between transmitting and receiving pulses may be established.

The velocity of sound in sea water varies with temperature, salinity and pressure. Echo-sounders are usually calibrated for nominal speeds of either

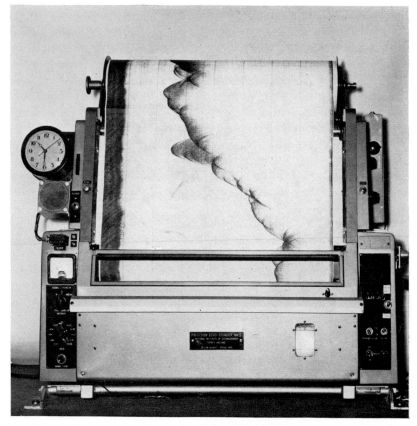

Figure 2.1. Precision Depth Recorder. The modified Mufax recorder on which echo-soundings or pinger signals are recorded. The helical rotating stylus is situated behind the lower edge of the paper chart, the chart moving upwards during recording (Copyright National Institute of Oceanography).

800 fathoms (1,463 m) or 820 fathoms (1,500 m) per second. For accurate measurements, especially in deep water, correction should be applied to the depth read on the sounder. Matthews (1939) has divided the oceans into 52 areas, for each of which tables are given of the necessary corrections. These tables take into account known variations in temperature, salinity and pressure at different depths, and are to be used only for computing vertical velocities and not those in a horizontal plane. More accurate corrections can be made by taking temperature and salinity samples throughout the

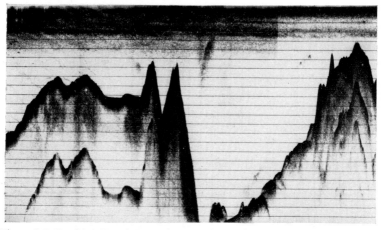

Figure 2.2. Precision Depth Recorder record. In this record of an irregular and steeply sloping sea bed a double echo, due to the returning sound wave being reflected at the sea surface and travelling again to the bottom, is clearly seen on the, left-hand side of the trace. Horizontal lines are at 100 fathoms (183 m) intervals, so that in this instance the chart width was traversed in 6 seconds (Copyright Smiths Industries Ltd).

water column and then calculating the actual sounding velocity (Wilson, 1960): alternatively, determinations of actual velocity can be made, in situ, using a special instrument, such as the Plessey Sound velocimeter, lowered on a cable.

Depth fixing of gear

Failure to take a sample when deep sea trawling or dredging is common (Menzies, 1964). Very often this seems to be due to the gear not reaching the bottom, but in other instances is due to snarling and entanglement which may often be the result of paying out too much wire.

The construction of steel cables is such that they tend to twist and untwist with varying loads, so that when heavy gear reaches the sea bed the consequent release of strain will cause the wire to twist. A ball-bearing swivel between the end of the wire and the gear will to some extent prevent the development of twisting strains in the wire, but if excess wire is paid out so that it lies slack on the bottom, there is a danger that it will twist around itself or the gear to form an entanglement which will not clear itself when the gear is raised off the bottom.

In shallow water in reasonably calm weather it will at once be apparent on board ship when the sampler has reached bottom, but for deep-sea work it is not only essential to measure the amount of wire paid out, but also desirable to measure the strain on the wire and the position of the gear relative to the bottom.

Tension and wire-length meters. In early deep-sea expeditions some form of elastic accumulator was often used to dampen the effects of sudden strains on the towing rope or cable (e.g. Menzies, 1964), and from the movement of the accumulator it was possible to obtain a measure of the strains developed. In deep-sea work the margin of safety between the strain on the warp and its breaking strain is often small, and it is therefore desirable to keep a

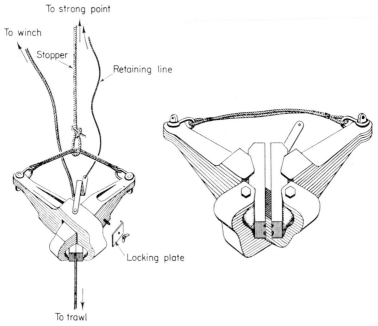

Figure 2.3. Warp-gripping 'nipper' as used on *Discovery* investigations. Left, viewed from underside; right, from on top. The retaining line prevents the nipper being carried away when the stopper breaks. The locking plate is only used for temporarily clamping to the trawl warp, and is then removed. The jaws have two grooves to accommodate different sizes of wire (e.g. for a tapered warp).

constant check on the warp loads. Kemp *et al.* (1929) describe a simple system in which the warp is gripped by a 'nipper' (Fig. 2.3) which is in turn attached to a Salter dynamometer recording the strain on a dial, but this system can only be used when the warp has been paid out, whereas the greatest strains are often developed during hauling, when the nipper cannot be used.

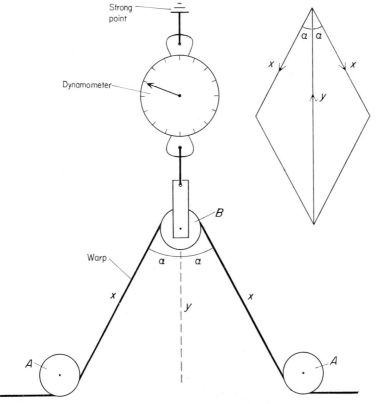

Figure 2.4. A simple method of warp strain measurement by deflection around a block attached to a spring dynamometer. *A*, fixed sheaves or bollards; *B*, block attached to dynamometer. The actual strain on the warp is calculated from the parallelogram of forces, in which the lengths *x* and *y* are proportional to the strains involved. The parallelogram is constructed by measuring the warp angle at *B* ($=2\alpha$) and drawing the diagonal *y* proportional to the force recorded on the dynamometer. The length *x* is then proportional to the warp strain.

Other simple strain recorders (Fig. 2.4) involve the deflection of the wire around a pulley to which a dynamometer is attached (e.g. Tydeman, 1902; Soule, 1951; Kullenberg, 1955), and such systems will record strains when the warp is being paid out and hauled.

In recent years strains have been recorded electrically by load-cells, the electrical resistance of which alters as load is applied. A suspended block incorporating a load-cell has been developed for stern-trawlers (White Fish Authority, 1964, 1970; now marketed by Kelvin-Hughes, London), and deck bollards incorporating load-cells have been developed on research

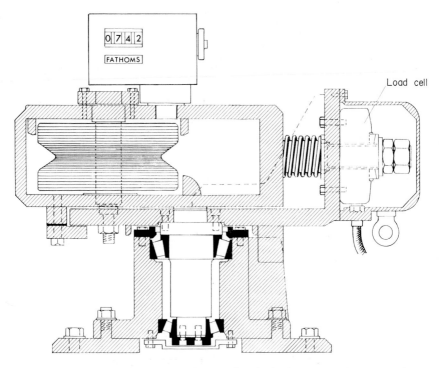

Figure 2.5. Section through strain-recording bollard on R.V. *Sarsia* (Marine Biological Laboratory, Plymouth). Strains exerted on the roller sheave are detected by the load cell, which is connected by electric cable to the recorder on the bridge. A mechanical fathom-meter records wire out. The spring adjacent to the load cell maintains contact between the sliding upper unit and the load cell, and is not concerned with strain measurement.

Figure 2.6. Photograph of the strain-recording bollard shown in Figure 2.5. The upper assembly can rotate through an arc to accommodate different warp angles (Photo N A Holme).

ships (Figs. 2.5; 2.6). The system lends itself to indication remote from the deck, to repeat indicators, graphic recording of changing loads on a chart recorder and to an overload alarm system which gives warning when a pre-determined strain is exceeded.

Tension recorders not only minimise the possibilities of overstraining and parting the warp but are also an aid to determining when the sampling gear has reached bottom. Shortly before the gear is expected to reach bottom, the winch is braked and a reading of the static load recorded. It will then be apparent from the chart record when the gear later reaches bottom, or in the case of a dredge, when it starts to bite into and sample the bottom. Examples of the use of a dynamometer for deep-sea dredging are given by Menzies (1964) for a spring-accumulator system, and by Sachs (1964) for load-cell recordings.

For shallow-water work, the warps are often marked off with twine ties at measured intervals to indicate length of warp and this system is to be preferred to any other when, as when otter trawling, it is necessary that two warps should be paid out to exactly the same length. Deep-sea wires are not so marked, and are commonly led round a measuring sheave which indicates the amount of wire paid out. Such meters have a resetting system so that the dials can be set to zero when the gear touches the water surface. There is inevitably some slip relative to the sheave during payout and hauling, and dials will need to be reset for each lowering. On small ships a simple mechanical meter (as made by Munro Ltd of London) will suffice, but for remote indication an electronic counter may be used. With this may be combined a tachometer to measure speed of lowering. In the Lebus spooling system wire is wound on to the winch drum so precisely that a measure of wire length is automatically obtained.

Pingers. Pingers (or other devices employing sonar) are essential for precise location of corers, grabs and cameras with relation to the bottom. The pinger itself consists of a cylindrical pressure-tight casing containing electronic equipment transmitting brief sound signals, of frequency 10 or 12 kHz, at the rate of precisely one per second. Signals from the pinger are recorded on a Precision Depth Recorder.

When used with an instrument lowered vertically the pinger is attached to the wire a few metres above the instrument (Fig. 2.7). Three sound signals are received from the pinger: (1) a direct signal transmitted up through the water from the pinger, (2) an echo, or echoes from the sampler, which will remain a constant interval from (1) throughout the lowering, and (3) an echo off the sea-bed, which may not appear until the pinger approaches bottom. As lowering proceeds the echo off the sea bed will converge towards signals (1) and (2), so enabling very precise location of the instrument in relation to the bottom. With an underwater camera it is possible to position it at the correct distance above the bottom in order to take photographs of the sea bed. Sometimes a counterweight mechanism is used to alter the pinging rate as bottom is reached, so giving even more precision (Laughton, 1957).

The pinger not only gives precise control over lowering, but in some instances it is also possible to see on the record whether the sampler has operated successfully. For example, Hersey (1960) has shown that after the free-fall corer has released the component echoes off the gear change, the distance between the direct pinger signal and the echo off the body of the corer increasing. Similarly, when operating the Holme grab which unwinds

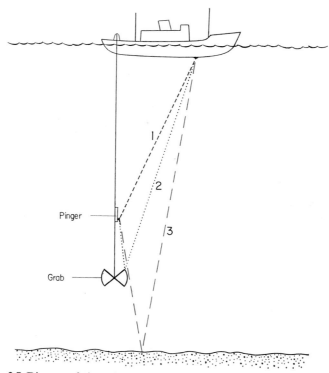

Figure 2.7. Diagram of pinger in use for grab-sampling in the deep sea. For explanation see text. Sound signals are normally received on the ship's echo-sounder transducer.

cable to close, the increased distance between pinger and grab echoes show up clearly (Fig. 2.8). In the example shown the counterweight release failed to actuate on the soft muddy bottom at first, and it was then necessary to 'bounce' the grab up and down, until the record showed that the release had actuated. Premature release of a grab or corer in mid-water while lowering would also be detectable in the same way. Bandy (1965) has shown how the echo off the large Campbell grab changes after closure and similar effects may perhaps be noticeable with other instruments.

Pingers are also useful for deep-sea dredging (Nalwalk *et al.*, 1962). The pinger is attached much farther up the wire, say 90 m above the dredge, so as to be well clear of the bottom. An echo from the dredge itself does not necessarily appear on the record, and lowering is continued until the pinger

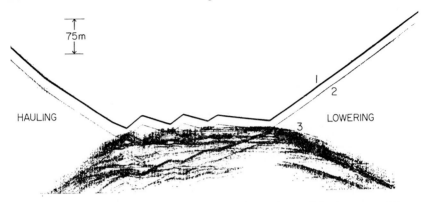

Figure 2.8. Record of pinger signals when working Holme grab in deep water. The grab had to be bounced on the bottom several times until an increased distance between pinger and grab echo showed that the grab had closed. 1, direct signal from pinger; 2, echo off grab; 3, sea bed echo.

is 30 m above bottom. It is then certain that the dredge is on the bottom, and towing is commenced, keeping the pinger at about the same distance above bottom by varying ship's speed or length of wire out.

Pingers undoubtedly save much time when working in the deep sea, and enable samples to be taken under conditions when they would otherwise not be obtained. When dredging on the continental slope or over other particularly rugged bottoms, however, it may be best not to risk the pinger but to rely mainly on dynamometer readings (see previous section).

Another example of the use of sonar for positioning is described by Blacker and Woodhead (1965), who used a headline transducer or 'netzsonde' to control the height of a towed underwater camera (see p. 64). The transducer was connected by cable to the ship's echo-sounder so giving on the trace a record of the height of the transducer above the sea bed. Normally used for controlling the depth of midwater trawls, the transducer was here attached to the body of a Gulf III high-speed plankton sampler, to which was also attached the underwater camera.

Aids for repeated sampling in one place

When grab sampling it is usually necessary to take several samples at a station; alternatively, there may be a need to return to the same place on subsequent occasions for repetitive sampling.

Ideally, samples should be taken with the ship at anchor, but in calm conditions it may be possible to take a series of samples with the ship drifting slowly, the position of each being checked by Decca Navigator or by other means. The extent to which this will be possible depends on the nature of the grounds—clearly any noticeable change in depth of water or the type of sediment brought up would indicate that more precision was needed.

In deeper water, or when it is impracticable to anchor, other methods of returning to the same place may be used:

(a)   Using any of the ordinary navigational aids described on pp. 12–13 to return on station after each haul. This is relatively simple with some means of position fixing such as transits, but when using Decca Navigator, return on station is facilitated if an enlarged Decca chart is prepared, or a Decca Automatic Track Plotter is available.

(b)   A marker buoy is anchored at the required position and the ship returns to it after each haul, or as necessary. Alternatively, positions relative to one or more previously laid buoys may be determined by radar or other means. It is now possible to moor buoys in very deep water, and unless accurate means of electronic position fixing are available in the area, this will be the best way of taking a series of samples at a station in the deep sea.

(c)   The use of transponders. These are electronic devices on the sea bed which act as reference points for accurate positioning of the vessel. These have been developed for precise positioning of oil rigs etc. over deep water. The transponders are excited by sound signals transmitted from the ship, the return signals being received by a number of hydrophones hanging below the ship's hull. The signals received are fed into a computer, which gives an immediate fix of the ship's position relative to the transponders, and impellers controlled by computer can be used for automatically keeping the rig on station.

Position fixing by sonar

Sometimes the positioning of samples is best made in relation to features of the sea bed. For example, it is customary to switch on the echo sounder when approaching a station, and should the echo trace show that either the configuration of the bottom or the depth are not as required, the ship can steam on until a suitable bottom is reached. When grab sampling, one would normally choose a smooth level bottom avoiding an irregular echo-trace indicating rock, whereas when rock dredging the latter may be just what is required. Particularly when working on the continental slope the final manoeuvres of the ship are likely to rely more on the echo sounder than on other means of navigation; even so the drift of the ship while lowering the gear may result in sampling from a depth or bottom feature other than that chosen.

On the continental shelf precise positioning of the ship in relation to bottom features is obtainable by the use of sideways-scanning sonar (Asdic). The transducer may be hull mounted, in a towed 'fish', or may be a portable unit clamped to the side of a launch. In some installations, used principally for mapping the sea bed, narrow-width beams are projected at right angles to the ship's course, while in others, used mainly for fish location, the beam can not only be tilted between vertical and horizontal, but can also be rotated to any bearing relative to the ship's head.

An installation with a series of beams projected at right angles to the ship is shown in Fig. 2.9. Sound signals transmitted from a hull-mounted trans-

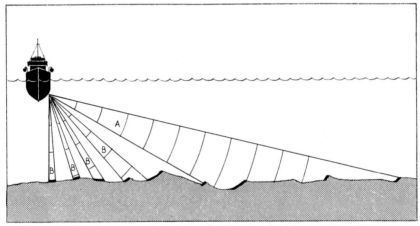

Figure 2.9. Plotting the sea floor by sonar. The sound originates at a point source on the side of the ship and spreads out as a main (*A*) and secondary (*B*) beams. Strong echoes return from the parts of the floor (black) facing the ship. The vertical beam gives a profile of the sea bed beneath the ship (Copyright National Institute of Oceanography).

ducer, stabilised against roll, are radiated in a narrow-width main beam, a vertical beam, and three intermediate side lobes between them. The gaps between the lobes enable mid-water fish traces to be distinguished, as in the corresponding spaces on the trace no bottom echoes will appear. The returning echoes are recorded graphically in the same way as echo-sounder traces, but owing to the oblique angle of the beam there is some distortion of the scale of the traces across the chart. This distortion increases in deeper water, for reasons of geometry. Normally the beams scan 750 m to one side of the ship, the transducer being tilted as required according to the depth of water. In the other direction the scale will depend on paper speed and ship's speed, any deviations due to variations in ship's course and speed affecting the accuracy of the plot.

Owing to the wide band on the sea bed scanned by oblique sonar, location of bottom features should enable the ship to position itself in relation to these without difficulty. This can be more readily achieved if the beam can be turned in any direction, and can also be turned to point vertically down. An outline of the technique used for sea-bed search and ship-positioning relative to bottom features is given by Yules and Edgerton (1964).

The long path necessarily traced by oblique sonar beams from the ship to the sea bed restricts the depth at which the sea floor can conveniently be examined. For deep-sea work the necessary slant range requires low frequency (6·5 kHz) transducers of very large size and high-power output, with the transducer towed beneath the ship at a depth of several hundred feet, in order to avoid the full effect of the thermocline, so that echo-ranging from a surface ship to the deep-sea cannot be undertaken with equipment at present generally available. However, the National Institute of Oceanography, Wormly, England, has made and obtained interesting results with sonar equipment of this kind (GLORIA) with a range of twelve miles, for examination of the continental slope and deep-sea floor (Belderson *et al.*, 1970).

Bottom-type analysis from sonar

Both the echo sounder and sideways-looking sonar (Asdic) are needed for analysing the structure and texture of the sea bed.

Where the sound is directed vertically downwards, the intensity of the returning echo is influenced by the nature of the bottom. Rock and gravel will give a stronger trace than sand or mud, although the interpretation of echoes of varying intensity is not easy. In addition, the bottom relief will tend to be different, rock bottom usually giving an irregular trace, while soft sediments will have a level or undulating surface. Interpretation of bottom

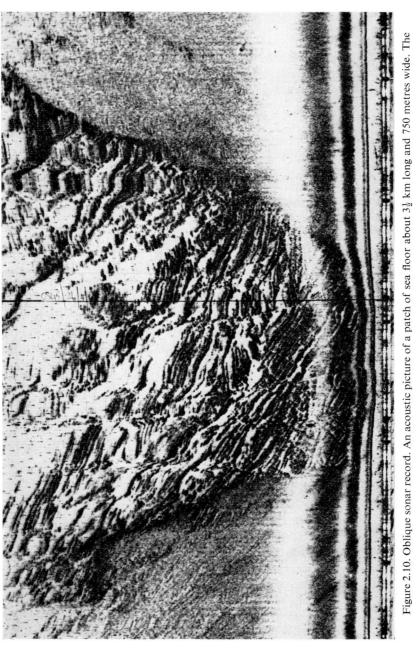

Figure 2.10. Oblique sonar record. An acoustic picture of a patch of sea floor about $3\frac{1}{2}$ km long and 750 metres wide. The different bands towards the lower edge correspond to the lobes of the asdic beam, that at the bottom corresponding to a vertical echo-sounding. The record shows a nearly flat sandy floor surrounding a ridge of slates. The continuity of individual beds is interrupted by fractures (Copyright National Institute of Oceanography).

texture from echo-soundings is discussed by Pratje and Schüler (1952), Chesterman *et al.* (1958), and Breslau (1965).

Hard rocks underlying soft sediments (not to be confused with double echoes—see Fig. 2.2) often show up on the trace, and the use of powerful sound sources such as 'sparkers' or 'boomers' (e.g. Edgerton *et al.*, 1964; Dingle, 1965) has enabled geologists to carry out continuous reflection surveys of features below the sea bed.

Sideways looking sonar, as described in the previous section, has enabled mapping of features on the sea bed to be carried out. Orientation of sand-waves and other features may be determined, features of the sea bed being distinguished by their range and from the intensity of the reflected sound (Fig. 2.10). The latter is dependent both on the slope of the sea bed, features normal to the beam giving the strongest reflection, and on the physical nature of the deposit. If the bottom contours are irregular it may not be possible to distinguish between these two causes, but on relatively smooth bottoms variations in the record will be mainly dependent on the grade of deposit. Even so, it will be necessary to take grab samples to check the deposit. The interpretation of sonar records of bottom features is discussed by Stride (1963), Stubbs (1963), and Belderson and Stride (1966).

Acknowledgments

The following have kindly read and commented on parts of this chapter:
Commander D P D Scott, R N, Hydrographic Department, Ministry of Defence, London;
A J Lee, Fisheries Laboratory, Lowestoft;
A H Stride, National Institute of Oceanography, Wormley, Surrey;
J S Catlow, Decca Navigator Co Ltd, London;
J N Ely, Kelvin Hughes Ltd, London;
A J Southward, Marine Biological Laboratory, Plymouth.

Thanks are due to the National Institute of Oceanography for permission to reproduce Figs. 2.1; 2.9; and 2.10, and to Kelvin Hughes, a division of Smiths Industries Ltd, for Fig. 2.2.

3

Measurement of the Physical
and Chemical Environment

J. B. Buchanan and Joanna M. Kain

SEDIMENTS

J. B. Buchanan

In some respects it is unfortunate that the acquisition of large quantities of bottom sediment is an unavoidable consequence of benthic sampling. This, together with the fact that sediment grain size is easy to quantify, has often led to the gross oversimplification of considering the granulometric characteristics of the sediment to be almost synonymous with the physical environment and any correlation between the animals and the granulometry to be the key to benthic ecology. Such a correlation, when demonstrated, is far from an answer but rather a statement of an ecological problem, which only an intimate knowledge of the biology of the individual species will resolve. Some animals, such as unselective mud swallowers living wholly within the sediment, may show a direct dependence on the nature of the sediment. To others, perhaps among the suspension feeders, the sediment may represent nothing more than a convenient support. The distribution of both sorts of animals may nevertheless show a clear correlation with sediment type. In the first case, the correlation is direct, but in the second, the correlation could be wholly indirect and the true determinants of the distribution would be found in that complex of factors, such as water movement, turbulence and suspended load, which as a whole and acting together represent the *sedimentary environment*. An analysis of a sediment is a means of quantifying the resultant of an essentially dynamic process from a sample taken at a moment of time. The nature of a sediment is determined by the complex interaction of a large number of factors which are conveniently classified in three categories: 1, factors determining source and supply of sedimentary material; 2, factors determining transportation; and 3, factors determining deposition.

30

If the interaction of the various factors remains stable over a period of time, then it can be expected that the sedimentary environment, and therefore the nature of the sediment, will continue substantially unchanged. If, on the other hand, any short term or long term change takes place in any one of the categories of factors, there will be a corresponding alteration of the sediments. It is beyond the scope of a handbook of this sort to give full treatment of the dynamic aspects of sedimentation but a number of concise accounts may be found in text-books of marine geology (e.g., Kuenen, 1965). The results of sediment analyses will be much more meaningful biologically if an attempt is made to relate them to the causative environment of sedimentation.

Many of the techniques of sediment analysis which are used by biologists have been borrowed from the geological discipline of sedimentary petrography. Although there may be a considerable overlap of interest, it should be remembered that the questions asked, and the answers sought by the two disciplines, may be widely divergent. If the results of sediment analyses do not furnish a recognisable correlation of ecological significance, the uncritical use of unmodified geological techniques may prove a time-consuming and wasteful exercise. Since few measurable sediment properties vary independently, the interpretation of a correlation, in terms of the causation of the distribution of organisms, presents a considerable problem. Two sediments with disparate grain size characteristics will also, in most cases, show demonstrable and related differences in many other physical and biological properties, such as: bulk density, porosity, capillarity, thixotropy, permeability, oxygenation, plasticity, content and nature of organic matter and bacterial count. Morgans (1956) provides useful notes on the treatment and analysis of marine sediments, and discusses these problems with particular reference to the biologist. Other relevant techniques may be found in Krumbein and Pettijohn (1938), Trask (1955), Ackroyd (1964), and Griffiths (1967), while Webb (1969) deals in particular with porosity and permeability and their relation to animal distributions.

Collection and storage of samples

The quantity of the sample required, and the means of obtaining it, must depend largely on the nature of the analysis contemplated and details will be considered under the heading of the various techniques. In some cases it may be sufficient to retain a small amount of sediment from the grab sample before sieving off the animals. On a patchy bottom this has the advantage of ensuring that both the animals and the sediment have come from the same locality. It has the disadvantages, however, that the sediment will often be disturbed, that the natural stratification will be destroyed and that some of the fine material may have been winnowed out of the surface layers by water movement during the ascent of the grab. If the distribution of a property with depth in the sediment is to be studied and the natural stratification observed, then a comparatively undisturbed core sample should be obtained. Sediment samples are best temporarily stored on shipboard or the field in convenient wide-mouthed glass jars, labelled internally as well as externally (see p. 161). The subsequent storage again depends on the techniques contemplated but for some analyses the jars together with their contents can be oven dried at 100°C, covered, and stored indefinitely. For others, air dried sediment is recommended for storage. If techniques require the use of raw sediment, and there is a substantial lapse of time between collection and analysis, the samples should be stored under refrigeration. Raw sediment, especially if taken from a highly organic mud, will rot if kept for any length of time at room temperature.

Particle size analysis

The essential equipment for analysis is a graded series of standard sieves suited to the intervals of the Wentworth scale. Much of the other equipment is to be found in the standard apparatus of most laboratories. A mechanical sieve shaker is useful but by no means essential. An electric beverage mixer is an ideal intrument for the mixing and dispersal of sediment samples. This should have a cup holding at least 500–600 ml with side baffles fitted and a close lid to prevent loss of material. As an alternative, the apparatus can be contrived from an ordinary laboratory stirrer and a glass beaker fitted with baffles.

The choice of grade scale

The object of size analysis is to obtain numerical, statistical and possibly graphical data, which will serve to characterise a sediment in terms of the frequency distribution of grain size diameters. Size is here considered as the independent variable. The particles which make up a sediment belong to that class of frequency distributions known as a *continuous distribution*. That is to say that there is a continuous distribution of sizes from the largest to the smallest with the independent variable increasing by infinitesimals along its range of values. Such a distribution does not lend itself to frequency analysis unless some arbitrary series of finite increments is imposed on the independent variable to convert it into a *discrete series* with no gradations between. The series of finite increments is known as a *grade scale*. Each grade class has an upper and lower limit of size, and analysis determines the abundance of frequency within the class intervals. Many arbitrary grade scales have been suggested and the choice should suit the convenience of the analysis. Most marine sediments may be expected to contain particles ranging from a fraction of a micron to several thousand microns. Since it is generally considered desirable to have closer grade intervals at the smaller of the spectrum, an arithmetic scale would result in an impossibly large number of grade intervals. This difficulty is largely overcome by adopting a geometric grade scale. There has been a tendency in recent years for increasing numbers of benthic ecologists and marine geologists to use the Udden scale as modified by Wentworth. The Wentworth scale is geometric, based on 1 mm and a ratio of 2 (Table 3.1). The class intervals can be decreased if required by using the ratio $\sqrt{2}$ or $\sqrt[4]{2}$ instead of 2 (Table 3.2). It is a fact, which will be shown later to have considerable convenience in graphical treatment, that in a geometric series, the logarithms of the numbers to any base will form an arithmetic series. A logarithmic transformation was applied by Krumbein to the Wentworth scale in order to produce an arithmetic series of integers. This is the so-called phi notation (Table 2) where $\phi = -\log_2$ of the particle

TABLE 3.1. Wentworth grade classification.

Name		Grade Limits	
		mm	μ
Boulder		Above 256	
Cobble		256–64	
Pebble		64–4	
Granule		4–2	
Very coarse sand		2–1	2,000–1,000
Coarse sand		1–$\frac{1}{2}$	1,000–500
Medium sand	Sand	$\frac{1}{2}$–$\frac{1}{4}$	500–250
Fine sand		$\frac{1}{4}$–$\frac{1}{8}$	250–125
Very fine sand		$\frac{1}{8}$–$\frac{1}{16}$	125–62
Silt		$\frac{1}{16}$–$\frac{1}{256}$	62–4
Clay		Below $\frac{1}{256}$	<4

TABLE 3.2. The Wentworth scale with the 2, $\sqrt{2}$ and ϕ notation.

	2 scale mm	$\sqrt{2}$ scale mm	ϕ
Sand	2	2	-1
		1·41	-0.5
	1	1	0
		0·71	$+0.5$
	0·50	0·50	$+1.0$
		0·351	$+1.5$
	0·250	0·250	$+2.0$
		0·177	$+2.5$
	0·125	0·125	$+3.0$
		0·088	$+3.5$
Silt	0·062	0·062	$+4.0$
		0·044	$+4.5$
	0·031	0·031	$+5.0$
		0·022	$+5.5$
	0·0156	0·0156	$+6.0$
		0·0110	$+6.5$
	0·0078	0·0078	$+7.0$
		0·0055	$+7.5$
	0·0039	0·0039	$+8.0$
Clay	<0.0039	<0.0039	

diameters in millimetres. The advantages of this procedure are to be found in graphical and statistical treatment. Only the Wentworth scale and the phi notation will be considered in the treatment of techniques which is to follow, but workers who wish to familiarise themselves with other scales should consult a text-book of sedimentary petrography (Krumbein and Pettijohn, 1938).

The observation of naturally occurring aggregates
In many raw sediment samples, much of the material may exist in various states of semiconsolidation in the form of faecal pellets, the tubes of dead polychaetes, etc. Naturally occurring aggregates of this sort may have a considerable ecological interest, but most standard techniques of sediment analysis result in their break-up and dispersal into individual grains which give no clue to the natural condition of the sediment. Since these aggregates tend to be vertically stratified in the sediment (Moore, 1931) the samples should be obtained by coring. The core can be extruded and sectioned at depth intervals.

For the analysis, the portion of wet untreated sediment is placed on the largest sand sieve (2 mm) and the sieve plus contents is 'puddled' gently in a white basin of sea water which conveniently fits the sieve diameter. The technique requires two basins. The material which passes the coarse sieve into the basin is transferred with the water to the next finer sieve in the other basin and so on. The material on each sieve can be washed into petri dishes and the aggregates counted, measured and, if desired, picked out for dry weight measurement. If the weight of aggregates is to be compared with the total weight of the sample, it will be necessary to dry and weigh all residues after the removal of the aggregates. This will naturally include all the material in the water which has passed the finest sieve. This can be recovered by filtration under gentle suction in a Buchner funnel using a washed, tared, hardened filter paper (e.g., Whatman No. 50), which is subsequently dried and weighed.

The rapid partial analysis of sediments

In conjunction with more extensive benthic surveys, sufficient information can often be derived from a measurement of the combined silt and clay content of the sediment. This involves an initial splitting of the sediment into a sand fraction (particles greater than 62 μ) and a silt-clay fraction (particles less than 62 μ). The sand fraction may be further divided through a series of graded sieves, but the initial splitting is achieved with the 62 μ sieve employing a wet sieving method. If several 62 μ sieves are available the method is rapid and large numbers of samples can be processed in a short time. Oven dried sediment can be used for this method.

1 Accurately weigh 25 g of oven dry sediment.

2 Place sediment with about 250 ml of tap water in the dispersal beaker and add 10 ml of aqueous sodium hexametaphosphate ($NaPO_3)_6$ (6·2 g/l). Break up the sediment with a glass rod and then stir mechanically for 10–15 minutes. Allow the sediment to soak overnight and restir for 10–15 minutes.

3 Wash the sediment suspension on to a 62 μ sieve placed in a white basin adding water until the sieve surface is submerged. Sieve by 'puddling' the sieve in the basin of water. From time to time, the material passing the sieve into the basin may be discarded and the basin filled with clean tap water until no further material is seen to pass, and the water remains clear against the white background of the basin.

4 Transfer the sieve and contents to a drying oven and dry rapidly at 100°C.

5   Gently remove the sieve from the oven and place over a large sheet of glazed white paper. Vigorously knock and agitate the sieve over the white paper; discard any material which passes and continue dry sieving till no further material can be observed on the white paper. If the material on the sieve has tended to 'cake' during oven drying, this should be gently broken up with a dry clean camel hair brush.

6   The initial splitting is now complete. Any material remaining on the 62 μ sieve may be regarded as the sand fraction. The weight of this material subtracted from original sample weight will give the silt-clay fraction by difference. If required, the sand fraction may be graded further through the sand sieve series.

The further analysis of the silt-clay fraction

After a sediment sample has been split on a 62 μ sieve, the sand fraction may be further graded by dry sieving. The material of the silt-clay fraction, which passes the 62 μ sieve, is generally of a size which is below the practical level for further sieving. If the silt-clay fraction has been retained and its further grading is considered essential, then it will be necessary to employ some form of sedimentation analysis. It should be noted that both the preliminary preparation and the actual mechanical process of sedimentation analyses can be very time-consuming. The principle of sedimentation analysis is simply that large particles will fall faster and further than small particles through a column of distilled water in a given time. By first assuming that all of the particles are spheres and that all have the specific gravity of quartz (2.65), it is possible to quantify the distance of fall in a given time for any particular diameter of particle by using the classic formula for settling velocities provided by Stokes' Law. The times of settling, for the Wentworth grade scale, computed from Stokes' Law, are given in Table 3.3 for a temperature of 20°C.

TABLE 3.3. Settling times in distilled water at 20°C.

Diameter (mm)	Settling distance (cm)	Hours	Time Minutes	Seconds
0·0625	20			58
0·0312	10		1	56
0·0156	10		7	44
0·0078	10		31	0
0·0039	10	2	3	0

Because of its simplicity and since it does not require any sophisticated apparatus, pipette analysis is generally regarded as a suitable method for benthic ecology. The essential apparatus for the analysis is a litre measuring cylinder, preferably of the stoppered type, and an ordinary 20 ml pipette which has a stem length, below the bulb, greater than 20 cm. The stem should be etched and well marked with two rings at distances of 10 cm and 20 m respectively from the tip. Approximately 30 cm of flexible rubber tubing should be fixed to the mouth end of the pipette. For most problems of benthic ecology, bearing in mind the time factor, it should be necessary only to divide the fine fraction into three grades: coarse silt (62–15·6 μ), fine silt (15·6–3·9 μ) and clay (below 3·9 μ). This can be achieved by taking only three pipette samples.

The mechanics of the analysis are simple. The dispersed silt-clay fraction is transferred to the litre cylinder with distilled water to make a suspension of exactly 1 litre. The sediment is suspended by shaking and turning the stoppered cylinder and when it is judged that the sediment is uniformly dispersed throughout the suspension, the cylinder is placed upright and a stop-watch started. From the moment of placing the cylinder upright, all of the particles will start to fall through the water column under the action of gravity and at the settling velocities appropriate to their individual diameters. If, as an example, particles of 15·6 μ are considered, Table 3.3 indicates that such particles will fall a distance of 10 cm in 7 minutes 44 seconds. After the lapse of this period of time, it can be confidently expected that the part of the water column between the surface and a depth of 10 cm will be free of all particles greater than 15·6 μ but that at the level of exactly 10 cm there will still be a representative amount of all particles less than 15·6 μ occurring in the same proportions as they did when the sediment was originally homogeneously suspended throughout the water column. If a 20 ml pipette sample is taken at the level of 10 cm after a lapse of time of 7 minutes 44 seconds and if the material in the pipette is subsequently dried and weighed, it should represent the weight of material less than 15·6 μ contained in a volume of 20 ml of the original suspension. This figure can easily be extrapolated by multiplying by fifty to obtain an estimate for the whole suspension. Provided that both the weight of material less than 62 μ and the weight less than 15·6 μ is known, it is simply a matter of subtraction to find the weight of material lying between the grade limits 62–15·6 μ. The analysis proceeds in this manner from the coarsest to the finest grades.

When taking a sample, the pipette is lowered very gently into the cylinder (preferably by mechanical means) to the appropriate mark just before the expiry of the time interval. The pipette can be held steadily at this depth by one hand resting on the top of the cylinder. To take a sample an even suction is applied by the mouth through the rubber tube attached to the pipette. When the pipette is filled to the mark the rubber tube is pinched with the free hand, the pipette is removed from the cylinder and the contents of the pipette transferred to a tared 50 ml crystallising dish. The sample is dried at 100°C but care must be taken to avoid boiling and possible spattering. The dried sample, cooled in a desiccator, should be weighed accurately to the third decimal place, preferably on an aperiodic balance. Some workers advocate the use of more elaborate suction devices for taking samples. These usually involve a suction pump and an evacuated aspirator, but after some preliminary practice, mouth suction produces adequately accurate results. In order to be confident of his results, each worker should first familiarise himself with the technique by comparing a series of replicate pipette samples taken from the same sedimentation grade.

Variation in temperature can lead to serious errors in pipette analysis. If the table of settling velocities computed for 20°C is employed, it is essential that the entire analysis is carried out at this temperature. A quartz particle of 50 μ diameter will show an increase of settling velocity of approximately 2·3% for each Centigrade degree rise in temperature. For this reason the sedimentation cylinder should ideally be immersed in a thermostatically-controlled water bath to within a few centimetres of its mouth. Even if such a bath is not available, it is still a good practice to immerse the cylinder in a water bath at the ambient temperature in order to buffer the effects of room temperature fluctuations. If the analysis is carried out in a room temperature which differs from 20°C, it will be necessary to recalculate a new table of settling velocities from the Stokes' Law formula. The formula may be expressed as:

$$V = Cr^2$$

where V = the settling velocity in cm sec^{-1},

    C is a constant, and

    r = radius of the particle in cm.

The constant $C = \dfrac{2(d_1 - d_2)g}{9z}$,

where d_1 = density of the particle = 2·65 (quartz),

    d_2 = density of water,

    g = acceleration of gravity = 980 cm sec^{-2}, and

    z = viscosity of water in dyne seconds cm^{-2} (1 dyne second cm^{-2} = 1 poise).

In the range of temperature 15–30°C, the density of water can be regarded as 1 without great loss of accuracy although the figure for viscosity varies considerably. The numerator of the equation for this temperature range may be conveniently regarded as 3234, so that $C = 3234/9z$.

The values for z over a wide temperature range can be extracted from physical tables of water viscosity. Most tables give the value in centipoises (0·01 poise), so that it will be necessary to divide the value by 100 before applying to the equation. It should also be noted that although most tables for settling velocities are calculated for the *diameter* of the particle in *millimetres*, Stokes' Law is calculated from the *radius* of the particle in *centimetres*. The values of C for 15°C and 20°C are $3·14 \times 10^4$ and $3·57 \times 10^4$ respectively.

When choosing the weight of sediment to start a pipette analysis, the aim should be to arrive at a suspension of silt and clay weighing approximately 25 g. That is to say, if the sediment contains 50% sand and 50% silt and clay, an initial sample of 50 g should be chosen to start the analysis. Because of this, no universal starting weight can be recommended and it is necessary to carry out a rapid partial analysis for silt and clay before embarking on the pipette analysis. The complete analysis is outlined below in seven stages.

1. Pretreatment
(i)   Weigh an appropriate amount of air-dried sediment to produce approximately 25 g of silt and clay fraction.
(ii)   Transfer the sediment to a litre beaker with 100 ml of 6 per cent hydrogen peroxide. Stand overnight and then heat gently on a water bath. Add further small quantities of peroxide until there is no further reaction. This process should effectively remove the organic matter.
(iii)   Wash the contents of the beaker on to a filter paper (Whatman No. 50) in a Buchner funnel. Wash thoroughly under gentle suction with distilled water to remove any electrolytes.
(iv)   Wash the sediment from the filter paper into the cup of the mechanical stirrer using a jet of distilled water and a camel-hair brush. About 200–300 ml of water should be used. Add 10 ml of sodium hexametaphosphate solution (6·2 g/litre aqueous), and stir for 10–15 minutes. Leave the sediment to soak overnight.

2. Initial splitting of silt-clay fraction
Stir the sediment again for 10–15 minutes and then transfer to the surface of a clean 62 μ sieve placed in a flat-bottomed white basin. Add about 300–400 ml distilled water sufficient to flood the sieve surface. The volume of water within the basin should on no account exceed 1 litre. Wet sieve the sediment by agitating and puddling in the basin of water until most of the fine fraction has passed. Lift the sieve and allow to drain over the basin. Transfer the sieve and its contents to a drying oven at 100°C.

3. Dry sieving of the sand fraction

Although the process of wet sieving will have removed most of the material less than 62 μ, a certain amount will have been retained by the water film on the sieve. It is therefore necessary to subject the sieve to a period of dry sieving. The first stage of this can be carried out by agitating the dried 62 μ sieve over a large sheet of white glazed paper and transferring any fine material which passes through to the suspension in the basin. When no further fine material is seen to pass, the contents of the sieve can be transferred carefully to the upper-most (coarsest) of a stacked series of graded sand sieves, taking care to gently brush all of the material from both surfaces and the pores of the 62 μ sieve with a fine sieve brush. Although the bulk of the silt-clay fraction will now have been removed it is still advisable to have a fresh 62 μ sieve at the bottom of the stack of sieves and care should be taken to use a pan below this finest sieve to catch the last of any fine material which may still pass. The stacked column of sieves may now be transferred to an automatic sieve shaker for a period of 10–15 minutes. If an automatic sieve shaker is not available, the column of sieves should be rocked and tapped with the flat of the hand until it is judged that sieving is complete on the topmost sieve. This sieve may then be detached and any doubts about the finality of sieving may be checked by agitating and tapping over a sheet of white glazed paper, and any material passing should be immediately transferred to the next finer sieve. When the finality of sieving has been checked, the material on the sieve should be emptied on to the sheet of glazed paper and any grains lodged in the sieve should be brushed out with a sieve brush. The fraction can then be transferred to the balance pan for weighing The analysis continues sieve by sieve through the series until finally any material passing the last 62 μ sieve into the pan is transferred to the suspension of silt and clay in the basin.

4. First pipette sample

The grading of the silt-clay fraction may now proceed. It will be assumed that the analysis takes place at 20°C. Wash the fine material in the basin into the litre cylinder using a large filter funnel and a wash bottle with distilled water. Make up the volume in the cylinder to exactly 1 litre with distilled water. Place the cylinder in the thermostatic water bath until the temperature has equilibrated at 20°C. Remove the cylinder, shake and turn to suspend the sediment evenly throughout the water column. Place upright and immediately withdraw a 20 ml pipette sample from a depth of 20 cm. Transfer the pipette sample to a tared crystal-lising dish and dry in the oven at 100°C. The weight of this material will represent the total amount of sediment less than 62 μ in the suspension.

5. Second pipette sample

Re-shake the suspension. Place upright in the water-bath and simultaneously start the stopwatch. A few seconds before the expiry of 7 minutes 44 seconds, lower the pipette tip to a depth of exactly 10 cm below the surface of the suspension. At exactly 7 minutes 44 seconds withdraw the 20 ml sample and transfer to a tared crystallising dish. Dry at 100°C.

6. Third pipette sample

Resuspend the sediment, replace the cylinder in the water bath and take the third sample after a time interval of 2 hours 3 minutes. Dry the sample.

7. Calculation of results

Wt. of first pipette sample+dish	31·799
Wt. of dish	31·317

∴ Wt. of material less than 62 μ in 20 ml suspension 0·482
∴ Wt. of material less than 62 μ in 1 litre suspension$=0.482\times 50$
$$=24.100 \text{ g}$$

Wt. of second pipette sample+dish	30·247
Wt. of dish	30·126

∴ Wt. of material less than 15·6 μ in 20 ml suspension 0·121
∴ Wt. of material less than 15·6 μ in 1 litre suspension$=0.121\times 50$
$$=6.050 \text{ g}$$

Wt. of material finer than 62 μ	24·100
Wt. of material finer than 15·6 μ	6·050

Difference: amount in 62–15·6 μ grade	18·050

Similar calculations are carried out for the third pipette sample to give the weight of material in the 15·6–3·9 μ grade together with the amount below 3·9 μ (i.e. the clay content). Finally the results of the pipette analysis are combined with the sieve analysis and the weights in each grade expressed as a percentage of the dry wt. of the total sample.

Graphical presentation and statistics of analysis data

Presentation of two variables

Two simple devices are available for depicting size frequency distribution data: 1, the frequency distribution histogram; 2, the cumulative frequency curve. Of these, the second is preferable since it allows the direct derivation of statistical data. The size of the particle grades should be laid off on the horizontal axis using the phi notation and arithmetic graph paper. By convention the phi values should increase positively to the right (i.e. particle diameters should decrease towards the right). At the upper limit of the first (largest diameter) class interval, an ordinate is erected equal in height to the frequency percentage in that class. At the end of the second class interval another ordinate is erected equal in height to the cumulative sum of the frequencies of the first two classes. At the end of the third, the ordinate should equal a height of the sum of the first three classes, and so on. The cumulative curve is in effect similar to setting each block of a histogram above and to the right of its predecessor. When complete, the ordinates are joined with a smooth curve. If the analysis of fine sediment has been incomplete at the small diameter end of the spectrum, the curve can be left open-ended, but for statistical purposes it is essential that at least 75% by weight of the sediment should have been graded.

An example of a cumulative curve derived from sieving analysis of a beach sand is shown in Fig. 3.1, and the analysis data given in Table 3.4. It should be noted that the cumulative frequency curve allows the comparison of sediments analysed by different sieve series, provided that the aperture interval between successive sieves is not too great.

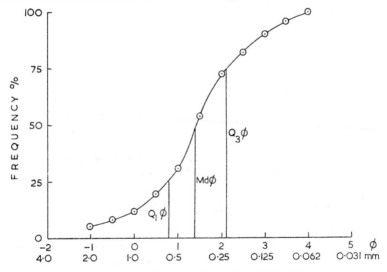

Figure 3.1. Cumulative curve of beach sand data from Table 3.4:
$$\text{Md}\phi = 1\cdot36 \quad QD\phi = (2\cdot10 - 0\cdot80)/2 = 0\cdot65$$
$$Q_1\phi = 0\cdot80$$
$$Q_3\phi = 2\cdot10 \quad Skq\phi = [(0\cdot80 + 2\cdot10)/2] - 1\cdot36 = +0\cdot09$$

Statistical treatment of two variables

It is often convenient to express the characteristics of the size frequency curve in terms of numbers. Three attributes of the curve are generally considered: 1, a measure of central tendency; 2, a measure of degree of scatter; 3, a measure of the degree of asymmetry.

The median diameter is a good measure of central tendency which can be determined easily from the cumulative curve by reading the phi value which corresponds to the point where the 50 per cent line crosses the cumulative curve. It is defined as the phi value which is larger than 50 per cent of the

TABLE 3.4. Sieve analysis data—Beach sand

mm	ϕ	% wt. on sieve	Cumulative %	Grade
4·00	−2·0	0	0	4·00
2·83	−1·5	0	0	4·00 −2·83
2·00	−1·0	5	5	2·83 −2·00
1·41	−0·5	3	8	2·00 −1·41
1·00	0	4	12	1·41 −1·00
0·71	+0·5	8	20	1·00 −0·71
0·50	+1·0	11	31	0·71 −0·50
0·351	+1·5	23	54	0·50 −0·351
0·250	+2·0	19	73	0·351−0·250
0·177	+2·5	9	82	0·250−0·177
0·125	+3·0	8	90	0·177−0·125
0·088	+3·5	6	96	0·125−0·088
0·062	+4·0	4	100	0·088−0·062

phi values in the distributions and smaller than the other 50 per cent. It should be abbreviated as $Md\phi$.

Although the median diameter gives an average value, it represents a central point but does not indicate the degree of spread of the data about this central tendency. A second measure, the quartile deviation, measures the number of phi units lying between the first and third quartile diameters, that is, between the 25 per cent and 75 per cent points on the cumulative curve where $QD\phi = (Q_3\phi - Q_1\phi)/2$. A sediment with a small spread between the quartiles is regarded as being 'well sorted'.

The quartile deviation, which measures the spread, does not give any indication of the symmetry of the spread on either side of the average. If there is a tendency for the data to spread on one side more than the other, this asymmetry is called skewness. The phi quartile skewness may be calculated from the equation $Sk_q\phi = [(Q_1\phi + Q_3\phi)/2] - Md\phi$. A positive value will indicate that the mean of the quartiles lies to the right of the $Md\phi$ and should be prefixed +, while a negative value would lie to the left and should be prefixed − to indicate negative skewness.

The values for the various statistical measures have been worked out for the curve in Fig. 3.1.

In some cases, particularly for the median diameter, it is useful to convert from the phi value to the diameter in millimetres. The most rapid way of doing this is to construct a conversion chart on graph paper (3 cycle log. *X* arithmetic) as shown in Fig. 3.2.

Chapter 3

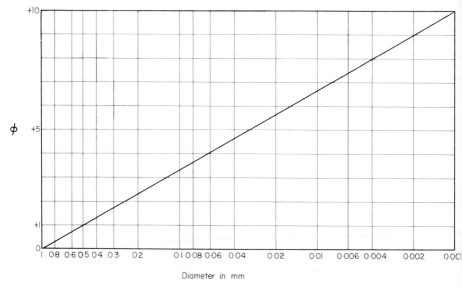

Figure 3.2. Conversion graph, ϕ to diameter in mm.

Presentation of three variables

In a rather different approach, a sediment can be characterised with respect to its percentage content of three variables, for instance, sand, silt and clay. This can be done by utilising the grade nomenclature of the Wentworth scale. If triangular graph paper is used, it is possible to represent the percentage content of three variables by a single graph point. When a number of different sediments are represented by points on the same graph, it is often possible to classify the sediments into groups which have regional ecological significance.

In practice, each of the three vertices of the triangular graph are labelled for one of the three variables. The distance from each vertex to its corresponding base is considered to be 100 per cent. If, for instance, a sediment contains 30 per cent sand, 60 per cent silt and 10 per cent clay, the plotting would proceed as shown in Fig. 3.3. Move a ruler 30 units up the sand axis and draw a faint line parallel to the base. Repeat the process moving 60 units up the silt axis and draw a second faint line parallel to the silt base. The transection of the two lines fixes the point which will automatically also be correct for the clay percentage.

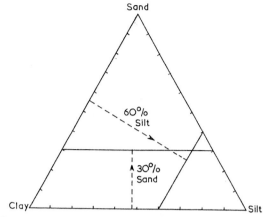

Figure 3.3. Plotting procedure for triangular graph—see text.

Another common function for the triangular graph, is to subdivide the entire field into classes for descriptive purposes. Two of many possible subdivisions are shown in Fig. 3.4, the one for sand, silt and clay, and the other for coarser sediments using gravel (particles > 2 mm), sand and silt + clay.

The measurement of some other physical properties

Porosity

Porosity is the percentage volume of pore space in the total volume of sediment. In a submerged sediment it measures in effect the volume occupied by water. Although the concept is simple, it is in fact difficult to measure with accuracy. Since porosity varies markedly with depth in the sediment, it is essential to obtain undisturbed cores for depth sectioning, avoiding core compaction during sampling. The determination of porosity involves the measurement of the volume of water in the wet sediment and the volume of the sediment grains. Both volumes may be measured indirectly by gravimetric techniques. The weight of water in the sediment can be obtained by washing the salt out of the sediment, drying, and subtracting the dry weight of washed sediment from the original weight of wet sediment. Assuming that the salinity of the interstitial water is similar to the overlying seawater, the weight can be converted to volume using sea-water density tables. The dry weight of washed sediment can be converted approximately to volume by

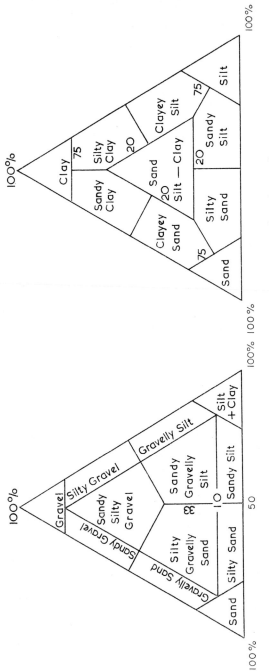

Figure 3.4. Possible methods of presenting sediment data as triangular graphs.

assuming a mean grain specific gravity of 2·65. More accurate sediment specific gravity measurements can be made by comparing the weight of the washed sediment immersed in distilled water with the dry weight in air.

Cores should be sectioned immediately on collection and each core section placed in a previously weighed, tightly covered weighing jar. The jar plus contents will be weighed in the laboratory to give the wet weight of the sediment. The wet sediment is then transferred by washing with distilled water to a centrifuge tube which has previously been weighed in air and also weighed completely immersed in water. Repeated centrifuging and decanting will effectively remove the dissolved salts. When free of salt, after the final centrifuging, the sediment and the tube should be weighed immersed in water after which the sediment is dried in the tube and finally reweighed in air. The displacement volume of the sediment and the volume of interstitial water can then be calculated.

Permeability

For sediments, permeability is usually understood as the rate at which water passes through a cylindrical section of core.

The coefficient of permeability P can be conveniently measured using a constant head permeameter (Fig. 3.5) P being calculated as follows:

$$P = \frac{QL}{hAt}$$

where
$Q =$ volume of water collected
$L =$ length of core
$h =$ head of water
$A =$ cross sectional area of core
$t =$ time

If all measurements are in c.g.s. units, P will be in cm sec^{-1}. A full treatment of permeability may be found in Frazer (1935) and some aspects of biological significance in Webb (1958 and 1969). In beach sediments, it may be valuable to measure permeability horizontally as well as vertically. Considerable differences dependent on the plane of coring have been reported by Emery (1960).

Capillary rise

Of particular importance in beach deposits, capillary rise was studied by Bruce (1928) for both graded and ungraded sands. The procedure is to

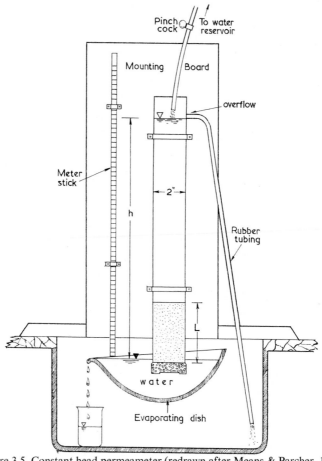

Figure 3.5. Constant head permeameter (redrawn after Means & Parcher, 1964).

arrange a number of drained sediment cores in a frame with their lower ends resting in a shallow dish of seawater and to measure the capillary rise against time. The temperature of the seawater must be kept constant in order to avoid viscosity changes.

pH and Eh

A concise account of the measurement and biological significance of pH and redox profile can be found in Fenchel (1969). In both cases, undisturbed core samples are required.

Temperature

Thermoprobes are available to geologists for measuring the temperature of sediments in situ but biologists will find that adequate results can be obtained by pushing a thermometer into the middle of a grab sample as soon as it is brought up. Sediments act quite effectively as insulating water bottles.

Other factors

A number of other physical factors may be measured, such as shear strength, plasticity and thixotropy. A good general account will be found in Emery (1960), but the biological significance of such measurements has not as yet been fully demonstrated.

The determination of organic matter in sediments

For the routine determination of organic matter in sediments, a rough estimation may be obtained by the loss of weight on ignition at 600°C of a dried sediment sample from which the carbonates have been previously removed by acid treatment.

For more accurate determinations, the organic nitrogen or organic carbon should be estimated. The most commonly adopted method involves the estimation of organic carbon using modifications of the Schollenberger chromic acid oxidation technique. In this, the sediment sample is digested with a chromic acid-sulphuric acid mixture and the excess of chromic acid not reduced by the organic matter is titrated with a standard ferrous salt. Two routine methods are available, (1) the method of Walkley & Black (1934) and (2) the method of El Wakeel & Riley (1956). There is little to choose between the methods, both give similar results and both are easy to operate.

The analytical procedure for the Walkley & Black method is as follows:

Reagents

N Potassium dichromate. Dissolve 49·04 g of reagent grade $K_2Cr_2O_7$ in water and dilute to one litre.
Sulphuric acid. Not less than 96 per cent with 1·25 g of silver sulphate added for every 100 ml of acid. (The silver sulphate removes the interference of chlorides.)
Phosphoric acid. At least 85 per cent.
Diphenylamine. Dissolve 0·5 g diphenylamine in 20 ml water and add 100 ml of conc. sulphuric acid.
N Ferrous sulphate. Dissolve 278 g of reagent grade $FeSO_4.7H_2O$ in water, add 15 ml of conc. sulphuric acid and dilute to 1 litre. Standardise by titrating against 10·5 ml potassium dichromate as described below.

Method

The sediment sample should be ground to pass a 0·5 mm screen. Transfer a weighed quantity of sediment not exceeding 10 g and containing 10–25 mg organic carbon to a 500 ml conical flask. The suitable quantity of sediment for the estimation can only be judged by experience of the benthic area being sampled. In practice a weight of about 1·5 g is often suitable. If, however, the sediment is very highly organic, it is possible that this amount will reduce all of the dichromate and leave none to be titrated. This situation will be immediately obvious at the commencement of the titration and can be corrected by a reduction in the weight of sediment used. If the titration value is less than 1 ml, the sediment weight should be reduced to one-third of the original weight. If on the other hand the titration value is in excess of 9 ml, the weight of sediment should be trebled. Add 10 ml of normal potassium dichromate followed by 20 ml of conc. sulphuric acid. Shake by hand for one minute, then place on a boiling water bath for 15 minutes. Cool, add 200 ml water, 10 ml phosphoric acid and 1 ml diphenylamine indicator solution. Titrate by adding ferrous sulphate from the automatic burette until the solution is purple or blue. Continue to add the ferrous sulphate in small lots of about 0·5 ml until the colour flashes to green. This occurs with little or no warning. Then add 0·5 ml dichromate to restore an excess of dichromate and complete the titration by adding ferrous sulphate drop by drop until the last trace of blue colour disappears.

The end point can easily be recognised to within one drop of ferrous sulphate. The colour is not always purple on adding the indicator at the beginning of the titration but the purple or blue always appears just before the end point. The original blue frequently does not reappear on the addition of 0·5 ml excess potassium dichromate but soon redevelops after the addition of the first drop or two of ferrous sulphate.

Calculation

One ml of normal dichromate is equivalent to 3 mg of carbon. The amount of carbon present in the sediment is therefore expressed by the equation:

$$\frac{V_1 - V_2}{W} \times 0{\cdot}003 \times 100$$

where V_1 equals the volume of normal potassium dichromate (10·5 ml),

V_2 equals the volume of ferrous sulphate in ml,

W equals the weight of soil taken.

The percentage recovery by this method varies according to the sediment type and is 75–90 per cent. For this reason it is undesirable to use a conversion factor to correct the results. Rather, the results are expressed as single value determinations and are designated 'Organic Carbon, chromic acid oxidation values'.

Nitrates interfere only if present in amounts in excess of one twentieth of the carbon content. Carbonates, even when they constitute 50 per cent of the soil, do not affect the results. Manganese dioxide may also be present (three or four times in excess of the carbon content does not introduce serious error). Interference due to chlorides is overcome by the addition of excess silver sulphate to the sulphuric acid. Elementary carbon is almost unattacked in this method so this source of error is eliminated. The presence of coal will invalidate the estimations and as yet there is no means of overcoming this difficulty.

Suspended matter and bottom waters

Most corers and some grabs bring up some of the water overlying the sediment, which for many purposes will be sufficiently uncontaminated to be used for analysis. Carey and Paul (1968) describe a modification of the Smith-McIntyre grab for collection of sediment and bottom water. Ordinary water sampling bottles of the type used for hydrographic work can be fixed to the wire to take samples about 2–3 metres off the bottom in calm weather. A number of horizontally mounted closing water bottles have been designed. Those that are operated by a messenger from the surface are suitable only for use at fairly shallow depths and in moderate sea conditions. It is difficult to place the bottle on the bottom and keep the wire taut enough for the messenger to slide right down. If the bottle is arranged to close automatically on bottom contact there is a risk that it will not have been flushed out adequately but the device described by Schink *et al.* (1966), which collects water samples at 1, 2, 3, 4, 5 and 6 m above the sea floor, and also takes a short sediment core appears to be satisfactory in this respect. Also, a modified Van Dorn type water sampler fitted with a bottom actuated trip (Fig. 3.6) has proved a useful method of obtaining water samples from a distance of about 0·5 m above the sediment-water interface. The most satisfactory principle on which to operate bottom water samplers is to use springs, triggered by bottom contact, to draw pistons or to inflate plastic bags.

Samples of the interstitial water of sands may be taken from undisturbed grab samples using a hypodermic syringe or similar device. The same technique can be used on the shore or by a diver. With fine cohesive sediments, squeezer or filter-press devices (Siever, 1962; Reeburgh, 1967) have to be used on samples taken into the laboratory. Care needs to be taken to avoid the contamination of the samples with the body fluids of organisms contained in the sediment sample.

The technique for gravimetric estimation of suspended matter has been well treated by Strickland and Parsons (1968) together with a number of chemical estimations and pigment analyses. The techniques involve the removal of particulate matter from the bottom water by membrane filtration using a vacuum pump. Subsequent analyses are colorimetric and require a good quality spectrophotometer.

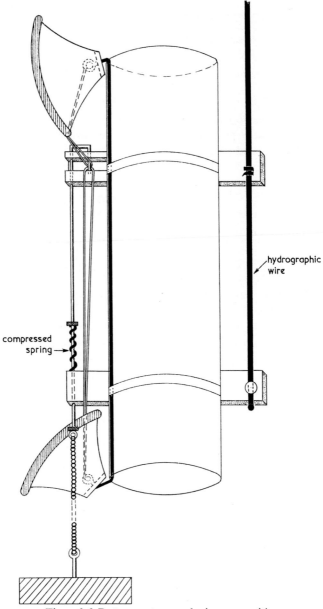

compressed
spring

hydrographic
wire

Figure 3.6. Bottom water sampler in open position.

MEASUREMENT OF UNDERWATER LIGHT
Joanna M. Kain

Guide to the literature

Although biologists have been interested in the penetration of light into natural waters for many decades, the practical difficulties associated with its measurement prevented frequent or accurate records until relatively recently. The interest of physicists in the optics of sea water has stimulated improved instrumentation as well as an increased understanding of the interactions of radiation and natural waters. This has resulted in a large crop of review articles during the last ten years.

Publications explaining in some detail the underlying principles and definitions include those by Tyler and Preisendorfer (1962) and Jerlov (1968). The latter is an extremely useful book although the bibliography is incomplete. Articles explaining some of the relationships of the many terminologies and units include Strickland (1958), Sauberer (1962) and Westlake (1965a). Those particularly describing or comparing techniques or instruments include Strickland (1958), and Jerlov (1963, 1965 and 1968). Some of the results of measurements are summarised by Holmes (1957), Strickland (1958), Duntley (1963) and Jerlov (1968). At a symposium in 1960 recent developments were outlined (Jerlov, 1961).

There are several properties of sea water which can be measured in relation to radiation and which may be of interest in classifying water types with different dissolved and particulate substances. The attenuation of an artificial beam is often measured in the laboratory or in situ with beam transmittance meters. Similarly scattering is measured with scatterance meters. References to these can be found in Jerlov (1968). Here it should be noted that beam transmittance is not equivalent to transparency in the sea, where scattered radiation is not lost.

Of most interest to workers in the benthos is natural irradiance, or radiant flux per unit area. Those interested in light available for benthic plant photosynthesis require information on total downward flux, in amounts measurable with instruments such as photovoltaic cells. Those interested in the response of animals to light may need information on irradiances as low as are measurable with the most sensitive instruments and although the total downward flux is important, its direction may also be of interest, particularly near the bottom where feeding is important.

Because the spectral composition of daylight is altered as it passes through water it is improper to measure it in terms of illumination which is associated with the wavelength response of the human eye. It should thus be termed irradiation and measured in energy units. For the same reason great attention has to be paid to the wavelength or wavelength band in which measurements are being made. The radiation at each wavelength is reduced exponentially with depth, the coefficient of extinction varying with the wavelength. The semi-logarithmic plot of total energy with depth is thus curved near the surface, where there is a wide range of wavelengths present, but straight in deeper water where the radiation is nearly monochromatic. The wavelength of maximum penetrance is particularly affected by Gelbstoff, or yellow substance (reviewed by Kalle, 1966) which is characteristic of coastal waters.

Irradiance is measured with a light sensitive detector which should be covered by a diffusing screen such as opal glass or perspex placed flush with the upper surface of the instrument or protruding slightly. The response of this type of collector is then proportional to the cosine of the angle of incidence. This cosine error is unimportant when measuring downward irradiance with a horizontal plate and in some cases algal fronds may almost act as cosine collectors. A more important error is the immersion effect. This is explained in detail by Westlake (1965a).

There are a number of types of instrument in use. The simplest, but with severe limitations, is the Secchi disc. This is discussed by Strickland (1958), Sauberer (1962) and Tyler (1968). Although the thermopile is less sensitive than other instruments in use it has the advantage that it responds equally to all solar radiation and thus indicates total energy. It has been used by Stephens and Strickland (1962). The group of instruments most commonly used in photosynthetic work are photovoltaic cells. The selenium barrier layer cell is the most popular, its spectral response being mainly within the photosynthetic range and high in the blue and green. Silicon cells have also been used recently and are useful at the red end of the spectrum. Photovoltaic cells are convenient to use and require only a galvanometer. There may, however, be a lack of linearity between the flux received and the potential produced. They have been used, for example, by Jerlov (1951), Cooper (1961) and Holmes and Snodgrass (1961). Photoconductive cells (e.g. cadmium sulphide) have recently been used, for example by Sasaki *et al.* (1966). These are sensitive and can be varied in their spectral response. They are more complicated to use however and require an external power source. The most important advance in instrumentation has been the photomultiplier tube.

This can be extremely sensitive and has been used with effect to 900 m in the sea and for the detection of bioluminescence (Clarke and Kelly, 1964). It requires a power supply. Underwater instruments using this tube are described by Sasaki *et al.* (1955), Clarke and Wertheim (1956), Boden *et al.* (1960) and Craig and Lawrie (1962).

It is sometimes desirable to integrate irradiance falling at a particular depth over a period of time. This has been achieved in instruments described by Snodgrass (1961), Currie and Draper (1961) and Draper (1961). Scalar irradiance (including all directions about a point) may sometimes be important to the benthos biologist. The instrument described by Currie (1961) measures this.

Radiance, or radiant flux from different directions, is measured with specialised instruments such as those used by Duntley *et al.* (1955), Lenoble (1958), Sasaki *et al.* (1962), Timofeeva (1962) and Sasaki (1964), The polarization of light in the sea has been studied by Waterman (1955), Ivanoff (1957) and Timofeeva (1962).

Light sensitive instruments are normally calibrated using a standard light source (requiring a constant voltage) but the sun (Johnson and Olsson, 1943) or a previously calibrated instrument may be used. It is important to use a wide range of irradiances during calibration.

The isolation of wavebands during measurements is fraught with difficulties. Coloured glass filters, singly or in combination, are most often used, and there are a number of standard types. The method of calculation of the relationship between the spectra of filter transmission, photocell response and energy source is clearly described by Westlake (1965*a*). As the spectral distribution of radiant energy alters with depth, the optical centres of most filters change. This band-width error can become important (Joseph, 1949). In very deep water leakage of any filter at wavelengths of apparently nil transmission can cause serious errors (Tyler, 1959). Interference filters are more reliable and although more useful with photomultiplier tubes, can be used with photovoltaic cells (Ivanoff *et al.*, 1961). Another method is the use of a spectroradiometer (Ivanoff, 1956; Lenoble, 1956; Tyler and Smith, 1966).

Simple measurement of irradiance

Most of the instruments in use have been constructed by the laboratories in which they have been developed. The most widely used and useful instrument from the biologist's point of view is the pair of photocells, one underwater and one on deck, used for measuring downward irradiance as a percentage of surface irradiance. A complete, though not ideal, instrument of this type is the 'submarine photometer' produced by G. M. Mfg. & Instrument Corp., 2417 Third Avenue, New York, N.Y., U.S.A., and marketed in Europe by Willy Gunther K. G., Nurnberg 9, Humboldstrasse 37/39, W. Germany. The construction of a similar instrument from more readily obtainable parts is relatively simple.

Two, preferably identical, selenium barrier layer photocells of about 5 cm diameter should be obtained. These may be 'potted' in epoxy resin but this cannot be relied upon as a waterproof seal in the sea. For one of the photocells a pressure-proof case should be made of brass or acrylic ('Perspex', 'Plexiglass') sheet. The lid should be held on with strong brass bolts or screws and sealed with a narrow rubber gasket or O-ring. The light sensitive area of the photocell should be below glass in a brass case and protected from all light except from a circular window directly above it in an acrylic case. On the outside of the case there should be a cylindrical well around this window, to contain three or four glass filters. The window should be completely covered by any filters used. The upper filter should be opal glass and the top edge of the well should be flush with this. Spacer rings should be used in place of filters when necessary, to keep the opal glass flush with the top of the well which should be provided with clips to keep the filters in place. The two-core cable connected to the photocell can be led to an underwater bulkhead connector (obtainable from Marsh & Marine, 5123 Gulfton Drive, Houston 36, Texas, U.S.A.) fixed in the wall of the case or passed through the wall with a permanent seal. This is fairly simple with an acrylic case if the cable is cylindrical. A hole of the same diameter as the cable casing is drilled halfway through the case from the outside. This hole is extended to the inside with a drill of a slightly smaller diameter. About 2 cm of acrylic tubing with an internal diameter just fitting the cable is glued to the case as an extension of the hole. The outer casing of the cable having been removed for a sufficient length for the cores to reach the photocell from the wall of the case, the cable casing is covered with epoxy resin glue and the cable pushed into the hole as far as it will go. When the glue has set it is preferable to fit a heat shrinking sleeve to the acrylic tube and a few centimetres of cable. The photocell case should be fitted with three horizontal arms and a bridle from which it is suspended from the ship.

The second photocell need not have a waterproof case but should be fitted with a similar filter holding system. It should be swung in gimbals but it may be hand held and kept horizontal by sighting along the top at the horizon. The cables from the photocells should be led to a galvanometer, preferably one each, but a single galvanometer may be used with a switching arrangement. The galvanometer should have several ranges, preferably allowing readings from 0·1 to 1000 μA. The output of most selenium barrier layer cells without filters is between 1 and 10 μA per μg cal/cm² sec. Neutral density filters should be used in high light levels to protect the photocells and reduce current.

Because the spectral distribution of energy in the sea varies with depth and a photocell is not equally sensitive throughout the spectrum, the use of such a cell in the sea without colour filters would lead to large errors. Schott filters are most commonly used (Jenaer Glaswerk, Schott & Gen., Mainz, W. Germany) but alternative filters of similar absorption spectra can be obtained elsewhere. A minimum of three should be used, usually Schott BG 12 (blue), VG 9 (green) and RG 1 (red). The visible spectrum can be measured more accurately with a more complete series of filters with narrower bandwidths. The relative response of the photocell to a given light source through a colour filter can be calculated by multiplying together the spectral distribution curves for photocell sensitivity, filter transmission (both supplied by the manufacturers) and the radiation. In the case of solar radiation the curves given by Taylor and Kerr (1941) may be used while manufacturers supply curves for artificial sources. Transmission is usually expressed as a percentage at each wavelength but photocell sensitivity and radiation may be expressed relative to the maximum which is taken as 1. The multiplication is performed by dividing the curves into equal wavebands and taking the product of the mean figure for each curve within each waveband. The result can be plotted as the response curve. When comparing the relative effect of different sources equal area curves should be constructed for the radiation from the sources. This should represent equal energy in the range considered (usually 400 to 700 mμ). Each of these curves is multiplied by the response and, if necessary, filter curve, and a sum taken of the products in all the wavebands. The sum gives the total relative response of the photocell to each source of a particular spectral distribution. This may be useful in making energy measurements with an instrument calibrated from one source only.

Because it is usually necessary to alter the optical set-up of a photocell to accommodate the appropriate filters, it is not usually advisable to accept the manufacturers' calibration which in any case is usually in illumination units.

The instruments may be calibrated in a physical laboratory using a standard lamp, or compared with an already standardised stable instrument such as a thermopile, in use at some meteorological stations. If a thermopile, measuring total solar energy, is used, its reading should be halved to obtain visible energy (400–700 mμ). For calibration the underwater cell should be flooded with a depth of pure water equivalent to at least the radius of the opal (Westlake, 1965*a*). Both should be horizontal when compared with a horizontal thermopile.

In making underwater measurements the sea photometer is lowered from the end of a boom projecting as far as possible from the side of the ship facing the sun. The upper surface of the instrument, i.e. the opal glass, should be horizontal and the suspending line vertical if it is used to measure the depth. A series of readings at different depths is taken first with one colour filter in place and then with each other filter. In each series the same colour filter is kept on the deck photocell. At each depth simultaneous readings are taken from each photocell. If only one galvanometer is available a series of readings are taken at each depth, alternating between the two cells, unless light conditions are very stable (e.g. with a cloudless sky). It is important to include as wide a depth range as possible because extrapolation of a logarithmic series of values can produce large errors. The results for each colour filter are calculated as percentages of the surface reading (given by the deck cell) and plotted on semi-logarithmic paper. If the total visible radiant energy variation with depth is required the percentage for each colour filter can be appropriately weighted after calculation of the relative response for a particular combination of filter and photocell. Surface energy measurements can be made with the deck photocell without filter, providing it has been calibrated under suitable conditions. However, because the effect of seawater on irradiance levels is of more lasting interest than the actual irradiances at a point in time, it is more usual to express underwater irradiances in the visible range in percentages of that at the surface. These can then be used in conjunction with known variations in surface irradiance.

4

Photography and Television

A. D. McIntyre

Introduction

In recent years the development of improved optical equipment suitable for underwater operation has introduced new possibilities for marine biology. Still, ciné, and T.V. cameras have been used to take single, stereoscopic, serial or continuous pictures of the sea bed, and the equipment has been hand-held and diver operated, or lowered vertically from the ship, or attached to towed gear, or even sited for long periods on the bottom. The arrangement of equipment has often been highly individualistic, the result of a particular approach to a specific job or situation, and the final set-up can be expensive and may require special expertise in operation. However, with the standardisation of techniques, less complex units are becoming available from stock, and the camera can be increasingly regarded as an established tool. This chapter does not attempt to describe technical detail, but indicates the range of equipment which has been used, and the kinds of problems which have been attacked, noting some of the advantages and disadvantages of underwater photography applied to benthos sampling, and listing references which may be helpful as points of entry to the field.

Photography

The use of cameras
Sampling with grabs or dredges is essential for benthos studies which require morphological examination of animals, accurate taxonomic determination, estimates of biomass, or detailed sediment analyses. However, on hard or uneven ground photography may be the only means of obtaining information, and even in areas where conventional benthos sampling gear operates well, photographs can provide valuable supplementary data on ripple marks and

surface patterns, or on the exact relations of animals to the deposit. Photography can also be useful in the initial examination of grounds at the planning stage of surveys for demonstrating the distribution of sediment types or animal aggregations, and a series of still or ciné photographs can indicate the reactions of organisms to each other or to the gear. Comparing benthos estimates made over a wide area by trawl, grab and camera, McIntyre (1956) concluded that for the less common animals of the epifauna the camera gave the most acceptable estimates and was able also to indicate the distribution

Figure 4.1. Distribution of brittle-stars in patches or scattered on rocks in a way which makes estimation by grab unreliable. Photograph taken in Loch Creran (Scotland) at 15 m depth by F.24 underwater camera (McIntyre, 1956). The camera trigger weight is seen at the top.

of the animals over the ground. Even for the more abundant epifauna species, the camera gave better results than the other gear for organisms which were distributed singly or in small or isolated patches as illustrated in Fig. 4.1. On the other hand, photographs are of little use for estimating infauna, and attempts to derive animal numbers from surface tracks or burrows in deep-water photographs can be positively misleading (Owen, Sanders and Hessler, 1967).

Since a clear field of view is essential, the most serious limitation to photography for bottom survey is the prevalence of turbidity in shallow waters round the coast and on the continental slope. In many places, especially in harbours and river mouths, visibility may be reduced to considerably less than half a metre, and even in deeper areas where water movements stir the deposit into suspension cameras may be of little use. It is sometimes possible to produce photographs in such conditions by replacing turbid water in the object field by clear water (Peau's 'turbidity eliminator'), but there are awkward practical problems, and it must be accepted that the photographic technique is often not applicable.

Schenck and Kendall (1954) cover the whole field of underwater photography and provide a bibliography of the older literature. Cross (1954), Barnes (1958), Craig and Priestley (1963), Edgerton (1967), Carrothers (1967), Brundza (1968) and Mundey (1968) outline various problems and give details of design and operation of units for particular purposes, while Stanton (1968) considers the characteristics of several types of film. The physics of underwater photography is discussed by Thorndike (1967) and recent advances in underwater lighting by Harford (1968). An extensive bibliography is produced by Eastman Kodak Company (Kodak pamphlet no. P-124) and this is brought up to date at intervals by the addition of new references.

The simplest application of underwater photography is in the use of hand-held, diver-operated cameras (see p. 78). This is obviously confined to shallow water of about 30 m, and not only provides a permanent record of what the diver can see, but also enables him to demonstrate the view to others, and to record rapid events which could escape his notice (Edgerton, 1963). This can be of value in studies of growth and colonisation of sedentary organisms on hard surfaces as well as in recording the distribution and movements of animals and the performance of gear. The limited working time available underwater to SCUBA divers imposes restrictions on such observations and Johnston, Morrison and Maclachlan (1969) have developed a photographic recording technique designed to make maximum use of each dive. W. M. Stephens (1967) describes some of the hand-held cameras at present available.

Turning to the use of remote equipment from a ship at sea, since much of the effort is involved in launching and retrieving the camera, it is economic to obtain a long series of exposures at each main lowering. The camera is often triggered by a weight suspended below the unit, so that when the weight touches bottom the flash, synchronised with the shutter opening, is set off; a signal by light or buzzer is received on the ship, and the film winds on to the next frame. The operator can immediately raise the camera a few metres while the ship steams or drifts to the next position. A camera of this type, described in detail by Craig and Priestley (1963) is shown in Fig. 4.2.

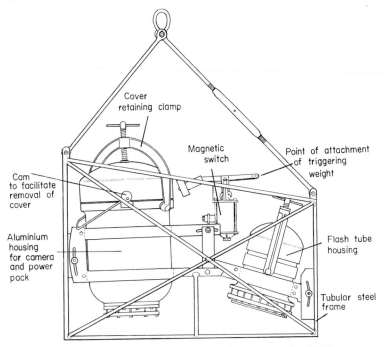

Figure 4.2. Mark V sea-bed camera of Craig & Priestley (1963).

For the observation of temporal changes at a single site, the placing on the sea bed of a camera set to take serial pictures at predetermined time intervals can give useful results. Mitchell (1967) describes an inexpensive system utilising a 16 mm motion picture camera in a simple underwater housing, which can expose one frame per minute for a period of over 6 hours. In a more sophisticated set-up, a recording camera can be arranged to revolve, covering 360° with eight exposures (J. B. Pearce, personal communication). The effects of the lights, and of the equipment itself, which constitutes an artificial reef, must be borne in mind in such work, and the settlement of algae and encrusting animals on the lens can be a difficulty if the gear is retained for long in the water.

While the camera may be lowered as an independent unit, valuable addi-additional information is obtained if it can be attached to or used in conjunction with other sampling equipment. Menzies, Smith and Emery (1963)

Figure 4.3. Bottom view of Campbell grab (as used by Wigley & Emery, 1967) with attached camera and high intensity light. Width of jaws (vertical dimension in photograph) is 57 cm. (From Hersey, 1967.)

describe a camera fitted inside a large bottom sampler—the Campbell grab, which covers an area of 0·56 m². Contact of a trip weight with the bottom activates the flash and camera shutter at about 1 m above the substratum, and further lowering lands the grab on the bottom. Although this arrangement provides only one photograph at each lowering, it does give a valuable sight of the undisturbed sea bed just before the grab bites. A similar system (Fig. 4.3) has been used by Emery *et al.* (1965) and by Wigley and Emery (1967) who discuss the additional information provided by such photographs, concluding that grab sampling alone tends to under-estimate the surface-living component of the fauna. A camera mounted in the weight of a piston coring apparatus is described by Ewing *et al.* (1967). This set-up used at depths of over 5,000 m, provided pictures of the sea bottom and, by time-lapse photography of the sediment cloud raised by the impact of the coring tube, gave information on the velocity and direction of the bottom currents.

Another means of combining photography with sampling is to attach the camera to the headline of a trawl or the frame of a dredge. The unit may involve a still camera set to make a series of exposures automatically (Fig. 4.4), or a ciné may be used (Craig and Priestley, 1963). These devices make it possible to correlate the catch with the type of bottom over a wide area, and in the case of epibenthic species, to estimate the efficiency of the gear. An ingenious system for obtaining serial pictures of the bottom is described by Blacker and Woodhead (1965), who mounted an automatic camera inside the body of a Gulf III high speed metal townet. With a depressor attached to the townet body, and also a transducer which recorded on the ship's echo sounder, it was possible to keep the gear within about a metre of the sea bed by small alterations of the ship's speed and/or the towing warp. The camera could be towed for over 30 km at a speed of 5 knots taking 1,000 exposures, and because it can operate so close to the bottom, it can produce results even in quite turbid waters. Development of this type of equipment is actively under way in several laboratories.

Stereoscopic cameras have also been used, and have obvious advantages in the interpretation of photographs. Owen (1967) describes suitable equipment.

In deep water, where there is little or no suspended matter, turbidity does not present a problem, and no loss of definition occurs over ranges of six metres and sometimes considerably more. Fig. 4.5, taken at 1,780 m depth, shows the high quality of photography possible in such conditions. Deep

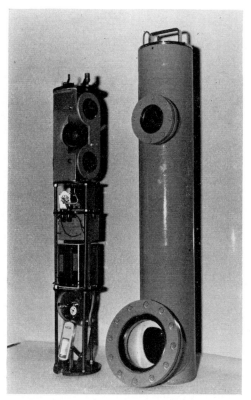

Figure 4.4. Trawl headline camera (Craig & Priestley, 1963). Internal unit on left, with camera, flash, batteries and control gear; camera case on right.

water cameras require water-tight cases able to withstand considerable pressures, and an acoustic transmitter ('pinger'—see Chapter 2) is usually attached to indicate when the gear reaches bottom. Examples of deep sea cameras used on a vertical wire are described by Edgerton and Hoadley (1955) and by Laughton (1957). Such equipment is now produced commercially and an instrument designed to operate to 9,000 m depth is illustrated in *Hydrospace* (Vol. 1, No. 3, 1968, pp. 44–45). It can be used as a freely suspended automatic camera, or may be triggered by a remote control switch. Single exposures can be made, or a series at regular intervals timed from 25 seconds to hours or even days.

Figure 4.5. Photograph taken at 1,780 m depth off New Jersey on a clayey silt sediment. (From Hersey, 1967.)

Laughton (1963) discusses the information which may be obtained from random photographs of the deep sea floor. He considers that they may be analysed under the headings (1) surface geology, (2) indications of current activity, and (3) benthic fauna, and in his account he studied some 2,000 photographs from a variety of habitats.

Towed cameras also are used in deep water, and particularly impressive results have been produced by a submarine sledge ('troika') especially designed for towing on a long cable on difficult bottoms (Laban *et al.*, 1963). Although operating a camera at great depths brings its own problems and frustrations, the results can perhaps be even more rewarding than in shallow water since the deep regions are inaccessible and less explored, and information from other sources, such as grab and dredge, is hard to come by.

The use of cameras in benthos studies is not confined to underwater situations. Aerial photography can provide useful information on certain environmental factors such as turbidity and wave action, and Wanless (1969) indicates its value in field studies in detecting exposed rock bottom and shoal development. Ellis (1966) has described a technique for intertidal surveys by aerial photography from a helicopter. Flying at a height of 60 m, he used twin 70 mm cameras and obtained photographic ground coverage of about 20 km per hour. During a 5-day period of spring tides in British Columbia he was able to survey about 300 km of coastline. Biological interpretations of the photographs (helped by working from stereopairs) was made possible by collecting specimens from transects, and from these surveys three major biotic zones could be distinguished and their distribution charted. From greater heights a wider coverage can be obtained, and the possibilities for the oceanographer of photography from high-flying aircraft or satellites are now being discussed (Ewing, 1966; Pardoe, 1969).

Interpretation of photographs

Great care is required in the interpretation of bottom photographs. It is possible to work from prints, but negatives or transparencies can also be studied, and these, especially if fine grain film is used, can be subjected to considerable magnification. Vevers (1951, 1952) examined negatives under a binocular dissecting microscope, with a grid to aid in counting large concentrations of animals, and a micrometer slide for length measurements. Negative size is important, and this can vary from about 13×11 cm down to the small frames of ciné film. Black and white film may be used and has the advantage of ease of processing so that errors or incorrect exposures can be adjusted immediately, but when lighting is constant and exposure can therefore be made more or less correct, colour film can be useful in distinguishing animals from the background, in helping with identification and in giving information about the deposit (Trumbull and Emery, 1967).

Because of the difficulty of resolving perspective on a single photograph it is not usually possible to plot the distribution of individual organisms. However Johnston, Morrison and Maclachlan (1969) describe a technique by which accurate plots can be made using a calibrated marker frame included in the photograph.

When making quantitative studies from serial photographs, particularly from deep water, it is important that every relevant frame should be included in the analyses, care being taken to avoid over-emphasis of the perhaps few frames of particular interest. Whenever possible, photographs should be examined in conjunction with material collected from the bottom by grab or dredge. Laughton (1957) illustrates the dangers of making interpretations of photographs without samples. Pictures from 1,430 m off Madeira showed boulders with parallel lines suggesting bedding planes of sedimentary rock. Dredging from the same area, however, produced similar boulders which showed that the 'bedding planes' were in fact corrugations on the cooling surface of a lava flow, the boulders being highly vascular basalt. Further discussion on the use and interpretation of bottom photographs can be found in the papers of McIntyre (1956), Emery *et al.* (1965) and Cabioch (1967).

Television

Until recently, underwater television equipment tended to be very expensive, bulky and difficult to handle, and the definition was less good than with photographic cameras, so its use was much restricted. The earlier problems and equipment are discussed by Cross (1954), and Barnes (1963) gives a comprehensive review.

The main advantage of underwater television compared with conventional photography is that of continuous viewing, which is of considerable value in the study of fish and active epibenthos, as well as in observing gear in action. It can also provide rapid appraisals of large areas of bottom. It suffers from the same disadvantage as photography, in particular that clarity of water is a limiting factor, and that nothing is brought to the surface for detailed examination. Further, the advantage of continuous viewing is to some extent offset by the need to use artificial light in most situations, and while this may present no problem when used with instantaneous photography, the lighting required for continuous viewing may well alter the behaviour of the organisms observed. This difficulty is a general one except in regions where water is exceptionally transparent, such as in the Adriatic, where Czihak and Zei (1960) have used a T.V. camera to depths of 45 m without artificial light.

In spite of these disadvantages the use of U.T.V. for biological work is increasing. Stevenson (1967) describes a unit mounted on the sea bed at about 20 m depth in the Straights of Florida off Bimini, consisting of a transistorised T.V. camera provided with two incandescent lamps of 300 watts each for night photography. A tilt-and-pan mechanism gave 360° horizontal and 60° vertical visibility. Associated underwater equipment included hydrophones and environmental sensors recording data on temperature, currents and turbidity. The system was controlled remotely from the shore base about a mile away. As well as giving valuable information on fish behaviour and sound production, the effect on the bottom of varying hydrographic conditions could be observed. For example, normally sandy bottoms were seen to acquire coverings of up to 15 cm of marl after hurricanes Further details of this underwater set-up are given by Kronengold and Loewenstein (1965) who also describe the use of cinematography from U.T.V.

The use of such sophisticated equipment sited permanently on the bottom is obviously restricted, and lighter mobile gear lowered from a ship has more general application. This has proved of value even in the poor visibility of Japanese waters (Nishimura and Hara, 1968) where it has been applied to fisheries research, and in the Baltic, where it has been used for ecological studies of submarine plants (Schwenke, 1965).

Figure 4.6. Hand-held underwater television camera.

Recent developments in construction and design have provided even more compact equipment and diver-held U.T.V. cameras (Fig. 4.6) are now available which weigh as little as 5 kg in air (4 kg in water) with associated deck equipment of correspondingly compact nature.

Acknowledgments

Thanks are due to Roland L. Wigley (Bureau of Commercial Fisheries, Woods Hole) and to members of the staff of the Marine Laboratory, Aberdeen, for assistance. Also, to the Marine Laboratory, Aberdeen, for Figs. 4.1, 4.2 and 4.4, and to Hydro Products, Billingham Corporation, for Fig. 4.6.

5

Diving

N. S. JONES

General application

The role of diving as a method of investigating the benthos has become increasingly important during the last 20 years and there is every sign that its use will continue to increase. Many of the marine biological and fisheries laboratories now have several staff members trained to dive, and some, such as those at La Jolla in California and Endoume near Marseille, have made very extensive use of diving in marine research. For an historical review see Riedl (1966, 1967). There have been a number of reviews of diving as a research tool (Riedl, 1963, 1967; Skarlato *et al.*, 1964; Bacescu, 1965; Clark, 1965; MacInnis, 1966; Pérès, 1966).

At the present time diving for purposes of biological research is almost entirely carried out using the aqualung (SCUBA) because of the freedom of movement which it provides and its relative cheapness. Where long periods of immersion are needed in shallow water, however, a surface-demand system may be an advantage. The techniques of diving, where training courses are not readily available, may be learnt by following the instructions given in various naval diving manuals or those of the British Sub-Aqua Club, and similar organisations in other countries (Poulet, 1962; U.S. Navy, 1963; Admiralty, 1964; Terrell, 1965; British Sub-Aqua Club, 1968).

The majority of biological investigations by free divers have been confined to hard substrates or to the epifauna (Hass, 1948; Drach, 1948, 1958; Pérès and Picard, 1949; Forster, 1954, 1959, 1961; Picard, 1954; Ernst, 1955; Baird and Gibson, 1956; Morgans, 1957, 1962; Laborel and Vacelet, 1959; Hiatt and Strasburg, 1960; Laborel, 1960; Kempf, 1962; Neushul, 1963; Neushul and Haxo, 1963; Randall, 1963, 1964; North, 1964; Leighton *et al.*, 1965; Turner *et al.*, 1965, 1966; Ledoyer, 1966*a*, *b* and *c*; Clarke *et al.*, 1967; Drew and Larkum, 1967; Jones and Kain, 1967; Vacelet, 1967). On some kinds of bottom diving is unrivalled by any method involving apparatus controlled from the surface; these include steep rocky slopes and cliffs, boulders and uneven surfaces, caves and canyons. Some quantitative or growth studies on sessile organisms and certain observations on behaviour can only be made by diving (Baird, 1958a; Abel, 1959, 1960, 1961; Sinclair, 1959; Carlisle, 1961; Limbaugh, 1961; Ebert and Turner, 1962; Randall, 1962; Bertram, 1966; Altman, 1967; Hartnoll, 1967). Diving is often a convenient method of obtaining specimens in good condition for laboratory work.

In general the techniques and apparatus used in the study of the benthos under water do not differ greatly from those used on the shore but the water medium imposes some special problems. It is not easy to perform work involving sustained hard physical effort when free diving, nor to exert much force in the use of tools. On the other hand the comparative lightness of many materials in water is an advantage to the diver, while buoyancy may readily be obtained by filling collapsible plastic bags with respired air or directly from a high pressure cylinder. The necessity normally to carry everything required for the duration of a dive limits the amount and size of apparatus which can be used unless it can be lowered from a boat. The problem of poor visibility in many areas may be severe and this increases the difficulty of recognising features on the bottom or of revisiting a site for recurrent investigation unless this is close to the shore or can be buoyed. On fine deposits visibility may be reduced to nil by the disturbance caused by the diver's movements.

Probably the most important factor that must be taken into account is the limitation imposed by the air supply. At present, unless special apparatus is used, the depth limit at which a free diver can carry out a reasonably long piece of work as opposed to a quick observation or collection of specimens is about 35 m, and for an investigation involving fairly lengthy periods under water 20 m could be considered the maximum without providing extra supplies of air for stage decompression. These are by no means the physical or physiological limits for free divers, even on compressed air, but for most research purposes they would be the practical limits. Cold water may also limit the duration of a dive but this can largely be overcome by wearing the more sophisticated kinds of protective clothing. In less than 10 m depth and in warm water long periods may be spent on the bottom without risk and much may even be accomplished by snorkelling. With a normal quantity of compressed air a dive may last between 20 and 90 minutes according to depth, but the development of cryogenic (liquid air) apparatus may greatly extend these times.

Exposure to wind-driven waves and swell and to tidal or other currents may affect the choice of a site. In many localities a diver may be able to work only at slack water of neap tides. The overriding consideration at all times should be the diver's safety, and in this respect institutions should take note of their responsibilities and ascertain that divers are properly insured against accident or loss of life and the institution itself legally protected against claims.

Recording and collecting

On rocks under water some quantitative estimates of the benthos may be made by line transects. It is not difficult to make a reel of non-corrodible materials to carry a line with intervals clearly marked, or a suitable measuring-tape may be used (Knight-Jones *et al.*, 1967). By leap-frogging with a line two divers can cover fairly long distances (Kain, 1962). For estimating numbers of large organisms a modified form of transect may be found useful, as described by Forster (1959) and Larsson (1968), when the diver swims along a line of known length previously laid out on the sea bed, holding before him a rod one or more metres long; one end of the rod is kept above the line and the organisms are counted as it passes over them. Quadrat frames of various sizes are also useful for quantitative studies, the smaller or more abundant the organisms to be counted the smaller the quadrat that must be used. These methods are, of course, useless for fast-moving animals. Small plants and sessile or slow-moving animals may be removed from within a quadrat frame by a knife blade or a scraper with a net bag attached as described by Kain (1960). The Finnish IBP-PM Group have produced a bag for sampling whole plants of larger algae with their attached fauna and flora; this is essentially a large fine-meshed net attached to a hand-held circular frame, the purpose of which is to hold the bag open, with a lower open-ended part round which a draw-string passes; the open end is placed over the plant, which is pushed inside by the diver, the plant detached and the string drawn tight beneath it. For collecting specimens generally netting or finer-meshed bags are most useful provided that they allow water to pass fairly freely but for keeping living specimens, especially of delicate organisms, in good condition impervious plastic bags or bottles are better.

The collection and counting of animals which are able to move rapidly present a difficult problem under water. Small fishes and crustaceans may sometimes be caught in nets or sucked into large cylinders by the backward movement of a piston in the bore. In some situations it is possible to kill or paralyse animals by ejecting rapidly working poisons or anaesthetics into the surrounding water (see p. 116). Large fish may be shot with spear-guns. However, it is impossible in many cases to arrive at an accurate estimate of the numbers present (but see Brock, 1954).

There is little need to detail methods of observation below water but the choice of recording instruments and materials may be important. For writing notes matt-surfaced, light-coloured plastic sheets (p. 161) are preferable, and soft pencils (with spares) whipped with string or bound with plastic adhesive tape and attached to the note-pad will be found satisfactory. Notes may be taken by an attendant on the surface through a telephone line, which may also be used as a safety line by a diver without a companion. Several bone-conducting transceivers have been produced which give reasonable sound reproduction. The most time-saving method of making records is by means of a tape-recorder enclosed in a water-tight case, as described by Breslau *et al.* (1962) or Fager *et al.* (1966). It is quite easy to construct a suitable case from clear perspex or plexiglass and controls may be adapted with a little ingenuity and the help of O-rings. For communication between divers and with the surface there are now a number of pieces of equipment in commercial production which give satisfactory results without cable connections over short distances but until these have stood the test of time it is best to seek advice from those experienced in their use.

On soft substrates the advantages over apparatus operated from the surface are less apparent, especially in the study of the infauna, but it is much easier for a diver to select the exact site of a bottom sample and to obtain deeply burrowing animals. For quantitative estimates of larger epifaunal animals and plants, quadrats are as useful as on a hard substrate (Jones and Kain, 1964). For the infauna some sort of corer may be used as described by Fager *et al.* (1966), Angel and Angel (1967) and Walker (1967), and as described by the Finnish IBP-PM Group (1969). The Tvärminne sampler consists of a steel cylinder enclosed at the top by a lid of stainless steel mesh and with a circular steel cutting plate with a handle. The open bottom of the cylinder is pushed carefully into mud or silt by a diver who excavates a pit alongside it. The cutting plate is then pushed through the pit into a slit near the bottom of the cylinder, thus cutting off the bottom of the sample.

The deposit and its contained animals may be sucked up by means of the apparatuses described by Brett (1964), Reys, *et al.* (1966), Barnett and Hardy (1967), Emig and Lienhart (1967) and True, *et al.* (1968) (see pp. 108–115). These may be used quantitatively when combined with a quadrat frame or

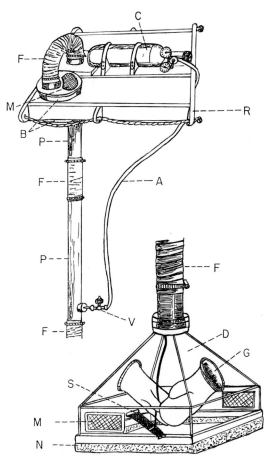

Figure 5.1. Finnish suction sampler for hard bottoms. *A*, air hose; *B*, plastic bucket, with open bottom covered with fine steel mesh; *C*, air cylinder; *D*, perspex funnel; *F*, flexible pipe; *G*, latex glove; *M*, stainless steel mesh; *N*, foam plastic; *P*, rigid plastic pipe; *R*, raft; *S*, scraper; *V*, air valve (Redrawn from Finnish IBP-PM Group. 1969).

cylinder, if necessary with knife edges hammered into the substrate, or forced in by water pressure as described by Barnett and Hardy. The Finnish IBP-PM Group have developed a sampler which can work on either of the principles described by Brett or Barnett and Hardy but for use on hard bottoms (Fig. 5.1). In this case the suction pipe is inserted into the top of a collecting funnel made of perspex with a foam plastic seal around the bottom edge. The funnel has small openings protected by steel mesh through which water can pass freely and a pair of rubber gloves fixed around holes in its upper sides. A diver can place the funnel on the rock and insert his hands into the gloves to remove plants and animals by means of a scraper. These are then sucked up the tube and retained by sieves (Finnish IBP-PM Group, 1969).

Fager *et al.* (1966) describe several methods for quantitative sampling of the epifauna and for studying distribution patterns.

Diving at night may be more productive than during the day as many animals leave holes and crevices and move around freely in the dark. Some are easier to catch when dazzled by a light (Wicklund, 1964; Starck and Schroeder, 1965). A variety of suitable underwater lights is available.

In shallow water and clear conditions diving may be used to compare the relative efficiencies of trawls, dredges and bottom samplers in action (Vyskrebezov, 1962; Parrish *et al.*, 1964; High and Lusz, 1966).

Studies of growth and reproduction and of recolonisation may be carried out with advantage by divers. It is sometimes necessary to mark individual plants or animals and this is usually a simple matter of attaching a numbered tag but calls for ingenuity in some instances to avoid damage to the marked organisms (for references on tagging and marking see p. 294).

A number of studies have been made of the physical environment of sessile benthic organisms, using apparatus placed by divers (Parker, 1965), and microhabitats may perhaps be investigated only in this way (Riedl, 1966).

Amateur divers may be employed for certain types of investigation. With some training, groups can collect specimens from or explore wide areas and undertake measurements of a fairly simple kind, while individuals who are not professional biologists may become competent observers. Supervision of such projects and care in interpretation of data obtained are essential.

Position fixing in diving work

Aids to navigation by divers have not yet been highly developed and finding or relocating position underwater is often a matter of some difficulty. Close to the shore it is usually possible to take marks from the surface on to objects out of the water with enough accuracy to make returning to a precise position on the bottom fairly easy in conditions of reasonable visibility. Starting from the shore there may be enough distinctive underwater features to enable the diver to follow a route. Where there is no current it is usually possible to rise vertically to the surface, from where location can be ascertained by the usual methods if a boat is available or by means of a hand-bearing compass carried by the diver if not, but at any distance offshore position finding by sextant or navigational aids such as Decca are not sufficiently precise to enable a diver to return to a site unless visibility is exceptional and the depth small.

Where there is doubt about finding a diving site repeatedly it should be buoyed. Unfortunately buoys are not ideal markers. Unless they are moored with heavy chain or wire they may not remain in position for more than a few weeks where there is much wave action or tidal movement, while in some places they may be interfered with. In a seaway a buoy may be in danger of being cut adrift by passing ships or if it is large be a danger to shipping.

Buoys must be firmly anchored, especially in a tideway, and concrete blocks provide a cheap and convenient method for anchorage when handling facilities are available although almost any heavy material available would be satisfactory. Concrete blocks may be used as markers on unstable bottoms (Jones *et al.*, 1965). Where buoys cannot be used it may be possible to lay out a wire or rope along the bottom leading to the site for work. The wire should be fixed at either end. From the shore this presents no difficulty but offshore it may be necessary for the diver to submerge at a position to one side of the wire and from there to swim over the bottom on a compass course until the wire can be seen. If the wire is long enough the chances of missing it are small. When a site has been lost through removal of a buoy or some other accident it may sometimes be found again by carrying out one of the methods of search outlined in several of the diving manuals (e.g. Booth, 1968).

In some circumstances objects on the bottom may be located by echo sounding or oblique sonar and this may be sufficient to enable a diver to visit a site repeatedly but the most accurate method of locating a position on the bottom is by means of a sonar beacon or pinger placed on the position and a pinger locater on the surface or held by the diver. A suitable instrument is sold by Hydro Products, California (see list of suppliers, p. 291).

Ancillary diving equipment

Ancillary equipment which has been developed includes various diving sleds and planes (Sand, 1956; Hold, 1960; Kumpf and Randall, 1961; Carpine *et al.*, 1965; Riley and Holford, 1965) which may be towed behind a boat and kept by the diver either on or above the sea floor. These are useful for surveys covering large areas, for mapping gross features or for searching. There are also several commercially produced self-propelled towing vehicles with suitable controls for divers.

Above all, photography is useful for recording the progress of experimental work below the water surface, for behavioural studies and for displaying organisms in their natural environment. Good results are more easily obtained by a diver in shallow water than with equipment lowered from a boat and he can approach places inaccessible from the surface. Several still and ciné cameras can be obtained with specially made water-tight cases, and cases with suitable controls incorporated can be made from perspex or its equivalent to suit the majority (see also p. 61). Cameras specially designed for underwater use, such as the 35 mm Nikonos with properly corrected lenses, are possibly easiest to use; with its electronic flash unit or with flash-bulbs this camera can give excellent results. On the other hand larger film sizes give more detail and for many purposes such cameras as the Rollei may be more suitable. For ciné work, except near the surface where daylight is sufficient, more elaborate and expensive lighting equipment is needed and any photographic work requires reasonably good visibility. In many places photography is only worth while occasionally when the amount of suspended matter in the water is small and it may be necessary to wait for the most favourable time. (For details see Riedl, 1954; Schenck and Kendall, 1954; Dobbs, 1962; Booda, 1967; Mundey, 1968; see also Chapter 4.)

Apparatus for underwater vehicles

To overcome the drawbacks of restricted air supply and to extend working time under water a number of experimental submerged bases filled with compressed gases and having life support systems have been constructed from which free divers can make excursions into the surrounding water without the need for immediate decompression. The depth to which divers can work from such underwater 'houses' and the length of time for which they can remain below the surface is still being extended. It is unlikely that such systems could be used much below 300–400 metres depth but it is certain that much valuable work on the benthos will be carried out from them in the future. They will always, however, be expensive to operate if the safety of the occupants is to be fully ensured (Dugan, 1965; Platt, 1965*a*, *b*; Cousteau, 1966; Spiess, 1966; R. W. B. Stephens, 1967; Nicholson *et al.*, 1968). On the other hand a simple reservoir of air as described by Williams (1968) is inexpensive and might be a great help in some underwater projects.

The depth to which divers can penetrate is also being currently extended by the use of special gas mixtures and submersible decompression chambers, but again the expense of operating these is likely to remain beyond the means of small laboratories, while the time available for work is short.

For investigation of the benthos at greater depths and for exploration of lesser depths the preferred method will no doubt involve the use of underwater research vehicles such as are now being developed, especially in the U.S.A. At present these are mostly experimental and little can be said about their capabilities. They lack well developed methods of taking and manipulating samples in sufficient numbers. These disadvantages will probably be overcome (Wischhoefer and Jones, 1968) but costs are likely to remain relatively high. Up to now they have mainly been used, when not simply on test, for exploration. Many valuable observations have, however, been made from Cousteau's diving saucer (Pérès, 1960*a, b*; Laborel *et al.*, 1961; Reyss, 1964; Guille, 1965; Shepard, 1965*a*) and this submersible at least has proved its worth in the field of benthos studies. The latest developments are best discovered by reference to such periodicals as *Undersea Technology* and *Hydrospace*.

6

Macrofauna Sampling

N. A. HOLME

Intertidal observation and collection

Study of the intertidal fauna and flora is in some ways easier than that of subtidal areas, but since the habitat is subjected to both aerial and aquatic climates, environmental factors influencing distribution are more complex. When visiting the shore it should be remembered that low tide is a dormant period for many animals, which are active only when covered by the sea. Also, certain predators invade the shore at different periods of the tidal cycle: fish and crustaceans at high tide, and man, birds, insects and sometimes rats or cattle at low tide.

For productivity studies it is necessary to express quantitative collections in terms of numbers, or biomass, occupying unit area as projected in plan on to a horizontal plane. The figures will then correspond to studies offshore which are related to quantities below unit area of sea surface. On gently sloping shores of soft sediment no conversions are required, but on irregular rocky shores the necessary conversions may prove difficult.

On sandy or muddy shores estimates of the standing crop of macrofauna and flora are made by driving a square sheet metal frame of appropriate area (perhaps 0·1 m² or 0·25 m²) into the substratum, the sediment within the frame being excavated to the desired depth. On some beaches water for sieving can be obtained by digging a hole near the sampling site, otherwise the sediment is placed in a sack or metal bath and carried or dragged to the water's edge for sieving. A plentiful supply of water is required for sieving; sometimes a nearby stream may be utilised, but if this is of fresh water it may damage the more delicate organisms. If no stream is available and the distance to low water mark is great it may be possible to arrange sampling for a time when the water's edge is not too far from the sampling position. Subsequent sorting is made easier if all traces of mud can be washed out of the sample when sieving.

It is not possible to indicate how deeply the area should be excavated. On some shores the majority of species and individuals occur in the top 15 cm, in others it may be necessary to excavate to 30 cm or more. Preliminary excavations should be made to find a suitable sampling depth. Since the majority of small individuals occur in the top 5–10 cm it may be possible to sieve the surface layers through a fine sieve, the deeper layers being passed through a coarser sieve (Pamatmat, 1968). In this way much unnecessary labour may be avoided.

The question of sieve mesh is discussed on pp. 158–160. On muddy shores it may be possible to use an aperture as small as 0·5 mm, but on sandy shores a coarser mesh of 1·0 or 1·4 mm may be necessary. Organisms which would pass the mesh employed can be collected by taking smaller volumes of deposit with a Perspex or glass coring tube, and by adopting the methods described for meiofauna on pp. 163–168.

At high tide fish and crustaceans invade the intertidal zone. These may be sampled qualitatively by shrimping nets, or by a small sledge such as described by Pullen *et al.* (1968). The Riley push net (Fig. 6.1 and Appendix p. 286) may be used in shallow water either just below the low tide mark, or on the flooded beach. If operated at a standard speed for fixed times it can produce comparatively quantitative data on small active animals such as juvenile flatfish. Some small sand-burrowing crustaceans such as amphipods swim freely in the overlying water at high tide, returning to their zones in the sand as the tide retreats (Watkin, 1941). These animals can be sampled by nets such as those described by Colman and Segrove (1955) (Fig. 6.2); Macer (1967), and others referred to on pp. 118 and 136–138.

It is usual to survey an intertidal flat by traverses running from high to low water mark, with sampling stations at regular intervals. Sometimes two or more samples are taken at each station to give an indication of the variability of populations. Since the surface of an intertidal flat is often more or less uniform in appearance, the question of possible bias in selecting the position of the traverse and of individual stations does not usually arise, although the presence of irregularities on the beach should be carefully observed, since these are often associated with turbulent conditions at particular tidal levels. On smaller areas, such as pocket beaches, the profile may be much more obviously irregular, and the various features—ridges and runnels, streams, pools of fresh or salt water should be taken into account in sampling. Surveying and levelling of intertidal transects are treated below.

Fig. 6.1a

Fig. 6.1b

Figure 6.1. (a) Riley push-net ready for use. (b) Push-net in use (Both photographs by courtesy of J D Riley).

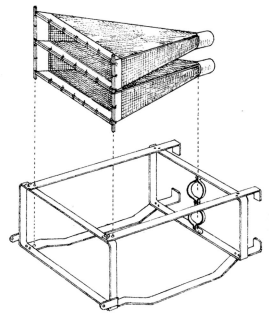

Figure 6.2. Bottom plankton net (Redrawn from Colman & Segrove, 1955).

On rocky shores sampling is carried out by means of square frames of heavy gauge wire laid on the substratum, the animals and plants within the frame being counted, weighed, or estimated in terms of percentage cover of the surface. Sometimes estimates may be made *in situ*, otherwise organisms must be scraped off for subsequent examination in the laboratory. For larger organisms a frame of 1 m² is suitable, but for smaller organisms or where the rock surface is irregular smaller frames of 0·1 m² (316 × 316 mm) should be used. A flexible frame might be appropriate on some rock surfaces. For counting small organisms like barnacles squares of 0·01 m² (100 × 100 mm) are suitable. For such counts a piece of thick (6 mm) perspex exactly 100 mm square and with a grid of 10 mm squares etched on is very convenient, allowing smaller areas to be counted, and also minimising the possibility of missing individuals or counting them twice. Besides organisms living on the rock surface, estimates should be made of crevice-living and boring species, and of those sheltering among weeds.

Stations should be spaced out at regular intervals along traverses from high to low water mark. The lack of uniformity of most rocky shore habitats will often make it necessary to make a number of estimates in different types of habitat (e.g. rock pool, rocks exposed/sheltered from waves/sun, crevices, under stones) at each station. Since such habitats cannot normally be selected by predetermined measurements, the question of bias will arise. Bias cannot be entirely eliminated when making such estimates, and indeed on a rocky shore having an almost infinite variety of microhabitats it is questionable whether it is possible to take a sample which is in any degree representative of a wider area. No general guidance on this problem can be given, each shore must be dealt with as the individual investigator sees fit.

Position fixing and levelling on the shore

The positions of stations or transects on the shore may be fixed by the usual surveying techniques as outlined, for example, by Southward (1965, Chapter 8). However, he has not emphasised the importance of positioning the levelling instrument exactly half-way between the two positions to be levelled, so eliminating any small inherent errors in the instrument, or errors due to refraction etc. A cheap and simple level which may be used by one person without assistance is described by Kain (1958). A fuller treatment of levelling techniques is given in the Admiralty Manual of Hydrographic Surveying (Admiralty, 1948). Other relevant references are Kissam (1956), Morgans (1965) and Zinn (1969). For repeat sampling, positions on a rocky shore may be marked with paint, marks chiselled into the rock, expanding 'Rawlbolts' inserted into crevices or by small concrete blocks cast *in situ*. On sandy and muddy shores positions may be marked by wooden posts driven deeply into the sediment. However, such posts may themselves cause some alteration of the environment. They may for example attract the attention of people gathering shellfish so that on an otherwise featureless flat the sediment surrounding the posts may receive more trampling than elsewhere. In such instances it may be best to position posts a known distance (say 20 m) from the selected position, the exact location of which is determined with a tape measure.

For intertidal organisms the duration of exposure at each low tide is important. This may be roughly determined from the zonation of plants and animals on the shore, and by observations of the length of time for which the selected sites are exposed over a number of low tides. Where tidal data are available the positions may be levelled to a bench-mark or other mark of known height; it will then be possible to calculate exposure from data given in the tide tables (e.g. Admiralty Tide Tables, Vol. 1, 1969 (European waters), pp. xii–xxvi. Hydrographer of the Navy, London. 1968, 359 p.).

In estuaries or in parts of the world where accurate tidal data are not available a series of observations on a graduated tide pole should be carried out, and positions on the shore can then be levelled in relation to the tide pole. Allowance should be made for spring and neap tides, the effects of wind and barometric pressure, and for river outflow in estuaries. It should not be assumed that the tidal curve follows a symmetrical harmonic curve, nor that tidal heights are necessarily the same on the two tides of one day (Doodson and Warburg, 1941; Lewis, 1964). On wave-exposed coasts levels are elevated through spray and swash, so that plants and animals will tend to occur much higher than on sheltered shores.

Useful literature

Although much descriptive material on sea-shore ecology has been published, there is no general work dealing comprehensively with sampling techniques. A helpful account, particularly for quantitative studies, is given by Southward (1965), and further information is contained in Dowdeswell (1959).

For descriptions of different intertidal habitats, often with some reference to quantitative data, the reader is referred to:

Rocky shores: Crisp and Southward (1958); Ballantine (1961); Moyse and Nelson-Smith (1963); Lewis (1964).
Aerial surveys: Ellis (1966).
Atolls: Wiens (1962).
Algae and associated fauna: Colman (1939); Wieser (1952); Gerking (1957); Forsber (1959); Gillespie and Brown (1966).
Fauna of submerged boulders: Lilly *et al.* (1953).
Crevice faunas: Morton (1954).
Sand and mud flats: Holme (1949a); Moore *et al.* (1968).
Salt marshes: Pomeroy (1959).
Mangrove swamps: Golley *et al.* (1962); Walsh (1967); Macnae (1967, 1968); Warner (1969).

Remote collection

Introduction

In recent years several reviews have appeared (Gunter, 1957; Thorson, 1957a; Holme, 1964; Hopkins, 1964; Reys, 1964) in which the equipment and techniques used for sampling the benthos are described. While choice of equipment depends largely on local conditions—the size of ship, whether sampling in exposed or sheltered water, depth of water, bottom deposit and the type of sample required—the multiplicity of samplers which have been described is evidence not only of such varying conditions, but of a widespread dissatisfaction with existing methods of collection. There is clearly a need for considerable improvements, particularly in quantitative sampling techniques, before any sampler can be unreservedly recommended. The problem is most acute for small boat sampling, because many instruments need to be rather heavy to sample effectively, and under these conditions some compromise in the direction of less quantitative sampling methods may have to be adopted. This section is concerned with methods of collecting the macrofauna; meiofauna is dealt with in Chapter 7, and phytobenthos in Chapter 11.

Dredging and trawling

Qualitative sampling of the macrofauna is carried out by means of dredges or trawls, which capture members of the epifauna, but which, because of their very limited penetration of the sediment, are not really suitable for sampling, even qualitatively, the burrowing fauna.

Dredges are of many kinds, the commonest being the naturalist's or rectangular dredge (Appendix, p. 282), used for sampling on rocks and for exploratory purposes where the nature of the bottom is not known. The dredge scrapes off animals attached to rock or brings up stones with attached animals, but on sediments it only samples a selection of the epifauna and it scarcely digs into the bottom unless this is of soft mud. The dredge has two hinged towing arms which come together at the towing point. One arm is shackled to the tow-rope, the other being joined by a weak link consisting of several turns of twine. If the dredge comes fast on the sea bed the weak link is intended to break, allowing the arms to open out and free the dredge. The strength of the weak link must be found by experience; for a heavy dredge three turns of 8 mm diameter manilla rope is about right. If synthetic rope is used there is a danger that the link may be made too strong so that it does not part when required. Knots in synthetic rope tend to slip and this is another reason for preferring natural fibre. More sophisticated links involving a shear pin are also available (Fig. 6.3). An alternative arrangement is to have a safety-chain connected to the back or side of the dredge (Fig. 6.4; see also Carey and Hancock, 1965) to retrieve it when a weak link at the towing point

approx. scale 0 2 4 6 8 10 cm

Figure 6.3. Weak link (UMEL) with holes for pins of different shear strength.

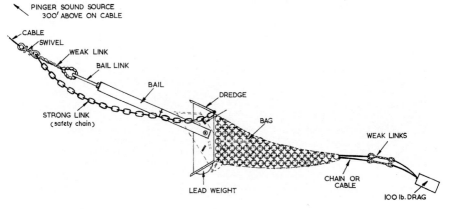

Figure 6.4. Dredge for rock-dredging in the deep sea, showing arrangement of weak link, safety chain and swivel. Note the bag made up of interlaced metal rings (Redrawn from Nalwalk *et al.*, 1962).

is parted. A swivel must always be inserted between towing warp and dredge (or any other gear), and this should be of a ball-bearing type when the towing warp is of wire.

The net bag is usually about half as deep as wide, the mesh varying according to circumstances. If made up by hand from trawl twine the mesh will be about 25 mm knot to knot, but machine-made netting of about half this mesh may be more suitable. In general, synthetic materials such as ulstron, or polyethylene, are best for such nets, particularly if they are used infrequently and are stored in damp surroundings. For nets in regular use, which wear out before they rot the cheapest suitable material, whether natural or synthetic, should be used. If a sample of sediment is required the netting bag should be lined with an inner bag of sacking, stramin or burlap. An impervious material like canvas should not be used, as water must be allowed to drain out when the dredge comes out of the water. In some cases (as with the anchor-dredge, Fig. 6.7), the bag can be an open-ended sleeve tied at the bottom with a cod-end knot, which is released to empty the sample. There is

Figure 6.5. Heavy rock dredge, without arms, showing bag of wire rope grommets (Copyright National Institute of Oceanography).

Figure 6.6. Oyster dredge, showing bag of interlaced alternate large and small iron rings (Photo N A Holme).

a danger, however, that if the bag is too deep it may burst when a heavy load is brought in.

For heavy-duty dredging over rocks or rough ground the dredge bag can be made of metal rings or wire grommets (Fig. 6.5). Bags of interlacing metal rings are commonly used on oyster and scallop dredges (Fig. 6.6) and for rock dredging for geological purposes a bag specially made up of links of flexible galvanised wire rope (as used industrially for safety nets) can be produced to order (e.g. from British Ropes Ltd, London).

When operating from a small boat where the dredge is hand-hauled, a rectangular dredge frame of length 300–380 mm is large enough (see Appendix, pp. 282). This can be towed on a rope, preferably synthetic, of at least 10 mm, and preferably 12 mm diameter. For larger boats with a power hoist, a dredge frame of length 450–600 mm is suitable, and a 750 mm frame for trawler-sized vessels. On ships equipped with winches, wire ropes will be used for working the dredge, and the diameter of these will be related to the size of ship and depth of water, bearing in mind that, in spite of weak links, very severe strains are exerted on the towing warp from time to time (see p. 155). In shallow water it is usual to pay out warp equal to $2\frac{1}{2}$–3 times the depth of water, but in the deep sea a factor of $1\frac{1}{2}$ times or less is all that is needed (p. 126) particularly when a pinger is used to show when the dredge is on the bottom (see p. 22). When dredging, the ship should drift, or steam slowly (1–2 knots), and a check should be made on the functioning of the dredge either by feeling the warp for vibrations, or by means of a strain gauge (see p. 18). The dredge would normally be towed along the bottom for 5 or 10 minutes, but in some circumstances (e.g. in mud or loose gravel) it may fill up at once and can be hauled almost immediately. Special techniques for deep-sea dredging are described on pp. 123–127.

Dredge frames with a bowed, oval or circular mouth are more effective than straight-sided dredges for digging into the sediment and sampling the burrowing fauna, but the penetrating powers of most are limited except in soft mud, so that only shallow-burrowing forms are collected. It is not possible to say which of the various shapes is more useful for a particular purpose and this will in any case depend on other factors such as weight of the dredge frame, length of towing warp, and speed of towing. Dredges with teeth are more effective for certain purposes (see Baird, 1959) but should be avoided if possible because they may damage the side of the ship or injure the crew. For deep-sea dredging the use of inclined steel diving plates to make the dredge sink more quickly is worth considering (e.g. Baird, 1955, 1959; Little and Mullins, 1964).

Beam, Agassiz, and otter trawls may be used for qualitative sampling of the epifauna. These nets are designed and rigged to skim over the surface of the bottom, and because of the large area covered are useful for collecting larger or scarcer members of the epifauna, and species of fish, cephalopods and crustaceans associated with or feeding on the bottom. The efficiency of such gear is discussed in Chapter 8.

The beam trawl is still used commercially on small boats for inshore fishing for shrimps, prawns, etc. The mouth of the net is held open by a wooden beam of perhaps 2–4 m length, with iron runners at either end. The net itself is a fairly long bag of mesh about 12.5 mm knot-to-knot, the lower leading edge of which is attached to a weighted chain forming a foot-rope which curves back behind the top of the net attached to the beam so that fish disturbed by the footrope cannot escape upwards. For small boat work the beam can be obtained in two jointed halves for easy stowage (see Appendix, list of suppliers).

The Agassiz trawl is virtually a double-sided beam trawl (Appendix, Fig. 3), and was designed for deep-sea collecting, where it is not possible to control which way up the trawl lands on the bottom. As compared with the beam trawl it suffers from the disadvantage that foot and head ropes, being interchangeable in function according to how the trawl settles on the bottom, are necessarily the same length. Consequently very few fish are caught by the Agassiz trawl, which is not therefore used commercially.

Both these trawls can be towed by two wire or rope bridles attached to a single tow rope. They are towed over the bottom with warp equal to about three times the depth, at speeds of 2–3 knots. Unfortunately the cross-bars or beams of either trawl are liable to be damaged if they meet an obstruction. A weak link and safety-chain as used for dredges should therefore be used when trawling on unknown grounds or in deep water. Besides animals retained in the cod-end many small organisms may be found attached to the net meshes, and these trawls usefully supplement the records obtained by dredging when making faunistic surveys.

Otter trawls used for commercial fishing also capture members of the epifauna but because of the rather wide meshes used only larger invertebrates are retained. The rigging, shooting and working of otter trawls is a complex subject best left to the professional fisherman. However, instructions for making up a small trawl are given by Steven (1952), and details of various fishing nets are given by Davis (1958) and by FAO (1965). FAO have also published a bibliography of fishing gear and methods (FAO, 1958).

When dredging or trawling it is possible to standardise speed and duration of tow, so obtaining estimates of population density which are of value for comparative purposes. However, it is well known that most dredges and trawls sample only a fraction of the animals lying on the surface of the sea bed (see p. 140), and the burrowing fauna scarcely at all, so that the results merely represent minimum densities present on the grounds. It is not very easy to control the exact time the gear is on the bottom, for the dredge or trawl will usually continue to drag along the bottom while it is being hauled, the distance depending on the drift of the ship under different weather conditions. Nevertheless, hauls of standard duration are commonly used for quantitative sampling of demersal fish, and may also prove useful for taking members of the invertebrate epifauna not adequately sampled by other methods. An account of the statistical methods used in fisheries biology is given by Gulland (1966).

A number of workers have fitted spiked measuring-wheels to beam trawl or dredge frames. These rotate in contact with the bottom, recording the distance travelled on a meter (e.g. Belyaev and Sokolova, 1960; Riedl, 1961; Wolff, 1961; Gilat, 1964; and Richards and Riley, 1967). They no doubt give a reasonably accurate figure for comparative purposes, but have not been widely used. The wheels and meter would seem to be rather easily damaged by obstructions on the sea bed. There is need for further research and development on devices recording the time during which towed gear is in contact with the bottom.

If the dredge bag is lined with closely-woven material to retain the sediment, quantitative data can be based on the numbers of organisms per unit volume of sediment. On soft grounds where the dredge sinks fairly deeply into the sediment and so takes a representative sample of the fauna from all levels, the results may prove satisfactory for comparative purposes, but the surface area represented will not be known. As an example of this method, Smith (1932) sampled the Eddystone shell gravel with a conical dredge fitted with a canvas bag. On deck, the dredge contents were tipped into a bath and from the middle of the pile a sample of known volume was taken for faunistic counts. On this ground the Petersen grab did not sample at all well, and Smith considered that in spite of its disadvantages the conical dredge gave a more satisfactory sample for comparative purposes.

Anchor-dredging. The anchor-dredge developed by Forster (1953) is one of the most useful instruments available for sampling sands and similar firmly-packed deposits. This dredge (Appendix, Fig. 2, and Fig. 6.7) has an inclined plate intended to dig in deeply at one place on the sea bed, and is not towed along as are other dredges. It is best used from a small launch fitted with power hoist, where it is more likely to work satisfactorily than on a larger ship. The anchor-dredge is shot and hauled in the same manner as a ship's anchor; it is most conveniently shot over the side, with the ship going astern, and provided there is sufficient way on the ship for the net to stream out during lowering it can usually be landed on the bottom right way up. As the

Figure 6.7. Forster's anchor-dredge. A strengthened version of that originally described. Note the net with tied cod-end, and a rectangle of hide below to prevent chafing (Photo N A Holme).

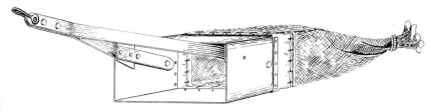

Figure 6.8. Double-sided anchor-dredge as described by Holme (1961). The wishbone towing arms are free to swivel or can be locked to one side if required. Note that the net is laced to a canvas collar bolted to the dredge frame, enabling easy changing of nets (Reproduced by permission of the Council of the Marine Biological Association).

ship drifts slowly astern warp equal to about five times the depth is gradually paid out. The inboard end is then made fast and the strain exerted as the ship is brought to a standstill drives the dredge into the sand to a depth of up to 25 cm (much deeper than most grabs penetrate). The ship then steams slowly ahead as the warp is heaved in so that the dredge is broken out from the bottom when the warp is almost vertical.

On ships over 10–15 m length the pull exerted after the warp has been made fast may severely strain either the dredge or the warp itself, so it is advisable to be prepared to pay out further warp if the strain becomes excessive, perhaps by leaving the brakes on the winch applied only gently. There is a tendency for the anchor-dredge to jerk out or be dragged through the sediment in such circumstances, and this will also occur if insufficient length of warp has been paid out.

The sample theoretically taken by Forster's dredge is wedge-shaped, and of area approximating to that of the digging plate, so that it may be used for semi-quantitative studies. However, there is always a possibility that it may drag along the bottom at some stage, so sampling a disproportionate number of surface-living species.

In deep water a double-sided anchor dredge which will work either side up may be used (Fig. 6.8). This does not have the same deep-digging powers as Forster's and tends to drag through the sediment. Even if it were possible to land Forster's dredge right way up in deep water it would be difficult, but not impossible, to manoeuvre the ship away from and then back over the dredge.

Sanders (1956) and Sanders *et al.* (1965) describe modified anchor-dredges for quantitative studies on the shelf and in the deep sea. The Sanders anchor-dredge is double-sided with two heavy angled digging plates (Fig. 6.9), between which is a wide horizontal plate which limits depth of penetration to 11 cm. The dredge is very heavy (225 kg) and is assumed to sink to its maximum depth in the sediment. Once the mouth of the dredge has become clogged with sediment, further material is rejected upwards out of the mouth. The quantity of sediment collected in the bag varies with the physical properties of different sediments, but estimates of population density are based on numbers per unit volume. Figures are converted to numbers per unit area on the assumption of an unvarying depth of penetration to 11 cm The accuracy of this method depends mainly on this last assumption, and observations by divers show that, in silt-clay sediments similar to those in the deep sea, the dredge does function in this manner. However, tested on sandy

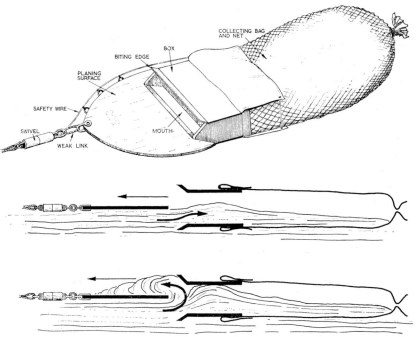

Figure 6.9. Deep-sea anchor-dredge, redrawn from Sanders *et al*. (1965). Above, general view of dredge; centre, movement of sediment into dredge before clogging; below, movement of sediment after clogging.

deposits the dredge did not dig to its full depth, so that results could not be expressed quantitatively.

The Sanders anchor-dredge is probably the only dredge which can sample in a reasonably quantitative way. However, with all towed instruments there must always remain some doubts as to the manner in which the contents of the bag are collected. Greater confidence, but not necessarily a more accurate sample, may be obtained by sampling with a grab or other instrument lowered vertically to the bottom.

Grab sampling

Quantitative samples of the animals inhabiting sediments are usually taken by a grab. The grab, which is lowered vertically from the stationary ship, captures slow-moving and sedentary members of the epifauna, and infauna down to the depth excavated by the particular instrument. There has been much debate on the depths to which animals burrow in the sea floor (e.g. MacGinitie, 1935, 1939; Thorson, 1957*a*, Holme, 1964, pp. 212–15): the majority appear to live in the top 10 cm, but some large animals burrow to 30 cm or more (Barnett and Hardy, 1967). Few of the grabs at present available are designed to dig much deeper than 15 cm, and in practice many take a maximum 'bite' of 10 cm or less on firm-packed sand, so that it is doubtful if even all the animals in the top 10 cm are adequately sampled. Moreover, with grabs taking a 'bite' which is theoretically semi-circular in cross-section (the orange-peel grab takes a roughly hemispherical sample), the area excavated decreases with depth. However, there is some effective sampling of animals below the actual 'bite' in the form of lamellibranch siphons, worm tubes or fragments of deeper living animals chopped off by the cutting edges.

For sampling the macrofauna, samplers covering a surface area of 0·1 or 0·2 m² are commonly used, several samples being taken to aggregate to 0·5 or 1 m² per station. Samples of this size are usually considered adequate for quantitative determinations, measurements of biomass etc. (see pp. 8 and 142), but do not adequately sample scarcer species, particularly of the epifauna. Moreover some faster moving species escape the grab altogether. It is therefore advisable to supplement grab estimates of the epifauna by hauls with an Agassiz or small beam trawl fitted with a fine-meshed net, or by underwater photography, television or diving.

In view of the manifest deficiencies, particularly as regards penetration of hard-packed deposits, of so many bottom samplers, it is not possible to recommend any single instrument as suitable for general use. Much will depend on such factors as size of ship and hoisting gear available, the type of sediment to be sampled, depth of water, and whether sampling in sheltered waters or in the open sea. A great variety of instruments have been described, and choice will no doubt depend largely on what is already available or can be obtained without difficulty.

It is proposed to consider briefly a number of samplers which are in general use at marine laboratories, some others used for special purposes or which may be used for calibration, and then to make some recommendations on choice of a sampler.

Petersen grab. This is a small version of the grab used commercially for dredging, unloading coal, etc. It consists of two buckets (Fig. 6.10), hinged together, which are held in the open position while being lowered. When on

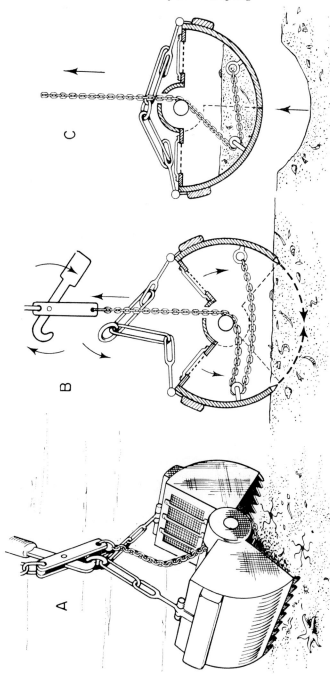

Figure 6.10. Petersen grab taking a sample on the sea bed (Redrawn from Hardy, 1959, and reproduced with permission from *Advances in Marine Biology, Vol. 2*).

the bottom, the lowering rope slackens, allowing a release to operate so that on hauling up the two buckets close together before the grab leaves the bottom. The grabs used by C.G.J. Petersen for his pioneer work on bottom communities in the Danish fiords sampled an area of 0·1 m², but a larger model covering 0·2 m² is more effective for sampling in the open sea.

The disadvantages of the Petersen grab for sampling in other than soft muds and in sheltered waters have often been discussed (e.g. Davis, 1925; Thorson, 1957a; Holme, 1964), and many attempts have been made to improve on the original design for sampling under open sea conditions.

van Veen grab. The van Veen grab (Fig. 6.11) improves on the Petersen grab in having long arms attached to the buckets, so giving better leverage for

Figure 6.11. van Veen grab ready for lowering (Crown copyright. Reproduced by permission of the Controller of H.M. Stationery Office).

closing the jaws. The arms also tend to prevent the grab being jerked off the bottom should the ship roll as the grab is closing. On the other hand the arms may pull the grab over to one side if through drift of the ship, the upward pull for closing is oblique. Thorson (1957*a*, p. 64) states that the van Veen grab is liable to premature release in mid-water during lowering, and modification of the release to a counterweight mechanism, as proposed by Lassig (1965) may be an improvement. However, there is a danger that the counterweight or its wire may get between the jaws when they close.

Many workers have used the van Veen grab, but as with the Petersen grab, experiences with the 0·1 m² size in the open sea may have been disappointing. Mr. L. Birkett successfully used a heavily-weighted 0·2 m² van Veen for his work in firm sandy deposits on the Dogger Bank.

Campbell grab. The Campbell grab (Figs. 4.3 and 9.2) is similar to the Petersen grab, but its greater efficiency is due to its larger size (0·55 m² area sampled) and weight (410 kg). It has been used by Dr Olga Hartman and others in the United States, and appears to work well, but its great weight would preclude its use from small ships or where an A-frame or similar device was not available to control its swinging on board ship.

Orange-peel grab. The orange-peel grab (Fig. 6.12) has been much used in the United States, also in France and Australia. It has four curved jaws closing to encircle a hemisphere of sediment. Penetration of the sediment is aided by the fact that the jaws each narrow to a point, but there appears to be some risk of loss of material between them, also from the top of the grab if a canvas cover is not fitted. Thorson (1957*a*, pp. 69–70) does not consider it a satisfactory quantitative sampler. The orange-peel grab is available commercially in a range of sizes.

Smith-McIntyre grab. (Smith and McIntyre, 1954.) This has hinged buckets mounted within a framework (Fig. 6.13), with powerful springs to assist penetration into the sediment. Two trigger-plates, one on each side of the frame ensure that this is resting flat on the bottom before the springs are released. Closing of the grab is completed as hauling commences by cables linked to arms attached to each bucket. The top of each bucket is covered with fine wire mesh to reduce the resistance and downwash on descent. In recent models each mesh top is in the form of a flap hinged along its outer edge to allow convenient access to the sample.

Figure 6.12. Orange-peel grab (left, open; right, closed) fitted with canvas hood to prevent washing out of sample. Area sampled by this model about 0·24 m², capacity about 70 litres (Copyright Allan Hancock Foundation of the University of Southern California).

Figure 6.13. Smith-McIntyre grab. Above, in open position, ready for lowering. Note the trigger plates on either side of the base, both of which must rest on the bottom before the release is actuated. Below, in closed position. Note the wire gauze tops to the buckets, allowing water to flow through freely during lowering. The threaded studs with butterfly nuts are for attaching lead weights (Photo A. D. McIntyre).

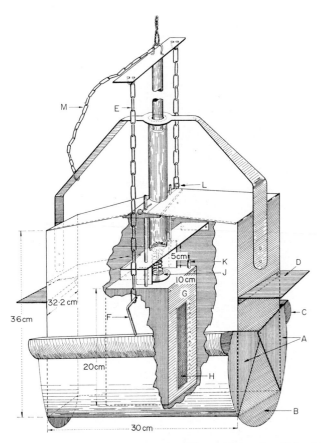

Figure 6.14. Bacescu sampler, consisting of an Ekman-type grab, within which is a square sounding tube. A, grab buckets; B, extension of side-wall of grab; C, lead weights attached to grab buckets; D, plates limiting depth of penetration into the mud; E, chains holding buckets open during lowering; F, hook on grab bucket to which chain is secured; G, square sounding tube; H, graduated slit, gauze-covered, for measuring length of core; J, spring-loaded valve; K, valve for extracting water sample from top of sounding tube; L, mechanism for releasing sounding tube from grab; M, safety chain. Dimensions shown are internal (Redrawn from Bacescu, 1957).

The Smith-McIntyre grab samples 0·1 m² and is of moderate weight (45 kg) so that it is suitable for use from a small ship. Provision is made for the addition of extra weights when required. On firm sands it penetrates to about the same depth as the 0·1 m² van Veen grab (see p. 143), but the greater reliability of its release makes it preferable to that grab for open sea conditions.

Many small grabs such as the Ekman and Birge-Ekman grab are suitable for use from a small boat on soft sediments, but since they cover an area of only about 0·04 m² are not very suitable for macrofauna sampling. They are described in the literature of fresh-water sampling techniques.

Bacescu sampler. (Bacescu, 1957.) This takes the form of a large Ekman grab, covering 0·1 m², inside of which is a square corer enclosing an area of 100 × 100 mm, sediment being retained both inside and outside the corer by jaws closing the bottom of the grab (Fig. 6.14). A pair of horizontal plates on the outside prevent the grab sinking too deeply. This grab simultaneously collects a large sample for macrofauna determinations and a smaller, stratified, sample for determinations of micro- and meiobenthos. It seems to work well in deposits in the Black Sea, but it is questionable if it would effectively sample sands or gravels in the open sea.

Baird grab. (Baird, 1958b.) This was designed for sampling the epifauna of oyster beds, etc. in sheltered water. It has two inclined digging plates which are forced together by springs and levers (Fig. 6.15). It covers an area of 0·5 m², and has been found to dig into sediments quite well, so having some application for sampling the infauna where a sample of large area is required. Since the sample is not covered on top it is not very suitable for open-sea work.

Holme grab. (Holme, 1949b.) This samples by means of a single semi-circular scoop rotating through 180° to take a sample. Its design minimises the chances of losing material through the jaws being wedged open by a stone, and as the closing mechanism depends upon the unwinding of about 7 m of cable from a drum, considerable mechanical advantage is obtained and the effects of sudden jerks on the wire when the ship rolls are minimised. Although sometimes considered awkward in use at sea, it takes as deep a sample as the other grabs on firm deposits. Later models (Fig. 6.16) have two separate

Figure 6.15. Baird grab, ready for lowering. The grab is triggered when the pendant arm (seen in the centre) touches bottom. Initial closing is by tension springs; the final closure by hauling in on the lever arms. Area sampled; 0·5 m² (From Baird, 1958b. Crown copyright. Reproduced by permission of the Controller of H.M. Stationery Office).

counter-rotating scoops (each covering 0·05 or 0·1 m²), enabling statistical studies on adjacent pairs of samples to be carried out (Holme, 1953).

Shipek sediment sampler. Although taking rather a small sample (approx. 205 × 200 mm) more suitable for meiofauna investigations, the Shipek sampler (Fig. 6.17) is included here because its method of excavating a sample is similar to the Holme grab. The single semi-circular scoop is actuated by powerful coiled springs which are released by a catch actuated by the momentum of a heavy weight when the sampler hits bottom. The scoop rotates

Figure 6.16. Holme's double-scoop grab, ready for lowering (cf. Holme, 1953). (Photo Service de Ciné-Photographie, Quebec.)

through 180° to take its sample. The Shipek sampler is used mainly by geologists, providing a useful small sample of sediment. It is easy to set, and seldom fails to take a sample.

Reineck box sampler. (Reineck, 1958, 1963.) This consists of a rectangular corer supported in a pipe frame, with a hinged cutting arm which comes down to close the bottom of the tube (Fig. 6.18). The instrument now available

Figure 6.17. Shipek sampler, with scoop closed (Photo R Swinfen).

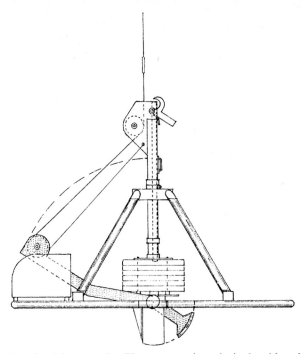

Figure 6.18. Reineck box sampler. The square coring tube is closed by a knife edge actuated by pulling up on the lever to the left of the diagram. An attachment can be fitted to show the inclination and compass orientation of the core (Redrawn from Reineck, 1963).

commercially samples an area 20×30 cm to a depth of 45 cm. It is a rather large and heavy piece of equipment, weighing over 750 kg complete with weights. A similar instrument is described by Bouma and Marshall (1964). Provided they can be handled on board ship these instruments should take satisfactory samples.

Okean grab. (Lisitsin and Udintsev, 1955.) The Petersen grab has a gauze-covered window at the top of each bucket to allow water to escape while the

Figure 6.19. The Okean grab, ready for lowering. The 0·25 m² grab shown here is weighted to 150 kg or more (Copyright Institute of Oceanology of the U.S.S.R. Academy of Sciences, Moscow).

grab is closing. This offers some resistance to swift lowering of the grab, which is highly desirable for deep-sea sampling. In the Russian Okean grab (Fig. 6.19) the tops of the buckets form hinged doors which are held open during lowering, and which are closed when the grab reaches the bottom. Very rapid rates of lowering are possible with the Okean grab, which has a counterweight release mechanism to prevent tripping in mid-water. Since there is nothing to limit penetration of this grab, it may sink below the surface in soft sediments. Okean grabs, in various sizes, are in regular use on Russian research ships.

Suction sampling

A number of samplers employ suction either to force a coring tube down into the substratum or to draw the sediment and its fauna up into a tube leading to some form of self-sieving collector.

Knudsen sampler. (Knudsen, 1927.) This was the first sampler to employ suction successfully to take a core of a size suitable for sampling the macrofauna. It consists of a wide coring tube, 36 cm in diameter and covering an area of 0·1 m², which is sampled to a maximum depth of 30 cm. A pump connected to the top of the coring tube is actuated by unwinding cable from a drum while the sampler is on the bottom. This has the effect of sucking the sampler down into the sediment. When all the cable has been unwound, strain is transferred to the wishbone-shaped lifting arms which invert the coring tube as it is lifted out of the sediment, so retaining the sample, although there may be some loss of small fauna through the mesh base on which the sample is retained.

The Knudsen sampler meets nearly all specifications for the perfect sampler, but tends to anchor itself in the sea bed so firmly that the cable may part when attempts are made to break it out of the bottom. Consequently it can only be used in rather calm weather, when it is a useful means of calibrating instruments which can be used under more rigorous conditions.

Barnett (1969) has described an improved model supported by a metal frame which reduces the chances of it falling over on the bottom, and this is shown in Fig. 6.20.

Brett sampler. Brett (1964) describes a diver-operated suction sampler in which sediment is sucked up a wide tube leading to a 3·2 mm mesh sample net. By driving a metal frame into the substratum and then sucking out the

Figure 6.20. Knudsen sampler fitted with stabilising framework to keep it upright on the sea bed (Barnett, 1969). The sampler is operated by unwinding cable from the drum at the top. This operates a pump which sucks the wide central coring tube down into the sediment. When hoisted off the bottom, strain comes onto the wishbone arm at the left, causing the sampling tube to invert as it comes out of the sediment (Photo P R O Barnett).

sediment within the frame, quantitative samples can be obtained. Power for suction is produced by a 3 h.p. engine at the surface which forces water down a pipe inserted axially into the wide collecting tube, suction being produced on the aspirator principle. The collecting bag is necessarily of a fairly wide mesh to prevent clogging.

With the aid of this sampler it is possible to excavate to depths of 20 or 30 cm, but there may be some difficulty in driving the frame sufficiently deeply to stop the sides of the hole caving in. In samples obtained in this way it is not possible to determine the position of individuals *in situ*, since all are mixed in the collecting bag, but by sampling successively deeper layers in the sediment it is possible to obtain some idea of their depth zonation.

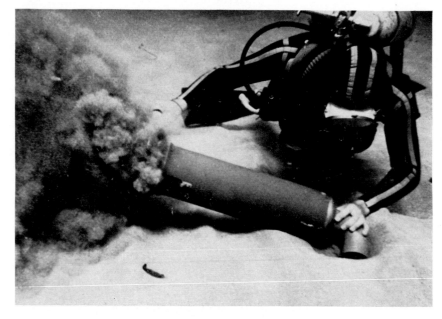

Figure 6.21a. Suction-sampler of Emig and Lienhart (1967) being operated by a diver.

The greater sampling efficiency of a suction sampler of this kind as compared with an orange-peel grab has been demonstrated by Massé (1967).

Emig and Lienhart's aspirator (Emig and Lienhart, 1967) has a suction pipe similar to that used by Brett, with filtration through a rigid cone of metal gauze, but suction in this instrument is provided by a propeller powered by a self-contained 12-volt electric motor and storage batteries within the instrument (Fig. 6.21a & b). Being independent of any connection with the surface it can be more easily handled by divers than Brett's sampler.

Barnett and Hardy's diver-operated sampler (Barnett and Hardy, 1967) makes use of suction both to drive a coring tube into the bottom and then to extract sediment from the area sampled. It consists of a sampling cylinder 60 cm tall with an internal diameter of 35.7 cm, covering an area of 0·1 m². In the first stage of sampling an air-lift is used to suck the corer into the sediment in the manner of the Knudsen sampler (Fig. 6.22). In the second stage the top of the corer is opened and an air-lift used to draw the contents upward through a long vertical suction pipe into an enclosed sieve of 1 mm mesh,

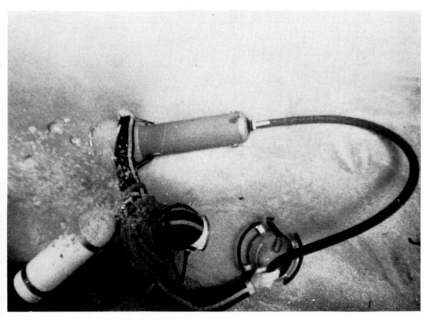

Figure 6.21b. For quantitative sampling a narrow (40 mm diameter) tube is used to suck up the contents of a cylinder which has been forced into the sediment (Photographs by C Emig and R Lienhart).

from which the sample falls into a polyethylene collecting bag (Fig. 6.23). Use of this sampler makes deep penetration (up to 60 cm) of firm sediments possible (see discussion in Massé, 1967).

The benthic suction sampler of True *et al.* (1968) employs a jet of water acting through a venturi to suck a coring tube of 0·1 m² area into the bottom, the sediment and fauna being sucked into a wire mesh collecting basket (Fig. 6.24). This instrument is not diver-operated, but is lowered vertically on a wire, power for the jet being provided either by a submerged electric motor with power cable to the surface, or by a pressure hose from the ship. Either method limits depth of operation, but this instrument has been successfully operated in deep water from a submersible (submarine) where the power cable was quite short.

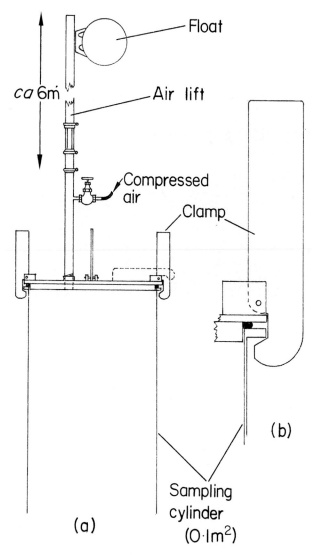

Figure 6.22. Diver-operated suction sampler of Barnett and Hardy (1967). a, b. Cross-section showing details of sampling cylinder. (Figures 6.22 and 6.23 redrawn from Barnett & Hardy, 1967.)

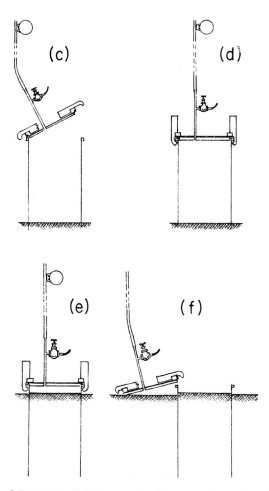

Figure 6.22 c–f. Barnett and Hardy sampler. First stage of sampling. The cylinder is driven by hand a few cm into the sediment (c); the lid is secured by clamp (d); water is pumped out of the cylinder, which is thus forced into the sediment (e); and the lid is removed (f) ready for stage 2.

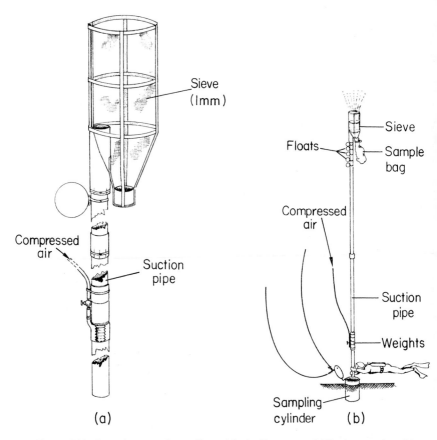

Figure 6.23. Second stage of sampling with the Barnett and Hardy sampler. (a) detail of suction pipe and sieve; (b) method of operation. The lid of the sampling cylinder is opened, and the sediment is drawn up the vertical suction pipe into a sieve, that retained by the sieve falling from this into the attached plastic bag.

The development of suction samplers represents one of the most important advances in sampling techniques in recent years. In particular the diver-operated samplers, such as that of Barnett and Hardy, provide an accurate method of quantitative sampling to whatever depth in the sediment may be required. They also provide a means of calibrating remotely-controlled samplers which must continue to be the standard method of sampling under open sea conditions both on the shelf and in the deep sea.

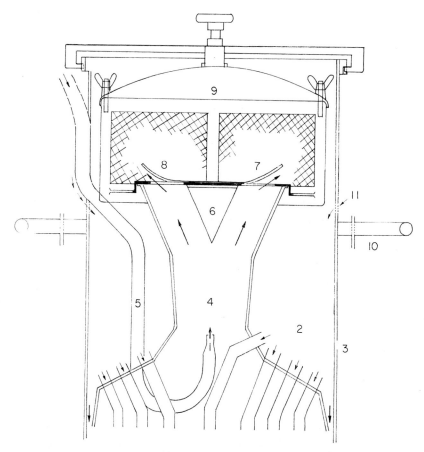

Figure 6.24. Benthic suction sampler, redrawn from True *et al.* (1968). Compensating water inlets stir up the sediment which is carried upwards through the venturi chamber into the gauze-lined collecting basket. 1, upward jet of water from nozzle; 2, compensating water inlets; 3, outer casing; 4, venturi chamber; 5, high pressure water source; 6, deflection cone; 7, flap valve; 8, collecting basket; 9, cover; 10, support frame and sample limiter; 11, main water inlet.

Other methods of sampling

Some species are not readily taken by conventional sampling gear such as dredges, trawls or grabs, either because they occur too sparsely to be represented in samples covering a limited area or because they live in habitats inadequately sampled by the instrument employed. Alternative methods, which do not necessarily sample other members of the fauna are available for such species. Techniques for underwater photography and television, of special value in estimating scarce members of the epifauna, are described in Chapter 4.

After storms burrowing animals are often washed in from shallow water on to the beach, and this may be the best means of obtaining some deep-burrowing species not readily taken by ship-borne samplers. Empty mollusc shells and other remains cast up on the beach are usually some guide to the nature of the shallow-water offshore fauna.

Fish stomachs often contain deep-burrowing or active members of the benthos seldom taken by sampling instruments, but as the fish are likely to have been feeding selectively little idea of the abundance of the prey species can be obtained by this means. Similarly, the stomachs of birds feeding in estuaries and salt marshes may show the presence of otherwise unreported species.

Species of fish and crustaceans which hide away in rock crevices may be taken by using one of the chemical fish collectors which drive them out of their hiding places. Some such as Rotenone are toxic, but the Quinaldine compounds (Gibson, 1967) have an anaesthetic action and usually cause no permanent damage. A bleach such as sodium hypochlorite may also be used. Talbot (1965) has employed explosives for a comprehensive survey of fish populations in coral reefs.

Tagging and marking techniques have been used for studies on the growth rate of certain benthic animals, particularly molluscs and Crustaceans of economic importance. They have also been used for studies of migration and population size among the more mobile or vagrant species of Crustacea. Methods and techniques are outside the scope of this Handbook. Many useful papers and references may be found in the Report of the North Atlantic Fish Marking Symposium (ICNAF, 1963), and a short bibliography, mainly of more recent publications, is given on pp. 294–295.

Free-living invertebrates may be captured in traps. Dead fish make suitable bait, or light lures may be used when fishing at night. Traps may be based on those used commercially; descriptions of different kinds of trap are found in the commercial fisheries literature, including Davis (1958) and Hardy (1954), and the use of light lures is described by Sasaki (1959). Traps for the deep sea have been described by Albert, Prince of Monaco (1932) and Isaacs and Schick (1960).

There is a need for more accurate means of estimating quantitatively populations of fish and motile invertebrates such as shrimps and prawns associated with the sea bed. These are usually sampled by trawling, but it is well known that the trawl gives a far from accurate estimate of density on the grounds. An attempt to sample such populations quantitatively has been made by Van Cleve, Ting and Kent (1966); see also Van Cleve and Ting (1962, 1963). Their sampler is a large cage covered with nylon netting which

Figure 6.25. Demersal animal sampler (reproduced, with permission, from Van Cleve, Ting & Kent, 1966) with door closed across the bottom after taking a sample. The curtain around the bottom, which is weighted, prevents the escape of fish on an uneven bottom. The electric cable powering the motors for closing the bottom of the sampler and for the water pump leads off to the left foreground. A van Dohrn water sampling bottle and bathythermograph (arrowed) are attached to the left side of the cage. For further explanation see text.

is lowered to cover an area of 8·6 m² of the bottom (Fig. 6.25). The cage is closed by a shutter running on rollers, driven by an electric motor. Powerful jets of water and a nylon bristle brush aid the capture and retention of more elusive members of the fauna. The large size and weight (1 ton) of this sampler indicates that its use will be restricted to occasions when adequate operating facilities are available.

For sampling plankton close to the bottom and smaller members of the epifauna many types of sledge net have been designed. Some are little more than simple plankton nets on runners (e.g. Myers, 1942), while others have opening and closing mechanisms and sometimes a meter to measure the quantity of water filtered (e.g. Bossanyi, 1951; Wickstead, 1953; Beyer, 1958; Frolander and Pratt, 1962; Macer, 1967; also Holme, 1964, p. 191). A sledge net (Fig. 6.2) for hand towing in the intertidal zone is described by Colman and Segrove (1955). Among sledge nets more specifically designed for collecting the superficial bottom fauna are the sledge net of Ockelmann (1964) and the much larger and heavier epibenthic sledge of Hessler and Sanders (1967). Ockelmann's net (Fig. 7.3) has a framework and runners of light alloy and a net adjustable for height above the bottom. It was designed for collecting newly-settled benthic invertebrates which are stirred up by a tickler chain, but has also given useful collections of many other small animals. Hessler and Sanders's sledge is of similar design (Figs. 6.26; 6.27), with a net 80 cm wide and 30 cm high. It has wide steel runners to stop it sinking too deeply into deep-sea muds, and its weight is 160 kg. There is no tickler chain but the net is set at such a height as to sample the surface of the substratum as well as the overlying water. Additional material stirred up when the towing warp is in contact with the bottom ahead of the sledge will also be collected. The epibenthic sledge has proved useful for sampling members of the deep sea fauna not readily taken by other means. Washing out of the sample has now been eliminated by incorporating a closing door in the mouth of the net.

Choice of a quantitative sampler

Choice of a sampler must necessarily be a compromise, based on individual requirements and the conditions under which sampling is undertaken. Some guidance is given here as to the possible best choices:

Sampling from small boats

This is a very real problem if the ship is too small to handle heavy gear. Scaled-down versions of grabs are usually not very effective, and a grab of

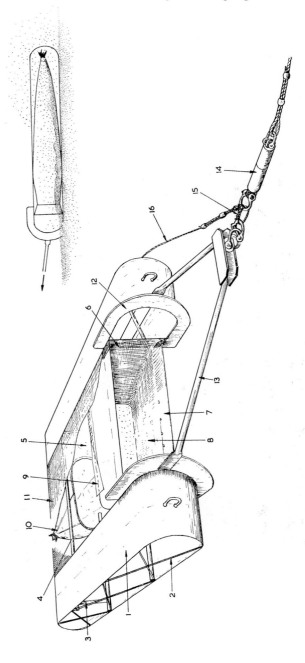

Figure 6.26. The epibenthic sledge, redrawn from Hessler & Sanders (1967). In this sketch much of the top protective wire screen and part of the anterior tubular cross-piece are cut away to show additional details. 1, runners; 2, 3, strengthening members inside runners; 4, tubular cross piece; 5, collecting net (nylon); 6, side-plate at mouth of net; 7, biting edge at top and bottom of net, adjustable for height; 8, canvas collar at front of net, which is tied by canvas flaps, 9, to the tubular crosspieces and struts; 10, net tied at posterior end; 11, heavy wire screen to protect net; 12, flange preventing mud entering net from the side; 13, towing yoke; 14, swivel; 15, weak link; 16, safety-line. The smaller drawing shows the mode of operation of the sledge.

Figure 6.27. The epibenthic sledge of Hessler and Sanders. For details see legend to Figure 6.26.

0·1 m² size is about the smallest which will sample effectively. When working in shallow water the importance of the diver-operated suction samplers described on pp. 108–111 must be emphasised. These are capable of taking as accurate and as deep a sample as can be obtained by any means, and are also useful for calibrating quantitative samplers used in deeper water.

For sampling from small boats unable to handle heavy gear the order of preference for different methods might be:
1 Diver-operated suction devices.
2 Forster's anchor-dredge. Although only semi-quantitative this digs much deeper than most grabs.
3 Smith-McIntyre grab, 0·1 m².
4 van Veen 0·1 m² grab, if the bottom is not too hard-packed.
5 Shipek sampler, although the sample covers only 0·04 m².

Deep penetration
Where deep samples to 30 cm or so are required, the following methods are available, again in order of preference:
1 Diver-operated suction devices.
2 Forster's anchor-dredge, taking semi-quantitative samples to 20 cm or more.
3 The Knudsen sampler, which takes cores up to 30 cm in length.
4 The Reineck Box sampler, which samples to 45 cm depth.
Heavy grabs such as the Campbell grab also sample deeply in soft deposits.

In situ examination of fauna
It is often helpful to examine the sample as it comes in to obtain some idea of the orientation and mode of life of the fauna.

With suction-type instruments, whether diver-operated or actuated by remote control, the sediment is sieved under water so that this is not possible. With most samplers, however, it is possible to determine the original position of the animals in spite of some distortion of the sediment during sampling. If the sediment is relatively undisturbed a small coring tube may be pushed in for sub-sampling for micro and meiofaunas.

Examination of the sample is best achieved if the top of the sampling bucket or core can be opened. This provision is not normally made on the Petersen and van Veen grabs, but it is in the Okean and in later versions of the Smith-McIntyre, which therefore give easy access to the surface of the sediment within the sampler. This also applies to the Holme and Baird grabs, although in the latter, the surface being uncovered, material is liable to be washed out during hauling.

With the Knudsen sampler the stratification is retained, but access to the top of the sample is not possible since the sampling tube is inverted.

General-purpose quantitative sampling

For general-purpose sampling from a moderate-sized ship capable of handling gear of 100–200 kg weight there is at present no agreement on the best instrument.

We believe that the Petersen and van Veen samplers, in the 0·1 m² size, can *not* be recommended for general use on the continental shelf, although in their 0·2 m² sizes reasonably satisfactory samples may be obtained. Although the orange-peel grab has been used with apparent success, particularly in the United States, Thorson (1957*a*, pp. 69–70) has criticised its use as a quantitative sampler, so that preference should be given to more precise instruments.

The most satisfactory general-purpose samplers seem to be the Smith-McIntyre grab (0·1 m²), and, for larger sampling areas, the Campbell grab (0·55 m²). The latter, however, weighs 410 kg and therefore needs appropriate lifting gear. Sanders's anchor-dredge (Sanders *et al.*, 1965) can also be recommended for quantitative sampling. In shallow water the diver-operated sampler of Barnett and Hardy (1967) will give a more accurate sample than any grab. The suction sampler developed by True *et al.* (1968) is perhaps too new for its capabilities to be confirmed.

If none of these methods will provide an acceptable sample, less quantitative collecting methods employing dredges or anchor-dredges must be employed.

Working sampling gear at sea

In the earlier part of this chapter comments have been made on the methods of using trawls and other towed gear on the continental shelf. Grabs or other instruments which are lowered vertically from an anchored or slowly-drifting ship require different techniques. It is important not to use too heavy a wire for the purpose: most grabs are not hydrodynamically shaped and sink rather slowly, so that if too heavy a wire is used it may form a loop below the grab, possibly causing kinking. For similar reasons the grab should be lowered steadily with gentle braking on the winch. This will also help to prevent the wire going slack as the ship rolls, so tripping the release on some samplers. As a guide to speeds of lowering, the Holme grab has been lowered at rather less than 1 m/sec, while the Okean grab, offering much less water resistance, has been lowered at speeds of up to 2·8 m/sec and hauled at 1·6 m/sec (Lisitsin and Udintsev, 1955).

As soon as bottom is reached (see below for determining this in deep water), the brake should be applied, and hauling commenced immediately. Any delay on the bottom will increase the wire angle if the ship is drifting, causing the instrument to be pulled out obliquely, making it sample less efficiently. It is very important to haul very slowly until the sampler has left the bottom: (a) because with most instruments closing is completed as hauling commences, and if the warp is suddenly jerked upward a grab may be jerked off the bottom while it is closing, (b) because in breaking out a sampler which has dug deeply into the bottom great strains are produced, which may cause the gear or warp to break. Once off the bottom the sampler may be hauled as fast as is convenient, assuming the surface of the sample to be covered to prevent washing out.

Some grabs can be worked on a 5 or 6 mm diameter wire (see also p. 153), but some workers prefer to use a rope, which overcomes many of the difficulties mentioned above. In particular it tends to drag behind the grab, so stabilising its descent and preventing premature release. On the bottom it is less likely to foul the gear (particularly if a synthetic rope less dense than sea water is chosen), and when hauling it can be surged around a capstan so that precise manual control of the closing and lifting operations are possible. The only disadvantages of rope as against wire are the possibility that the rope may get cut, and storage problems due to greater bulk of the rope.

As with all marine gear, a swivel, preferably ball-bearing, must be inserted between the warp and the gear.

Deep-sea sampling

Successful sampling in the deep sea with a grab, trawl or dredge on the end of several kilometres of wire requires special skills, for as Menzies (1964) has emphasised the proportion of failures, particularly with towed gear, has been high. The positioning of the gear underwater is dependent upon the manoeuvres of the ship, the diameter of wire used, and the speed with which it is lowered. Sampling in the deep sea is a time-consuming operation and presupposes a research ship of adequate size, equipped with a deep-sea winch. The importance of selecting the best size of wire on which the gear is lowered has already been indicated and in deep-sea work this may make all the difference between success and failure. Many ocean-going research ships are equipped with a wire of 10–12 mm diameter, often tapered (see Chapter 9), for carrying out rock dredging and coring in the deep sea, but such a wire may prove too heavy for working lighter grabs, which can conveniently be worked on a 6 mm wire. The Okean grab has been successfully worked on a 4·7 mm wire on Russian ships.

If the wire is of small diameter and the grab fairly heavy, it may be possible to detect when bottom is reached by a lessening of strain on the wire. This can sometimes be observed by movement of an accumulator spring, or may be recorded more precisely on a strain gauge (p. 18). A meter wheel recording wire out is some guide when lowering, but owing to slip of the wire against the wheel and likelihood that the wire is not vertical, it is only a rough guide as to when the grab may be expected to reach bottom. Either through motion of the ship or weight of wire out it is often not possible to detect when bottom is reached, so for precise control a pinger should be used on the wire a short distance above the grab (p. 22). The pinger record may also show when the grab closes, so possibly saving much time on abortive hauls. Sampling in deep water is so expensive of ship's time that a pinger should be used whenever practicable.

Dredging or trawling in the deep sea is particularly difficult and Menzies (1964) has considered in detail the methods of carrying this out successfully, although his review does not include the use of pingers. The main difficulty in deep-sea dredging and trawling is to land the gear on the bottom without the wire fouling the gear or becoming entangled in itself. The gear may be lowered with the ship stopped, but preferably with some way on. In either case it is necessary to keep some strain on the wire at all times to prevent it becoming entangled. The gear will sink rather slowly so that it is preferable for the ship to be moving through the water slowly—sufficient way to un-wind wire from the winch and to keep the net streaming through the water being all that is necessary. If towed any faster it may never reach bottom. A weight is sometimes attached to the wire a short distance ahead of the dredge to give a more horizontal pull, and this may aid descent of the dredge. As a guide to speeds of lowering, on the Swedish deep-sea expedition (Nybelin, 1951) the otter trawl was lowered at speeds up to 0·7 or 0·8 m/sec and hauled at about 0·4 m/sec.

Little and Mullins (1964) have shown that diving plates increase the speed of descent of a beam trawl, reducing the amount of wire paid out. At depths between about 1000 and 5000 m the average wire out/depth ratio was 2·56 (range 1·67 to 3·40) without diving plates, but only 1·54 (range 1·07 to 2·08) with the plates fitted. Towing speeds varied between about 1 and 3 knots.

If the net is not streamed through the water during its descent not only is there a risk of the towing cable winding around it, but the net itself may become wrapped around the mouth of the frame so that it cannot sample properly. These difficulties were overcome by Menzies (1964) by enclosing the net within a rigid cage and by encircling the chain bridles with a steel pipe. A cage enclosing the net (Fig. 6.27), or a rigid net of wire mesh have been used on other nets for deep-sea work. When using an ordinary dredge in deep water the net can easily be kept open by one or two lengths of thick polyethylene pipe, as used for water supplies, lashed lengthwise inside the net. Lengths of the same pipe could also be used to stop bridles from becoming twisted. A heavy weight on the end of the net bag (Fig. 6.4) will also prevent the bag wrapping round the dredge frame.

When working a dredge or trawl in the deep sea, failure to take a sample may be due to too little wire being paid out so that the gear does not reach bottom, or too much so that the slack lying on the bottom is not taken up and the gear is not towed at all. Kullenberg (1951, 1956; see Fig. 6.28) has

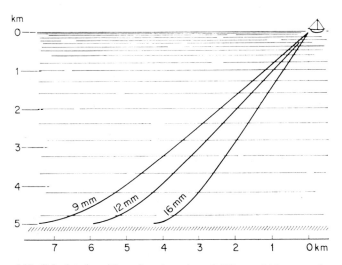

Figure 6.28. Calculated position of towing wires of different thicknesses when deep-sea trawling (Redrawn from Kullenberg, 1956).

calculated the lengths of towing wire of varying diameters required for deep-sea trawling at different depths, but it is helpful if some positive signal can be received when the gear touches bottom. A strain gauge can be useful, but a pinger placed some distance up the warp is of even more value, preventing the paying out of excessive lengths of wire. When dredging at slow speeds of about 1 knot a ratio of wire out/depth of water of between 1·10 and 1·20 is required (e.g. Laughton, 1967). When dredging in this way with wire equal to little more than the depth of the water, one must remember to correct soundings for the velocity of sound in sea water (p. 16), and that the dredge is not immediately below the ship and so may be in water of a different depth from that indicated on the echo sounder.

Exploration of canyons on the continental slope requires special techniques. Where the bottom is steeply sloping it may not be possible to get a reliable sounding, because of echoes from the side walls of the canyon, and it may be difficult to place the gear in the required location on the sea bed. Unless the canyon is particularly well charted, and accurate position fixes can be obtained, working any type of gear may be hazardous. Because of the risk of loss it is inadvisable to use expensive instruments like pingers, and indeed pinger signals may give a false impression by failing to give a return echo from vertical cliff-faces towards which the gear may be drifting. Cousteau's diving saucer has been successfully used for exploration of submarine canyons (Shepard *et al.*, 1964; Shepard, 1965*b*), and an ingenious device for photographing the side walls of a canyon is described by McAllister (1957). The latter would seem to be appropriate only for fairly shallow water and where the topography of the canyon is well known.

For general-purpose collecting on the slope and in canyons a sturdy rock-collecting dredge (Fig. 6.4), with safety link should be used. This should be lowered vertically from the ship, which then drifts or steams slowly towards the canyon wall. Manoeuvring of the ship at slow speeds is more easily accomplished if the ship is steaming against the surface current. Exploration of canyons can only be carried out in good weather, and even then frequent losses of gear are to be expected.

One other aspect of deep sea sampling has been emphasised by Hessler and Sanders (1967) who point out that often much of the sample may be lost by winnowing (washing out) of the lighter components during hauling. Wherever practicable the sample should be covered when hauling. When sampling sediments it is best if the net bag is lined with closely woven material which will retain the sediment. Many of the smaller organisms which might otherwise be washed away are brought to the surface still within the sediment which not only gives mechanical protection but also buffers against sudden temperature changes as the sample is hauled through warm surface waters.

The relative sparsity of the deep sea fauna and the risk that a grab will not close, so wasting much time, have encouraged the use of dredges and other towed gear such as the epibenthic sledge of Hessler and Sanders. These almost invariably obtain large samples, often rich in species and individuals, and so provide more material to work on than could otherwise be obtained from the deep sea in the necessarily limited amount of ship's time available (see also p. 10).

ADDENDUM: HYDRAULIC JET DREDGES
E. I. S. Rees

High pressure water jets are frequently used in salvage and mining operations to clear away sand and mud. The same principle was first used in the mid 1940's to improve the digging power of clam dredges used off the coast of North America (Parker, 1966). Water jets were arranged to loosen the sediment ahead of the dredge blade and so prevent the sediment from clogging the dredge bag. The same approach may be used by the benthic ecologist who wants to sample the large but sparsely distributed species of the infauna.

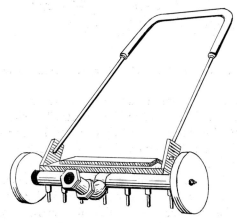

Figure 6.29. Hydraulic clam rake (Redrawn from Bourne, 1967).

The simplest application of the jet principle is seen in the hydraulic clam rake (Fig. 6.29). This is a valuable tool for gathering large samples of fragile molluscs from intertidal flats (McPhail and Medcof, 1962; Bourne, 1967). Breakage is reduced and sampling is more complete than when the molluscs are dug out with a fork. At the opposite end of the scale of complexity the cockle harvesting dredge developed by the White Fish Authority (U.K.) uses a jet-powered lift pump to raise the catch to the surface as well as to loosen the cockles from the sand (World Fishing, 1967). The jet lift works on the same principle as the venturi cones used in the benthic suction samplers of True, *et al.* (1968)—see p. 111.

The largest commercial clam dredges have blades 2·13 m wide and are supplied with over 680 m³/h of water (Standley and Parker, 1967). The water supply for these dredges and for the 1·22 m dredge used for exploratory fishing (Fig. 6.30) is equivalent to 3·1 to 3·6 m³/h/cm blade width. The miniature version of this type of dredge used by Castanga (1967) (Fig. 6.31)

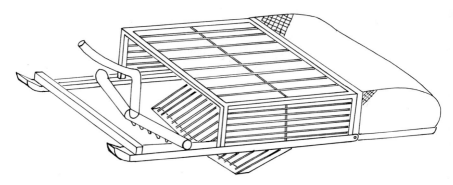

Figure 6.30. Hydraulic clam dredge (see Parker, 1966).

has a 46 cm blade and seems to have been operated with a water supply equivalent to less than 0·45 m³/h/cm blade width. The clam rakes appear to use about 0·6 m³/h/cm blade width while the cockle harvester uses about 1·1 m³/h/cm blade width. The figure given for the cockle harvester does not include the water needed for the lift pump.

The pressure differential at the manifold is about 4–5 kg/cm² with the large clam dredges and the cockle harvester (Standley and Parker, 1967; Parker, 1967, and World Fishing, 1967). To achieve this pressure pumps developing 5·6–9·1 kg/cm² have to be used to overcome the friction in the long delivery

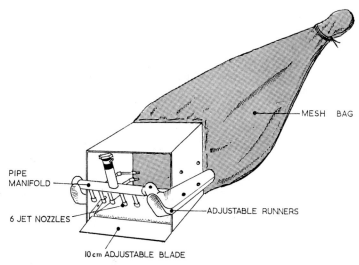

PIPE
MANIFOLD

MESH BAG

6 JET NOZZLES

ADJUSTABLE RUNNERS

10 cm ADJUSTABLE BLADE

Figure 6.31. Hydraulic sampling dredge (Redrawn from Castanga, 1967).

pipes. The clam rakes operate satisfactorily with a manifold pressure of 1·4–1·8 kg/cm². Standley and Parker (1967) found that the optimum nozzle diameter was 17·5 mm, but most of the smaller dredges have had nozzles of 9·5–12·5 mm diameter. The manifold pipes and delivery nozzles are apt to get blocked from time to time. The equipment therefore needs to be built so that it can easily be stripped down for cleaning.

Pumps and delivery hoses are naturally arranged to match the size of the dredge. For example, a pump developing 110 hp was fitted on board the research vessel when a 1·22 m dredge was being used for exploratory fishing (Standley and Parker, 1967; Fahlen, 1967). Compared to this Castanga (1967) used a portable pump of only 2·5 hp with his 460 mm sampler. Delivery hoses of 150 mm or occasionally 200 mm diameter are used with the big clam dredges. The cockle harvester and Castanga's sampler have delivery hoses 63 and 38 mm diameter respectively. Rubber hoses are most commonly used but reinforced plastic and canvas fire hoses have also been used with the smaller gear.

Owing to the difficulty of handling large diameter hoses and the energy losses due to friction, dredges operated by pumps on the surface vessel are limited to depths of less than about 50 m. A submersible pump mounted directly on the dredge has been used by Standley and Parker (1967) to overcome this problem. A 65 hp pump on the dredge gave better results than a 110 hp pump on the surface vessel. If the pump is mounted on the fore part of the dredge and if the intake is sited well above the ground and screened it can be kept clear of sediment that could clog it. Submersible pump dredges have obvious applications for use with undersea vehicles if they can be supplied with enough power.

Pump operated venturi type suction devices may also be mounted on sleds to provide a vacuum device for sampling small agile benthic organisms (Allen & Hudson, 1970).

Hydraulic pumping causes considerable disturbance to the deposit, and the question of damage to the benthic community arises. This has been studied by Bybee (1969) in relation to hydraulic pumping for ghost shrimp (*Callianassa californiensis*) in the intertidal zone of a southern Californian estuary. He concludes that in this area pumping was not harmful if regulations laid down by the regulating commission were adhered to.

7

Meiofauna and Microfauna Sampling

A. D. MᴄIɴᴛʏʀᴇ

Any instrument or method suitable for sampling macrofauna will usually in principle be suitable also for the smaller organisms. The reviews of Gunter (1957), Thorson (1957a), Holme (1964) and Hopkins (1964) are therefore relevant, as well as Chapter 6 above. Additional references are given in the benthos bibliography (McIntyre, 1970) and sampling of small metazoans is discussed in a review by McIntyre (1969), and in Hulings & Gray (1971).

Meiofauna

The main difference between sampling for macrofauna and meiofauna is that because of the much higher numerical density of the latter, smaller samples are usually adequate. These can be obtained by subsampling from a larger volume, but this can introduce errors or inaccuracies, so that whenever possible a sample should be collected which can be examined entire.

The permanent members of the meiofauna, such as nematodes, copepods, gastrotrichs, turbellarians, kinorhynchs and tardigrades are present throughout the whole year, and have a wide distribution both horizontally and vertically. If specific animals are required in large numbers, or if particular groups only are to be studied, it may be useful to deal with quite large quantities of deposit. Wells and Clark (1965) working on intertidal sand, dug out 3,000 ml of sand at each station to sample copepods, and Higgins (1964) used a sledge-dredge on subtidal mud for kinorhynchs. For qualitative sampling on the beach, a general impression of the meiofauna can be obtained by simply digging a trench and allowing water to accumulate in it. Actively swimming animals are then scooped from the water with a fine plankton net, and the more sedentary or adhesive forms are collected by

131

sampling sand grains from the trench. A refined version of this procedure, the 'méthode des sondages' is often used on tideless beaches to concentrate animals from the level of the water table (Delamare-Deboutteville, 1960). Alternatively, sand can be added to filtered sea water (preferably containing anaesthetic) in a bucket, and after stirring this is poured through a fine sieve. Such techniques are useful in the field and deal qualitatively with quite large areas or volumes, but for quantitative work small samples are usually required, and these are most conveniently obtained in cores of some description.

In intertidal areas or in very shallow water where the apparatus can be operated by hand, a tube or pipe of any available material may be adapted for use, the diameter chosen depending on the volume and depth of sample required. In many intertidal habitats a diameter of 2–4 cm has been found to give samples which can be sorted entire. Tubes of transparent material such as perspex are useful because the intact sample can be seen throughout its entire length and the distribution of the soil components as well as any changes in the packing of the core can be noted. In collecting the sample, the tube is simply pushed or tapped gently into the ground, the top is plugged, and the tube withdrawn, the bottom then being plugged if the sample is to be transported. In practice this simple method can usually produce a sample of 30–40 cm length, but if the sediment core tends to slide or break on withdrawal of the tube it may be necessary to excavate a trench round the tube and plug the lower end before raising it. In some deposits, especially if a narrow tube is used, forcing the tube into the bottom results in shortening of the core and distortion of the sample. If this occurs, it is convenient to attain the depth to be sampled by a series of shorter cores, a trench being excavated to the lower end of each successive sample, exposing a new horizontal level at which the next core is inserted. In this way deep layers may be sampled step-wise, as described by Bush (1966). In some deposits, where stones or shells are present, or when very deep cores are required in single lengths, the tube may have to be hammered into the bottom, and a metal corer is then probably required. McIntyre (1968) used a metal tube halved longitudinally, with the two parts held together by a collar, so that the entire core could eventually be exposed for examination and processing. For very deep work Renaud-Debyser (1957) devised a completely demountable corer, square in cross-section. Each of the four sides consisted of a metal sheet, 100 cm long, 5 cm wide and 1 mm thick, and each was slotted so as to slide within the other sides. Since the sides can be inserted one by one into the sand, little pressure is required, and shortening of the sample does not occur. Cores as long as 1 m can be obtained, and the removal of the sides gives easy access to the sample.

In removing the sample from a standard core tube, it is best to allow the core to slide down into the collecting vessel since this causes less disturbance than pushing out with a piston. Fenchel (1967) describes a method by which the top stopper of the core tube is replaced by a bored cork fitted with a short glass tube attached to a length of rubber tubing closed by a clamp. Opening and closing the clamp allows the core to slide down inside the tube step-wise. Alternatively, more control may be obtained by compressing and releasing the top rubber bung with the fingers. If the deposit is of dry sand and the column tends to break rather than slide evenly, a small quantity of filtered sea water carefully added to the top helps to keep the column intact. In samples from muddy ground, the lower part of the core may form a plug of clay, and the sample must then be pushed out from below with a piston. This method is less satisfactory, since it compresses the core, and in most samples causes water and particles to mix from one layer to another. These effects can be minimised by selecting a tube length as close as possible to the sediment length required. On muddy grounds, short cores are usually adequate since most of the animals live in the upper layers, and below 6–8 cm there is little life (Rees, 1940; McIntyre, 1968). On sand, however, with interstitial species extending to great depths, cores of 20–30 cm may be required to collect the bulk of the fauna, and animals are known to exist in considerable numbers even below 50 cm (Renaud-Debyser, 1963).

In subtidal areas, core tubes again provide the most suitable means of general sampling for the permanent meiofauna. In shallow water, where SCUBA divers can work, some of the techniques used on the beach can be highly satisfactory. In deeper water, or when divers are not available, samplers which can be lowered from a boat are required. Of the variety of coring devices available the open-barrel gravity corer is the most suitable type, but these, being designed for geological work, are usually large and heavy. A light instrument, such as that described by Moore and Neill (1930), which is simply a tube constructed to fall vertically and penetrate by its own weight is useful, and can be adapted to take one or more samples of various diameters (Fig. 7.1). An easily constructed corer for use in mud is illustrated in Appendix Fig. A6. Comparable instruments constructed to take multiple cores have been described by Krogh and Spärck (1936) and Fowler and Kulm (1966), while a multiple version of the Moore and Neill corer is illustrated

Figure 7.1. Moore & Neill (1930) corer (Photograph A D McIntyre).

by Holme (1964, Fig. 27). On soft sediments, especially where a layer of clay is present to plug the bottom of the tube, good samples up to 40 cm long can be obtained. On very soft bottoms the corer may fill completely or even bury itself in the deposit, spoiling the sample. In such areas the instrument should be lowered to a few metres above the bottom and then the warp should be paid out quickly so that the corer falls free under its own weight into the sediment. The optimum distance for this free fall, which may be determined by trial and error, will depend on the instrument as well as on local conditions. Burns (1966) showed experimentally that for corers of

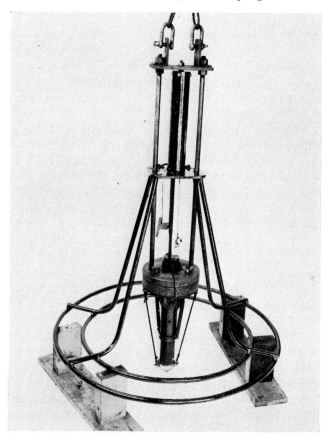

Figure 7.2. Craib (1965) corer, with ball closing device in position (Photograph J S Craib).

about 25–50 kg weight and approximately 4 cm inside diameter, the optimum free fall distance was 2–3 m.

Coring on sand is more difficult with a light instrument, and a retainer, such as that described by Mills (1961) or Fenchel (1967) is usually required to prevent loss of the sample on hauling. A built-in closing device is an important feature of the instrument designed by Craib (1965). This is essentially a frame-mounted core tube, 5–7 cm in diameter, which is forced into the bottom by weights (Fig. 7.2). The rate of penetration is controlled by a hydraulic damper, and this, combined with a slow initial approach, ensures minimum disturbance of the light superficial layer of sediment. Samples of 15 cm length are produced, and thanks to the spherical closing device which retains the core, good samples have been reported from sediments ranging from hard sand to soft mud. The apparatus weighs 44 kg and can be used from a small boat. Its main disadvantage may be that since it must stand upright for a short period while the tube is penetrating there may be difficulties in bad weather, on uneven bottoms, or in deep water. The problem of core shortening already referred to may be more serious in subtidal work if only because it may pass unnoticed. Recent unpublished work in Scottish sea lochs has shown that shortening can begin to occur on some muds whenever the core tube penetrates deeper than 6 cm. The effects of shortening on the efficiency of collection are discussed on p. 145.

In the absence of a suitable corer, it may be acceptable to collect cores from a grab sample. The grab must be such that it can be opened from the top so that vertical cores can be taken by hand (see p. 121). Cores should be taken only when it has been possible to keep the grab upright with little disturbance to the surface sediment of the sample. The Bacescu sampler (p. 103) which is a grab with a built-in core tube was designed for such work. This procedure is useful when comparison is being made of macro and meiofauna from the same area.

While cores of one kind or another are suitable for sampling the permanent meiofauna (animals always present in the substratum and usually in large numbers) they are not necessarily the best collecting devices for temporary meiofauna. This category includes juvenile stages of larger forms such as molluscs, polychaetes and echinoderms, and while these can be very abundant, they are seasonal in occurrence, often patchy in distribution, and usually restricted to the superficial deposits. Dredge sampling is thus useful and the instruments described by Mortensen (1925) and Ockelmann (1964) are suitable. These are simply dredges on runners (Fig. 7.3), designed to disturb and skim off the sediment surface which is then collected in a fine net. A dredge of this kind is at best only semi-quantitative although a 'supergadgeted' version described by Bieri and Tokioka (1968), and fitted with a flow meter and pedometer seems to represent a considerable advance. If fully quantitative data are required, a known surface area and depth must be sampled. While this can be done by subsampling from a standard grab haul, some devices have recently been designed with quantitative collections of temporary meiofauna particularly in mind. Muus (1964) describes an instrument which cuts out the top 2–3 cm of deposit below a surface area of 150 cm^2

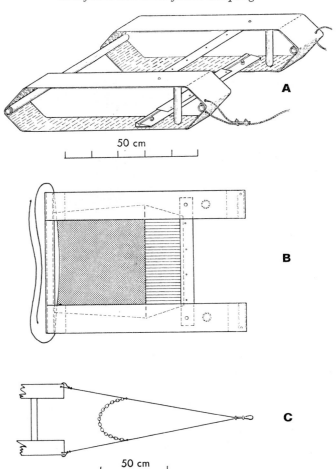

Figure 7.3. Ockelmann (1964) detritus-sledge. (A) parallel-perspective view (no net); (B) view from above; (C) view from above, showing wire bridles and tickler chain (Redrawn from Ockelmann, 1964).

and collects it in a nylon bag (Fig. 7.4). In operation, this 'mouse-trap' releases and closes after penetrating the bottom and it is claimed that no downwash is caused which might disturb the surface deposit. Its total weight is 25–30 kg and it can be used from a small boat. Corey and Craib (1966) considered that the Muus sampler was not suitable for such animals as

Figure 7.4. Muus (1964) sampler (Photo Bent J Muus). For explanation see text.

amphipods, isopods and cumaceans which became free-swimming when disturbed. To overcome this difficulty they describe another device, rather more complicated, which samples a surface area of 0·05 cm² to a depth of 3 cm. It releases and closes automatically when the lowering rope slackens, and the design of the instrument prevents any disturbance of the sea bed during initial penetration. Finally, the Shipek sampler (p. 104), covering about 400 cm², might usefully be employed for meiofauna work.

Microfauna

For qualitative work on Protozoa most of the methods and samplers described above for meiofauna are satisfactory. When quantitative estimates are required it is usually possible to work with even smaller volumes of deposit than used for meiofauna counts, because of the very high numbers of microfauna often present. Core tubes are again most satisfactory for quantitative work. Fenchel and Jansson (1966) found tubes of 1·3 cm internal diameter to be adequate at intertidal sites in the Baltic Sea, but a sample size appropriate to the population densities in the area should be selected on the basis of preliminary trials.

Willemoës (1964) gives details of equipment originally designed to collect small samples of benthic diatoms, but which has been used for Protozoa. It consists of plexiglass tubes, each covering a surface area of 3 cm², mounted singly or in threes. Each tube contains a piston with a solid rubber ball attached to its lower end by a length of perlon fishing line. On lowering, the tube penetrates the deposit by the weight of the unit and the operation of hauling pulls the piston up the tube and the ball closes the end, retaining the sample. Depth of penetration 'may be several cm' but the weight of the apparatus is not given, and there is no discussion of how the surface of the deposit is affected by the perlon line or by the down-wash due to the piston ring.

8

Efficiency of Benthos Sampling Gear

Dredges

Sampling efficiency is a useful concept only when referring to quantitative or semi-quantitative gear. Most dredges, defined as collecting instruments which are towed along the bottom, are at best semi-quantitative. When used to collect fauna living on or just above the bottom, the efficiency of a dredge, judged by its ability to capture all the animals within its sweep, is usually low. The performance will vary with the configuration and nature of the bottom and since several types of bottom may be encountered on any given tow, it is difficult to allow for these variations. Other complicating factors are the behaviour of the ship, the length of warp, and the speed of towing—increased speed above a low level usually reduces catches. Further, the type of warp used can be most important. Wire, with a weight in water greater than the drag, can increase the effective weight of the dredge on the bottom, while rope, with the drag greater than the weight and a consequent backward and upward catenary, can produce a lift. The fitting of depressors or diving plates, and the proper use of teeth on the leading edge can increase efficiencies (Baird, 1959). Attempts have been made to use various fitted pedometers to measure the exact distance covered by the dredge on the bottom (see also p. 92) and this should help to quantify the results.

The behaviour of the animals themselves is also of considerable importance and if interest is concentrated on only one species, with a consequent reduction in the range of habitat and behaviour encountered, then it should be possible to make appropriate gear modifications to produce increased efficiency. Yet Dickie (1955) has shown that dredges specifically designed to capture scallops had an efficiency of only 5 per cent on uneven inshore grounds and just over 12 per cent on smoother offshore areas. Again, juvenile stages of a flatfish (*Pleuronectes platessa L.*) have recently been the subject of population studies in Britain, and gear has been developed for their capture. Since they occur on relatively flat sandy bottoms in shallow water where their behaviour can be observed by divers, it may be expected that high gear efficiencies should be possible. Riley and Corlett (1966) used a 4 m beam trawl and found it worked best when towed at a speed of 35 m per minute with three tickler chains attached. Efficiency ranged from 33 to 57 per cent, and even for fish in their first year of life it varied considerably at different times of the year, depending on the size and age of the fish. Efficiencies of this order, however, seem to be exceptional for dredges, and when total fauna is considered, a value nearer 10 per cent is probably more realistic, even when the gear is fitted with a pedometer (Richards and Riley, 1967).

The one towed benthos sampler which appears to be acceptably quantitative for the in-fauna is the modification by H. L. Sanders of the Forster anchor dredge (see p. 94). The principle is that a wide flat plate behind the towing connection determines the digging depth of an open box frame with an attached collecting bag. Knowing this digging depth, measurement of the volume of deposit collected allows calculation of the surface area sampled. A version of this instrument weighing 39 kg and digging to 7·6 cm (Sanders, 1956) has been used for shallow water work, and a larger model, 225 kg, digging to 11 cm (Sanders *et al.*, 1965) for deep water.

Grabs

The concept of efficiency is more meaningful for true grabs, which may be defined as instruments lowered on (ideally) a vertical warp from a stationary ship, to take a deposit sample of a given surface area. In this context the term efficiency tends to be used loosely to cover various purely functional aspects of an instrument's general performance and digging characteristics, as well as its ability to produce an acceptable picture of animal number and distribution. Although all these uses of the term are obviously related, they should not be confused.

Performance. Considering first the functional aspect, this refers primarily to the ability of an instrument to perform consistently and correctly according to its design in all conditions of deposit, depth and weather. These features are perhaps better covered by the word 'reliability' rather than by 'efficiency' and are best judged by the volume of deposit collected, so that an instrument which filled to capacity on every haul would be regarded as completely reliable within the limits of its design. The first requirement for reliability is that the grab must land on the bottom in a condition to operate properly. Any grab which is activated by the slackening of the warp when the gear strikes the bottom will tend to be set off in mid-water by the roll of the ship, and so may be difficult to use in bad weather or deep water. An instrument which is not stable when in an upright position on the bottom, or which must sit at rest for a time to collect the sample (e.g. the Knudsen sampler) may be upset by strong currents or by the pull of the warp. Once correctly on the sea bed, a grab-type instrument covers a known surface area, and assuming it can be raised by a reasonably vertical warp, and not pulled laterally off the bottom (the skill and experience of the operator is often important here and comments on the use of grabs at sea are given on pp. 122–123), then the extent to which it attains its maximum digging depth (and greatest volume of sample) depends largely on the weight of the instrument and the nature of the substratum. On soft mud most grabs will fill completely, but on the most difficult bottoms of hard-packed sand conventional grabs will merely scrape the surface if not adequately weighted, and even those instruments which achieve some initial penetration by spring loading (Smith and McIntyre, 1954; Briba and Reys, 1966) will be raised off the bottom by the springs if they are not heavy enough. If all these factors are satisfactory, the volume of deposit will serve as an index of the depth of penetration, but will not give an absolute measure unless the exact shape of the bite is known. Table 8.1 gives volumes of deposit collected by various grabs as reported by a number of authors, and indicates the range of variation which may be expected depending on the type of deposit, the size and weight of the instrument, and the way it is handled.

Given that a particular type of grab is fully reliable as discussed above, one would further wish to know, still dealing with the functional aspect, how well its design allows it to collect the deposit below the surface area it covers. This is the sense in which Birkett (1958) used 'efficiency' and he defined it as the ratio between the volume of sediment collected and the theoretical volume, which is calculated by multiplying the area covered by the deepest penetration. This could perhaps be called the index of digging performance.

In recent years a new type of bottom sampler has been introduced, working on the principle that the deposit can be raised by jets of air or water (see pp. 108–115). Such samplers tend to have a high digging performance (especially if operated directly by divers) since they can lift all the deposit to a given

TABLE 8.1. Volumes of deposit collected by various grabs.

Note: The volume sampled per 0·1 m² is equal to the mean depth of penetration in cm.

Grab	Area covered (m²)	Wt. (kg)	Deposit	Range (litres)	Mean vol. (litres)	Vol. per 0·1 m² surface	No. of hauls	Authority
van Veen (chain rig)	0·2	60	Fine sand	10–25	17·0	8·5	5	Ursin, 1956
,,	0·2	60	,,	7–14	10·0	5·0	4	,,
,,	0·2	60	,,	3–22	9·9	5·0	63	Ursin, 1954
,,	0·2	60	,,	—	5·5	2·8	—	Reys, 1964
,,	0·2	60	,,	—	6·2	3·1	5	Birkett, 1958
,,	0·2	60	Coarse sand	6–25	14·6	7·3	28	Ursin, 1954
,,	0·2	60	Muddy sand	4–21	11·1	5·6	71	,,
,,	0·2	60	Clayey sand	6–22	11·4	5·7	28	,,
,,	0·2	60	Sandy clay	13–28	21·6	10·8	14	,,
van Veen (warp rig)	0·2	60	Fine sand	—	9·0	4·5	5	Birkett, 1958
Petersen	0·2	140	Fine sand	—	8·5	4·3	19	Ursin, 1954
van Veen	0·1	40	Sand	3–11	6·7	6·7	30	Lie and Pamatmat, 1965
,,	0·1	45	Fine sand	<1–6·0	3·4	3·4	165	Smith and McIntyre, 1954
,,	0·1	45	Shell gravel	<1–6·0	4·5	4·5	15	,,
,,	0·1	45	Mud	<1–3·5	2·1	2·1	9	,,
,,	0·1	45	Soft mud	9–16	13·0	13·0	110	McIntyre, 1961
Smith-McIntyre	0·1	45	Fine sand	1–7	3·9	3·9	53	Smith and McIntyre, 1954
,,	0·1	45	Shell gravel	4–7	5·0	5·0	9	,,
,,	0·1	45	Mud	2–5	3·0	3·0	9	,,
,,	0·1	—	Hard sand to fine silt	7–16	8·0	8·0	720	Banse (personal communication)
Knudsen	0·1	—	Fine sand	18–26	22·0	22·0	9	Ursin, 1956
Holme Sampler	0·05	110	Muddy gravel	—	5·4	10·8	3	Holme, 1949b
,,	0·05	110	Muddy sand	—	2·7	5·4	20	,,
Large orange peel	0·25	86	Firm fine sand	—	8·5	3·4	—	Reys, 1964
Small orange peel	0·1	20	,,	—	4·0	4·0	—	,,

penetration depth from within their area of operation. In contrast, it was until recently considered that the biting profile of grabs with horizontally placed spindles was more or less semicircular and that the digging performance of such grabs was therefore low, since the deepest part of the bite sampled only a fraction of the surface area covered by the open jaws. Recent observations (Gallardo, 1965; Lie and Pamatmat, 1965), however, indicate that the profile is more nearly rectangular, and that divergencies from a true rectangle can be explained in terms of the closing mechanisms of the various grabs. Thus the Petersen and van Veen, which have an upward leverage as the jaws close, tend to leave a hump of deposit in the middle of the sampling area, while the Smith-McIntyre, with a downward pull on the arms as the jaws close, digs deeper in the middle of the sampling area and thus for the same initial vertical penetration as a van Veen, takes a rather larger volume. These grabs thus appear to have a better digging performance than had been supposed, and on hard packed sand (the most difficult ground to sample) this can be increased by the addition of extra weights to the instrument.

Efficiency of capture. The second aspect of efficiency is more complex and relates to the ability of the gear to collect the fauna so as to give a reasonably accurate picture of its density and distribution. This may be called the efficiency of capture. Few studies have been made of how efficient a particular grab is in capturing all the fauna below a given surface area. This was attempted for an 0·1 van Veen grab by Lie and Pamatmat (1965) who compared grab collections taken at high tide with hand-dug samples of the same unit area at low tide. They showed that for the most abundant species there were significant differences between the two sets of samples in only 8 out of 37 cases.

Efficiency of capture may be defined as the ratio of the number of animals in the volume of deposit collected by the grab, to the number present in the same volume *in situ*. By using as the denominator of this ratio the same volume as was collected rather than the theoretical volume based on a rectangular bite, the ratio excludes the functional efficiency of the grab and deals only with its ability to capture the fauna available to it.

One possible cause of low efficiency of capture is that the down-rush of water caused by the grab's descent may disturb the surface of the deposit and result in the loss of superficial fauna. Smith and McIntyre (1954) considered that the use of gauze on the upper surface of their grab reduced this, producing higher catches of small crustaceans on sandy grounds, and this is supported by experimental work by Wigley (1967) who studied the behaviour of the grabs by motion pictures. On muddy grounds this may be an even more serious problem, and it is probable that most sampling instruments, even when landed carefully on the bottom, will not sample adequately the fine surface layer. Apart from this aspect, even a sampler which is fully reliable as described above, i.e. one which consistently takes its maximum volume, may not be most suitable for every job. For example one with a low or medium maximum penetration will not sample adequately the deep burrowing animals and an instrument which covers only a small surface, no matter how efficient as a machine, may be quite unsuitable for sampling widely dispersed fauna.

In conclusion, selection of the most 'efficient' grab involves consideration of reliability, digging performance, and capture efficiency which are in turn influenced by such factors as the size of sample required, the type of deposit likely to be sampled most, the depth of water, the prevailing weather conditions, the handling facilities available, and the experience of the operator.

Corers

From the purely functional aspect, coring devices have a high digging performance and most tend to be relatively reliable in that a particular instrument of a given weight will usually provide consistently similar lengths of core, depending on the type of sediment sampled. The main difficulty may be the loss of the core during ascent, and on sandy grounds a core retainer is usually required (see p. 135).

As a means of providing quantitative data on the fauna, the main criterion of a corer's efficiency must be the accuracy with which the collected core represents the sediment column as it was *in situ*. A peculiarity of gravity open-barrel corers is that the length of the core retrieved may be considerably less than the penetration depth of the tube into the sediment. The shortening ratio (core length: penetration distance) may be 0·5 or less for long cores, and this ratio depends on the weight and dimensions of the corer as well as on the type of sediment. The work of Emery and Dietz (1941) suggests that the shortening is due to wall friction and that some time after initial penetration the corer begins to act as a solid rod pushing downwards or sideways the sediments in front of it so that they eventually enter the core tube either incompletely or in layers of reduced thickness. Shortening may have important implications with regard to animal counts. It will not affect estimates of total fauna provided the core is sufficiently long to sample completely the strata where most of the animals are concentrated, and this will almost certainly be the case on soft grounds. But shortening may affect studies of the vertical distribution of the fauna, since segments cut from successive levels down the core may not correspond with the same levels on the sea bed. An additional complication inherent in the use of cores is that on removal of the sediment from the tube, some vertical redistribution is almost inevitable (see p. 133). Finally, although the downwash of a corer is less than that of a grab, it may well have a significant effect. This is illustrated by recent work (unpublished) from the Marine Laboratory, Aberdeen, in a Scottish sea loch on mud at 30 m depth. SCUBA divers using perspex tubes of about 2 cm diameter found it almost impossible to collect a core which retained all the flocculent material at the mud surface. The same difficulty was encountered with larger tubes of 4·3 cm diameter—even the most gentle approach of the corer to the sediment caused a disturbance and some of the superficial layer was lost. Only when tubes of about 10 cm diameter were used could completely intact cores be obtained. These observations suggest that even apparently undisturbed samples from a gravity corer may be less than satisfactory, and that it may seldom be possible with remote gear to collect the sediment-water interface without loss.

In conclusion, the most efficient corer will be the one which samples with the least shortening and the smallest surface loss, and from which the sediment can be removed with the least disturbance.

9

Aids and Methods For Working Benthos Samplers

E. I. S. REES

Boat facilities

Benthos sampling gear has been worked from all types and sizes of boats from dinghies to large ocean-going research vessels, and even from sledges working over holes through the ice. Large vessels have the stability for working heavy gear on a vertical wire, but may suffer from a lack of manoeuvrability at slow speeds when towing trawls or dredges. Small boats on the other hand are often more suitable for towed gear since they can alter speed more quickly and are more likely to be brought to a standstill should the gear become fouled on the bottom, whereas a larger vessel having greater momentum would tend to travel on and part the towing warp or seriously damage the gear.

Small dredges and trawls can be worked from boats of about 4 m length upwards, and even small grabs can be used from boats little bigger than this. For example, the Smith-McIntyre grab has been used from a gantry at the stern of an 8 metre boat (sufficiently small to be towed by road trailer) and it should usually be possible to rig up a davit or A-frame to lift 0·1 m² grabs on boats larger than about 4–5 m length. Greater weight can be handled over the stern than over the side of a conventional hull, but a catamaran hull could provide exceptional stability where the overall size and weight of the boat must be kept low. Sampling from such small boats is not easy, particularly where no power hoist is available, and would normally be restricted to sheltered waters. Sorting of the catch in an open boat is facilitated if it is possible to arrange a tray across the gunwales to enable the sample to be washed down with the waste draining over the side.

On larger vessels the requirements for operating benthos sampling gear do not differ greatly from those for other oceanographic work. For working vertical gear provision for slow speed manoeuvring of the ship to maintain a vertical wire is highly desirable, and for towing, great flexibility of control at slow speeds. Both kinds of operation are made easier if the ship is equipped with such aids to manoeuvring as bow thrusters, active rudders, kort nozzles, or controllable pitch propellers.

If the ship is equipped for stern trawling it would seem logical to use the stern for all towed gear, and also to lower vertical gear from the same part of the ship. But where there may be a need to manoeuvre the ship back over the gear, either because it has come fast, or in the normal operations involved in anchor-dredging (see p. 92), side working may be preferred. Similarly, when working vertical gear, like suction samplers, which have to remain on the bottom for periods of 30 seconds or more while they are operating, side-working is to be preferred to minimise the risk of the wire fouling the propeller.

Precise manoeuvring when working all kinds of gear is aided if the navigating officer on the bridge is able to see at what angle the warp is leading from the ship into the water.

Winches

Light grabs and small dredges can be hauled by hand when working in shallow water, but if much sampling is to be done a power hoist of some kind is almost essential. A powered capstan head is an aid to hauling ropes on a small boat, but larger vessels should have a mechanically driven winch, the most important feature of which, apart from adequate power, is the ability for speed variation down to zero. Other requirements are ability to pay out under power—useful when lowering a light grab before there is sufficient wire out to pull the wire off the winch drum—and the ability rapidly to reverse the drive when a grab or similar instrument reaches bottom. It is also an advantage if the winch is stalled by loads over a predetermined value, and that hauling should recommence as soon as the load eases. At present, hydraulic winches seem to meet such requirements better than those driven by other methods, and these have been fitted on many research vessels in recent years (Huse, 1961). Some electric winches have overload circuit-breakers which may be triggered at a crucial moment, and not all can be run at very slow speeds. Other methods of powering winches such as small petrol engines and hybrid systems with petrol or diesel engines, powering a small hydraulic pump and winch can be used for temporary installations. On large research vessels, electro-hydraulic hybrid systems may be used to avoid excessively lengthy pipe-work and to allow specialised winches to be demounted more easily. It is very important for the winch operator to have a good view of the operations. The current trend on both small trawlers and research vessels designed mainly for biological work is to have the main winch controlled from a console in the wheel-house. This saves manpower and increases the precision with which dredges can be towed.

Derricks and A-frames

Most fishing vessels are provided with derricks which can be used for handling grabs or lifting dredges inboard. Normally the derrick is set to plumb just outside the rail and the gear is swung in and out manually. The derrick must be set up fairly high, which tends to give the grab a dangerously large arc through which it can swing as the boat rolls (Holme, 1964, Fig. 29, p. 225). This can to a considerable extent be overcome by using a jockey pulley system as designed by L. Birkett and shown in Fig. 9.1. When grabs and other awkward pieces of gear are being constructed they should if possible be fitted with handles, or points for fixing restraining ropes.

Sometimes it will be found that the trawl gallows are sufficiently high to allow grabs to be swung in through them. Gallows or A-frames that can be swung in or out with hydraulic rams are extremely useful. The largest types of these, the Unigan gantries, have been fitted to a number of middle-water stern trawlers and to some research vessels in recent years. Smaller versions have been fitted on the quarters of several ocean-going research vessels (Fig. 9.2) or in place of the fore-gallows on side-trawler type research vessels. Most use a pair of hydraulic rams, but small versions with a single ram fixing overhead to the deckhouse have been tried. Hydraulic rams have most often been fitted inboard of the A-frame, but deck space can be saved by fitting them on the outboard side (Fig. 9.3). Normally a roller sheave is hung from the hydraulic gantry in the usual way, but sometimes a roller has been incorporated into the top bar of the gantry to allow the sheave to move within the scope of a large accumulator spring. For small installations, hand-driven worm-drive (as on lifeboat davits) can be used for operating A-frames or davits.

Warps

When gear has to be hauled by hand or over a capstan head natural fibre or synthetic ropes should be used. Synthetic ropes are very strong, and the

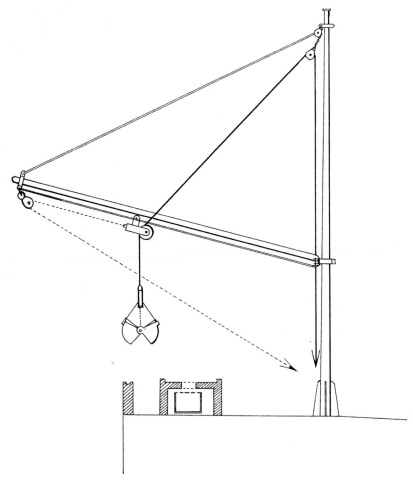

Figure 9.1. System for outhauling grab using jockey pulley (cf. Figure 6.11).

choice of a suitable size is determined more by ease of handling than by the breaking strain. The minimum diameter for hand-hauling is 10 mm, but 12 mm or larger should be used if possible. Synthetic ropes made of poly-ethylene (e.g. 'Courlene') or 'Ulstron' float in water and are therefore less likely to get entangled with the gear on the sea bed. Plaited ropes are prefer-able to the normal three-strand construction as they do not twist under

Figure 9.2. Working deck of *Velero IV* showing pneumatically-operated gallows. An orange-peel grab (with canvas hood) is seen below the gallows, and a Campbell grab is seen on the right (Copyright Allan Hancock Foundation of the University of Southern California).

strain. The only disadvantages of synthetic ropes are their greater bulk in storage as compared with wire, and the possibility that they may get cut. Advantages of using a rope for working grabs in shallow water have been given on p. 123.

Most dredging and grab work is carried out with galvanised steel warps. Hydrographic wire of 4 mm diameter and 6×7 construction (Fig. 9.4) has a breaking strain of about 950 kg and can be used for working light vertically operated gear in shallow water. However, the margin of safety is small should the gear get entangled on the bottom, and such wire should not be used for towing gear, except from a very small boat.

Larger size warps for dredging, trawling or grab sampling are commonly of 6×19 construction (Fig. 9.4), which has greater flexibility for its size than

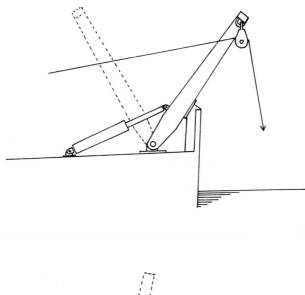

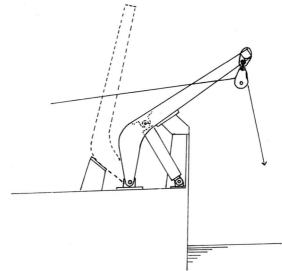

Figure 9.3. Swinging gallows with inboard and outboard rams.

Figure 9.4. Cross-section of two types of steel cable commonly used for oceano-graphic work. Left, 6×7, with central fibre core. Used for hydrographic wire. Right, 6×19, with central fibre core. For dredging, trawling and grab sampling.

6 × 7 construction. General-purpose warps are made from steel with a nominal breaking strength of 145 kg/mm², but for deep water work where maximum strength is required higher tensile steel of 180 or 200 kg/mm² is used. Such warps are only slightly more expensive, but are rather less flexible than the normal grade. A selection of ropes and warps for different purposes is given in Table 9.1.

TABLE 9.1. A selection of ropes and wires for different purposes. Specifications of individual brands should be checked from manufacturers' data. Steel rope data kindly supplied by the Gourock Ropework Co., Port Glasgow, Scotland. All steel ropes with a central fibre core.

Material	Diameter (mm)	Strength of material (kg/mm²)	Construc-tion	Breaking strain (kg)	Use
Manila (natural fibre)	16	—	3 strand	2000	Hand or capstan-hauled ropes for dredging, etc.
Ulstron (synthetic)	12	—	3 strand	1930	,,
	12	—	8 plait	1930	,,
	16	—	3 strand	3302	,,
Polyethylene (synthetic)	12	—	3 strand	1524	,,
	16	—	3 strand	2794	,,
Galvanised steel	4	180	6×7	957	Hydrographic wire, light corers and grabs
,,	6	180	6×19	1990	Grabs up to 100 kg.
,,	8	145	6×19	2850	Grabs. Light dredges
,,	11	145	6×19	5390	Heavy grabs. Dredging on continental shelf
,,	11	180	6×19	6690	Grabs, dredges. Shelf and continental slope
,,	12	145	6×19	6420 ⎤	Otter-trawling, dredging.
,,	16	145	6×19	11400 ⎬	Size according to that of
,,	20	145	6×19	17800 ⎟	ship
,,	24	145	6×19	25700 ⎦	

The length of wire that a winch drum will hold may be determined as follows, using a factor of 0·85 of the wire diameter to allow for the way the successive layers fit together:—

$$\text{Number of turns per layer} = \frac{\text{Width of drum}}{\text{Wire diameter}}$$

Median diameter 1st layer = Drum diameter + wire diameter.
Median diameter subsequent layers = Median diameter 1st layer + (Wire diam. × 0·85).
Wire length of each layer = π × median diameter of layer × No. of turns.

$$\text{Number of layers} = \frac{(\text{Cheek diameter} - \text{drum diameter})}{(\text{Wire diameter} \times 0\cdot85)}$$

Total length = Σ Lengths at each layer.

For deep-sea dredging a tapered warp is commonly used, as the wire nearest the surface has to support the weight of wire paid out in addition to towing strains. Tapered warps, often several km in length are specially made, usually of high tensile steel cable. For example, the R.V. *John Murray* (Natural Environment Research Council, London) has a 9000 m wire, mainly for geological coring, with the following specification:

Galvanised flexible steel wire, nominal breaking strength 190/205 kg/mm². Fibre core.

1st section: 1,500 m, 13 mm diameter, 6/19 construction, breaking strain 10,262 kg.

2nd section: 3,000 m, 12 mm diameter, 6/17 construction, breaking strain 9,043 kg.

3rd section: 4,300 m, 11 mm diameter, 6/12 construction, breaking strain 7,824 kg.

Wires of galvanised steel are preferred for most purposes to stainless steel because while galvanised wires show their age by rusting and can be discarded, the more expensive stainless wire tends to suffer from metal fatigue and may part suddenly. Recent development in plastic impregnated wires (see list of suppliers, Norsemann Ltd) may prove useful in prolonging the life of steel warps.

A safety factor of about 5 times is commonly specified for marine gear. This is taken to mean that the normal lifting or towing strains do not exceed one-fifth of the nominal breaking strain. A considerable margin of safety is needed to cope with shock loads when a dredge snags in fairly shallow water, even if a weak link is fitted to it. When working in deeper water the strain on the wire is more constant because its catenary dampens any sudden jerks. In practice, when dredging from a medium sized trawler in shallow water the working load is likely to be between perhaps 500 and 1,000 kg, with shock loads up to 1,500 kg or more. When dredging in deeper water the working strain is usually only a little more than the weight of wire out, so that in 1,000 m the load on an 11 mm wire would be about 1,500 kg with shock loads up to about 2,000 kg. Under such conditions and in deep water it is impossible to maintain a 5 times safety factor, and one must rely on a strain gauge (p. 18) to keep a check on wire tension, and weak links on the gear to release when tension becomes excessive. The greatest strain usually occurs during hauling, and here an overload device on the winch will prove its worth.

Sheaves and pulleys must be of adequate diameter for the wire in use. For ships' blocks the *overall* diameters for wires of different size are:

Wire diameter	Sheave diameter
Under 16 mm	254 mm
16 mm	305 mm
18 mm	356 mm
20 mm	356 mm
22 mm	406 mm
24 mm	406 mm

These diameters are rather less than those specified for lifts, hoists etc.

The cheeks of blocks must be of adequate width to allow swivels, shackles, chain etc. to pass through. Ordinary bushed bearings soon seize up, and roller bearings (with adequate grease points) should be used whenever possible. Measuring sheaves (p. 22) must have roller bearings, and the diameter of the groove should be checked from time to time as steel wires wear the sheaves rapidly, causing inaccuracies in measurement.

10

Treatment and Sorting of Samples

L. BIRKETT and A. D. MCINTYRE

Introduction

A benthos sample on collection usually consists of a volume of sediment from which the animals must be extracted. In meiofauna work, samples are often quite small, sometimes of the order of 10 ml, and such samples may be ready for immediate extraction. Macrofauna samples on the other hand may vary in size from a few to many litres, and the extraction process is often divided into two stages, the first being done in the field with a view to reducing the bulk of material taken back to the laboratory where the second stage of separation takes place. This chapter considers first the treatment of macrofauna samples, and then deals with special methods for meiofauna.

Macrofauna

Initial treatment

At sea the standard procedure is to receive the bottom sampler on deck on a wooden or metal-lined sieving table or hopper, which should be so designed that the sampler can be emptied and the contents washed through a sieve without loss of material. A measure of the total volume of deposit collected is often required since this helps to assess the performance of the gear. The volume may be measured either by using a dip stick before emptying the sampler, or by arranging that the contents pass first into a graduated container. Methods of dealing with the sample have been reviewed by Holme (1964) and vary from the simple arrangement of McNeely and Pereyra (1961) which consists of washing the sample through a nest of sieves with a hose, to the elaborate set-up described by Durham (in Hartman, 1955) in which a mechanical shaker agitates a graded series of screens under a set of sprinkler heads. A smaller hopper (Fig. 10.1) for general use has been described by

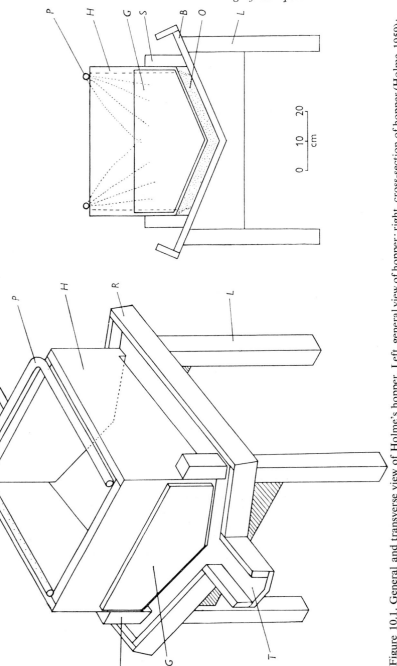

Figure 10.1. General and transverse view of Holme's hopper. Left, general view of hopper; right, cross-section of hopper (Holme, 1959); *P*, pipes supplying jets along top of hopper; *H*, side-wall of hopper; *R*, retaining wall at side of base (*B*); *T*, spout; *G*, rising gate; *S*, short legs supporting hopper off base; *L*, legs; *O*, sediment seen through gap between hopper and base (Reproduced by permission of the Council of the Marine Biological Association of the United Kingdom).

Chapter 10

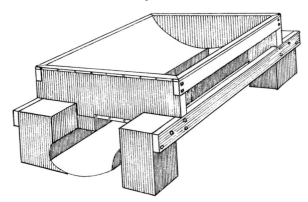

Figure 10.2. Combined grab cradle and wash trough (Redrawn from Carey & Paul, 1968)

Holme (1959), but there is probably no single set-up which would be satisfactory for the full range of sampling instruments and working conditions, and it may be desirable to modify an existing pattern appropriately to suit particular needs, or to construct a new unit such as the combined grab cradle and wash trough (Fig. 10.2) designed by Carey and Paul (1968) for the Smith-McIntyre grab.

The surface area of the sieve may to some extent depend on detailed design of the sieving table or hopper, but unless the sample is to be washed through slowly in small sections, the sieve must be of a certain minimum size to allow adequate sieving space and prevent clogging by the sediment. For samples of more than a few litres a sieve of at least 30×30 cm is desirable. Washing can be done by single or multiple jets from a hose but unless this is very gentle, and therefore time consuming, it can damage the animals. A gentler method is described by Sanders *et al.* (1965) by which the sample in a large vessel with a spout about one-third of the way up is swilled with continuously running water and the suspended sediment and fauna are passed out from the spout through a sieve. If the animals are required in especially good condition sieving should be done by hand, the sieve being gently agitated in water so that a flow takes place from below as well as above.

The mesh size of the sieve used is of critical importance, and should be determined at an early stage in the planning. Sieves with either round or square apertures may be used, but the square mesh is probably to be preferred since it has a higher percentage open area and this is the type in general use for soil analysis, so that a wide range of sizes to standard specifications is available. In practice mesh sizes have usually varied from roughly 2 mm to about 0·5 mm, although even finer apertures have occasionally been used to capture juvenile stages or to make maximum use of deep sea samples. The effects of different meshes on the results are referred to by McIntyre (1961) and Driscoll (1964). Jónasson (1955) showed that in the case of one particular species a small decrease in mesh size from 0·62 to 0·51 mm resulted in a 47 per cent increase in numbers, and stressed that the use of too large a sieve could produce an erroneous picture of seasonal peaks in animal numbers. In a more detailed study, Reish (1959) passed five grab samples from a shallow water muddy ground through a series of 11 sieves with apertures varying from 4·7 to 0·15 mm. His data have been recalculated in Table 10.1 to show cumulative percentages for the main species and groups. If only molluscs were required, a screen of 0·85 mm which separated about 95 per cent of the individuals in his samples would have been suitable, but a very fine screen was required for nematodes and crustaceans. Analyses of polychaetes into species show the variation which can occur within a single taxonomic class. Thus about 95% of *Lumbrineris* were found on the 1·0 mm mesh, but to attain this level of separation for *Cossura candida* required a mesh of 0·27 mm. When the overall assemblage is considered it appears that a 0·27 mm mesh was needed to collect about 95 per cent of all individuals. On the other hand, if only the biomass is considered, Reish found that over 90 per cent was retained in the 1·4 mm sieve. While these results clearly apply only to the ground studied, they emphasise again that the sieve selected must depend on the purpose of the survey.

In general, it is suggested that a 0·5 mm sieve should be used for macrofauna whenever possible, but on coarse grounds this may retain too large a volume of material. The mesh selected will then depend both on the grade of the deposit and on the size range of the animals to be collected. The use of a mesh corresponding to one of those proposed in the International Standard (ISO) is recommended, and a choice should be made from one of the following apertures:

2·00, 1·40, 1·00, 0·71, 0·50 mm

In areas where coarse deposits necessitate the use of wide-meshed sieves, it may be useful to collect additional samples of smaller volume for the assessment of macrofauna passing these sieves.

TABLE 10.1. Number of specimens retained on graded screens, and cumulative percentages (calculated from Reish, 1959).

Mesh sizes in mm	4·7	2·8	1·4	1·0	0·85	0·7	0·59	0·5	0·35	0·27	0·15	Total
Nematoda	—	—	—	—	—	1	2	6	26	456	90	581
%	—	—	—	—	—	0·2	0·5	1·5	6·0	72·0	100·0	
Nemertea	2	7	6	3	5	2	—	1	—	—	—	26
%	7·7	34·6	57·7	69·2	88·5	96·2	96·2	100·0	—	—	—	
Polychaeta:												
Lumbrineris spp.	8	10	33	9	3	—	—	—	—	—	—	63
%	12·7	28·6	81·0	95·2	100·0	—	—	—	—	—	—	
Dorvillea articulata	—	—	22	52	30	5	4	2	2	2	—	119
%	—	—	18·5	62·2	87·4	91·6	95·0	96·6	98·3	100·0	—	
Prionospio cirrifera	1	6	23	100	115	30	18	10	—	1	—	304
%	0·3	2·3	10·0	42·8	80·6	90·1	96·4	99·8	99·8	100·0	—	
Capitita ambiseta	3	6	29	104	109	23	21	13	2	—	—	310
%	1·0	2·9	12·3	45·8	81·0	88·4	95·2	99·4	100·0	—	—	
Cossura candida	—	—	1	11	129	100	157	265	88	105	10	866
%	—	—	0·1	1·4	16·3	27·8	46·0	76·6	86·7	98·8	100·0	
Other Polychaeta	10	23	27	38	31	10	11	7	4	5	2	168
%	6·0	19·6	35·7	58·3	76·8	82·7	89·3	93·4	95·8	98·8	100·0	
Crustacea	3	—	—	—	2	—	1	3	5	3	—	17
%	17·6	17·6	17·6	17·6	29·4	29·4	35·3	52·9	82·4	100·0	—	
Mollusca	5	4	7	5	2	—	—	1	—	—	—	24
%	20·5	37·5	66·7	87·5	95·8	95·8	95·8	100·0	—	—	—	
Pisces	1	—	—	—	—	—	—	—	—	—	—	1
%	100·0	—	—	—	—	—	—	—	—	—	—	
Total	33	56	148	322	426	171	214	308	127	572	102	2479
%	1·3	3·5	9·7	22·5	39·7	46·6	55·3	67·7	72·8	95·9	100·0	

Subsequent sorting

Having reduced the sample to a manageable size by initial sieving, the sorting of the animals from the residue may proceed. If the final extraction is done soon after collection, and near the sampling site, sorting live material may be possible, with the advantage that movement of the animals helps in their detection, especially if they are small. But frequently it is necessary after the initial sieving in the field to preserve the collections for later sorting. In such circumstances it is important to ensure adequate labelling. It may be convenient to number the tops or sides of the jars with a waterproof marker, but even if this is done, a properly annotated label strong enough to withstand water and preservatives should be placed inside the jar. A suitable paper is goatskin parchment, obtainable from Wiggins Teape and Alex Pirrie Ltd, Gateway House, Watling Street, London EC4. Alternatively, sheet plastic with a matt surface, which may be marked with pencil, can be used, and this is particularly suitable for sediment samples. Rigid PVC sheet such as *Vybak* or *Cobex*, obtainable to order with a matt surface, in a thickness of 0·010 or 0·020 in (0·025 or 0·050 mm), and in various colours should be used (Obtainable from G.H. Bloore, see list of suppliers, p. 291. Rather thicker plastic of the same kind is useful for underwater notebooks.)

For preservation at this stage formalin is normally used, and this can conveniently be diluted with sea water. While a 10 per cent solution of commercial formalin (equivalent to 4 per cent formaldehyde) is suitable for histological purposes, for general storage the strength may be reduced to between $2\frac{1}{2}$ per cent and 5 per cent formalin, providing that the volume of preserving solution is considerably greater than that of the specimens. In very large samples, perhaps containing much gravel, care should be taken that not only is there sufficient preservative but that it is adequately mixed throughout the material. Since formalin tends to become acidic with storage and cause damage to the specimens, a buffer such as borax or hexamine is often added to the preservative. These substances have been criticised for causing disintegration of labels, or for producing a precipitate, and in plankton samples sodium acetate is sometimes used. However these problems are at present being considered by SCOR Working Group number 23, and pending their report it is perhaps least damaging to prevent acidity by addition of marble chips to the formalin. Although bulk treatment is satisfactory for general samples, if specific animals are required in good condition for fine work, such specimens should be extracted and dealt with separately whenever possible. Alcohol is often used for later storage of samples, but it is less satisfactory for initial field preservation because of its volatility, because its mixing with sea water produces a precipitate, and because it may bring about the separation of lamellibranchs from their shells.

If the study is restricted to major species or to large animals, hand-sorting may be straightforward. This is best done in glass trays below which alternately black and white material can be inserted to provide varying backgrounds suitable for discerning different types of animals. If every animal must be extracted this can be a time-consuming task, and may severely restrict the extent of the sampling. It is often useful to divide the sample into fractions by agitating the light material into suspension and pouring through a fine sieve. This separates small fauna (such as crustaceans and polychaetes) together with the fine debris, leaving large or heavy animals behind in the main sample.

The two chief methods sometimes used to ease the work of sorting macrofauna are flotation and elutriation. A flotation technique has been described by Birkett (1957). The sample, in carbon tetrachloride covered with sea water in a large vessel, is agitated with a stirrer. Most of the living animals float up on the carbon tetrachloride and lie at its interface with the water, from where they can be collected on a strainer. The process takes only a few minutes and may be repeated if it appears that animals remain trapped in the sediment. Quite large specimens float up, and only heavy, thick-shelled species, such as some of the larger bivalves, fail to do so. These species are likely to be uncommon, and can quickly be removed by hand. Unfortunately, organic detritus also floats, so the method is often unsuitable for muds and silts. Since carbon tetrachloride vapour is dangerous if inhaled, the liquid must always be covered with a layer of water, and the operation should be carried out with adequate ventilation. Trichloroethylene ('trilene'), which is less toxic, has been suggested as an alternative.

Elutriation involves passing a continuous stream of water up through the sample in a tall tube with an overflow onto a fine screen. The flow rate is adjusted so that the water agitates the sample and carries up the small animals but not the sediment. An apparatus suitable for macrofauna, which is described by Lauff *et al.* (1961), utilises both water and air jets. Elutriation and flotation techniques are used in meiofauna extraction and are discussed in more detail below.

Meiofauna

Methods available for extraction of meiofauna vary according to the type of sediment and depend on whether extraction is qualitative—to obtain representative specimens—or quantitative—to extract every organism possible for detailed counts. Extraction can be done on either fresh or preserved samples. If the vertical distribution of the fauna is to be studied it is essential that division of the sample into appropriate sections should be done immediately on collection since changes within the sample (e.g. in packing, water content, temperature) can rapidly alter the vertical distribution of the fauna.

Live material

Whenever possible meiofauna should be extracted from the sediment alive, because moving animals are much more easily seen and because certain groups, such as turbellarians and gastrotrichs, may be difficult or impossible to identify if roughly preserved.

For qualitative extraction the sample can be allowed to stand in the laboratory in sea water and the deposit examined at intervals when organisms which come to the surface (often aggregated away from the light) can be pipetted off. Stirring the sample or bubbling air through it, brings certain types of animals (such as kinorhynchs and small crustaceans) on to the surface film of the water, from where they can be scooped off using a wire loop or blotting paper. For deep-living fauna the sample may be shaken and decanted, preferably using an anaesthetic as described below.

For quantitative extraction of living material from fine sediments it is usually convenient to divide the sample into two fractions using a fine sieve. A mesh of 62 or 50 μ is appropriate since one of these is usually accepted as defining the upper limit of the silt-clay fraction of the sediment, but even finer meshes, 30 or 40 μ, are often used to ensure that most of the fauna is retained in the sieve residue. When sieving meiofauna it is important always to use filtered water to prevent contamination of the sample with organisms which might be present in, for example, the deck water supply of a research vessel. The residue is hand-sorted under a stereoscopic microscope, attention always being paid to the surface film of the overlying water. This is of particular importance in the case of some groups such as Kinorhyncha, which tend to be caught by surface tension. What passes through the sieve includes most of the silt-clay fraction of the deposit, along with the smallest meiofauna, mainly juvenile stages. Normal hand sorting from such fine material is difficult, and an appropriate technique involves stirring the sample into uniform suspension in a measured quantity of water and withdrawing a known volume in a graduated pipette. The volume thus subsampled should be related to the size of the sorting dish so that the settled subsample covers the bottom of the dish with a layer of deposit only a few grains thick. When viewed by light from below, living animals can easily be seen either directly by their movement or by the track they leave. Counts from the subsample are adjusted to give an estimate for the total volume of water, and this is added to the sieve-residue count to obtain a value for the original sample. The section of the sample awaiting examination must be kept under suitable conditions of temperature and restricted light so that the animals remain in good condition. The whole procedure is time-consuming, and restricts the number of samples which can be dealt with, but it does permit an accurate count of the fauna in fine muddy deposits.

For coarser, sandy deposits, a number of more convenient procedures are available. Satisfactory quantitative extraction can be done by repeatedly shaking and decanting the sample; if necessary, through an appropriate sieve or filter. Best results are obtained if the whole sample is first treated with an anaesthetic, since many interstitial animals tend to attach to sand grains when motion occurs. A solution of magnesium chloride isotonic with sea water is widely used—75·25 g $MgCl_2$. 6 H_2O dissolved in 1 litre of distilled water is approximately isotonic with sea water of 35 per mille salinity. (Since this salt is very hygroscopic, a solution is more accurately made up by heating the salt to constant weight at 500–600°C, 35·24 g of the anhydrous salt being used to make 1 litre of solution.) This is sufficient to relax the fauna without adverse effects after several minutes' treatment, but 10 per cent alcohol is also satisfactory.

Elutriation is a more sophisticated and perhaps more efficient version of the decanting procedure. Its use for macrofauna separation has already been noted, and Boisseau (1957) introduced it for meiofauna work. A possible set-up is illustrated in Fig. 10.3. This indicates the use of a small pump with a by-pass to control the pressure, but alternatively pressure can be provided by raising the reservoir high enough to provide a head, or by direct attachment to a suitable tap and the water need not be recirculated. Filtered water should be used in the reservoir, or a filter must be introduced into the direct system to prevent contamination of the sample. The time required for elutriation depends on the size and nature of the sample. Samples of 20 ml can

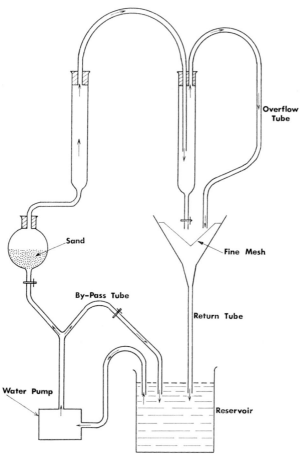

Figure 10.3. Boisseau-type apparatus for elutriation of sand, closed-system arrangement. For discussion see text.

usually be completed in a few minutes. The fauna is collected on a fine sieve and the flow should be arranged to meet the sieve surface at an oblique angle to minimise the loss of animals roughly the same cross-section diameter as the sieve mesh. Any such loss may be further reduced by the addition of a second sieve below the first. Elutriation carries over most of the light fauna, but the residue should be examined for heavier organisms (molluscs, ostracods) which may have been left behind and which can be extracted by hand.

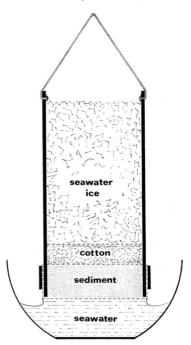

Figure 10.4. Apparatus for separating interstitial fauna from sand by seawater-ice method (Redrawn from Uhlig, 1968).

Other methods possible for extraction of living animals were originally developed for terrestrial work, and make use of the activity of the organisms themselves in response to changes imposed by the operator on their physical conditions. For example, Overgaard (1948) induced a temperature and moisture gradient in soil cores by heating them in an earthenware cylinder over a water bath. Worms moved upward into a layer of cooled sand on top of the soil and were separated by washing and decanting. By an alternative method, improved by O'Connor (1955), the soil samples were heated from above by an electric bulb and worms moved downwards into a column of water from which they could be drawn off and collected. A comparable technique was developed by Uhlig (1966, 1968) specifically for marine work. The sediment is placed in a tube on a nylon gauze base which just dips into filtered sea water in a collecting dish (Fig. 10.4). Crushed sea-water ice is added to a layer of cotton wool on top of the sediment, and as the ice melts, organisms move down into the collecting dish. Uhlig considers that movement of the animals is due more to the salinity and the streaming action of the water than to the temperature gradient. The method has certain limitations, and can be applied only to sandy sediments which have a capillary structure. Most of the smaller forms leave the deposit and concentrate in the collecting dish but nematodes and some of the larger animals are not extracted quantitatively, and the sediment should later be elutriated or decanted to obtain complete extraction. The sea-ice technique has recently been used successfully even in tropical situations (J. B. J. Wells—personal communication).

Preserved material

While live extraction is the ideal, the number of samples involved, or the distance of the laboratory from the sampling site may make this impossible, and the entire sample (or the sections into which it has been divided) should be preserved in 5 per cent formalin for storage or transport.

Most of the techniques available for live samples may also be used on preserved material but the final process of sorting tends to be less certain because the smallest animals are difficult to detect when not in motion. It is therefore useful to stain the entire sample before extraction. Rose bengal has frequently been used for this purpose, and a strength of 1 g in 1 litre of water, formalin or alcohol imparts sufficient colour after several hours' immersion. Hamilton (1969) describes a method developed in freshwater work, by which the samples are stained in rhodamine B and examined under longwave ultraviolet light. Most invertebrates fluoresced a brilliant orange, and in the presence of mud sediment and debris, time required to sort small organisms could often be reduced to about one-third of the normal time.

Decantation or elutriation can be used for preserved sand, but for muds sieve separation is required, and the fraction passing the finest sieve must usually be discarded since hand sorting of small animals, even when stained, from a silt-clay mixture, is usually unacceptably time consuming. Although these techniques for preserved samples are generally adequate, occasional live samples should be examined if possible to help with interpretation of the preserved material, and to allow identification of the more delicate forms.

The flotation technique, already referred to for macrofauna extraction can be used for meiofauna samples in either fresh or preserved condition, but since live animals tend to cling to debris, and since some of the solutions used can cause distortion of the organisms, it is probably best to work with preserved material. The basis of this technique is that if the specific gravity of the animals is significantly different from that of the bulk of the sediment, it is possible to separate the animals from the sediment in a liquid of suitable specific gravity. Various liquids have been used—sugar solution (Anderson, 1959), magnesium sulphate (Lydell, 1936), sodium chloride (Lyman, 1943) and zinc chloride (Sellmer, 1956). Dillon (1964) used carbon tetrachloride, which had been found suitable for larger animals, but for use with meiofauna he added first a detergent to prevent small objects being imprisoned by water globules. The best liquid for a particular sample will depend on the type of animal to be removed and on the material composing the bulk of the deposit. Anderson, for example, working with samples rich in organic debris, found the specific gravity of this to be greater than 1·12 and that of the invertebrates to be less, so a sugar solution adjusted to specific gravity 1·12 floated off his animals. Sellmer, on the other hand, wished to separate small bivalves, specific gravity 1·65, from sand grains of specific gravity 2·6 and used a 75 per cent solution of zinc chloride of specific gravity 2·1. When the animals have been raised to the surface of the liquid, they may be skimmed off on a fine mesh or concentrated by centrifuging (Teal, 1960). Although these flotation techniques have been widely discussed, most of the appropriate solutions are dangerous, unpleasant or expensive, and many workers find them unsuitable for general use.

Microfauna

Much of the previous section on meiofauna applies also to microfauna, except that live material must nearly always be used. Mare (1942) has used dilution culture methods, similar to those of soil microbiologists, to enumerate protozoa of subtidal mud, but she recognised that the technique was of value only for comparative purposes, and could not be used to give absolute numbers. The sea-water ice method of Uhlig is suitable for concentrating ciliates and flagellates from sand and has been used for quantitative work by Fenchel (1967). It cannot, however, be used in non-capillary sediments containing mud, silt and clay. For such sediments it is necessary to resort to direct counts on small samples, but since the microfauna is often confined to the extreme surface layer it may be found possible after a preliminary examination of deeper sections, to deal with only the top few millimetres of deposit unless the sulphide system is also to be studied.

11

Phytobenthos Sampling and Estimation of Primary Production

F. E. ROUND AND M. HICKMAN

Introduction

Primary production may be defined as the formation of organic molecules from relatively simple inorganic sources utilising either light energy (performed by bacteria, algae, lichens and angiosperms in the marine environment) or chemical energy (certain bacteria only).

The marine phytobenthos includes all the associations of organisms involved in the above processes and living at or closely associated with the many solid/liquid interfaces. The greatest bulk of phytobenthos occurs in the intertidal and shallow subtidal regions where both photosynthetic and chemosynthetic associations are involved. Below the limit of penetration of photosynthetically usable light only the chemosynthetic bacteria are involved. The primary producers live on or in the silt, sand or rock; attached to the macroscopic algae, angiosperms and animals associated with these interfaces; or even on the under surface of permanent sea ice.

Probably the greater part of the primary synthesis is by various algal groups although occasionally bacteria can be significant, as on some sandy sediments. Angiosperms are relatively scarce except in some tropical regions and lichens are mostly confined to the upper intertidal. Relatively few studies of marine primary productivity by the phytobenthos have been made and hence wherever applicable we shall refer also to techniques designed for freshwater studies since the same principles are involved. Considerable testing and development work is required on all aspects and the following should be treated merely as a working outline around which studies can be planned. In order to enable comparison of primary productivity in different regions it is essential that the habitats and plant associations are adequately defined and if two or more primary producing associations live in close association these should either be separated or studied as an aggregate. Also it is essential that methods should be standardised or the data presented in such a way that valid comparisons can be made.

Definition of habitats

Habitats themselves can be defined from a physico-chemical stand-point without reference to the organisms. Habitats occupied by the phytobenthos start on the upper shore where sufficient sea spray is deposited to form substrata suitable for colonisation by halophytic plants. Obviously in some localities this supratidal zone merges into the realm of the terrestrial ecologist and an upper limit must be set in each individual project. The intertidal zone tends to form the next easily definable gross habitat and can be relatively accurately defined from tide tables and direct surveying of the shore (see pp. 84–85). The subtidal zone may be divided into that occupied by the photosynthetic plants (down to the limit of penetration of photosynthetically usable light), and the effectively dark regions occupied only by chemosynthetic plants. The boundary between these will vary with season and turbidity of the water column. For precision and ease of comparison the substratum should be clearly defined together with as much information as possible on angle of slope, aspect, length of tidal exposure, etc.

Inorganic substrata

(a) **Hard.** Rock surfaces, intertidal and subtidal. Geological formation is rarely quoted hence it is difficult to assess the importance of this factor, but topography, angle and degree of bedding, friability etc. are important in the description of this habitat. Rock faces and rock pools are quite separate habitats and subject to different environmental stresses. Hard artificial substrata, e.g. concrete, may be of importance at some sites. On some shores loose stones which may be moved to varying degrees by wave action, constitute a further habitat for primary producers. These are undoubtedly difficult to study but they are productive often of both microscopic (e.g. diatoms and Cyanophyta) and macroscopic associations (e.g. large Chlorophyta, Phaeophyta and Rhodophyta). (Aleem, 1950a and Castenholz, 1963.)

(b) **Soft or mobile.** Sand, silt and various intermediates, intertidal and subtidal. Again where possible some information on geological origin, composition, grain size and organic content is desirable, and it is important to distinguish between sand and silt. Beds of inorganic remains of biogenic origin such as those derived from shell fragments or calcareous remains of algae are also colonised by primary producers. Calcareous algae detached from their substratum are known to continue photosynthesis and this must be taken into account. Microscopic associations are primarily of diatoms and dinoflagellates but some Cyanophyta and Chrysophyceae may also occur. Macroscopic siphonaceous Chlorophyta are especially common on sediments in the tropics. (Brockmann, 1935; Aleem, 1951; von Stosch, 1956; Round, 1960; Bodeanu, 1964.)

(c) **Ice.** This forms a relatively stable habitat for algal primary producers, mainly diatoms. (Bunt, 1963, and Apollonio, 1965.)

Organic substrata

(a) **Algae.** Some microscopic and most macroscopic algae frequently support a rich flora. These host plants are either attached to the hard inorganic substrata or grow in silt and sand but a few are free-living (e.g. some populations of *Sargassum*). They are abundant in intertidal and subtidal habitats.

(b) **Angiosperms.** Although only a small number of angiosperms grow in the subtidal zone they can be very abundant and form a stable habitat for algae, as do plants of salt marshes and mangrove swamps (e.g., *Enteromorpha, Caloglossa, Bostrychia*).

(c) **Epibiotic on fauna.** Primary producing algae live attached externally. Many sedentary animals (e.g. limpets) and a few motile species living associated with the above inorganic and organic substrates support dense microscopic and macroscopic algal floras.

(d) **Endobiotic in fauna.** This habitat is occupied by a number of algae and is of great importance in some regions. The host may be associated with sand/silt shores, e.g. *Convoluta*, or with hard inorganic substrates, e.g. corals.

In some instances the above gross habitats occupy considerable uninterrupted areas but usually they tend to be intermixed, adding complexity to the study. Furthermore, there are smaller niches within these habitats and some will be considered in the next section.

Definition and recognition of primary producing associations

The term association is here used in the sense defined by Hutchinson (1967) 'an assemblage of species that recurs under comparable ecological conditions in different places'. Two vital concepts are involved, firstly the recognition of these assemblages and secondly definition of 'comparable ecological conditions'. To some extent the recognition of the assemblages is simplified if the habitats are clearly defined as above and even more precisely if the individual niches are recognised. The assemblage, however, can be defined without recourse to descriptions of the habitat. For example, there are associations attached to inorganic sand both in the intertidal and subtidal zone and these are recognisable from habitats throughout the world. There is another totally different series of associations which live amongst the sand but which are unattached to the sand grains and capable of movement through the deposit. The definition and recognition of these two groups of assocations is important in considering their primary productivity which can be estimated separately for the two associations at any one site, or combined. If the latter approach is employed it is important to recognise that the data from two *totally unlike* associations are being combined. The species composition of, for example, associations attached to sand grains will vary somewhat from place to place according to local conditions but the life form of the species and probably many of the species themselves will be common.

The number of associations recognised will increase as detailed work expands and strictly they are definable only from the dominants, subdominants and other species present. They can, however, be classified according to niches which they occupy in the gross habitats defined above and this is extremely helpful.

Associations growing on hard inorganic substrata

These are the *epilithic* and *endolithic* associations (*epilithon* or *endolithon*).

A series of epilithic associations which may contain pure stands of microscopic species of encrusting Cyanophyta, Chrysophyta, Chlorophyta, Phaeophyta, Rhodophyta, diatoms or mixtures of these groups coats the surface of rocks. Some may be confined to sloping rock surfaces, others to rock pools. Data for these in the intertidal are scarce and in the subtidal even scarcer.

Macrophytic growths of Chlorophyta, Phaeophyta, Rhodophyta and lichens occur attached to rock surfaces. These associations are fairly well described in intertidal habitats and are now being increasingly documented for the subtidal by divers—however relatively little data have been obtained for biomass or productivity purposes.

Endolithic associations occur particularly on soft (often calcareous) rock and penetrate into it but even the pores and crevices in hard rock and corals are colonised. These associations which comprise certain Cyanophyta, diatoms and Rhodophyta have received little attention.

Associations on soft or mobile inorganic substrata

(a) Associations attached to sand particles (*epipsammic*) consist mainly of attached diatoms and bacteria with occasional Cyanophyta and Chlorophyta. The species involved are often minute and taxonomically difficult. Similar associations probably grow on calcareous shell and algal fragments but as far as we are aware have hardly been investigated.

(b) Associations moving on and in the surface sediments (*epipelic*) consist primarily of motile diatoms, but occasionally also of filamentous or coccoid Cyanophyta, dinoflagellate and euglenoid flagellates. They grow on sand and silt, both in the intertidal and subtidal. Wherever silt accumulates on other substrata, e.g. on stones, rocks or plants the epipelic association is liable to exist as a contaminant or may completely replace the true association of the substrata. The species often undergo rhythmic vertical movements. (Pomeroy, 1959; Bodeanu, 1964; Round and Palmer 1966; Round, 1966; Palmer and Round, 1967.)

(c) Associations living within the sediment (*endopelic*) are relatively un-unknown—diatoms occurring in mucilage tubes and motile or semi-motile species living beneath the surface on sandy shores and not moving vertically. (Williams, 1963, Round, in preparation.)

(d) Associations of larger algae or angiosperms rooted in sediments (*rhizobenthic*) consist of species of Chlorophyta, Phaeophyta, Rhodophyta or angiosperms. These are more common in tropical zones.

Associations growing on other living organisms

(a) The *epiphytic* associations which are found attached to plants are composed of species of Chlorophyta, Phaeophyta, Rhodophyta, Cyanophyta and Bacillariophyta. In some habitats species from other associations may become entangled amongst these—this flora has been termed *metaphyton* in freshwater studies and the term is equally applicable to the marine environment. Thalloid algae are often coated with diatom epiphytes and measurement of the primary productivity of e.g. *Ceramium* spp. growing on *Chorda*, *Laminaria* etc. could often include a considerable contribution from the diatoms.

(b) Similar species of algae occur in the *epizoic* associations which are found attached to shells and the surfaces of animals. These have been little investigated.

(c) *Endophytic* species which grow within other algae or angiosperms consist of Chlorophyta, Phaeophyta and Rhodophyta. Primary production is likely to be estimated together with that of the host, but densely colonised hosts may not assimilate carbon at the same rate as uncolonised hosts. As far as we know no studies have been undertaken on these combinations of species.

(d) *Endozoic* associations, actually growing within animals, have been studied because of an intrinsic interest in the kinds of symbiotic organisms and also because in the economy of coral reefs the endozoic algae contribute considerably to primary production.

Bacteria are likely to be involved in many of the above associations—a conspicuous example being the occurrence of purple sulphur bacteria on intertidal sands.

Field sampling techniques

The pre-requisite of field sampling is that the algal associations and the niches they occupy be recognised (see previous section) in order that wherever possible well-defined associations can be collected and mixed associations recognised when field separation is impossible, e.g. epiphytes on larger algae. Preliminary field surveys may be necessary to determine the extent and heterogeneity of the associations, and to fix sampling stations.

Biomass and production studies will rarely be possible on plants left *in situ* in the habitat.

(a) **Macrophytes.** In most instances these will have to be removed to the laboratory. Removal of whole plants attached to rock is difficult but if removal of individual pieces of rock is possible and does not drastically affect the sampling area, this is desirable since losses are more likely to occur if sampling is undertaken in the field. Holdfasts must be included in the samples. In the case of plants embedded in silt the underground 'rhizomes' should be removed at the same time, similarly the root systems of angiosperms such as *Zostera*. Plants can be sampled completely for weight, volume, chemical component analysis, or individual plants can be marked and growth measured directly. Rate of production can be related to rate of colonisation of cleaned areas but this is a somewhat artificial measure. Sampling of epiphytes usually requires the removal of the host plant to the laboratory. Some are loosely attached and therefore samples should be taken with the minimum of disturbance, preferably by enclosing the plant in a sampling device whilst still in position under the water. Even in apparently rough water there is often an easily lost diatom flora especially of long chain forming species, e.g. *Rhabdonema*. Transport to the laboratory may free other species from the substrata and these need to be added to the biomass still attached to the plant.

(b) **Sediments.** Sampling of sand and silt in the intertidal is relatively simple since cores can be removed and transported to the laboratory. In some instances the motile epipelic flora can be removed in the field by the use of fabric or lens tissue as described on pp. 176–179. The proportion of the total flora removed by this technique requires determination for each sediment type. Cores can also be obtained from underwater sediments, but care should be taken to avoid water movement as the sampling apparatus approaches the surface of the sediment since some of the surface forms may be washed away. (See p. 146.)

(c) **Hard surfaces.** Microscopic, epilithic species can be scraped off rocks, but rough surfaces are difficult to deal with and underwater surfaces do not appear to have been sampled. Much development work is needed before satisfactory sampling techniques can be recommended. Films of plastic material, e.g. collodion have been used (Margalef, 1949) but the algae so collected are liable to be damaged and therefore difficult to identify.

Contamination of all benthic associations by phytoplankton is likely although this may only be serious when there are massive phytoplankton blooms. Under normal circumstances the contaminating cells from the water bathing the benthic associations will be negligible since the density of cells at the surface/liquid interfaces is many times greater than the density of phytoplankton in the same volume of water. However, during decline of heavy phytoplankton populations, dying and dead cells can accumulate rapidly and may bias cell counts unless recognised and discounted. They will also contribute pigments, though these may be degraded forms rather than the active forms (see p. 183). Owing tot he special environmental conditions in the benthos, phytoplankton remains rarely stay active for more than a few days.

Areal sampling. Since by definition the benthic associations occur at inter-facial niches it is obviously desirable to express results on an area basis which for productivity measurements should be related to sea surface area (p. 80). Sampling of known areas of sediments is relatively simple in the intertidal but difficult in the subtidal. Dredges are too crude for almost all algal popula-tions and coring devices sampling known areas are essential (see p. 133). Macrophytic growths require to be sampled from marked quadrats. The angle of slope, degree of shading, degree of wave action etc. should be recorded. On ice surfaces the algal associations penetrate the ice and volumes must also be sampled.

Artificial substrata. Numerous experiments, frequently related to fouling and pollution have employed artificial substrata (glass, plastic, concrete, etc.) to study rates of colonisation under different ecological conditions. The algal flora tends, however, to be a somewhat specialised one although similar associations can sometimes be recognised on adjacent natural substrata. Undoubtedly much valuable information can be gained from this approach though it *cannot* be directly translated into productivity of the adjacent surfaces which over a period of time may support rather different associations growing at differing rates.

Separation of live populations from substratum, and estimation of biomass from cell counts

Epipelic algae
Diatoms can be isolated from damp intertidal sediments by placing a piece of fabric on the surface, and allowing time for the phototactic algae to move up into it. Eaton and Moss (1966) used lens tissue for this purpose, and they review earlier work. Another method frequently used in the laboratory is to make a suspension of the algae and sediment and to count the organisms in an aliquot of the suspension in a counting chamber. This direct method has

been used by Aleem (1950b), and Hopkins (1963) for core samples. Plante (1966) used a technique which involved separation of diatoms and fine detrital material gravimetrically by ascensional water flows, followed by differential centrifugation in liquids of differing densities.

In another technique for epipelic algae, a sample is mixed in the laboratory to disperse the algae. It is then poured into dishes, and coverglasses are placed on the damp sediment surface. The algae move up on to the underside of the coverglass, which can be removed from the sediment surface and placed on a slide for counting and identification of the algae (Round, 1953).

Eaton and Moss (1966) developed a quantitative technique of defined accuracy for sampling and estimating epipelic populations under a wide range of field conditions. Methods for sampling shallow and deep water were developed and three possible methods of estimating numbers of algae in field samples were studied: (i) direct counting, (ii) use of coverglasses, and (iii) lens tissues.

Samples can be taken from sediments in shallow intertidal pools etc. using a glass tube—diameter 0·5 cm—stoppered by a finger at the upper end and with the lower end placed on the surface of the mud. By releasing the finger, and simultaneously drawing the lower end of the tube across the mud surface, the tube fills with a mixture of surface and overlying material. Results with this method are qualitatively reproducible but the area sampled is not known (Round, 1953). Cores have been used in some cases. Aleem (1950a), Hopkins (1963) and Round and Palmer (1966) used short open-ended cylinders and took cores by hand from intertidal areas. For shallow waters, Perspex (acrylic plastic) cylinders, 9 cm diam. and 35 cm long or long enough to reach above the water surface, can be pushed into the sediment to delineate a known area. The sediment from within the cylinder can be removed by suction into a polyethylene bottle attached to a glass tube which is moved over the sediment surface. It was found that the suction prevented preferential uptake of either small or large sediment particles. Samples could be easily obtained from substrata of widely differing textures. In deeper waters, mechanical corers have to be used before the surface sediment can be removed by suction. The main requirement is that the surface of the core should be disturbed as little as possible.

Samples from underwater sites often contain far more water than sediment, and to separate this the sample is allowed to settle in the laboratory in the *dark*. This ensures that the flagellate groups which tend to be phototactically attracted to the water surface also sediment out. After 5–7 h the supernatant water is removed, using a pipette or pump. Losses here were estimated to be less than 1 per cent of total numbers of diatoms present. The sample is now vigorously shaken to thoroughly mix the sediment and algae. The mixture is poured into a petri dish or other suitable vessel of known area to give a depth of 0·5–1·0 cm, the remainder of the sample being dried to a constant weight at 105°C. Squares of lens-cleaning or other suitable tissues (experimentation may be needed to find the ideal tissue and size for each particular sediment) are placed on the surface and the sample left for at least 12 h.

The time of final harvesting is important because the epipelic populations show strong diurnal vertical migration rhythms (Round and Palmer, 1966; Palmer and Round, 1967). It has also been found that where the algal populations migrate vertically under laboratory conditions in phase with tidal cycles occurring simultaneously in the field, the timing of the migratory cycle must be determined by preliminary sampling and, hence, harvesting time adjusted accordingly. Samples in the laboratory should not be subjected to artificial illumination at night; instead they should experience a normal light/dark cycle (Round and Eaton, 1966).

As mentioned earlier, coverglasses can be placed on to the surface of sediment which has been poured into a suitable container of known surface area and then the following day the coverglasses can be removed with forceps. Counting can be achieved by placing the coverglass on to a slide; however, since the majority of the epipelic algae are motile, it is not satisfactory to count them alive. Placing the coverglass on to a drop of 40 per cent glycerol prevents movement and overcomes this difficulty without rendering the algae unrecognisable. The algae can then be identified and counted. Numbers increase toward the edge of the coverglass, because the algae tend to migrate whilst it is on the mud surface. This would suggest that some deoxygenation occurs under the middle of the coverglass. Also any sediment sticking to the underside of the coverglass will obscure the algae, thus making counting difficult, and also inaccurate. When counting by this method one should use standard traverses to ensure reproducibility, although Eaton and Moss (1966) found that even when this was done an error always remained.

Williams (1963) used silk fabric to trap epipelic algae from marine mudflats, then separated them for counting by washing the fabric with water. This is satisfactory for such organisms as pennate diatoms, which readily wash off, but flagellates etc. may not, and whilst suitable for field use the technique described below is more suitable for laboratory studies.

Eaton and Moss (1966) investigated the possibility of using cellulose tissues instead of coverglasses or fabric to trap the algae. They studied eight commercially-available types of cellulose. It was found that a double layer of Grade 105 lens tissue (J. Barcham Green Ltd, Hayle Mill, Maidstone, England) trapped twice as many algae as the others from all types of sediment. This type of tissue is recommended for all such work. Results showed that up to 87·5 per cent of algae were removed by the tissues. Samples containing euglenoid flagellates can also be harvested readily, as can samples containing mixtures of diatoms, volvocalean and euglenoid flagellates and blue-green filamentous algae. This tissue method was found to be much better than the coverglass method in efficiency of harvesting, estimation of species proportions and adaptability to different associations of algae. Also it is readily adapted to production studies using both oxygen and carbon [14] (see p. 189).

Eaton and Moss (1966) developed a technique for counting the algae. Tissues of 2×2 cm were placed on the sediment surface and removed the following day; these were then placed in 3 ml 40 per cent glycerol in Lugol's iodine solution which kills, stains and preserves the algae. When stored in the dark the algal pigments last longer. The addition of 5 per cent formaldehyde is desirable for long preservation, as the iodine will gradually lose its preserving power. Very delicate and small flagellates were distorted by glycerol and sometimes by iodine. Thus other methods need to be developed for preservation and enumeration of the small and delicate algae. Tissues are broken up using a pair of dissecting needles. A known volume (0·020–0·025 ml) is transferred to a slide and counted under the microscope.

Squares of lens tissue (5 × 5 mm) mounted directly in a drop of 40 per cent glycerol have also been used. The lens tissue is first pulled apart with dissecting needles and coverglasses are then placed on the sample and the algae counted. This technique is useful where sites are relatively homogeneous. The use of larger lens tissue reduces the errors caused by heterogeneous populations.

If diatoms are present it is desirable to retain material for subsequent identification. Duplicate tissues can be removed from the sediment and placed in 10 ml conical tubes together with 5 ml dilute chromic acid. Tubes are then immersed in a water bath at 100°C for 1 hr. Lens tissue and other organic material is destroyed by the acid. This leaves only clean diatom valves and other mineral particulate matter. The residue is then washed by successive centrifugations and re-suspensions until neutral to litmus paper. Afterwards it can be made up to 10 ml, and 1 ml portions put on to 0·75 in (1·9 cm) circular coverglasses, allowed to dry, and the coverglasses mounted in

Mikrops 163. Diatoms can then be identified and also their numbers estimated, allowing for the fact that nearly every diatom is split into two separate valves during cleaning. However, for a quantitative estimation the permanent mount method is subject to gross errors in estimation of quantity and quality of epipelic diatoms, therefore it is only useful for identification purposes. (Eaton and Moss, 1966.) Tissue traps and temporary mounts are recommended for further quantitative estimates.

As mentioned earlier a method of estimation involving a suspension of the algae and associated sediment particles and counting of the organisms in an aliquot of the suspension in a counting chamber has been used. However, there are many problems and unless the sample is very rich in algae it is difficult to obtain a reliable count.

Epipsammic algae

In shallow water the method of Eaton and Moss (1966) can be used to sample the surface sediment. The apparatus enables samples to be taken from a known area, delimited by a plastic cylinder pushed into the sediment, followed by removal of the sediment into a polythene bottle by suction. In deep waters mechanical corers can be used.

The non-epipsammic flora should be removed by repeatedly swirling the sediment with filtered water. The non-attached epipelic, planktonic algae and detrital material is swept into suspension and can be decanted off, whilst the epipsammic flora remains attached to the sand grains, which being heavy compared with the epipelic algae and detrital material readily sediments out. For cell counts of the epipsammic algae, a standard volume of this cleaned sand is taken, and placed in twice its volume of filtered water. This is then subjected to sonication in a Burndept BE 297 Ultrasonic cleaner for 10 minutes to remove the algae from the sand grains. It is advisable to cool the sonication bath with ice to prevent heating of the sample and subsequent cell breakage. Ten minutes has been found to be the optimum time for sonication, working with an epipsammic flora from a lake—90·5 per cent of the population is removed in this time with no breakage of cells. Sonication time beyond 10 minutes does remove more algae, but after 12–15 minutes cells tend to be broken up. Experimentation is needed to determine the optimal system for removing the algae from each sand type because some algae may adhere so strongly that a weak acid treatment may be necessary. The aqueous suspensions of the algae are next made up to a standard volume. Aliquots of known volume can then be placed on a slide and direct microscope counts can be made or a standard volume can be placed on a coverglass, dried and mounted in Microps, Hyrax, Naphthrax etc. Sediment used is dried to a constant weight at 105°C so that all estimates of cell numbers can be related to the area sampled. (Round, 1965, Moss and Round, 1967.) Counting errors calculated by Moss and Round were small—the coefficient of variation ± 7.9 per cent for a series of 10 replicate samples. As with epipelic algae, dead epipsammic cells can be distinguished from live cells. The dead cells either have no contents or the contents are considerably contracted. Only live cells should be counted for use in correlations with chlorophyll estimations, C^{14} uptake, etc. For identification purposes the above method can still be used or the sand grains can be boiled in hydrogen peroxide or sulphuric acid to free the diatoms from the sand grains.

Epiphytic algae

The micro-epiphytic algae growing on the large algae can be removed by sonication as in the removal of the epipsammic flora. However, with this material a much higher percentage of the algae is left on the host plant. Sonication for periods longer than 10 min again tends to cause breakage of the cells. The algae growing on hosts such as *Laminaria*, *Fucus*, etc. could be scraped off using a sharp scalpel or razor, making sure that host epidermal cells are not removed in the process. If the population scraped off is very dense and clumped, these clumps can be broken down by sonication for 10 min. In both methods the algae are placed in known volumes of filtered sea water.

If difficulties arise in measuring the surface area of the host plants, the cell counts can be expressed on a cell/g dry weight of host basis or ash dry wt basis, even though this produces its own problems in that dry weights of different plants are not directly comparable. The simpler the shape of the host plant the easier it is to estimate the surface area.

Cell counts can be made by placing a known volume (0·020—0·030 ml) on a slide under a coverglass and counting all cells in a standard traverse across the coverglass. Alternatively, sub-samples may be pipetted into a sedimentation tube and counted, after the addition of iodine, using an inverted microscope (Lund *et al.*, 1958). It is advisable to dilute the algae to a suitable degree since dense populations cannot be counted accurately. Also, this method is hampered by any detrital material which also sediments.

Estimation of biomass from chlorophyll extracts

Two techniques have been used, spectrophotometry and fluorimetry, but the former has been more popular.

The most commonly employed method for the estimation of pigments is that of Richards with Thompson (1952) by absorption spectrophotometry. It is referred to as the 'trichromatic method', as it involves measurement of absorbency at three different wavelengths for the calculation of chlorophylls *a*, *b* and *c*. Creitz and Richards (1955) and Parsons and Strickland (1963) proposed a few minor changes in the equations used to calculate the amounts of pigments on the basis of re-determined specific absorption coefficients. However, in all these cases these equations depend for their validity on the absence of pheo-pigments in the extracts. According to Strickland and Parsons (1968), pheophytins are generally absent from the open ocean phytoplankton; however, large amounts of these compounds will probably be found when dealing with benthic communities. Therefore, in these latter cases, the method described by Moss (1967a, 1967b) or that described by Lorenzen (1967) should be employed. These methods provide an estimate of the amount of chlorophyll *a* and pheophytin *a* in the extract.

The accuracy of the trichromatic equations is decreased by changes in the absorption spectra that occur on conversion of chlorophylls to pheophytins. These changes at 645 and 630 mμ are fairly great and these are the principal wavelengths used in the calculation of chlorophylls *b* and *c*. Therefore, in the presence of pheophytins of chlorophylls *b* and *c*, the estimations of these chlorophylls by the trichromatic method will be unreliable. However, at 665 mμ (wavelength for chlorophyll *a*) there is no appreciable change in the absorption in the presence of pheophytins *b* and *c*. Secondly, this wavelength is affected only slightly by the presence of different proportions of chlorophyll *b* and *c*. This has been recognised by Odum *et al.* (1958) and Talling and Driver (1963) who in their simplified equations used absorption only at 665 mμ to estimate chlorophyll *a* and pheophytin *a*, where the extract is assumed to contain only these two components. Moss (1967b) gives modified equations for a two component system in which no chemical reaction is occurring at the given wavelength; from these, the amounts of chlorophyll *a* and pheophytin *a* can be calculated.

As Moss (1967b) says, meaningful estimations of chlorophylls *b* and *c* in the presence of their pheophytins will be achieved by either extending the trichromatic method to a hexachromatic one, in which pheophytins, as well as chlorophylls are estimated, or by using separation methods such as that devised by Parsons (1963) for chlorophyll *c*.

It should be pointed out that the amount of organic material associated with a given quantity of plant pigment is very variable. Therefore, when relating cell numbers to chlorophyll *a* estimations, cell volume should also be taken into account.

Until methods are developed which will enable reliable results for chlorophyll *b* and *c* and their pheophytins to be obtained, the method of Moss (1967a and b) for chlorophyll *a* and pheophytin *a* and the method of Parsons (1963) for chlorophyll *c* are recommended. If chlorophyll *c* is to be determined, Millipore filters should be used (Strickland and Parsons, 1968).

A summary of the extraction procedure, etc. is given in Strickland and Parsons (1968) and the restrictions they list apply to benthic algae.

Routine methods for pigment estimations

Epipelic algae—adapted from the method of Eaton and Moss (1966). The algae have to be separated from the sediment for accurate estimations of chlorophyll *a* because large amounts of detrital pigment degradation products occur in many sediments compared with the amount in living epipelic algal populations. The tissue trapping technique can be used to trap the algal population prior to pigment extraction and estimation. Cropping can be achieved by placing large double layers of lens tissue, on the sediment surface in petri dishes prepared as described on p. 179. Tissues are removed the following day and placed on small pieces of Whatman GF/C glass filter paper and left to air dry in the dark for approximately 3 h. They are then placed in ground-glass stoppered bottles, together with a small amount of analytical quantity anhydrous magnesium carbonate, plus a suitable volume of 90 per cent acetone (aqueous, of analytical purity). Because of the risk of small amounts of water being left on paper and tissues, the volume of acetone added should be as large as practical to minimise this error. The addition of magnesium carbonate prevents degradation of the pigments during extraction. The samples are extracted at 3–4°C in complete darkness for approximately 20 h. If large numbers of algae with thick cell walls or mucilage sheaths are present, grinding or homogenising may be necessary.

The acetone plus extracted pigments is then centrifuged at 3000–4000 rev/min to sediment out any magnesium carbonate and other interfering particles. The absorbances at the selected wavelengths are then measured as quickly as possible on the spectrophotometer (Moss, 1967a, b, Lorenzen, 1967, Strickland and Parsons, 1968).

To each centrifuge tube 10 drops of 10 per cent hydrochloric acid is then added, the tubes are shaken and left to stand in the dark for 10 min, before adding a small amount of magnesium carbonate and re-centrifuging. This process converts all the pigments to their degradation products. Each sample is then read again on the spectrophotometer at 430 mμ and 410 mμ (Moss, 1967a and b). (Using Lorenzen's method the samples are read again at 665 mμ after acidification.)

The results for epipelic algae should be expressed as mg chlorophyll/m². The amount of chlorophyll *a* and pheophytin *a* can be calculated using the equations of Moss (1967a) and then converted to m² (see sampling section and section on separation of algae from substratum).

Epipsammic algae. The washed sand grains are extracted with 90 per cent acetone as previously described and chlorophyll *a* and pheophytin *a* measured by the absorption spectrophotometric method of Moss (1967a and b). The coefficient of variation of replicate samples was ±4 per cent for freshwater material (Moss and Round, 1967).

Epiphytic algae. For removal of algae see p. 181. Samples of algae which have been removed either by sonication or scraping are made up to a suitable volume before filtering through Whatman GF/C glass filter paper. A suitable aliquot of 90 per cent acetone is then added. In most cases it is advisable to grind the filters in a homogenizer to ensure complete extraction because many epiphytic algae have thick mucilaginous sheaths. Then follow the procedure described for epipelic algae.

Cryophytic algae. Again, algal standing crop can be estimated using chlorophyll extraction by collecting ice and allowing it to melt, filtering, extracting, etc. (Apollonio, 1965; Bunt *et al.*, 1966).

Macro-algae and angiosperms. These can also be estimated by the chlorophyll technique. However, more macro-techniques would have to be employed, for example, grinding in 90 per cent acetone and sand to extract the pigments. Only sections of the larger plants can be used, and the mucilaginous and rubbery nature of some of these algae may present problems.

Estimation of production

The most direct and in many cases the most satisfactory method of estimating production is by the increase or decrease in the standing crop over a measured interval of time. In this case, production is measured in terms of changes in biomass, which can be expressed in several ways, e.g.:
(a) increase in the area of substratum covered
(b) increase in volume of organisms
(c) increase in wet weight, i.e. fresh weight
(d) increase in dry weight
(e) increase in ash-free dry weight, i.e. loss on ignition.

These methods have been used, in one form or another, for the study of the production of macroscopic marine plants, which undergo a regular growth cycle throughout the seasons. However, these methods are less suitable for measuring the micro-algae of the epipelic, epipsammic, epiphytic or epilithic communities. Here chlorophyll estimations are more useful for standing crop (biomass) estimations while O_2 and C^{14} techniques are more accurate and give instantaneous production rates.

Ecologists studying primary production have generally used the technique first described by Gaarder and Gran (1927) which involves measuring the rate of change of dissolved oxygen in samples enclosed in glass bottles. The titrametric Winkler method is usually used but techniques using oxygen electrodes could be applied. This method provides an approximation to natural production because the bottles can be placed back 'in situ' and, therefore, receive the same illumination and temperature as the surrounding water.

In such experiments the dissolved oxygen concentration is influenced by the respiration not only of the plants but also of the fauna and the large bacterial flora which may develop in water enclosed in bottles. A darkened bottle is normally used to correct for respiration, and thereby obtain a measure of gross production. By the Winkler estimation an oxygen content of 0·05 ml/l and assimilation of 0·02 mg/l can be detected with reasonable accuracy. Therefore, the oxygen technique is quite efficient if the sample is rich enough.

The most recently developed experimental method of estimating primary production involves measuring the uptake of radioactive carbon (C^{14}) by the plants, and there is now a considerable literature reviewing methods and data obtained from the use of this technique (e.g. Steemann Nielsen, 1952;

Ryther and Vaccaro, 1954; Ryther, 1956; Lund and Talling, 1957; Strickland, 1960; Goldman, 1963; Pomeroy, 1963; Strickland and Parsons, 1968). According to Goldman (1963) 'the rate of carbon fixation at the level of primary producers currently provides the best assessment of the interactions of the host with the physical, chemical and biological factors which determine the actual fertility of any environment'. Photosynthetic organisms are more important than chemosynthetic ones; the latter usually playing a minor part in productivity (Kuznetsov, 1956; Steemann Nielsen, 1960).

In this technique the carbon-14 is added to the suspended plant sample in the form of bicarbonate or carbonate; the sample is then exposed to light for a definite number of hours, and the amount of carbon-14 incorporated is determined by measuring the radiation emitted. The uptake of C^{14}-carbonate is assumed to measure the uptake of total carbonate, as a fraction of the whole, and hence the rate of photosynthesis can be evaluated. A dark bottle blank, as in the oxygen technique, is also used. This gives a fractional correction which is roughly independent of the number of cells present, and which generally amounts, in work with phytoplankton, to approx. 1 per cent of the rate of photosynthesis measured under optimum conditions. However, when studying the productivity of benthic communities the total uptake of C^{14} in the dark is greater. Grøntved (1960) found that the carbon-14 uptake in the dark averaged approximately 10·5 per cent of the total uptake of carbon-14 in the light in two-hour experiments using a mixture of sand, epipsammic algae and unfiltered sea water. In the suspensed fraction of the sample the fixation in the dark is relatively great, averaging 13·6 per cent of the total fixation in light by this fraction, whereas in the sand fraction the average percentage is 8·5 per cent. Grøntved also found that the dark fixation varied greatly in the various experiments, and the average figures from different fjords varied rather widely. This is not altogether surprising since the sample material, besides containing autotrophic organisms, contains heterotrophic flagellates, fungi and quantities of bacteria adsorbed to particulate matter. In view of these features, the dark fixation of carbon-14 does not seem to be particularly large.

Routine methods

Epipsammic algae. Grøntved (1960, 1962) in his studies of the productivity of the epipsammic flora of a Danish fjord devised an experimental technique whereby C^{14} was added to a sub-sample of benthic algae in bottles which were then incubated. Since unfiltered sea water was used the fraction of the total assayed C^{14} fixed by the epipsammic producers had to be calculated after allowing for fixation by the other primary producers which were present. Self-absorption of the radiation by the sediment particles was estimated by several methods of radio-assay of filters before and after removal of large inorganic particles. Grøntved expressed the results as potential rate of production because the experiments were not performed *in situ*.

Steele and Baird (1968) and Baird and Wetzel (1968) have also developed techniques for studying the production of the epipsammic flora. As in the method of Moss and Round (1967) the detrital material plus epipelic algae was removed by shaking the sand in filtered water, followed by decanting. This was performed once or twice. The method involves incubating the washed sand grains with $Na_2C^{14}O_3$ *in situ* followed by decanting off most of the water, and filtering into a *Stefi* filter funnel fitted with glass fibre filter paper. The sand is then rinsed with filtered sea water and an excess of sand placed in planchettes (aluminium—23 mm diam, 2 mm depth). After allowing the sand to dry in a carbon dioxide-free desiccator it is mixed and levelled to fill the planchette to the rim. The radiation from the sand sample was counted using a thin end-window G.M. counter (counts were corrected for background radiation and normalised to a reference source). In natural conditions it is highly probable that the sand surface will be mixed to a varying degree depending on depth, whether the site in question is exposed or sheltered, and the state of the sea during the exposure period. Baird and Wetzel (1968) therefore performed experiments where bottles were shaken every 15 minutes during a 4-hour exposure to try and simulate this effect; this resulted in a lower uptake and they concluded that movement of the sand does not enhance primary production. Correction factors were also calculated to allow for the effect of loss by self-absorption and back-scattering of the C^{14} within the sand. Two methods were employed. The first involved using C^{14}-labelled benthic diatom cultures. Filtered aliquots of these alone and also aliquots added to dried sand grains were counted to a minimum of 2,500 counts. The corrected counts for the filtered samples should be proportional to the volumes filtered indicating no self-absorption. Zero thickness activity could then be calculated and assuming that the absorption of the counts from the culture mixed with the sand grains is similar to that of the counts from the attached diatoms then a factor, F, is calculated from the ratio of the two counts; this can be applied to calculate zero-thickness activity (counts)/min/g sand of labelled natural populations. This factor, of course, will be specific for the type of sand, geometry and type of G.M.

counter employed in the determination. The method was repeated using a standard laboratory culture of *Phaeodactylum*, giving results which did not differ appreciably from those for benthic diatoms or from the results obtained using the second method of counting the labelled natural populations in gas phase. In this alternative method the organic carbon of the labelled samples was converted to CO_2 by van Slyke wet oxidation, collected in the ionisation chamber, and radio-analysed in gas phase with a recording electrometer system (Nuclear-Chicago-Model 6000), Wetzel (1964). The factor F obtained was essentially the same as obtained by the previous technique. However, statistical errors in the first method arise from count variation of aliquots of the culture, and the count variation of the sand when mixed with the culture. When combined these gave a standard deviation $\pm$ 1·2 for F and with gas phase counting, the errors associated with the efficiency determination are very small. Further work involving estimating the productivity of an epipsammic flora has been done by Hickman (1969) and Hickman and Round (1970). The epipsammic algae are separated from the epipelic algae + detrital material following the method of Moss and Round (1967). Aliquots of washed sand are then placed in glass bottles and filtered water and the C^{14} source added and exposed to light; dark bottle controls are also set up. After the exposure period, usually 3 h, the algae are removed from the sand grains by sonication (see previous section). A suitable aliquot (25 ml) is then filtered through Millipore HA filters and the radioactivity counted. Other aliquots of sand are dried and weighed so that the results can be converted to a m^2 basis. Corrections for self-absorption are made by reference to a $BaC^{14}O_3$ curve. The weight of material on the filter is too variable to consider adapting the culture method of Baird and Wetzel (1968) for calculating correction factors for self-absorption. In this method there are no large sand grains on the filter, as on shaking the bottles before filtering to suspend the algae in the water the heaviest sand grains sediment out.

The oxygen technique can also be used to study the productivity of epipsammic algae by adding to each bottle an aliquot of washed sand, and filtered water, followed by exposure for a number of hours to light, and then the amount of dissolved oxygen can be estimated titrimetrically by the Winkler method (Hickman, 1969).

Epipelic algae. No-one has yet tried to separate the epipelic population from marine sediments, and then estimate its productivity. Previously, workers have used bell jars placed directly over the plants on the sediment in intertidal zones and then used the oxygen technique or the carbon-14 technique (Pomeroy, 1960).

Filtered water may be placed in the bell jars to eliminate the phytoplankton primary producers. If unfiltered water is used then a correction factor must be applied. On hard bottoms a band of flexible rubber may be put around the bottom of the jar to act as a seal (Odum and Odum, 1955). The changes in dissolved oxygen are usually estimated by the Winkler method; it is possible to obtain a continuous record of the changes in oxygen tension by using a platinum-silver oxide polarographic electrode with a suitable recording potentiometer (Carritt and Kanwisher, 1959; Kanwisher, 1959).

The carbon-14 technique has also been used in a similar manner (Wetzel, 1963, 1964) in a shallow lake in which the littoral zone consisted of small, angular pebbles. There is no reason why this could not be adapted to marine habitats, although in more exposed places there would be problems. Wetzel placed plexiglass chambers on the sediments using a short rotational movement so that the chambers were actually worked into the sediment. These were sited along transects perpendicular to the shoreline. Carbon-14 was injected into the chambers underwater and then the chambers were sealed. A 4-hour incubation period was used. Afterwards, the chambers were removed by working a plate under the open end which allowed the removal of the whole sample, which comprised an undisturbed core of the superficial sedimentary material plus the overlying water. The latter was removed using a large syringe, followed by freezing the upper centimetre of the sediment in a desiccator. The organic material was then oxidised to CO_2 by van Slyke combustion for radio-assay in gas phase, which circumvents the problems involved in self-absorption of the radiation of the carbon-14.

Hickman (1969) has developed a method of studying the productivity of the epipelic algae by separating the algal population from the sediment. The algae are trapped in double layers of lens tissue (Eaton and Moss, 1966). The lens tissue is then placed with filtered water in glass bottles plus a suitable aliquot of carbon-14. The bottles are incubated *in situ* for 3 hours. To remove the algae from the lens tissue the bottles are shaken 20 times very gently, so as not to break up the lens tissue. Cell counts of the algae directly after removal from the sediment by the method of Eaton and Moss (1966) can be compared with the counts from the lens tissues which had been in the bottles for 3 h followed by shaking by inversion, and thus the percentage removed by this technique can be estimated. A suitable aliquot (usually 25 ml) of the incubated sample is filtered through Millipore HA filter membranes, for subsequent counting. Self-absorption can be corrected for by comparison with a $BaC^{14}O_3$ curve. Again the culture method of Baird and Wetzel (1968) cannot be adopted for calculating self-absorption correction factors because the variation in weight of the algae and sediment on the filter is too great. This will be due to differences in the sediment, and in some cases whether or not any undetected animals are present in the sediment which may move through and over the sediment surface thus moving sediment particles on to the lens tissue. This method enables separation of the algal population from the sediment.

The method can also be adapted for use with the oxygen technique, estimating the dissolved oxygen by the Winkler method, although lens tissue of larger area has to be used. In this technique the algae need not, however, be removed from the lens tissue. The value of these techniques lies in the easier manipulation and increased accuracy resulting from removal of the algae from the sedimentary material which itself tends to absorb C^{14} or oxygen.

Epiphytic algae. Two methods can be employed:

(i) Small pieces of the host plus the epiphytic algal population can be placed in bottles together with filtered sea water and the C^{14} source, then incubated either *in situ* or in an illuminated water bath. After incubation the microscopic epiphytic algae can be removed from the host by ultra-sonication or large algae removed by dissection of the host. Encrusting and creeping algae, e.g. *Melobesia*, may require the development of special techniques. As mentioned earlier, sonication only removes a percentage of the algae and some are removed more easily than others; therefore, it will be necessary to use cell count data in conjunction with C^{14} data, counting the number of cells removed by sonication and also those remaining on the host. After sonication the microscopic algae can be filtered and then counted and the radioactivity of a sub-sample determined.

(ii) If the host plant lends itself to scraping, the epiphytic algae can be removed in this way. This will remove a much higher percentage of cells than sonication but in some cases it is difficult to prevent contamination from pieces of the host material which themselves may absorb some C^{14}. The scraped-off cells can then be incubated with filtered sea water and the C^{14} source. Again an aliquot can be filtered through a membrane filter and counted.

Each host plant will present its own problems, and these methods will have to be modified accordingly. Many marine algae contain large amounts of mucilage and this will present problems owing to possible uptake of C^{14} by the mucilage and also by the bacterial and fungal populations which will probably be associated with the mucilage.

Macrophytes. Algae and angiosperms. As mentioned on p. 185 the most direct, and in many cases the most satisfactory method of estimating the production of the larger marine algae is by the increase or decrease in the standing crop (measured as fresh or dry weight) over a measured interval of time. Here production is measured in terms of biomass change. The ways of expressing this are given on p. 196.

The fresh weight may be defined as the weight of the plant immediately after being collected, and after superficial water has been shaken off (Baardseth and Haug, 1953). However, intertidal algae may lose water by evaporation at low tide, therefore these should be placed in sea water until the lost water is replaced and the weight is constant. The errors involved when determining fresh weight are:

(i) loss of water during exposure at low tide;

(ii) water adhering to the surface of the algae;

(iii) loss of water during transport and handling of the material before weighing.

Dry weight determinations should be carried out by air-drying the algae, and then, depending on the size of the algae or sample collected, all or a known proportion of the air-dried material is ground to a powder and dried at 100–150°C for 16 hours or to a constant weight (Baardseth and Haug, 1953). From the weight of the samples, the total dry weight can be calculated. The errors of dry weight determination can be attributed to:
(i) incomplete removal of water;
(ii) loss of material during the drying process—this can be avoided by careful handling;
(iii) respiration or other destructive processes during the time the material is kept covered before weighing. This is probably insignificant in the majority of cases.

The biomass data can then be related to the area of substratum and to a time interval, providing the samples were quantitatively taken on an area basis in the first place, i.e. taken from within quadrats of known dimensions.

In some members of the Laminariales in which the blade grows from the base the rate of growth can be estimated by punching holes in the blade

(Parke, 1948). Allowance has to be made for concurrent growth of the stipe which is lengthened by primary growth and thickened by secondary growth (Kain, 1963).

In the detailed study of Knight and Parke (1950) on *Fucus vesiculosus* and *F.serratus*, areas of the shore varying in extent from 1 m² to broad strips 16 m wide running through the entire fucoid zone were cleared of algae and animals. The sizes of the plants in the new recolonising populations were then measured over a time period. Several difficulties in this approach are apparent. Eggs from plants in the vicinity of the experimental area are shed continuously over a long period, so that the cleared areas become colonised by plants of differing ages. In this study the longest plants were measured at intervals on the assumption that the longest would be the oldest in such a mixed population. However, there is great variation in the vigour of the germlings, competition between the germlings, and variation due to where the germlings grow, i.e. on flat exposed surfaces or in more sheltered rock crevices. There was also a high mortality rate or de-population rate.

A second method was also used which involved marking certain plants *in situ*. Numbered chicken or hen rings were attached to the plants. Very small plants were marked by small celluloid tablets with a split into which the frond could be inserted. Very large numbers of plants had to be tagged because of the high de-population rate. The tagging of large plants was of little use because of the large amount of frond breakage.

In *Fucus*, linear growth alone is not a full measure of growth since dichotomy of the fronds and lateral frond development occurs simultaneously with linear extension. An attempt was made to estimate this development by recording the degree of 'bushiness' by counting the number of frond apices at the same time as recording the length. Here again there was great individual variation.

South and Burrows (1967) used measurements of overall and submeristem length together with maximum diameter to assess the growth of *Chorda filum*, i.e. the vegetative growth of the plant throughout the year. Again the results showed that linear increase is a poor guide to the actual amount of tissue produced. However, from such studies growth rates and cycles can be recorded and followed over a time period as long as the limitations of such methods are realised. Norton and Burrows (1969) applied similar methods to *Saccorhiza polyschides*.

It is not usually possible when using the carbon-14 and oxygen techniques to enclose the plants within containers pressed into the substrate. Therefore, the algae have to be removed from the rock and placed in incubation chambers. However, manipulation of these larger marine algae from the surface is difficult and in deeper water impossible, since sampling from the surface damages the plants and further the samples cannot be taken from a known area. Therefore, the whole operation of sampling and placing the plants in the incubation chambers should take place at the site and underwater. The plants should be placed in the incubation chambers at their growing site since many of these plants are adapted to low light intensities, and only brief exposures to the more intense surface light could seriously alter subsequent metabolic rates and could cause irreversible damage. The water used for the incubations should be taken from the same location as the plants in order to keep conditions as close as possible to natural. Filtered sea water should be used where possible or a correction factor applied if a large phytoplankton population is present. A further point not always recognised is that on all the larger algae there will be an epiphytic algal population; therefore this has either to be removed (p. 190) which in many cases would be impossible without seriously damaging the host, or its productivity estimated separately and this subtracted from the result obtained by incubating the host plus the epiphytic population.

As mentioned in an earlier section, changes in dissolved oxygen in light and dark bottles have been extensively used to determine the photosynthesis of both marine and freshwater phytoplankton, but has rarely been used for submerged marine macrophytes under field conditions.

Some marine benthic algae, particularly those in deeper water, require fairly lengthy incubation periods before there is a significant change in oxygen concentration. This lengthy incubation period, i.e. greater than 6 hours, will be accompanied by increases in bacterial populations on the surfaces of the incubation containers coupled with depletion of critical nutrients and stagnation. Therefore, the incubation containers should be sufficiently large to hold a large volume of water relative to the plant volume to prevent stagnation.

An important limitation and source of error in the application of the oxygen technique to macrophytes arises from internal storage and utilisation of oxygen produced by photosynthesis. The latter will probably occur in deep benthic plants where rate of oxygen produced and rate of oxygen consumed are very nearly equal (compensation point). Also the use of stored oxygen for respiration during periods of darkness can occur without affecting the concentration of dissolved oxygen of the incubation water under natural conditions. In all cases where oxygen techniques are employed, careful consideration must be given to possible sources of error and the results must be interpreted extremely carefully. Johnston and Cook (1968) and Johnston (1969) used the oxygen technique to study the primary productivity of *Caulerpa prolifera* in waters around the Canary Islands. Light and dark incubation bottles were used while the oxygen concentration changes were measured with a polyethylene-lead-silver electrode system.

C^{14} techniques developed for use with phytoplankton can be adapted for these macrophytic benthic associations. However, because of the very weak radiation, self-absorption by the plant tissues occurs and major changes in counting techniques are required. At the end of the incubation period with C^{14} the plants can be placed in polyethylene bags and quick-frozen between blocks of solid carbon dioxide for transportation to the laboratory. If samples are being taken for biomass estimations at the same time, these should be taken at similar transect intervals to those of the productivity estimations. The transects for both should be perpendicular to the shore in as many areas, and including as many different types of associations as possible.

Self-absorption problems of C^{14} radiation can be circumvented by the van Slyke wet oxidation technique for the conversion of organic carbon to carbon dioxide followed by radio-assay in gas phase. The production rates can then be calculated in a proportional manner as in the techniques for phytoplankton. Before oxidation the plants should be subjected to fumes of concentrated hydrochloric acid for the removal of extra-cellular carbon-14 precipitated as carbonates.

Johnston and Cook (1968) also used the C^{14} technique. They incubated fronds of *Caulerpa prolifera* with carbon-14, washed the fronds and placed them in 80 per cent ethanol. Radioactivity was measured in a Packard Tricarb Scintillation Counter.

Photographic techniques can be used to estimate the production and loss of plant material of macro-algae when the plants can be tagged in the field or when permanent quadrats can be placed over areas which can then be photographed at intervals throughout the year. Seasonal increments and losses can then be determined. Techniques of this kind are applicable to deeper waters where there is less depopulation than in tidal regions and where in deep waters the diver is able to spend only relatively short periods before facing serious physiological dangers. Johnston *et al.* (1969) have developed a quantitative photographic technique that requires no formal knowledge of photo-

grammetry, no specialised cameras and no plotting machines to plot distribution and cover of particular plants. The underwater procedure is fast and
flexible to allow the technique to be used in deep waters and under difficult
diving conditions.

Laboratory and ship-board measurements of primary production—
Illuminated constant-temperature incubators
The incubators enable measurements of activity to be made other than by
exposure in the natural body of water. The potential advantages when working aboard a ship include the saving of ship time after samples have been
taken, greater ease of manipulating samples under laboratory conditions,
and standardisation and control of conditions of light and temperature.
However, there are disadvantages, which include the impossibility of being
able to reproduce fully the conditions of light in the natural habitat, particularly with respect to spectral modification, angular distribution with depth
etc.; and also effects detrimental or otherwise of high light intensities present
near the water surface are not taken into account or alternatively they are
increased unless precautions are taken.

There are two types of incubators, those using ambient light (natural sunlight), or constant light (fluorescent, incandescent light), and each type can
be used in 3 ways: (i) without light filters, (ii) with spectrally neutral light
filters, and (iii) with spectrally selective light filters. For both types a large
temperature-controlled water bath is required. Examples of suitable baths
for which sunlight has been used as the light source are described by Sanders
et al. (1962). The incubator should be exposed to ambient solar radiation,
and located so as to minimise possible shading. It may be necessary (Jitts,
1963) to use a selective filter or glass plate to remove ultra-violet radiation
and possibly attempt some further simulation of the spectral modification of
underwater light. Examples of incubators involving the use of artificial light
source are described by Steemann Nielsen and Jensen (1957), Doty and Oguri
(1958, 1959), Talling (1960) and McAllister *et al.* (1964).

In measuring the light to which the samples are exposed determinations of
irradiance (energy flux: e.g. in calories/cm^2/min, langleys/min or kerg/cm^2
sec) are greatly preferred to determinations of illuminance (e.g. lux, foot-
candles) with a photometer, as the latter will possess a selective spectral
response unrelated to the action spectrum of photosynthesis. Such methods,
although developed for use with phytoplankton, can be adapted for work
involving the benthic communities.

Expression of productivity data

In productivity studies it is often difficult to compare the primary production of different communities and habitats because of the nature of the habitats, and the different methods employed by different workers. Therefore, methods will have to be developed which will allow direct comparisons of results.

It is also important to have a standardised terminology when discussing productivity results to avoid misinterpretation when comparing results. Theoretical discussions of various definitions are given in Thienemann (1931), Lindeman (1942), Ivlev (1945), MacFadyen (1948), Yapp (1958), Odum (1959) and Westlake (1963). Westlake (1965b) recommends definitions of biomass, primary production, primary productivity, gross and net productivity, standing crop, crop and yield, which are in basic agreement with the theoretical definitions but modified for common usage. The question of terminology has been discussed at several IBP meetings and some general agreement on symbols, terms and definitions has been reached (*IBP News*, No. 10, 1968). This is further referred to by Ricker (1968, pp. 2–3) and is discussed in detail in relation to secondary production on pp. 198–204 of the present handbook.

The units used to express results should give an indication of either the actual values determined or the validity of the results. For example, productivity of epipelic and epipsammic algae should be expressed as mg C fixed or O_2 evolved/hour/m^2 or day/m^2. However, with epiphytic algae where the surface area of the host plant cannot be estimated the results will be best put on a host-weight basis. The weight of host per unit area can be estimated and from this the epiphyte production can be expressed on an area basis. However, estimations from epiphytes growing on one host will not be comparable with those on another host. Those hosts whose surface area can be estimated with reasonable precision should have epiphytic productivity expressed as a rate per unit area of host.

The units for biomass, defined as weight per unit area should be in g/m^2 or kg/m^2 (Westlake, 1965b). Such estimates are not normally made on microscopic populations; instead the weight of pigment is estimated (see p. 182).

To avoid misunderstandings the time units for productivity should be related to the actual period considered. For example, Doty and Oguri (1957) showed that with phytoplankton there exists a daily rhythm of photosynthesis. There is a gradual drop after midday and increase from sunrise to midday. Therefore, time interval and time of day of *in situ* incubations should be stated and also investigations to determine whether or not a diurnal rhythm exists should be carried out.

12

Energy Flow Measurements

D. J. Crisp

Introduction

Investigations of the benthos must initially be concerned with the species and communities present in various types of deposits, their feeding mechanisms, reproductive habits and rates of growth. Such an approach, though qualitative, is an essential preliminary to the investigation of a new area and will lead to the application of more quantitative methods by which estimates of the abundance of commoner organisms and ultimately of the total amount of living matter or biomass can be made. Maps have been prepared showing the variation in the total quantity of living organisms (biomass) over large areas of sea bed in the form of contours of equal biomass per unit area of bottom (isobenths). A number of examples of such surveys are given in Zenkevich (1963).

Measurement of biomass alone, important though it may be in comparing the immediately available standing crop from place to place, is quite inadequate for the purpose of predicting the predation rate or the fishery yield that a benthic community does, or could, sustain over a long period. For these purposes the rates of production of organic matter by the various members of the benthic community and their trophic dependence on one another or on sources outside the benthos must be known. The distinction between rate of production (or productivity) of organic matter by an organism or a community and the standing crop, consisting of the organism itself or the community, is fundamental. The reader is warned against some confusing uses of the term 'productivity', especially in the early literature. Zenkevich (1930) for instance defines 'isobenths' as 'contours of equal bottom productivity', but means in fact contours of equal standing crop.

The most comprehensive form that investigations of production can take is the measurement of the flow of organic matter and energy through each component of the ecosystem. The interdependence of the various parts of the marine ecosystem is made clear by dividing the flow sheet between trophic levels starting with the primary producers which utilise solar energy and fix inorganic nutrients (first trophic level), passing through the herbivores (second trophic level), the carnivores (third trophic level) and leading ultimately to the decomposers. The principles of energy flow are well described in Odum (1959) and Phillipson (1966).

The relation between standing crop and yield, whether to the next trophic level or to man, can be considered at each level for the complete ecosystem (e.g. Teal, 1962) or more conveniently the problem can be broken down into individual projects in which each species playing a significant part in the energy exchange at a given trophic level is studied separately (e.g. Kuenzler, 1961). The relationship between standing crop and yield for species of economic value has become a most fruitful area of study wherever the rates of predation or harvesting are important, and has led to notable advances in the theory of optimal fishing rates (Beverton and Holt, 1957; Ricker, 1958).

Less effort has been put into studies of benthic production but the same basic concepts apply and the same advantages can be reaped. For the organism or the ecosystem, food is measurable in terms of energy; hence computations of energy flow can be employed to assess actual and potential yield of exploitable benthic species, to predict means of increasing productivity, and to estimate the contributions made by benthic communities to predatory species occupying other habitats.

The zoobenthos functions mainly at the second and third trophic levels which are among the more easily measurable components of an ecosystem. Measurement of primary production of phytobenthos is dealt with separately in Chapter 11.

Terminology

It is often difficult to compare the results of energy flow studies by different authors because of the differences in the use of terms defining the various purposes for which energy is used or conserved by the organism and because of differences in the units by which the energy or biomass is measured. Although it would be inappropriate to recommend a rigid terminology it is essential that the meanings of terms used in this handbook should be quite clear. Since the concepts of quantitative ecology are universal, the terms and symbols recommended generally by IBP can be used for benthos studies.

It is useful to reserve the term 'productivity' for *potential* rate under ideal or stated conditions, and to use the term 'production' for the actual rate of incorporation of organic matter or energy (Davis, 1963). In reporting rates of production the trophic level should be stated and also whether production refers to the whole ecosystem, to a group of species, or to a single species.

Biomass (B)

Biomass is defined as the amount of living substance constituting the organisms which are being studied. Alternative terms found in the literature are 'standing crop' or 'standing stock'.

Biomass can be expressed in units of volume, mass or energy and may refer to the whole or to part of the organism. Biomass is normally determined in relation to a particular unit used to measure the environment, usually its area but sometimes its volume. If, for example, the biomass is being related to the depth below the surface of a sediment, the amount of living matter must be expressed per unit volume of sediment at the stated depth. Usually the whole biomass is summed throughout the depth of the deposit and is then expressed as the biomass per unit area. This approach is particularly applicable where most, or all, of the living matter lies near the surface of the sediment.

The definition of biomass in terms of living substance raises serious difficulties because of the many ways in which the living tissue can be measured. The units in which biomass can be expressed may be divided into:

1, crude units of biomass;
2, units measuring the mass of living tissue only; and
3, units measuring the energy content of the living tissue.

1. Crude units. Biomass of aquatic organisms is most simply measured by weighing the organisms whole after mopping off the external water and emptying the water from cavities external to the animal (e.g. mantle cavity of molluscs). On board ship this may be the only available method short of preservation, which has its disadvantages (see below, p. 235). Wet weight can always be converted at a later stage into a more fundamental or refined measure of living matter by conducting a suitable calibration measurement in the laboratory (p. 234). Biomass may also be measured as the live volume of the animal, measured directly by displacement, and can similarly be converted into more refined units. If any part of the animal is excluded from crude measurement of biomass (e.g. the shells of hermit crabs and molluscs, tubes of polychaetes, etc.) this should be made clear.

2. Units of mass of living tissue only. It is usual when expressing biomass in a more refined manner to exclude those parts of the animal that are non-living. Such components as water and salt, the calcareous matter of the integument or skeleton, the whole of the protective houses not connected with the body (e.g. shells of hermit crabs, tubes of polychaetes and anemones) and heavy inorganic sediments present in the guts of such animals as the echinoids and polychaetes are clearly not part of the living organism. Some biologists (e.g. Thorson, 1957b) recommend excluding also the organic epidermal structures such as the heavy shells of crabs and lobsters. It is clear that there is no sharp demarcation between living and non-living matter in the constitution of the animal nor is there always available a simple technique for removing the non-living parts. Therefore, every worker must draw the line as seems appropriate for the particular animals being studied and for the purpose of the problem in hand. The one imperative is that those parts of the animal that are excluded from its biomass should be clearly stated so that valid comparisons can be made between various investigations.

When non-living parts have been removed, the water evaporated off by drying and the ash weight of inorganic matter measured and allowed for, the remaining mass represents the dry ash-free organic matter which is regarded by many workers as a good measure of the living substance. It can be expressed in units of biomass (dry ash-free weight) in kilograms, grams or milligrammes as appropriate.

An alternative to expressing biomass in terms of ash-free dry weight is to make the assumption that the nitrogen content is proportional to the quantity of living matter and to analyse the tissues chemically for nitrogen. Since the results of a nitrogen analysis vary slightly with the method used, the method should be stated and preferably included in the unit, e.g. biomass (mg Kjeldahl nitrogen). (See p. 265.)

3. Units of energy of living tissue. Measurement of biomass in terms of the energy released from the tissues when they are fully oxidised to water and carbon dioxide overcomes the philosophical problem of defining what are the 'living' and 'non-living' parts of the animal. In general, such non-living components as water and mineral matter do not yield any energy on combustion. Furthermore, energy units have precisely the same meaning for all organisms. Since energy is a conservative principle, the energy changes between parts of the ecosystem are exactly accountable by the first law of thermodynamics. A convenient and widely used unit of biomass in terms of energy is the kilogramme calorie (kcal) and the unit of biomass per unit area is conveniently expressed as kcal/m². The SNU (Standard Nutritional Unit) employed by Stamp (1958) and others is equal to 10^6 kcal and may be more suitably used for large areas. (It is unfortunate that the internationally accepted system of units (SI) recommends that the calorie be replaced by the Joule. Almost all existing thermochemical data are quoted in terms of calories and this unit is therefore likely to continue in use throughout the period of IBP.)

When biomass is to be measured in energy units it is usually necessary to measure the caloric content, or heat of combustion per g dry weight, of the biological material either directly by burning it in a bomb calorimeter or indirectly by determining its approximate chemical composition as protein, carbohydrate, and lipid and applying known average values of caloric content for each component. Details of methods are given on pages 267–275. When the average caloric content of the organic matter is known, the biomass expressed as dry ash-free weight can be converted quite simply into biomass expressed in energy units.

Energy flow (dB/dt). Energy flow refers to rates of change of biomass. It is divisible into a number of separate processes which together constitute the whole passage of matter or energy into and out of the organism, population, or ecosystem under investigation. The appropriate IBP terms and symbols for the components of energy flow for heterotrophic organisms are as follows:

Consumption (C) Total intake of food or energy.

Egesta (F) That part of the consumption that is not absorbed but is voided as faeces.

Absorption (Ab) That part of the consumed energy that is not rejected as faeces.

Excreta (U) That part of the consumption that is absorbed and later passed out of the body as secreted material, usually in an unwanted form as, for example, in the urine. Many organisms produce a number of other exudates such as milk, mucus, shed cuticle, nematocysts etc. which are released from the organism under various circumstances. All such exudates, with the exception of gonoproducts, will be regarded as parts of the 'excreta' in this work. The combined energies $F+U$ are sometimes referred to as *rejecta*.

Assimilation (A) That part of the consumption that is utilised for physiological purposes, namely, for production (including gonoproducts) and respiration, but excluding *rejecta*.

Production (P) That part of the assimilated food or energy that is retained and incorporated in the biomass of the organism but excluding the reproductive bodies released from the organism. This may also be regarded simply as 'growth'.

Respiration (R) That part of the assimilated energy that is converted into heat either directly or through mechanical work performed by the organism.

Gonad output (G) That part of the absorbed energy that is released as reproductive bodies. Because of its great importance in survival and recruitment this part of the energy flow is separated from excreta (U) and production (P) though some authors might regard it as being a contribution towards either of these elements of energy flow.

Yield (Y) This term is used in a narrow and varied sense as that part of the production or excreta utilised by man or by other predators. It may refer to only part of the organism (e.g. crop yields, milk yield) or it may refer to a fraction of the individuals in a population which are consumed by a predator or harvested by man (e.g. yield of fish of a particular species).

Hence, assuming conservation of energy we may write the following equations:

Consumption, $C = P + R + G + U + F$ (1)
Absorption, $Ab = C - F = P + R + G + U$ (2)
Assimilation, $A = P + R + G$ (3)

It should be noted that if biomass is expressed in energy units it must be conserved and the above relations hold true. On the other hand, if biomass is expressed in units of mass, the loss of weight during respiration and excretion (e.g. as water, carbon dioxide and ammonia) is usually not taken into account and the above equations, since they involve R and U, are not applicable.

All the above components are measured in units of energy flow, dB/dt, where B is the biomass. But since changes in biomass, like biomass itself, must be referred to a defined part of the ecosystem, the energy flow will usually need to be defined either (1) as the change in biomass of a given area of the system, as in the case of a community living in a defined habitat or a population occupying a stated area, or (2) as the change in biomass as a fraction of the existing amount of standing crop present.

In definitions of the type (1) the energy flow will be expressed as energy per unit of time, per unit of area. For example, a population of *Nephthys incisa* occupying 1 square metre of bottom was found by Sanders to produce 9·34 g dry weight of biomass per year (Sanders, 1956). The units here are g m^{-2} year^{-1}.

In definitions of type (2) the production would have to be measured per unit biomass standing crop. Taking the same example, Sanders found that the standing crop amounted on average to 4·32 g m^{-2}. The result would then be expressed as a rate of change of biomass of 9·34 g m^{-2} year^{-1} in respect of a biomass of 4·32 g m^{-2}. The units of biomass can then be cancelled and the result expressed more simply as 9·34 g m^{-2} year$^{-1} \div 4·32$ g m$^{-2} = 2·16$ year^{-1}. It will be seen that since the rate of increase in biomass is measured in terms of biomass, the dimensions of energy flow are simply reciprocal time. It is, in fact, desirable to express the rate of change of biomass and the amount of standing crop biomass in the same units wherever possible, so that energy flow can be expressed in a form which does not involve the units in which biomass itself is measured.

The most widely used unit of time for energy flow studies is the year. It is convenient because (a) the organisms usually return to the same nutritional and reproductive state after a year and (b) the population structure may sometimes return to a similar form and a similar level after a year has elapsed. These two factors tend to minimise changes in the biomass between its initial and final condition and thereby facilitate the calculations.

It is worth pointing out that all the components of energy flow as defined in Eq. (1), (2) and (3) must be regarded as thermodynamically equivalent forms of energy; all of them, including the term for energy spent through respiration and activity (R), refer strictly to the heat content of the system measured in relation to the fully oxidised form of the organic material (carbon dioxide, water) as the assumed zero energy state. There is no substance whatever in the claim that the division into components of production and respiration afford a basis for distinguishing between free energy and entropy changes in the living system as stated in Phillipson (1966). Slobodkin (1962) had correctly pointed out that the concept of entropy and free energy change is not yet applicable to energy flow studies.

To use heats of combustion from bomb calorimetry as a measure of the energy content of organic matter does, however, suffer from one minor source of ambiguity. Unlike the products of combustion of compounds of carbon and hydrogen, those of nitrogen, phosphorus and sulphur are imperfectly known and cannot therefore be exactly defined as they should be. Fortunately, the error attributable to the formation of different oxidation products in the measurement of the caloric content of biological materials containing these minor constituents is likely to be much smaller than the other errors encountered in energy flow studies.

Coefficient of assimilation efficiency

The ratio of the food absorbed into the organism to the total amount of food ingested is defined as the 'efficiency of assimilation'. It is obvious that the IBP definition of 'assimilation' as 'physiologically useful energy' is not strictly consistent with the normal use of the term 'Assimilation efficiency'; the definitions on pp. 201–202 would logically lead one to replace the term 'Efficiency of Assimilation' by 'Efficiency of Absorption' which is what is normally implied.

$$\text{Coefficient of efficiency of Assimilation (Absorption)} = \frac{Ab}{C} = \frac{C-F}{C} \quad (4)$$

It is obtained by measuring the amount of food ingested and faeces egested over an interval of time sufficiently long to be representative of the steady state. It can be defined as a ratio either of dry ash-free weights, or better, as a ratio of energies. These ratios will differ, since the caloric content of food and faeces will not usually be the same. If λ_C is the caloric content and w_C the average weight of the food ingested in unit time and λ_F, w_F, corresponding values for the faeces,

Assimilation efficiency (by wt.) $= (w_C - w_F)/w_C$

Assimilation efficiency (by energy) $= (\lambda_C w_C - \lambda_F w_F)/\lambda_C w_C$

The basis of measurement of the efficiency of assimilation (absorption) whether by weight or by energy must therefore be stated.

When assimilation efficiency by weight is measured it is essential that ash-free values should be used and therefore the ash content of both food and faeces must be measured. If ash is not taken into account, an ash intake at an average rate w_a will lower the apparent value of assimilation efficiency (by weight) from $(w_C - w_F)/w_C$ to $(w_C - w_F)/w_C + w_a)$.

On the other hand if assimilation efficiency is measured in energy units by direct weighing and calorimetry of food and faeces, it is not essential to take ash into account, provided that it is sufficiently small in amount and of such a constitution as to be calorimetrically negligible (see p. 200). The presence of ash can be neglected because the energy measured with the ash present (viz. $\lambda'_C w'_C$, $\lambda'_F w'_F$) can be shown to be the same as that measured in terms of ash-free energy ($\lambda_C w_C$, $\lambda_F w_F$) since

$\lambda'_C(w_C + w_a) = \lambda_C w_C$ (no energy from combustion of ash w_a)

$w_C + w_a = w'_C$ (increase in dry weight of food due to ash, w_a)

Therefore, $\lambda'_C w'_C = \lambda_C w_C$; and similarly, $\lambda'_F w'_F = \lambda_F w_F$.

Coefficient of growth efficiency

Growth efficiency may be defined as the total energy of production of body tissue and gonads ΔB, ($= P + G$), as a fraction of the energy of food ingested (C).

$$\text{Coefficient of growth efficiency} = \frac{\Delta B}{C} = \frac{P + G}{C} \tag{5}$$

Growth efficiency ratios should be based on energy content rather than wet or dry weight because the storage of smaller quantities of high energy reserve, such as fat, is not necessarily a less efficient mechanism than the storage of larger quantities of low energy reserve, such as carbohydrate. If the caloric content of the tissues is not known and therefore ΔB and C can be expressed only as wet or dry weight, the term 'conversion rate' is recommended.

The efficiency of growth is high in juveniles but usually declines rapidly with age (see Jørgensen, 1962; Carefoot, 1967b). Even in rapidly growing embryos utilising yolk, the growth efficiency rarely exceeds 75 per cent. Values in excess of 70 per cent should therefore be viewed with some suspicion.

Growth efficiency varies also with the rate of food consumption because the fraction available for increase in biomass ($P + G$) will decrease as the ration decreases, priority being given by the organism to activities connected with body maintenance and food searching (R). Thus, for example, Gerking (1955) found that the growth efficiency of the Bluegill, measured in terms of nitrogen content, increased with the ration up to a maximum of 33 per cent. Most of the information dealing with the relationship of growth efficiency to food ration in aquatic animals refers to experiments with fish but it is desirable that these concepts should be applied more widely to nutritional studies of benthic and other organisms.

The rate of food consumption which allows maintenance activities only to be performed but no increase in biomass ($P + G = 0$) is termed the 'Maintenance ration', C_m.

When the maintenance ration is known, the net or partial growth efficiency can be defined as the rate of increase in biomass for a given increase in ration above the maintenance level.

$$\text{Partial growth efficiency} = \frac{\Delta B}{C - C_m} = \frac{P + G}{C - C_m} \tag{6}$$

Coefficient of ecological efficiency

The term 'ecological efficiency' is employed as a measure of the efficiency of energy transfer from one trophic level to the next. The simplest definition is the fraction of the energy consumed at a given trophic level (n) that is exploited by a predator at the next trophic level ($n+1$). Referring to the yield to predator as Y_n,

$$\text{Ecological efficiency} = \frac{Y_n}{C_n} = \frac{C_{n+1}}{C_n} \tag{7}$$

A different definition is given by Ivlev for the 'Dynamic ecotrophic coefficient', ε. The denominator is replaced by the production term for the first trophic level:

$$\varepsilon_{n+1} = \frac{Y_n}{P_n} = \frac{C_{n+1}}{P_n} \tag{8}$$

A fuller discussion of these and related coefficients is given in Ricker (1968).

Energy budget

The equation of the total energy budget is

$$C = P + R + G + U + F$$

and it applies to any system where all energy sources are included in the left-hand side and all energy sinks to the right-hand side. The energy budget can be applied to an individual animal and, with increasing difficulty and complexity, to a population of a single species operating at a given trophic level, or to all the organisms constituting a multi-habitat ecosystem.

Not infrequently a single species population partakes of energy exchanges at more than one trophic level—for example a filter feeding organism may consume primary producers (algae) or herbivores (microcrustacea). This complication is immaterial provided that the above equation is rigorously applied. First, the limits of the system which is being investigated must be clearly defined; for example, a single species population of stated biomass, or one occupying a stated area. Secondly, all the items of the energy budget must be entered into the equation once and once only. In particular the novice should be wary when measuring the production term P, to avoid the fallacy of counting increase in biomass twice over, first as growth of tissues and later as mortality or yield to predator. To avoid such errors the experimenter should always attempt to write an equation of the above form, to see that it includes all possible exchanges of energy in the system.

Since the energy budget must balance, should any one of the terms be particularly hard to measure, it may be omitted and found by difference. However, it is much better, whenever possible, to estimate all the terms and use the equation as a check on the accuracy of the flow sheet. Most of the energy budgets that have been prepared for large scale ecosystems, even when they could be checked in this way, have not balanced at all closely. Nevertheless even the crude approximations hitherto obtained are preferable to no estimates at all.

Measurement of production

For some practical purposes the production term in the energy budget, P, is the only one that is essential. It is also frequently the most important quantity to be measured in fundamental studies of ecosystems and productivity.

There are two different approaches in the measurement of the total secondary production by a population of animals, which must be clearly distinguished.

The first method is to add all the growth increments of all the members of the population as they occur during the period under consideration, say one year ($t=1$). If we write G_i as the mean instantaneous relative growth rate of an individual of weight (or biomass) w_i, then the total production is given by the equation

$$P = \sum_{t=0}^{t=1} \sum_{0}^{N} G_i \, w_i \, \Delta t \qquad (9)$$

where

$$G_i \, \Delta t = \frac{1}{w_i} \left(\frac{dw_i}{dt} \right) \Delta t$$

is the relative growth increment of individual i during the interval Δt, and w_i

is the weight of this individual at this time. The sign $\overset{N}{\underset{0}{\Sigma}}$ implies the summation of $G_i\,w_i$ for all surviving individuals during the time interval Δt, which is assumed to be sufficiently short for G_i and w_i not to change appreciably.

The sign $\overset{t=1}{\underset{t=0}{\Sigma}}$ implies the summation of the population production increments over the whole set of time intervals Δt from the start of the survey ($t=0$) until one year later ($t=1$).

The second approach is to ignore growth processes and instead to consider the fate of the biomass that has been produced during the period of the survey. The organic matter or energy that is produced will either remain as living matter at the end of the survey, or have died, or have been predated. If B_0 were the standing crop biomass at the start and B_1 the standing crop biomass after one year then clearly

$$P=(B_1 - B_0)+M=\Delta B+M$$

where M is the mortality due to all causes, including any yield Y.

If we write the instantaneous mortality rate from all causes for an individual i of weight w_i, as Z_i, then the expectation of death over the interval Δt will be $Z_i\,\Delta t$, and the expected loss of biomass through mortality $Z_i\,w_i\,\Delta t$. The corresponding summation for all mortality losses during one year will then be given by an expression similar to that for production.

$$M= \overset{t=1}{\underset{t=0}{\Sigma}}\ \overset{N}{\underset{0}{\Sigma}}\ Z_i\,w_i\,\Delta t$$

$$\therefore\ \ P=\Delta B+ \overset{t=1}{\underset{t=0}{\Sigma}}\ \overset{N}{\underset{0}{\Sigma}}\ Z_i\,w_i\,\Delta t \tag{10}$$

In applying either of the expressions (9) or (10) it is necessary to have both growth and mortality data as functions of the weight of the individual. In equation (9), the growth rates must be known and the number of individuals surviving must be known at each time interval. In equation (10), the mortality rates must be known and the weight of each individual at each time interval. The information necessary is illustrated in Fig. 12.1. In this diagram, time in years is plotted on the abscissa and the average weight of all remaining individuals N from a single recruitment, $\bar{w}$, $(=\sum\limits_0^N w_i/N)$, is plotted on the ordinate.

It is assumed here that all individuals begin to grow at $t=0$ and that their weight is then virtually zero. The curve can be taken to represent the mean growth rate of a single age class of small larvae of negligible weight recruited at time $t=0$. Also plotted is the survivorship of recruits, starting at N_0 and dropping steadily on account of mortality from all possible causes including yield, predation and natural mortality. We may now apply equation (9) to obtain the growth increment over a small interval of time Δt during the first year of life of the recruitment. The summation of the weight increment for each individual i, $\sum\limits_0^N G_i w_i$, has now been simplified by having values for the average weight, $\bar{w}$, since the mean growth increment for all individuals is the slope of the growth curve $(d\bar{w}/dt)$ multiplied by the time interval Δt. Hence the total increment for the population is $N(d\bar{w}/dt)\Delta t = N\Delta\bar{w}$, where N is the number of survivors at time t, and $\Delta\bar{w}$ is the growth increment as shown in Fig. 12.1. The total production by all individuals during their first year of life is therefore obtained by the summation for one year.

$$P_1 = \sum_{t=0}^{t=1} N\,\Delta\bar{w} \tag{11a}$$

This summation gives a valid measure of production over any period from t_1 to t_2, the more general form of equation 11a being:

$$P_{(t_1-t_2)} = \sum_{t=t_1}^{t=t_2} N\,\Delta\bar{w} \tag{11b}$$

If $t_1 = 0$ and $t_2 = \infty$ the production will be estimated for the whole life of all survivors of the initial recruitment

$$P_\infty = \sum_{t=0}^{t=\infty} N\,\Delta\bar{w} \tag{11c}$$

Employing instead the second approach and applying equation (10) in place of (9), the instantaneous relative mortality rate Z_i is given by the expression

$$Z_i = \frac{1}{N}\frac{dN}{dt}$$

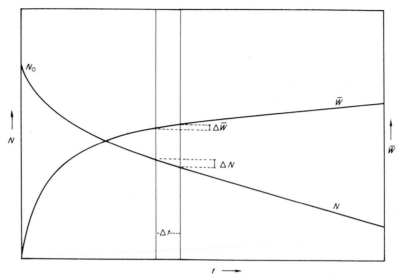

Figure 12.1. Curves of survivorship (N) against time and of mean weight $\bar{w}$ against time for a single recruitment N_0 of individuals of negligible weight at settlement.

where $- \mathrm{d}N/\mathrm{d}t$ is the slope of the survivorship curve as shown in Fig. 12.1. Hence the number of individuals dying during the interval Δt will be the product of the instantaneous mortality rate and the time interval, summed over the whole population:

$$\sum_{0}^{N} \frac{1}{N} \left[\frac{\mathrm{d}N}{\mathrm{d}t} \right] \Delta t = \Delta N$$

and the loss of biomass during this time will therefore be $\bar{w} \, \Delta N$.

The mortality loss of the recruitment during the first year of life, M_1, is found by summing over time intervals from 0 to 1 year:

$$M_1 = \sum_{t=0}^{t=1} \bar{w} \, \Delta N$$

The biomass increment of standing stock, ΔB, created by the end of the first year will be $N_1 \bar{w}_1$, where N_1 is the number surviving with average weight $\bar{w}_1$, that of an average one-year-old individual. Equation (10) then gives

$$P_1 = N_1 \bar{w}_1 + \sum_{t=0}^{t=1} \bar{w} \, \Delta N \qquad (12)$$

The estimation of production by growth increment (Eq. 11) has been associated with Allen's graphical method (Allen, 1950) described in Ricker (1968, pp. 183–186). The estimation of production from mortality plus residual biomass (Eq. 12) was employed by Sanders (1956, p. 393). His computation of total production falls short of the true value because the contribution by individuals more than three years old was not included, the data not extending beyond year class 2.

The results of equations (11) and (12) indicate that only the relation between N, the number of living survivors, and $\bar{w}$, the mean weight of survivors at corresponding times, need be known to compute production. Fig. 12.2 shows this relationship. The summation of production by growth increments (Eq. 11) $\sum_{t=0}^{t=1} N \, \Delta \bar{w}$ is shown hatched vertically in Fig. 12.2A while summation of mortality increments $\sum_{t=0}^{t=1} \bar{w} \, \Delta N$ is shown hatched horizontally and the product $N_1 w_1$ (see Equation 12) is shaded black (Fig. 12.2B). The unshaded areas under the curves of Fig. 12.2 A & B represent the production by individuals surviving for one year or longer. It is clear that both growth and mortality approaches for estimating production (Equations 11 and 12 respectively) give the same answer.

Furthermore, the ultimate production by the original recruitment when all have died ($t = \infty$, $N = 0$) is the same whether growth or mortality increments are measured. It follows from Eq. 12 that when $t = \infty$ and $N = 0$, $\Delta B = 0$ and therefore

$$P_\infty = \sum_{t=0}^{t=\infty} N \, \Delta \bar{w} = \sum_{t=0}^{t=\infty} w \, \Delta N, \qquad (13)$$

which is the total area under the curves A & B, Fig. 12.2.

Note that the curve of survivorship against mean weight is quite different from a size-frequency histogram of the population, and should not be confused with a size frequency curve. Whereas the latter includes many age groups and relates frequency to size at a given moment of time, the mean weight-survivorship curve refers to a single recruitment and covers a period of time equal to the whole or part of the life of the individuals. Furthermore,

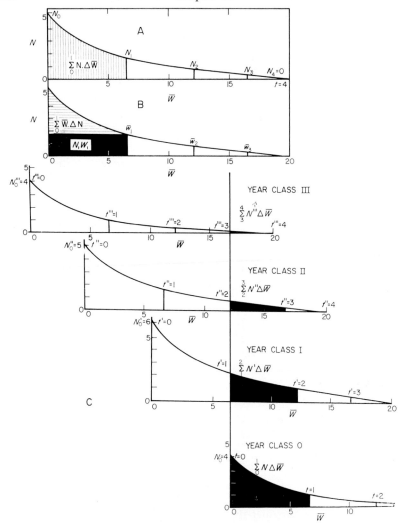

Figure 12.2. Curves of survivorship (N) against mean weight $\bar{w}$. $N_1 N_2 N_3 \ldots$ and $\bar{w}_1 \bar{w}_2 \bar{w}_3 \ldots$ are the values of survivorship and mean weight at the end of the first, second and third year of life respectively.

(A) Production during first year, summed as growth increments $N \triangle \bar{w}$ (vertical shading).

(B) Production during the first year, summed as mortality losses $\bar{w} \triangle N$ (horizontal shading) plus increase in biomass $N_1 \bar{w}_1$ (black).

The unshaded areas represent production in subsequent years.

(c) Separate curves of survivorship—mean weight during year 0 of recruitments from year 0 and previous years.

The total production during year 0 from each constituent recruitment is shown in black.

although size frequency histograms may have a number of peaks or modes, the mean weight-survivorship curve must show a continuous decline in numbers with increasing weight.

The precise meaning of the production term P_∞ in equations 11c and 13 is also important. It is the production by a population of N_0 recruits from the time of settlement up to the time that they have all died. The production therefore extends over a period equal to the maximum longevity of the species. An actual population will usually contain recruits settled at intervals over several years and the summation $P_\infty = \sum\limits_{t=0}^{t=\infty} N\,\Delta\bar{w}$ can be equated to the annual production of such a real population only under certain exceptional conditions. In a real population during any particular year, say year 0, there would be present a number of year classes contributing to production, whose original recruitment numbers 0, 1, 2, years previously might have been N_0, N'_0, N''_0, the number of primes referring to the age class. Figure 12.2C shows by shading which parts of the integrated growth-survivorship curves of each of these age classes should be included to give the actual production in year 0. It will be seen from Figure 12.2C, that if the annual recruitment is the same each year $(N_0 = N'_0 = N''_0)$ and the growth-mortality relationship continues along the same course in successive years, the production by all age groups in year 0 will be equal to the total production by the recruits of any one year throughout their life (P_∞). It is only when the population exists in such a steady state with constant annual recruitment, growth and mortality, that Equation 13 can be applied to all the current age classes of a particular year to estimate production by integrating a single continuous growth frequency curve. Otherwise the annual production will vary from year to year and will be equal to

$$P_{\mathrm{ann}} = \sum\limits_{t=0}^{t=1} N_0 \mathrm{d}\bar{w} + \sum\limits_{t=1}^{t=2} N'_1 \mathrm{d}\bar{w} + \sum\limits_{t=2}^{t=3} N''_2 \mathrm{d}\bar{w} \dots \text{etc.} \qquad (14)$$

Application of production equation

Method 1. Estimation of production by stock with no recruitment. If there is no recruitment to the stock, the measurement of production can be carried out quite simply by counting the numbers of stock surviving (N) and measuring the mean weight ($\bar{w}$) of a sample at intervals of time close enough to be

TABLE 12.1. Growth and survivorship of a hypothetical population recruited April, 1969, to illustrate computation of production

I	II	III	IV	V	VI	VII	VIII	IX	X	XI	XII	XIII	XIV
Date	Time from April 1 '69 t (years)	Mean individual weight $\bar{w}$ (mg)	Population density N (thousands m^{-2})	Standing Crop $N\bar{w}$ (kg m^{-2})	Average value of N over period $\frac{1}{2}(N_t+N_{t+\Delta t})$	Average mean wt over period $\frac{1}{2}(\bar{w}_t+\bar{w}_{t+\Delta t})$	$-\triangle N$	$\Delta \bar{w}$	ΔP $(=N\Delta\bar{w})$	ΔM $(=\bar{w}\Delta N)$	$\sum_0^t \Delta P$	$\sum_0^t \Delta M$	$\sum_0^t \Delta M + N\bar{w}$
1969													
April 1	0	0·2	100	0·02	—	—	—	—	—	—	—	—	—
May 1	0·08	5	60	0·30	80	2·6	40	4·8	0·38	0·10	0·38	0·10	0·40
June 1	0·17	30	24	0·72	42	17·5	36	25	1·05	0·63	1·43	0·73	1·45
July 1	0·25	90	20	1·80	22	60	4	60	1·32	0·24	2·75	0·97	2·77
Aug. 1	0·33	200	18	3·60	19	145	2	110	2·09	0·29	4·84	1·26	4·86
Sept. 1	0·42	350	16	5·60	17	275	2	150	2·55	0·55	7·39	1·81	7·41
Oct. 1	0·50	480	15	7·20	15·5	415	1	130	2·02	0·42	9·41	2·23	9·43
Nov. 1	0·58	600	14	8·40	14·5	540	1	120	1·73	0·54	11·14	2·77	11·17
Dec. 1	0·67	590	13	7·66	13·5	595	1	-10	-0·14	0·60	11·00	3·37	11·03
1970													
Jan. 1	0·75	580	12	6·96	12·5	585	1	-10	-0·12	0·58	10·88	3·95	10·91
March 1	0·92	610	10	6·10	11	595	2	30	0·33	1·19	11·21	5·14	11·24
May 1	1·08	630	8	5·04	9	620	2	20	0·18	1·24	11·39	6·38	11·42
July 1	1·25	660	3	1·98	5·5	645	5	30	0·17	3·23	11·56	9·61	11·59
Nov. 1	1·58	700	2	1·40	2·5	680	1	40	0·10	0·68	11·66	10·29	11·69

I	II	III	IV	V	VI	VII	VIII	IX	X	XI	XII	XIII	XIV
1971													
May 1	2·08	710	1	0·71	1·5	705	1	10	0·02	0·71	11·70	11·00	11·71
Nov. 1	2·58	720	0·5	0·36	0·75	715	·5	10	negl.	0·35	11·70	11·35	11·71
1972													
May 1	3·08	730	0·2	0·15	0·35	725	·3	10	negl.	0·22	11·70	11·57	11·72
Nov. 1	3·58	740	0·1	0·07	0·15	735	·1	10	negl.	0·07	11·70	11·64	11·71
1973													
May 1	4·58	755	0	0	0·05	747	·1	15	negl.	0·07	11·70	11·71	11·71
									11·70	11·74			

Method of calculation:

Mean population between April and May $= \dfrac{100 + 60}{2} = 80$ thousand/m^2 (Column VI)

Increase in weight $\triangle \bar{w} = 5 - 0·2$ mg $= 4·8 \times 10^{-6}$ kg (Column IX)

Production increment $\triangle P = N \, \triangle w = 80 \times 4·8 \times 10^{-3}$ kg m$^{-2} = 0·38$ kg m^{-2} (Column X)

Mean weight between April and May $= \dfrac{(0·2 + 5·0)}{2} = 2·6$ mg (Column VII) $= 2·6 \times 10^{-6}$ kg

Decrease in population $\triangle N = 100 - 60$ thousands/m$^2 = 40 \times 10^3$ m^{-2} (Column VIII)

Mortality increment $\triangle M = \bar{w} \triangle N = 2·6 \times 40 \times 10^{-3} = 0·104 \simeq 0·10$ kg m^{-2} (Column XI)

Columns XII and XIII are obtained by summing the Production and Mortality increments month by month giving a total production of 11·7 kg/m^2 by both methods of computation. (Foot of Columns X–XIV.)

able to draw a smooth curve of survivorship against mean weight. The total number of stock present and the mean weight can be found by techniques described below (see page 243). Method 1 is applicable to a non-breeding stock of organisms allowed to grow in a confined area, such as a group of fish fry in a pond (see Ricker, 1968, pp. 183–6). It can also be applied to any identifiable recruitment of a species whose population density and mean weight can be measured continuously.

The following hypothetical example is given to illustrate the graphical method of computing production, biomass increase and mortality, based on Equations 11, 12 and 13.

The data are given in Table 12.1. Columns I–IV represent the growth in size and decline in numbers of a fairly dense population of small organisms, such as molluscs or crustaceans, having a maximum net weight of less than a gram and an initial population density N_0 of 10,000/m². The mean weight and population size are plotted against time in Fig. 12.3, which corresponds in form to the curves in Fig. 12.1. It can be seen that the numbers fall rapidly at first, then more slowly, until the end of the first year of life when the population is quickly eliminated. Growth is rapid at first; after six months there is

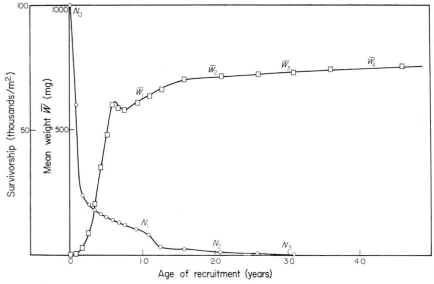

Figure 12.3. Population and growth curves for a single recruitment, based on data from Table 12.1.

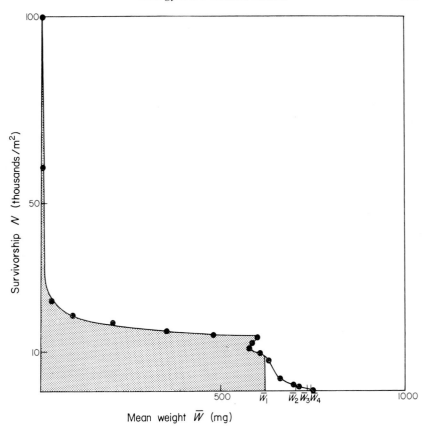

Figure 12.4. Plot of survivorship N against mean weight $\bar{w}$ for the recruitment described in Table 12.1 and Figure 12.3. Shaded areas give the production during the first year of life of the recruitment.

a marked decrease in weight, which might be caused by reproduction; thereafter growth is slow.

Fig. 12.4 shows the curve of N against $\bar{w}$, the area under which, if summed graphically, can be found to be 11·7 kg m^{-2}, which represents the total production by the 100,000 individuals initially recruited to the square metre quadrat. The computation can also be made arithmetically as demonstrated at the foot of Table 12.1. The production figures in Columns XII and XIV are based on the growth increment (Eq. 11a) and mortality (Eq. 12) approaches respectively, and agree as expected. The computation shows that, with this type of growth pattern, nearly all the production is completed before the end of the first year. (See the shaded area of Fig. 12.4.)

Stocks with recruitment. The factor that greatly complicates the assessment of production in a natural population is recruitment. In an isolated stock with no recruitment, survivorship, N, can be equated to the total population. This is clearly not so when recruitment takes place. In the extreme case where new individuals are recruited continuously at the same rate that older individuals die off, there would be no evident change in the population numbers, mean weight or standing stock biomass.

Method 2. For stocks with recruitment, age classes separable. The problem of production assessment in a population with steady or intermittent recruitment can be overcome if the age classes are separately recognisable. The stocks belonging to each year class can then be regarded as separate isolated populations, the survivorship and mean weight of which can be measured and integrated as in Method 1. The total production in any particular year can then be obtained by applying Equation 14. Methods of separating age classes are described on page 226.

In deriving the productivity equations, and in presenting growth-survivorship curves, it was assumed for simplicity that all members of a recruitment started at zero time (Figs. 12.1 and 12.2). In fact recruitment does not take place instantaneously. Whereas the numbers of all other age groups will fall continuously, the number of individuals less than a year old (by convention called 0 group individuals) will increase when recruitment starts, reaching a maximum as larval settlement on the benthic habitat begins to slow down. Such a curve is shown in Fig. 12.5a. However, the application of the summation $N \Delta \bar{w}$ is still valid for 0 group individuals so long as the quantity of biomass introduced by settling larvae is negligible, which is nearly always so. Since the changes in N and $\bar{w}$ are generally more rapid for 0 group individuals, more frequent sampling may be necessary for them than for the older, more slowly growing, age groups.

An example of the application of Equation 14 to compute the production of a population in which the age groups have been separated, counted and weighed at intervals, is demonstrated in Table 12.2 and Fig. 12.5. The kind of data obtained is given in Columns I to IV of the table and the values of N and $\bar{w}$ are plotted in Fig. 12.5, the 0 group being shown inset because of the

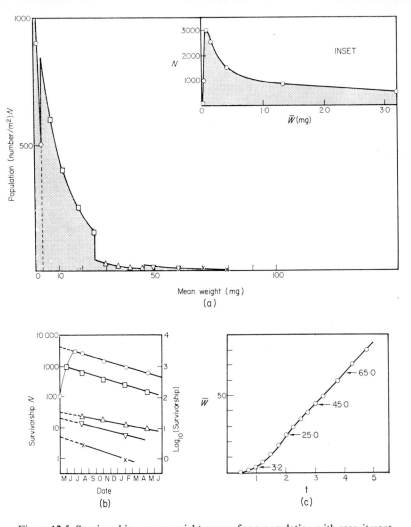

Figure 12.5. Survivorship—mean weight curves for a population with recruitment.

(a) Plot of N against $\bar{w}$ for each annual recruitment. The discontinuous curves are: ○, year class 0 (first year individuals); □, year class I; △, year class II; ▽, year class III; ×, year class IV. Inset. Plot of N against $\bar{w}$ for first year individuals. The rise in N represents the period of recruitment.

(b) Log survivorship—time curves from the slopes of which the specific mortality rate can be determined. The lines extrapolated back to the datum month of initial recruitment allow the value of N at the beginning of each year to be estimated. Extrapolated values of N are given in parenthesis against month V in column III of Table 12.2.

(c) Plot of mean weight $\bar{w}$ against time, using data for different age classes given in Table 12.2. The lack of any discontinuity indicates the assumption that growth rates do not vary significantly between successive annual recruitments. Arrows give mean weight at the end of each year after recruitment.

TABLE 12.2. Computation of production for a population with recruitment, age classes distinguishable.

I	II	III	IV	V	VI	VII
Sampling date (month)	Year class	Number in year class N (m^{-2})	Mean wt. per individual $\bar{w}$ (mg)	Wt. increment since previous sample $\Delta\bar{w}$ (mg)	Mean no./m^2 during period Δt N (thousands)	Production increment $\bar{N}\Delta\bar{w}$ (g m^{-2})
V	0	100	0·01	—	—	
VI		1,000	0·04	0·03	0·505	0·015
VII		3,000	0·07	0·03	2·00	0·06
VIII		2,500	0·15	0·08	2·75	0·22
XI		1,500	0·40	0·25	2·00	0·50
II		900	1·32	0·92	1·20	1·10
V		500	3·20	1·88	0·70	1·31
V		N_1' (900)			$\sum\limits_{0}^{1} N\Delta\bar{w}$	3·205
VIII	1	600	6·80	3·6	(0·75)	2·70
XI		400	12·0	5·2	0·50	2·60
III		250	18·0	6·0	0·325	1·95
V		150	25·0	7·0	0·20	1·40
V		N_2'' (32)			$\sum\limits_{1}^{2} N_1'\Delta\bar{w}$	8·65
VIII	2	24	30	5·0	(0·028)	0·140
XI		18	35	5·0	0·021	0·105
II		12	40	5·0	0·015	0·075
V		10	45	5·0	0·011	0·055
V		N_3''' (22)			$\sum\limits_{2}^{3} N_2''\Delta\bar{w}$	0·375
VIII	3	14	50	5·0	(0·018)	0·09
II		6	60	10·0	0·010	0·10
V		N_4'''' (5)			$\sum\limits_{3}^{4} N_3'''\Delta\bar{w}$	0·19
VIII	4	3	70	10.0	(0·004)	0·04
II		1	80	10·0	0·0020	0·02
					$\sum\limits_{4}^{5} N_4''''\Delta\bar{w}$	0·06
Total Annual Production (excluding 5th and later year classes)						12·48

much larger numbers present. It will first be noted that the mean weight-survivorship relationship differs from that of Fig. 12.4 in being discontinuous. This results from the year classes belonging to different recruitments. It is assumed in the table that settlement begins in May, which is therefore taken as the month at which each year class begins to grow. As in Table 12.1 the calculation of growth increments is based on the equation:

$$\int N \mathrm{d}w = \Sigma \tfrac{1}{2} (N_t + N_{t+\Delta t}) \Delta w;$$

the value of $\tfrac{1}{2}(N_t + N_{t+\Delta t})$ is given in Column VI.

Since production by each year class must be assessed separately, a difficulty arises in applying the above approximation to obtain the mean of the last value of survivorship of one year class, (i), in this example in May, and the first value of survivorship of the next year class, $(i+1)$, in August. Assuming that the year begins and ends in May, it is necessary to extrapolate the $i+1$ year class survivorship back from August to the beginning of growth year in May. For extrapolation of survivorship data (and, if the interval is long, for interpolation also) it is advisable to assume that survivorship follows a logarithmic law, $N = N_0 e^{-Zt}$. A plot of $\log_{10} N$ against t will then give a straight line from which the value of N in the preceding May can be estimated with reasonable accuracy on the basis of the data for the rest of the year, $i+1$. The lines for $\log_{10} N$ against time are shown in Fig. 12.5b, and the entries in Table 12.2 (Columns III & VI) based on extrapolation are shown in brackets. Since by this method a discontinuous series of curves must be used for survivorship and growth, the break being made at a datum month corresponding to the time of recruitment, the mean weight of each year class at this time needs also to be known. It can reasonably be assumed that, unlike the rate of recruitment, the mean growth rate is not likely to differ markedly from year to year, so that a continuous curve can be constructed from the data of Table 12.2 as is shown in Fig. 12.5c. The average weight reached at the end of the year (in May) by individuals of the first, second and nth year classes can then be read off from this graph and the integrations of each separate year class can be carried out between the limits of these values of $\bar{w}$. Vertical lines are shown in Fig. 12.5a at the datum month where the integrations are interrupted. If the areas under each of the separate weight-survivorship curves in Fig. 12.5 are integrated, they will be found to agree with the totals given by the approximate arithmetical integration in Column VII of the table.

Method 3A and B. Assessment of production for stocks with recruitment, age classes not separable. When it is impossible to recognise age classes it becomes necessary to measure growth rates or mortality rates as a function of size and season and to carry out a summation throughout the year for each size class present. Method 3A amounts to a direct application of Equation 9 modified by the introduction of grouping into size classes.

$$\text{Annual Production} = \sum_{t=0}^{t=1} \sum_{0}^{n} f_i\, G_i\, \bar{w}_i\, \Delta t \tag{15}$$

where G_i is the weight specific growth rate of size group i, $\bar{w}_i$ the mean weight of the size group and f_i the number of individuals of this size group existing in the population during the period Δt. The fraction of total standing stock biomass within the size class i is therefore $f_i\bar{w}_i$. The symbol f_i is used in place of N because it no longer represents a survivorship continuous throughout the period of the summation. The growth rate cannot necessarily be obtained from the population size distribution data because the rate of recruitment into the size class f_i is not known. Growth rates must therefore be obtained independently by observations on isolated individuals or groups of individuals whose identity can be established throughout the period of measurement. The methods of measuring growth rates are described below (pp. 235–238).

Details of the method of computation are best given by means of an example. A hypothetical population is divided into three size classes on the basis of length. The numbers per 100 square centimetre quadrat are assumed to have been sampled on five occasions which include four growth periods over one completed year. The relative growth rates required are assumed to have been obtained for each period of the year and are given at the head of Table 12.3. The raw data are next shown: against each date are given the population density per quadrat and the mean weight of those individuals in the sample belonging to each size class. The computation is given in detail for size group 1. The year is divided into four periods separated by the sampling dates and the density and mean weight of the size class during each of these periods is assumed to be the average of that at the beginning and the end. These values are shown in Columns III and IV and their product shown in Column V represents the average biomass during the period. The growth increment is then obtained by multiplying the standing stock biomass by the relative growth rate G_i and time interval Δt. The total production by this size group during the year will be the sum of these increments and the total annual production by the population is obtained by adding that of each size group as shown in the foot of Table 12.3.

TABLE 12.3. Computation of productivity for a population whose age classes cannot be distinguished.

Specific growth rates independently measured. (See pp. 235–238)

	Length class		
	0–5 mm	5–10 mm	10–15 mm
Dates	G_1 (year $^{-1}$)	G_2 (year $^{-1}$)	G_3 (year $^{-1}$)
21.IV–2.VII	50	20	5
2.VII–4.IX	60	30	6
4.IX–21.IV	20	10	2

Population density and mean weight data for three size groups.

	Size group 1		Size group 2		Size group 3	
	Density	Mean	Density	Mean	Density	Mean
	(per	wt.	(per	wt.	(per	wt.
Dates	100 cm^2)	$\bar{w}_1$ (mg)	100 cm^2)	$\bar{w}_2$ (mg)	100 cm^2)	$\bar{w}_3$ (mg)
21.IV	2,000	0·1	300	5·1	60	17·6
2.VIII	1,200	0·5	250	5·7	60	18·1
4.IX	400	0·55	200	6·3	40	16·0
21.XII	200	0·6	160	6·0	60	17·0
21.IV	1,000	0·15	320	4·6	80	18·0

Computation for size group 1.

I	II	III	IV	V	VI	VII
		Mean		Biomass B_1	Specific	Produc-
	Time	frequency f_1	Mean	per m^2	growth	tion
Period of	interval	(thousands	wt.	$f_1\bar{w}_1$	rate G_1	$G_1 B_1 \triangle t$
year	$\triangle t$ (years)	m^{-2})	$\bar{w}_1$ (mg)	(g m^{-2})	(year^{-1})	(kg m^{-2})
21.IV–2.VII	0·22	160	0·30	48	50	0·530
2.VII–4.IX	0·20	80	0·525	42	60	0·505
4.IX–21.XII	0·31	30	0·575	17	20	0·105
21.XII–21.IV	0·27	60	0·375	23	20	0·120
				Total production by size group 1		1·26

Summary of results of similar computations for other size groups.

Period $\triangle t$	Production by size group in kg m^{-2}			Total during period $\triangle t$
	1	2	3	
21.IV–2.VII	0·530	0·655	0·120	1·305
2.VII–4.IX	0·505	0·810	0·105	1·420
4.IX–21.XII	0·105	0·205	0·050	0·360
21.XII–21.IV	0·120	0·205	0·065	0·390
Total by size group	1·26	1·875	0·340	3·475
				Total annual production

Clearly the larger the number of size groups and growth periods employed in the assessment, the more closely will the summation approach its true value. In order to limit the amount of calculation, the population was assumed to have been divided into only three size groups. This is, in fact, rather too coarse a division and, as a result, the relative growth rates differ too much for accurate assessment. However, the example illustrates quite characteristically the important fact that the very small numerous and fast growing young stages of size group 1, though easily overlooked in the samples, may be responsible for much more production than the more prominent but more slowly growing mature individuals of size group 3.

Method 3B should be mentioned for completeness. If independently assessed mortality rates are available, production by a population with indistinct year classes can be obtained by applying a modification of Equation 10 in which i is one of the size classes into which the population has been divided.

$$\text{Production} = \sum_0^1 \sum_0^n f_i Z_i \bar{w}_i \, \Delta t + \Delta B \tag{16}$$

It will be seen that, unlike the corresponding Equation 15 based on growth increments, Equation 16 includes a term ΔB for the net change in biomass of the population. In using this method therefore, size specific mortality rates are not sufficient and must be augmented by measurements of the difference in the standing stock between the start and the finish of the annual survey.

It is usually more difficult to obtain information on mortality rates, than on growth rates. The use of this method may, however, be appropriate when most of the production is accounted for by larger individuals and where mortality rates can be approximated. For example, if the rate of harvesting accounted for a large fraction of mortality and was known, mortality rates could be estimated. If the population is in a steady state condition with no appreciable change in standing stock from year to year ($\Delta B = 0$), then the production measured from the growth integral and the mortality integral of Equations 15 and 16 respectively, should be the same. Kuenzler's attempt to obtain agreement between growth and mortality estimates for a population of *Modiolus demissus* (Kuenzler, 1961) was not very successful, however.

Note that the methods based on Equations 15 and 16 have a wider application than to a classification only in terms of size. They can be used equally for species where age classes can be distinguished or to any division of the population into a number of sub-groups, i, provided that each of the sub-groups is reasonably homogeneous in regard to instantaneous growth rate or mortality rate.

Stratified sampling

Production by a single species population, being a function of the individual rates of growth, will vary with climate, habitat and population structure. In computing production by Equations 15 and 16 above, the assumption is implicit that growth rates depend chiefly on individual size and the season of the year. In fact there will probably be significant differences in growth rate, not only from year to year but also between the various habitats that the species occupies, and over its latitudinal range. The investigator hopes that his estimate of production will be representative of the species as a whole in its natural environment and therefore usually selects a large study area which includes the full range of habitat variation available to the species and in which therefore growth rates and production may vary greatly from place to place. Under these circumstances the principle of stratified sampling should be applied. (See p. 4.) .

The whole area should be divided into sub-areas of different habitat type on the basis of factors likely to influence growth, mortality and population structure. If these are well chosen, the sub-areas will each contain a more homogeneous population, with individuals whose size-dependent growth rates are more consistent than those in the study area treated as a whole. Separate measurements of production should be carried out in each habitat type. These estimates can then be multiplied by the fraction that the habitat type occupies as part of the whole study area, thus obtaining the value of the production of the study area as a whole.

Stratified sampling has the following advantages:

1 It provides information on differences in production between different parts of the study area.

2 If the survey of the relative areas occupied by the different habitat types is accurately carried out, stratified sampling should greatly improve the precision of the estimate of production for the study area as a whole.

3 Stratified sampling allows the possibility of predicting the productivity of other areas, where the balance of habitat types is different.

As examples of the kind of sub-division that is desirable, a benthic habitat might be separated into sub-areas on the basis of the type of deposit, since some deposits will favour certain species over others. The littoral habitat might with advantage be divided into different zones in relation to chart datum since organisms immersed for longer periods will be likely to grow faster and to suffer greater predation than those exposed to the air only for short periods.

Multi-species studies

In the study of the production of all the species present in a selected habitat, unless an *in situ* measurement of total production can be made (see p. 262), each component species must be dealt with separately. This would be an enormous task, but for the fortunate circumstance that often arises in which only a few species account for most of the biomass and probably also for most of the production. If these species are obvious, the main effort can be concentrated on them and the data for the species whose contribution is relatively small need not be gathered with the same accuracy. In very rough estimates the minor species can be ignored altogether. It must be remembered, however, that in general the smaller in size are the individuals of a species, the more rapid is likely to be their growth and metabolism and the greater the part they will then play in the energy flow of the ecosystem. This principle applies to protozoa and bacteria as well as to higher organisms.

Methods of separating age groups

Separation by means of growth marks

It has been shown that the measurement of population production is made much easier if it is possible to determine the age of the individual. Unfortunately, overt growth marks are carried by only a minority of species and these are confined to two main groups of organisms, fish and bivalve molluscs. Methods of ageing have been most fully studied in fish where growth zones or growth checks can be recognised on the hard parts, such as the scales, opercula, otoliths, spines and vertebral centra (Ricker, 1968, Chapter 5). It is possible that methods of age determination in other invertebrate groups with hard permanent skeletons may be developed (e.g. in echinoderms).

Annual growth checks are related to fluctuating seasonal conditions and are therefore commonly encountered in temperate and arctic forms but are rarely found in tropical forms. Growth checks may be caused, not only by seasonal changes in the environment, but also by any event which might have a traumatic effect on growth, such as accidental disturbance of the habitat, disease, or the stress of breeding. It is essential therefore not only to establish beyond doubt that the marks used for determining age are in fact laid down annually, but also to be able to distinguish them from all other marks caused by extraneous factors. Usually such adventitious marks are fainter and do not fit into the regular series of spacings that characterise the annual marks. The Ford-Walford technique (Walford, 1946) offers a convenient method of displaying the regularity of the intervals between annual growth marks (see p. 240).

In any collection, particularly among the older age classes, some individuals are likely to be difficult to age with certainty. They should be placed in the class to which they seem most probably to belong on the basis of apparent age and size. It is unwise to discard such doubtful specimens from production estimates because they may belong predominantly to certain age classes and their absence would then produce a systematic error in the result.

Separation by means of size-frequency histograms

The majority of benthic invertebrates are soft bodied forms or forms that regularly shed their external skeleton. In such animals the year classes can be identified only on the basis of size-frequency histograms.

When the length or weight of a large number of individuals constituting a complete sample of a population is measured and the number of individuals found within a stated size interval plotted against size, the result is a size-frequency histogram. Usually a series of peaks or modes can be distinguished. The modes may result from irregularity in the rate of recruitment of the population. Hence, if there is an annual pattern of recruitment, the modes will probably represent separate year classes and the position of the mode along the size axis affords an approximate measure of the mean size of that year class.

Unfortunately, growth rates may vary greatly between individuals, especially if the habitat is not uniform, while the rate of growth itself usually declines with age. Consequently, only the first few modes are likely to remain distinct, those representing the older age classes becoming merged. In using this method of distinguishing between age groups, great care must therefore be exercised to ensure that the sample size is sufficiently large to authenticate the modes, especially those representing the older age groups. Where doubt exists simple statistical methods (e.g. χ^2 analysis) should be employed to establish that the apparent frequency fluctuations are not likely to have arisen by chance. Furthermore, should independent data exist on growth

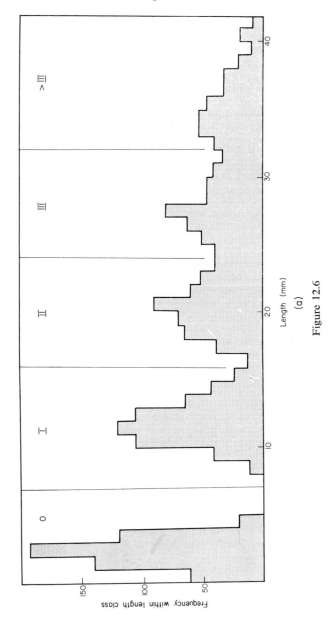

Figure 12.6

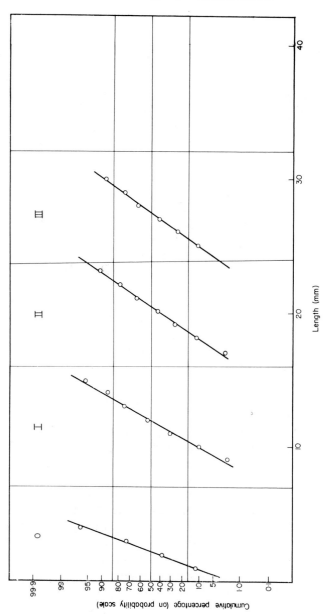

Figure 12.6. Separation of age groups by size-frequency histograms.

(a) Size-frequency histogram for a population with at least three distinguishable age classes.

(b) The same data plotted as cumulative curves on probability paper.

rates, it can be used as a further check by comparing the size at a given age with the position of the supposed mode.

Fig. 12.6a shows a size distribution that would allow at least the first three modes to be distinguished. The O group is quite distinct and the individuals belonging to it can be classed with reasonable certainty. The remaining age groups overlap to an increasing extent and there is no way of determining the year class of those individuals whose size lies in the region of overlap. The complete separation of the 1, 2 and 3 year groups must therefore be arbitrary. The simplest method is to draw lines of separation perpendicular to the size axis at the points where the component distributions intersect (vertical lines, Fig. 12.6a). The individuals can then be approximately separated into their age classes by identifying the age class with the size classes falling between the vertical lines. It will be seen from Fig. 12.6a that no separation at all is possible, not even by this approximate method, for individuals more than three years old. Fortunately the contribution to production by the larger and slower growing groups is relatively small and the greater part of the total production can be measured from data on the younger age groups whose numbers and mean weights can be obtained with reasonable accuracy. The production by the younger age groups can be measured using the survivorship-mean weight integration described under method 2 (p. 218), but the contribution of the larger size groups can be assessed only by methods 3A or B which require independent measurement of size specific growth rate or mortality rate. (p. 222).

An alternative to plotting histograms is to add the percentage frequencies to one another, starting with the smallest size groups, to obtain a cumulative percentage frequency curve. The cumulative percentage frequency relating to a stated size is the proportion of individuals in the total population having a size equal to or less than that stated. If the cumulative percentage frequency is plotted on the percentage scale of 'probability paper' against the size or weight to which it refers, any mode fitting the normal distribution curve will approximate to a sigmoid curve or a straight line (Harding, 1949). The successive modes can be more effectively transformed into straight lines, which are displaced from one another along the size axis, if a cumulative percentage plot is made for each, using arbitrary lines for separating the modes as in Fig. 12.6a. The modal value is the point at which these lines, extrapolated where necessary, intersect with the cumulative frequency value of 50 per cent. The slope of the line can be used to construct the best normal curve of distribution fitting the histogram. This will be the curve with a standard deviation equal to the distance between the values read off the size axis corresponding to 50 per cent and 16 per cent (or 50 per cent and 84 per cent) on the cumulative percentage frequency curve. Fig. 12.6b shows the data of Fig. 12.6a drawn on probability paper and indicates how this method linearises sections of the cumulative frequency curve and allows the positions of the modes to be determined more objectively.

Growth rates

Productivity measurement frequently requires a knowledge of the rate of growth in terms of dry weight or energy; the latter can be obtained from the dry weight if the caloric content is known (see p. 267).

It would be extremely inconvenient to have to measure the dry weight of the large number of individuals (see p. 207) either in population production studies or in growth measurements. Moreover, to obtain individual growth rates a method of measurement must be employed that does no harm to the animal, so that its weight can be measured at intervals of time. Instead of measuring dry weight directly, it is much easier to measure the length of the animal or of some hard part of the animal, such as the length of the shell of a bivalve, the carapace length of a crustacean, or the scale, otolith or operculum length of a fish. A separate series of experiments must first be carried out to establish the relationship between the selected measure of length and the ash free dry weight. Alternatively, volume or wet weight can be measured and converted to dry weight.

Length-weight conversion for animals with hard parts
A large number of typical animals of all sizes, extending over the full range required for later predictions, should be used to correlate length to weight. The length of the relevant part of each specimen is then measured and recorded, the specimen oven dried to constant weight, then ashed in a muffle furnace, and the weight of ash subtracted from the dry weight to obtain the ash free weight of the individual (see p. 200). When the organisms are small it may be advantageous to dry and weigh a number of individuals of similar length and to use average weight and average length for the purposes of correlation. The relationship required is obtained by regressing $\log_{10}$ (dry weight) on $\log_{10}$ (length).

TABLE 12.4. Length—dry weight conversion.
Individuals selected of similar length, oven dried and weighed
to obtain mean length *l* and dry weight *w*.

I *l* (mm)	II *w* (mg)	III $\log_{10}l$	IV $\log_{10}w$
1·25	$1·0 \times 10^{-2}$	0·10	$\bar{2}·00$
2·2	$1·1 \times 10^{-1}$	0·34	$\bar{1}·04$
3·8	$6·2 \times 10^{-1}$	0·58	$\bar{1}·79$
6·3	1·5	0·80	0·17
10·6	8·7	1·02	0·94
15·8	28·1	1·20	1·45

The values from columns III and IV are plotted in Fig. 12.7a
giving a line of slope 2·9 and intercept on the $\log_{10}w$ axis of $-2·1$.
Therefore $\log_{10}w = 2·9 \log_{10}l - 2·1$.

The procedure can be illustrated from a hypothetical example given in
Table 12.4. The basic data are shown in Columns I and II; these are transformed to their logarithms in Columns III and IV and are plotted against
each other in Fig. 12.7a. Alternatively, if log-log graph paper is available, the
raw data can be plotted directly. If the part of the organism chosen for
measurement provides a suitable index, the points when plotted in this form
will approximately fit a straight line. The best fitting line is then either drawn
by eye or by calculation using the least squares regression analysis and the
appropriate formula thereby obtained. This will be in the form

$$\log_{10}w = a + b \log_{10}l \text{ or } w = al^b$$

where *w* is the dry weight, *l* the length of the selected part of the animal; *a* is
a constant and *b* an exponent having a value of the order of three. If the
selected part of the animal grows in proportion to the whole of the organism,
b should be exactly 3; usually, however, it is slightly but significantly different
from 3. The coefficients in the above formula, particularly *a*, may change
seasonally with the condition of the animal; it is therefore desirable to repeat
the calibration experiment several times during the year.

Volume – dry weight, and wet weight – dry weight conversion for soft bodied animals

The lengths of soft bodied animals are usually difficult to measure precisely,
and since weight is roughly proportional to the cube of the length, any errors

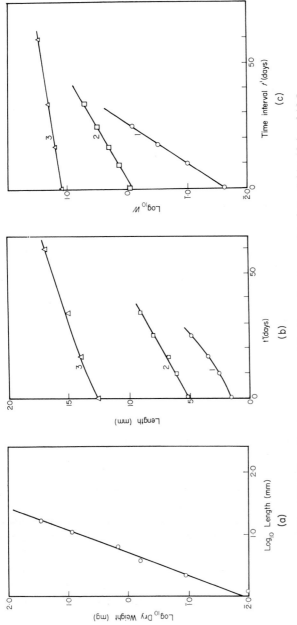

Figure 12.7. Growth rate measurement for three size classes, data from Tables 12.4 and 12.5.

(a) Plot of $\log_{10} l$ against $\log_{10} w$ for length (l)—dry weight (w) conversion. (See Table 12.4.)

(b) Length plotted against time in days, (t') to obtain specific growth rate $d \log_e w/dt'$. (See Table 12.5.)

(c) Growth curve plotted as $\log_{10} w$ against time, t', to obtain specific growth rate $d \log_e w/dt'$. (See Table 12.5.)

made in measurement of length will be greatly exaggerated when transformed to weight. It is better therefore to use volume or wet weight for animals that are difficult to measure. The volume of large irregular animals can be readily obtained by displacement of water, but the results are usually less accurate than those obtained by weighing. When large numbers of animals have to be weighed, it is almost essential to have an automatic type of balance. Any external water should be removed from the animal by blotting it dry on filter paper before weighing. Volume measurement is, however, sometimes more rapid and convenient if an automatic balance is not available.

Unfortunately there is no constant relationship between the wet weight and dry tissue weight, even for a given phylum or class. Thorson (1957) provides a survey in tabular form of dry weight as a percentage of wet weight. Animals without calcareous skeletons average about 17 per cent, those with skeletons (prosobranchs, lamellibranchs, echinoderms) are generally below 7 per cent. For all purposes but the roughest of estimates the appropriate relationship must be determined for each separate species.

The weight of organic matter in the shells of the molluscs, crustaceans, and other animals may form a substantial fraction of the total organic matter present (e.g. Kuenzler, 1961) and must therefore be included in the dry organic weight. The hard parts of such organisms can also be included when wet weight is measured if this is found convenient, provided of course that the same procedure is adopted when correlating wet weight to ash-free dry weight. The procedure for obtaining the relationship between volume, or wet weight, and dry weight is exactly the same as for the correlation of length to weight except that the exponent b in the resulting formula will have a value close to one.

$$\log_{10}w = a + b \log_{10} \text{[Wet Weight or Volume.]}$$

Measuring animals of variable shape

Some animals with hard parts are very variable in shape; individuals of the same species of barnacle, for example, may be tall and columnar or broad and flat. In such cases, a part of the animal may provide a better index of its size than any of its major dimensions. In the case of the barnacle this is true of the opercular valves. When no single part can be found to serve as a good index of the animal's size, two or more measurements in different dimensions may be necessary. For example, bivalves such as mussels can be measured in terms of their length from the anterior (umbo) to the posterior margin. But a short mussel which is very thick laterally and high dorso-ventrally may be much heavier than one which is longer and thinner; hence length alone offers a poor criterion of biomass. In such cases it may be worthwhile to use a product of length, breadth and height to provide a 'volume index' which will correlate better with dry weight than any single measurement.

Preservation

It is most undesirable to preserve samples for the above laboratory studies in alcohol or in formalin between collection and weighing, though on a small ship in rough weather this may be unavoidable. Preservation leads to chemical changes which alter the dry organic weight and the caloric content; formalin, unless neutralised, may destroy calcareous skeletons. Deep freezing is a much preferable method of holding biological material for laboratory investigations.

Measurement of growth rates

1. Direct measurement of growth rate

There are considerable problems in making continuous observations of animals living freely in the sea, but slow moving and sedentary forms present on the surface of hard substrata, which can be visited regularly by diving, can sometimes be photographed, identified and measured from time to time. Sessile forms attached to submerged frames, to piers, or suspended from an experimental raft may be recovered mechanically and measured. Live boxes containing small mobile organisms inevitably place restrictions on their movements but may provide conditions close to those in nature. In the inter-tidal zone it is quite easy to photograph or measure individuals of sedentary species at regular intervals of time or to mark and recapture slowly moving gastropods such as periwinkles, top shells, drills and whelks.

For the majority of soft bodied benthic invertebrates, however, direct measurement of growth rate can only be carried out in captivity. They need suitably aerated and flushed aquaria, with the appropriate bottom deposit in the case of burrowing forms. Even if the animals can be kept healthy, it is extremely difficult to simulate natural conditions in regard to food supply. For example, it may be difficult to be sure that sufficient micro-algal food is provided for a filter feeding organism, while a predator may be given more prey and grow faster in captivity than in nature. As an example of the great divergence of growth rates when different diets are used, Carefoot's (1967*a*) experiments with *Aplysia punctata* may be cited. Measurements of growth rate in the laboratory should therefore be regarded strictly as a basis for productivity measurements under laboratory conditions only. To apply the growth rates measured in the laboratory to estimate production in field conditions must, unfortunately, always be regarded with some suspicion.

2. Growth rate measurement from size-frequency histograms

As described above (p. 227) the modal size in a frequency diagram may indicate the approximate mean size of a year class. The positions of the modes cannot usually be fixed with great precision but if a time series of histograms is available in which the modes progress along the size axis, a plot of length (or weight) against time can be constructed. From this the population growth rate can be computed. Although growth rates measured from size frequency histograms are likely to be crude and possibly inaccurate, they do correspond to growth measurements under entirely undisturbed natural conditions.

3. Growth rate measurements from size distribution of animals of known age

Growth rates of certain fish, bivalves and any other animal with clear annual rings can be measured with considerable accuracy. From a large single collection of specimens of all sizes, those of normal shape and whose age can be determined with certainty should be selected, those of doubtful age or unusual shape being discarded. In ageing the specimens the convention is adopted that the age group corresponds to the number of growth rings laid down. Thus the 0 group has no growth ring, age group 1 has a single ring and so on. Growth marks are usually laid down in winter. If so, 1 January can be taken arbitrarily as the date of the growth mark (1 July in the southern hemisphere) and the mean lengths measured can be related to age on the date of collection. Thus, if the collection were made on 1 July (in the northern hemisphere), the individuals with one growth ring could be classed as 1·5 years. Hence by making several measurements during the year it would be possible to interpolate on the growth curve the values for length corresponding to years and fractions of a year. In the 0 and 1 age classes, where the growth increment is large, this additional information may prove useful. In measuring the average size of each age group it is desirable to use equal sample numbers, including at least 10 individuals from each age group, though naturally the older age groups become progressively less common in the sample.

In making measurements of a characteristic length of each individual (e.g. the greatest length of the shell) it is most important to define and measure precisely the same feature. When several hundreds of individuals have to be measured the operation is repetitive, tedious and sometimes tricky; the operator should therefore use calipers or a suitable mechanical jig wherever possible rather than to rely on measurements judged by eye. Where sexes can be distinguished, separate data of size against age for each sex should be collected and, if they do not differ significantly, the results can later be combined. Usually differences in growth rates are more likely to be attributable to environmental than to sex differences, and therefore if the habitat is exposed to considerable variation in such factors as tidal current, prey availability, or emersion, growth curves for individuals collected under different environmental conditions should be compared. (See stratified sampling, p. 225.)

4. Growth rate measurement by back calculation of lengths at a previous age
In this method a series of characteristic lengths are measured, corresponding to each of the growth rings present, so that the size of the animal itself at the time each growth ring was formed can be back calculated. This method is particularly valuable when only a few individuals are available for study or when the history of the growth of a particular individual is required. In fish, to which this method has been extensively applied, growth marks are present on relatively small parts of the animal such as the scales, otoliths etc. and the relationship between the dimensions of these parts and the length of the fish may be complex and variable; Ricker (1968) should be consulted for details. In bivalves, the group with which this method will mainly be concerned in benthic work, the growth rings are on the shell itself and no transformation is necessary for back calculation, the shell length measured on the rings representing the actual size of the shell at an earlier age. Back measurements from growth rings can therefore be used to determine the growth increments of the younger age groups in years previous to the year of collection. If the population structure can be assumed to be similar it would then be possible to calculate variations in production in successive years from a single year's observations.

Population and individual growth rates
The results of growth rate determinations by the four methods outlined above are not equivalent. Methods 1 and 4 deal with the growth of individuals and provide data on individual growth rate. Methods 2 and 3 deal with the increase in mean length of a given age group of the population and therefore

measure the population growth rate. The two concepts are different and the values will not necessarily be the same. If mortality among the larger individuals of a given age group were greater than among the smaller individuals, the mean weight of the population would not rise as fast as the weight of an individual that survived. Individual growth rates and population growth rates are therefore equal only if mortality is independent of size.

How great an error would be caused by using the wrong growth rate is not exactly known but the error is likely to be small compared with the other inaccuracies in population sampling and the natural variations in production. Nevertheless, when production is estimated by classification into size groups (p. 222) (Equation 15) it is the individual growth rate that should strictly be used and either the direct method of measurement or back calculation from growth rings is therefore to be recommended.

When estimating production in a population where the age classes can be identified, the integration of the survivorship-mean weight curve for each year class is free from any possible error through confusion between individual and population growth rate.

Computation of growth rate

A direct plot of length against age usually results in a sigmoid curve. The curve is not directly applicable to production estimates; it must first be transformed into a rate of increase of dry weight or energy using a formula of the type $w = al^b$ such as that obtained by the method described on page 232 and illustrated by Table 12.4. The values of $\log_{10}w$, derived from measurements of length, wet weight, or volume, are then plotted against time, and the weight-specific instantaneous growth rate, G, can be obtained from the slope of the line at any point.

$$G = \frac{d \log_e w}{dt} = 2 \cdot 303 \frac{d \log_{10} w}{dt} \qquad (17)$$

Table 12.5 illustrates the method as applied to consecutive measurements of the length of individuals of the same species as that used to establish a length-weight relation in Table 12.4. Columns I to III give the raw data for the smallest size class 0–5 mm. Column IV is the estimate of $\log_{10}w$ based on the equation derived in Fig. 12.7(a):

$$\log_{10}w = 2 \cdot 9 \log_{10}l - 2 \cdot 1$$

In Fig. 12.7(b), curve 1, the length l is plotted against time, t', and in Fig. 12.7(c) curve 1 the same data are plotted as $\log_{10}w-t'$ to give a line from which G can be calculated by Equation 17.

TABLE 12.5. Computation of specific growth rate.

A. Lengths of identified individuals of similar initial mean length l_1 and belonging to size class 1 measured on the dates given and averaged.
Equation relating dry weight to length:

$$\log_{10} w = 2 \cdot 9 \log_{10} l - 2 \cdot 1$$

I Date	II Time interval (days) t'	III Mean length l (mm) 0–5 mm class	IV $\log_{10} w$ calculated from above relationship
2.V	0	1·5	$\bar{2}$·40
12.V	10	2·5	$\bar{1}$·00
19.V	17	3·5	$\bar{1}$·48
27.V	25	4·9	$\bar{1}$·90

The values in columns II and IV are plotted in Fig. 12.7c curve 1 giving a line of slope of d $\log_{10} w/dt' = 0 \cdot 059$ days^{-1}.

$G_1 = $ d $\log_e w/dt$, where t is measured in years $= 0 \cdot 059 \times 2 \cdot 303 \times 365$ $= 50$ years^{-1}.

B. Data for larger size classes:

Date	Time interval (days)	Mean length 5–10 mm class (2) (mm)	Mean length 10–15 mm class (3) (mm)
2.V	0	5·1	12·5
12.V	10	6·0	—
19.V	17	6·7	14·0
27.V	25	8·0	—
5.VI	34	9·0	15·0
1.VII	60	—	17·0

These data are transformed to $\log_{10} w$ and plotted in Fig. 12.7c curves 2 and 3 giving, respectively, slopes of 0·024 and 0·006 corresponding to estimates $G_2 = 20$ years^{-1} $G_3 = 5$ years^{-1}.

Figs. 12.7b and c include also the lines for the two larger size groups computed in the same way from the data given in Table 12.5B.

A method based on measuring the slope at a particular point of the plot of $\log_{10} w$ against age is satisfactory only if the curve approximates to linearity, as do those in Fig. 12.7c. This is the situation when the growth rate of a particular size group is measured over a relatively small growth increment. But when the

TABLE 12.6. Length-age data for a hypothetical bivalve with a length-weight relation $\log_{10}w$ (g)$=2\cdot7\log_{10}l$ (cm) $-1\cdot6$.

I Age class (years)	II Mean shell length (cm)	III Estimated value of $\log_{10}w$ from length-weight relation
0	1·3	$\bar{2}$·70
1	3·55	$\bar{1}$·89
2	5·35	0·37
3	6·8	0·64
4	7·9	0·83
5	8·8	0·94

growth curve covers the whole life of the animal it has considerable curvature making it very difficult to draw and measure accurately the slopes of tangents. Table 12.6, Columns I and II provide typical data for the average length of successive age groups of a bivalve. Note that the average length of individuals of year class 0, which includes all those captured before the first growth ring has been laid down, has a finite value. Consequently, zero length on the growth curve (Fig. 12.8a) starts before zero age; a result of the convention adopted for defining age classes. The length-age curve shows a considerable change of slope and when transformed to $\log_{10}w$ (Column III Table 12.6, and Fig. 12.8b) the curvature is further increased. The slopes shown at values of $\log_{10}w$ corresponding to $l=2\cdot5$, 5 and 7·5 cm respectively would be very difficult to measure accurately and they can give only an approximate estimate of G. (Table 12.7, Columns II and III.) To overcome this difficulty the data may be presented in a form which gives a straight line, the Ford-Walford plot.

Ford-Walford Plots

It has been found that the section of the sigmoid growth curve in which the growth rate is declining can often be fitted to the Bertalanffy (1934) equation:

$$l_t = L_\infty - (L_\infty - L_0)e^{-Kt} \tag{18}$$

where L_0 and L_∞ are constants representing length at zero age and maximum possible length respectively. Clearly the equation will not fit lengths of young individuals and does not predict zero size at zero age. If $t=n$, an integral

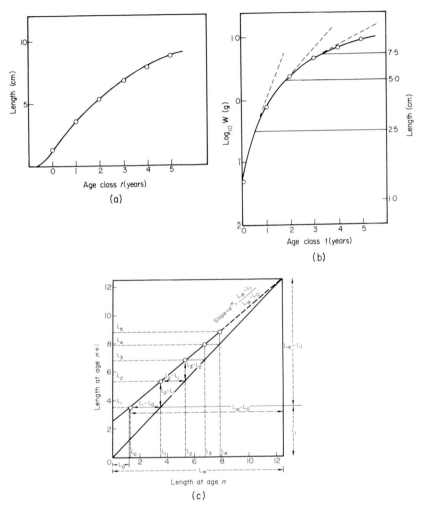

Figure 12.8. Growth rate measurement for a complete growth curve using Ford-Walford plot.
   (a) Length of shell plotted against time.
   (b) Log_{10} (dry weight) plotted against time.
   (c) Ford-Walford plot.

TABLE 12.7. Estimation of specific growth rate G, directly from the tangents to the growth curve of $\log_{10}$ (dry weight) – time (see Fig. 12.8b and column III), and from the Ford-Walford plot (see Fig. 12.8c and Column IV) The Ford-Walford plot gives $L_\infty = 12 \cdot 5$, $L_0 = 1 \cdot 25$, $K = 0 \cdot 23$. The weight-length relation (Table 12.6) gives exponent $b = 2 \cdot 7$.

I Length, l cm	II d $\log_{10}w/dt$ (approx.)	III $G = 2 \cdot 303$ d $\log_{10}w/dt$ years^{-1}	IV $G = bK[L_\infty - l]/l$ years^{-1}
2·5	1·2	2·8	2·48
5·0	0·4	0·9	0·93
7·5	0·2	0·46	0·41

number of years, then the ratio of annual increments for successive years can be shown to be constant:

$$\frac{l_n - l_{n-1}}{l_{n+1} - l_n} = e^K$$

Hence if l_{n+1} is plotted on the ordinate against l_n on the abscissa (Fig. 12.8c) the points can be shown to fall on a straight line of slope e^{-K}, which cuts the line drawn at 45° through the common origin of l_n and l_{n+1} at the point where $l_n = l_{n+1}$, that is at the value of L_∞. The constant L_0 can be read off the plot of l_{n+1} against l_n from the value on the abscissa where the line intersects l_1 on the ordinate. This presentation of growth rate data, known as the Ford-Walford method, allows information such as that obtained by methods 3 and 4 above (and as given in Table 12.6) to be combined, enabling accurate estimates of the three growth constants L_0, L_∞ and K to be made. From these the length and relative growth rate at any age can be computed, as follows:

Differentiating Equation 18:

$$dl/dt = (L_\infty - l)K$$

Differentiating weight-length transformation equation, $\log_e w = b \log_e l + \log_e a$:

$$d \log_e w/dl = b/l$$

hence the weight specific growth rate G is given by:

$$G = d \log_e w/dt = \frac{d \log_e w}{dl} \cdot \frac{dl}{dt} = b K [L_\infty - l]/l$$

The value of K can be obtained from the relation:

$$K = 2 \cdot 303 \; \log_{10} \frac{L_\infty - L_0}{L_\infty - l_1}$$

Fig. 12.8c illustrates the Ford-Walford plot of data from Table 12.6 and Table 12.7 shows how a more accurate value of G can be obtained from the Ford-Walford constants.

Methods are available for the mathematical computation of production using the constants of the fitted Bertalanffy equation and the size specific mortality rate Z in place of the empirical summation methods outlined in this chapter. They have been used for theoretical analyses of fish production (Beverton and Holt, 1957; Ricker, 1968, p. 88). There is no reason why the same principles should not be applied to benthic production where the theoretical equations of growth and mortality fit the observational data.

Population density

In all methods requiring data on the survivorship of stock, N, a method of obtaining a census of the stock is necessary. There are two classical methods available: mark and recapture and direct enumeration.

Mark and recapture methods are useful for mobile animals which can be tagged and sampled on a large scale; they have been widely applied in fishery research but are rarely useful for benthic studies unless bottom dwelling, actively swimming fish and crustacea are included and can be investigated on a massive scale. The methods described in Ricker (1968) would be applicable to such organisms; see also the bibliography on pp. 294–5.

Where direct enumeration can be employed, as is possible for the sedentary or nearly sedentary organisms in the benthos, more precise information can be obtained with less effort.

Benthic species must usually be counted by means of quantitative sampling using one of the more reliable samplers to collect a quantity of deposit representing a constant area of the sea bed. When the animal being sampled shows great variation in density from place to place or between substrate types, it is important to sample the same area and habitat on all occasions in order to reduce sampling errors. If the sampler cannot be relied upon to take a constant area of the substratum but can be relied upon to collect up to a consistent depth below the surface, the volume of deposit collected can be used as a measure of the amount of habitat searched and the population density expressed in numbers per unit volume.

In habitats favourable to the investigator, such as the intertidal areas and the shallow sublittoral accessible by diving, hand sampling of quadrats may be possible and visual or photographic methods be applied.

Mortality rates

In assessing production by methods 1 and 2, mortality data must be collected in the form of survivorship-time curves for single stocks (method 1) or for age classes (method 2). If instantaneous mortality rates are required they can be obtained by plotting $\log_{10}N$ (where N is the number of a stock or the specified age class surviving in unit area of the substratum) against t, the time of sampling. Not infrequently a particular age group may predominate in the population. This age group should be chosen for mortality measurements in order to increase the numbers of survivors (N) in each sample and so to reduce the sampling error. Furthermore, survivorship of a year class of exceptional strength can be followed through a longer period of time than an average year class.

The type of graph obtained from survivorship data has already been shown in Fig. 12.5b; it was previously used to demonstrate extrapolation (p. 221). Plots of survivorship against time are sometimes called 'catch curves' since, if harvesting has a significant effect, the curve will descend more sharply if the animal is heavily fished. When recruitment is taking place, the catch curve may contain a rising segment, as shown by the uppermost curve of Fig. 12.5b representing the 0 year class. This segment cannot of course be used to measure either mortality or recruitment since both are taking place at once. Where recruitment can be assumed to be absent, for example in the case of first or higher year classes, or when measurements are taken outside the season of settlement, the slope of the curve of $\log_{10}N$ against time allows the instantaneous mortality rate Z to be measured.

$$Z = \frac{1}{N} \frac{dN}{dt} = d(\log_e N)/dt = 2 \cdot 303 d(\log_{10} N)/dt$$

Thus in Fig. 12.5b the slope of $\log_{10}N$ against t for the year group 1 is $-0 \cdot 8$. The age specific mortality rate, Z, is therefore $2 \cdot 303 \times 0 \cdot 8 = 1 \cdot 84$ years^{-1}.

An annual mortality rate is sometimes quoted. This may be defined as $(N_0 - N)/N_0$ and will be equal to $1 - e^{-Z}$. For the year group 1 in Fig. 12.5b the annual mortality rate will be $0 \cdot 84$.

Although annual recruitment may vary from year to year, when the mortality rate is measured from consecutive values of the *absolute numbers* of an identifiable year class found in unit area or unit volume of the substratum on successive occasions, the only limit to the accuracy of the method is the error associated with the method of census. The presence of later recruits will not confuse in any way the enumeration of the survivors of a previous age class.

However, when it is not possible to obtain samples representing a standard area or volume of the substratum, the only method of measuring mortality may be in terms of year class frequencies, that is the *relative fraction* of the total sample collected attributable to each year class. Since this is a *relative* and not an *absolute* measure of the strength of the year class, uneven recruitment will lead to a serious bias in the apparent mortality rate. Thus, should the rate of recruitment be high in a particular year, the whole population will increase and the proportion of all other year classes will drop. A spurious impression will be created of increased mortality rate. Similarly, over periods of poor recruitment, mortality will be under-estimated. This method of measuring mortality rate will be valid only if recruitment is regular or if the slope of the catch curve based on frequency is measured over a sufficiently long period of time to even out irregularities in recruitment.

Where there are no criteria for age determination, natural mortality rates are very difficult to determine. They may theoretically be found by observations on marked individuals which can be regarded as age classes and the change with time in their rate of recapture, R, could be used to obtain a mortality estimate from the relationship:

$$Z\Delta t = (R_t - R_{t+\Delta t})/R_t$$

However, for this method to be successful very large numbers of marked individuals must be added over an area that is very great in relation to the movements of individuals in the population. Otherwise dissemination will be confused with mortality. The size of such an operation would usually have to be so large that it is unlikely to be applicable to the great majority of benthos investigations.

Changes in recovery *frequency* (the number of marked individuals as a fraction of the total number of individuals in the sample) can be measured more easily because, unlike measurements of recovery per unit area, they are unaffected by variations in the size of the grab samples. However, they would yield mortality rates which would suffer from bias if recruitment were irregular for the same reasons that relative year class frequencies provide an unsatisfactory basis for mortality measurements. In view of the difficulty of obtaining independent measures of mortality rates, production estimates should normally be based on measurement of growth increments.

Reproductive output

The production of eggs and sperm or of living young, together with the material associated with them (egg capsules, seminal fluid etc.), may be regarded as part of the process of growth and indeed many authors include it in the assessment of total production. The measurement of reproductive output often involves a separate series of experiments and computations and is therefore treated separately in this handbook.

It is virtually impossible to measure the reproductive output of most benthic species by making observations entirely in the field, but a preliminary study should be made where information is not available to establish the natural breeding season, whether the animal breeds once a year or more frequently, and the age or size at maturity.

If the species can be kept healthy and fed in the laboratory, the relation between reproductive output and the quality and amount of food intake can be examined. Examples of such studies are Marshall and Orr (1961), Paine (1965) and Carefoot (1967a, b). Laboratory observations, however, can give only an approximate idea of what occurs in the field since the conditions may be different from those in nature in some adverse respect, or they may sometimes be more conducive, for example by allowing the animal to obtain food with less expenditure of energy in searching.

For the purpose of measuring reproductive output, animals can be divided into two main categories; those which produce a single brood over a very short period of time once every year and those which breed over an extended season. The former class are characteristic of high latitudes and their reproductive output is relatively easily assessed. The latter are typical of warmer climates and the measurement of their reproductive output often presents considerable difficulty.

Annual breeders

Two basic methods are available; if the brood is shed in a form that can be handled (e.g. viviparous young, egg strings or capsules that can be collected and weighed in their entirety) the direct method can be used. If the reproductive output cannot be collected in a tangible form it is necessary to resort to the indirect method. This is necessary in the case of females producing minute planktonic eggs, and for sperm production by males.

Direct method. When there is a single annual brood it is usually possible to distinguish between gravid and spent individuals. Gravid females of widely ranging size should be brought into the laboratory just at the commencement of the spawning season. Sometimes animals are induced to spawn by the change from field to laboratory conditions, sometimes a spawning stimulus can be applied (e.g. rise of temperature, increase or decrease in illumination, the presence in the water of the reproductive products of other individuals). The eggs or young from each individual that spawns should be collected and the length or weight of the parent recorded. The reproductive products can either be weighed wet, the wet weight being converted to dry weight by means of an independently derived formula (as for whole animals see p. 234), or each separate spawning can first be dried and then weighed. The ash weight and caloric content of spawned products may also need to be measured, hence the dried material obtained from the spawn should be collected, homogenised, and kept for this purpose. Eggs generally contain high energy materials and their caloric content may therefore be considerably higher than that of the parent.

From these data a graph should be constructed showing the biomass of the reproductive products as a function of the biomass, dry weight, or length of the parent. Generally, the weight of the brood is roughly proportional to the weight of the parent for all individuals whose size exceeds that at which maturity is reached. Since, for annual breeders, this graph will represent the total annual reproductive output in relation to the size of the individuals, the only other information required to calculate the reproductive output is the size frequency of the population at the breeding season, and, in order to allow the number of actively reproducing females to be determined, the proportion of fertile females in each size class. The reproductive output by the females of the population will then be obtained from the frequency of females of each size class multiplied by the energy output for females of this size, as read off from the graph.

Unfortunately, the reproductive output of the males cannot be determined in this way, and though it is often neglected in energy flow studies, the losses are probably not always inconsiderable. They can sometimes be determined by the method described in the next section.

Indirect method. The energy present in the tissue of the gravid male or female before spawning must be almost equal to the energy of the spent individual plus the energy of the reproductive products. If the biomass of fully ripe males and females can be determined in relation to a characteristic length and the biomass of just spent individuals similarly determined, the difference will represent the reproductive output. When individuals in the population breed closely in synchrony, the loss of biomass can be deduced from the curve obtained by plotting against time, for each sex, the average values of individual biomass (preferably in energy units) for each age class or size class. The curves should show a discontinuity between the beginning and the end of the breeding season equal to the loss of energy at reproduction.

The weight lost during breeding is sometimes expressed in the form of changes in the ratio of weight to the cube of the length and referred to as 'coefficient of condition' or 'condition factor'. As an alternative to measuring changes in the weight or energy of the whole animal, ripe and spent ovaries (or *vesiculae seminales*) can be dissected out and weighed with reference to the size of the animal from which they were obtained.

Continuously breeding species

Species which breed throughout, or for a large part of, the year will not necessarily show any discontinuity in the curve of growth or in their condition factor resulting from any sudden loss of reproductive material. Frequently a steady state exists within the animal, the loss of weight through the shedding of reproductive products being made good continuously by assimilation. Sometimes, when assimilation cannot keep pace with breeding, the animal may gradually become spent and, in consequence, a gentle discontinuity may appear on the growth curve and a slight change be recorded in the condition factor. However, this change does not represent the whole reproductive output but only the lack of balance between assimilation and reproduction. If the indirect method, as described above, is applied in such situations it may grossly under-estimate the reproductive output.

If the reproductive products are in a form that can be collected and weighed it is possible to adapt the direct method to a continuously breeding species.

When the reproductive products are in the form of egg capsules, egg strings or egg masses produced at regular intervals of time, it may be possible to relate the dry weight of the egg mass produced to the size of the parent. It is then only necessary to record brood frequencies at different seasons and integrate over the year. The annual reproductive output can then be obtained from the frequency of females belonging to the post-maturity size classes, the size specific brood weights for each class of females and the total number of broods per year.

Brood frequencies may be established in various ways.

(a) When the breeding cycle is synchronous and rhythmic, frequent monitoring of the state of the gonad of field samples will enable brood frequencies and the proportion of individuals breeding at each season of the year to be established. Rhythmic breeding cycles in intertidal and shallow water species are often synchronised to lunar or semi-lunar periods, and if this can be established it may assist in estimating the number of broods.

(b) Where the female retains developing eggs until the next brood is due, and where the time between egg laying and hatching (brood period) can be determined by observations on ovigerous females kept in aquaria, the number of broods in the field population can be determined by sampling the population at regular intervals for the proportion of ovigerous females. The frequency of ovigerous females should then be plotted against time and integrated over the year or appropriate part of the year. The total number of broods in the population can be obtained by dividing this integral by the brood period. If there is a considerable variation in brood period at different seasons, it will be necessary to measure the number of broods during each season using the value of brood period that applies.

(c) Occasionally, direct observation of brood succession in known individuals is possible in the field (e.g. Crisp and Davies, 1955). If the planktonic eggs are sufficiently large, as in some species of *Littorina*, it may be feasible to strain them from the water with fine plankton netting and count the numbers produced daily in the laboratory. However, the criticism cannot be avoided that the rate of shedding of the eggs may not be characteristic of that of the animals in the field. The laboratory population, being kept under unnatural conditions, may become out of condition, though this can be minimised by frequently renewing the animals kept in captivity. On the other hand, abnormal increases in the rate of egg laying may be induced as a result of bringing the animals into the laboratory through shock or changes in the environment.

It is usually likely to be necessary, as in the case of brooding species, to establish the approximate relation between rate of egg laying and size; to obtain the size frequency structure; and to assess the proportion of females breeding in the field, in order to compute the total output by the natural population.

Where viviparous young are produced over a long period of the year, but are sufficiently large to be collected and weighed, the method outlined in this paragraph can also be applied (e.g. Heywood and Edwards, 1962).

The measurement of brood output in animals with planktonic eggs that are not readily collected and weighed and in which reproduction occurs steadily over a long period of time cannot at present be achieved. The same applies to the loss of sperm and seminal fluid from the males of such species. No information can be obtained from the size of the ovary or testes because eggs and sperm are being matured and shed continuously and the output cannot be related to the biomass of the reproductive organs. No firm recommendations can be put forward for measuring the reproductive output of organisms with this type of breeding since no satisfactory study on these lines has yet been carried out. Unfortunately such examples are likely to be very commonly encountered among warm temperate and tropical benthic species.

Other losses of energy

Largely on account of the difficulty in their measurement, losses of energy in forms other than reproduction and respiration have largely been ignored by ecologists. Where the nature of the nitrogenous excretory products are known, it should not be difficult to measure the rate of nitrogen excretion in the laboratory, but it is generally assumed that losses in the form of low energy nitrogen compounds are unimportant.

This is certainly not true of organic secretions. Teal (1957) claimed that about 60 per cent of the total energy loss of the planarian *Phagocata* was in the form of mucus, while McCance and Masters (1937) found that the mollusc *Archidoris* secreted its own weight of mucus (wet weight) in five hours. Kuenzler (1961) determined that the amount of energy lost as byssus threads by trapped specimens of *Modiolus demissus* amounted to 2–3 per cent of the total energy assimilated and about half the losses through reproductive effort.

Other forms of energy loss that need to be taken into account in a full energy budget are exuviae of crustaceans, the tests of Larvacea, and the tube building materials of polychaetes. No general method can be put forward.

Ingestion and egestion

Benthic communities consist mainly of filter feeders and detritus feeders, macro feeders being in a minority. Assimilation rates are difficult to measure directly in both of the predominant groups and there are few satisfactory studies of energy flow in typically benthic species.

With few exceptions, rates of ingestion and egestion can be measured only in the laboratory. There are, in principle, two types of methods available:

Direct method

The food ingested and the faeces produced by the animal over a sufficiently long period of time to establish continuity are measured directly.

Indirect method

The concentration of an indigestible marker present in, or artificially incorporated into the food, is measured in both food and faeces, together with the rate of faecal production.

If w'_C is the dry weight of food ingested in unit time including the weight of marker and w'_F the weight of faeces egested in unit time, ϕ_C the weight fraction of the marker in the food and ϕ_F the weight fraction of the marker in the faeces, it follows that, since the marker is conserved,

$$w'_C \phi_C = w'_F \phi_F$$

if w_C is the dry weight of food alone consumed in unit time and w_F the dry weight of egestion of faeces alone in unit time then

$$w_C = w'_C (1 - \phi_C) \qquad w_F = w'_F (1 - \phi_F)$$

It follows that the rate of consumption of food alone can be estimated by the relation:

$$w_C = \frac{w'_F \phi_F (1 - \phi_C)}{\phi_C}$$

The rate of egestion is given by the formula:

$$w_F = w'_F (1 - \phi_F)$$

The assimilation efficiency is given by the ratio:

$$\frac{\phi_F - \phi_C}{\phi_F (1 - \phi_C)}$$

It will be noted that the assimilation efficiency can be obtained without measuring either ingestion or egestion rate.

This method has obvious advantages when, as is often the case, it is more difficult to collect and measure by difference the food consumption than to collect and weigh the faeces. The simplest marker is the organic ash content of the food itself, though the method is very inaccurate and perhaps unreliable if the amount of ash present is small. Conover (1966) has employed this method for measuring the ingestion rates of copepods.

Since the method assumes that all the ash absorbed in the food is present in the faeces it is essential to be sure that this is in fact the case; calcareous skeletal material ingested by carnivores might be absorbed in the gut and not appear in the faeces. Indeed, the same may apply to the ash component of the food of any organism. Soluble salts, which constitute much of the ash of some soft bodied animals, might be absorbed and later excreted through the skin, gills or kidney of the predator. Artificial markers added to the food are likely to be more reliable. Chromic oxide is used in such studies: it is not absorbed, it is not normally present in significant quantity in the food, and it can be accurately determined chemically.

Consumption by filter feeders

It is not difficult to measure the rates of filtration of filter feeding organisms by observing the rate of removal of small particles from fine suspensions. The subject has been recently fully reviewed by Jørgensen (1966). Most filter feeders are believed to clear a constant volume of water in unit time independently of the concentration of food particles, provided that it is not too high. Consequently, to obtain the ingestion rate the filtration rate must be multiplied by the dry weight or energy per unit volume of the suspension. This is done by separating the cells from a known volume of suspension by centrifugation or filtration, and obtaining the ash-free dry weight and the caloric content. The filtration rate is measured by following the concentration of food particles in the water containing the organism over a period of time. If C_0 is the original concentration, C_t the concentration after time t, V the volume of the water in millilitres, w the weight of active filter feeding organisms, the filtration rate per unit weight of the animal is given by:

$$F = \frac{0 \cdot 43 \, (\log_{10} C_0 - \log_{10} C_t)}{w.t} \text{ ml/unit time}$$

Care must be taken to maintain the cell suspension in a uniform state by stirring, but the stirring must be sufficiently gentle to prevent faeces and pseudofaeces from being re-suspended in the experimental vessel. It is often an advantage to place the animals on a gauze mesh in order to allow the faeces to drop through. Allowance must also be made for cell multiplication or cell sedimentation during the experiment. A satisfactory method of control is to use another suspension of the same concentration in a similar dish treated in the same way but without animals present. The concentration in the control suspension can be substituted in the above formula for C_0.

When a number of readings are taken at intervals of time, values of $\log_{10}(C_0/C_t)$ should be plotted against time, a straight line being fitted to the values either by eye or by the least squares method. The slope of this line, S,

$$S = \mathrm{d} \log_{10} \left[\frac{C_0}{C_t} \right] / \mathrm{d}t$$

can then be substituted in the above equation for

$$(\log_{10}C_0 - \log_{10}C_t)/t$$

The goodness of fit of the points to the line is an indication of the extent to which the animals have been filtering steadily and independently of cell concentration; if the line is markedly curved, the experiment should be continued until a straight line results, or be abandoned. Sometimes one or more of the individuals in the experiment has the siphons closed for the whole or part of the time. Allowance should be made for this in the calculation, by adjusting w to include active animals only. The animals must be well spaced out in an ample volume of suspension, otherwise they may filter each other's effluent, rather than the suspension.

Rates of filtration per unit weight are likely to vary with the size of the animal, the temperature and other environmental conditions such as the movement of water over the animal or the presence of food material in the water.

The concentration of particles in the suspension, usually in the form of microalgal cells from monoculture, can be measured by counting them visually in a haemocytometer cell of known area and thickness. Recently the Coulter counter, which counts electronically the change of conductivity when each cell passes through a narrow orifice, has been employed for this purpose. In using this instrument there is always the danger that mucus secreted by the animals or by the algae may upset its operation by causing the cells to clump and block the orifice.

Instead of counting cells individually, their property of light absorption may be used to measure routinely the concentration of a suspension. It will be noted that the equation for filtration rates relies on the change in the ratio of the initial to final concentrations of the particles in the suspension. Therefore any quantity proportional to concentration can be used in place of concentration. The optical density of cell suspensions is commonly used, but a linear relation should first be shown to hold good by measuring the light absorption of a series of dilutions of the suspension. Any reliable light absorptiometer is suitable for such measurements, but an instrument which incorporates a cell with a long optical path will enable a range of more dilute suspensions to be used, corresponding more closely to cell concentrations in nature.

Somewhat different methods should be used in the case of filter feeders that utilise larger organisms such as micro-crustacea as their food. Such organisms can be counted individually using a photoelectric counter of the type described by Mitson (1963). A suitable volume of sea water containing micro-crustacea is put through the apparatus and counted. It is then poured into the aquarium containing the filter feeding organisms. Many micro-crustacea, such as the nauplius larvae of *Artemia salina* which are commonly used for feeding, react to light and the water in the aquarium must therefore be continuously stirred to ensure that the food is evenly distributed. After the time allowed for feeding, the water containing food organisms is again poured through the photoelectric counter and the number of organisms ingested can be found. The dry weight and caloric content of the micro-crustaceans can be measured by applying the usual methods to a large mass of individuals strained off on plankton silk after having been counted with this apparatus.

The pigment present in the larvae may sometimes be used to measure rates of ingestion. Ritz and Crisp (1970) applied a light absorption method for measuring the uptake of micro-crustacea by barnacles, the pigment voided in the faeces being used as a marker, taking into account that only half the pigment ingested is normally voided. The photoelectric counting apparatus was used to correlate the optical density of the pigment extracted from the faeces with the number of *Artemia* nauplii consumed during the feeding period.

In making suspension rate measurements, it should be borne in mind that many filter feeders have mechanisms for rejecting part of the food, with the result that when the suspension is too concentrated for their needs, or contains unwanted material, part of the food available is not consumed. Under natural conditions, therefore, when the animal is presented with a variety of suspended particles, some more nutritious than others, the particles actually ingested may have a much higher energy content than that of the remaining particles left in the suspension, some of the less nutritious material being removed in the pseudofaeces. Similarly some suspension feeders which utilise living plants and animals damage part of their prey in addition to that which they ingest. Such behaviour complicates the measurement of ingestion rates, and poses the question whether one should regard as 'consumption' the total loss of food organisms to the predator or only that part of the suspension which ultimately passes through the oesophagus.

In view of such difficulties in measuring the actual rate of ingestion by filter feeders some authors have used the summation equation of energy flow (Equations 1 and 2, p. 202) to determine consumption or absorption by adding together all the forms of energy utilisation. (For example, Kuenzler, 1961, on *Modiolus demissus* and Jørgensen, 1962, in measuring the assimilation by larval and juvenile bivalves.)

Consumption by detritus feeders

The difficulties of measuring directly the rate of food intake by detritus feeders has led investigators to use the indirect method given above. Heywood and Edwards (1962) measured the rate of faecal production by the fresh water snail *Potamopyrgus jenkinsi* and the difference in the amount of organic carbon present in the mud and faeces, thereby allowing rates of ingestion and absorption to be calculated. The population consisted of mature animals assumed non-growing and absorption was of the same order as the sum of respiration and reproductive loss. Odum and Smalley (1959) investigating the periwinkle, *Littorina irrorata*, and Teal (1962) investigating the fiddler crab, *Uca*, adopted a similar approach.

Consumption by macro feeders

Many carnivores can be kept in the laboratory and fed quantitatively on prey organisms. Carefoot (1967a, b) fed carnivorous nudibranchs *Dendronotus frondosus* and *Archidoris britannica* on polyps of *Tubularia* and pieces of the sponge *Halichondria* respectively. The large herbivore *Aplysia punctata* was fed on various seaweeds. The direct method was applied by providing the animals with a known weight of food and weighing the remains of the food and the faeces after each day's feeding. The feeding of *Archidoris* caused the remains of the food to be badly fragmented and therefore the indirect method was applied, using the siliceous spicules as a food marker. Silica was estimated chemically in the food and faeces. Teal (1957) fed the flat worm *Phagocata* on whole oligochaetes.

A particularly ingenious example of the measurement of food uptake in the field is described by Paine (1965). The large opisthobranch *Navanax inermis* swallows its prey, consisting of other molluscs, whole. The remains of the shells of the prey in the gut of recently caught *Navanax* can be recognised and measured. By this means the energy content of each item of prey can be calculated. The rate of ingestion can then be calculated from the energy derived from an examination of gut contents, divided by the rate of gut clearance observed in aquaria.

Energy losses by respiration

The direct calorimetric measurement of the loss of energy in the form of heat resulting from biochemical oxidations and various motor activities, though appealing to the purist, has hitherto been regarded as impracticable for small animals because of the low rate of heat output. It is much more convenient to measure oxygen uptake during respiration and to convert this into the energy equivalent of the food that is presumed to have been oxidised. Strictly, therefore, the energy equivalent of a given rate of oxygen uptake will vary with the kind of food source utilised by the animal. However, by good fortune, if the food is fully oxidised, the variation in energy equivalent for a given oxygen consumption, termed the oxy-calorific coefficient, between different kinds of food is small.

Table 12.8 gives the oxy-calorific coefficients for converting oxygen uptake into energy for the three main types of nutrient. In view of the other errors involved in the measurement of energy losses through respiration, the assumption that 1 ml of oxygen at n.t.p. is equivalent to 4·8 calories is sufficiently close for all practical purposes. It is equivalent to Ivlev's (1934) value expressed in alternative units of 3·34 cal per milligram of oxygen (1 mg of oxygen at n.t.p. occupies exactly 0·7 ml).

TABLE 12.8. Oxycalorific values of different energy sources.

Source	Cals/ml oxygen at n.t.p.
Protein	4·73
Fat	4·69
Carbohydrate	5·05
Approximate mean	4·8

Some authors have converted oxygen uptake into the dry weight of food utilised, but this is not generally to be recommended. Although oxy-calorific energy equivalents are similar, the weights of nutrient corresponding to 1 ml of oxygen consumed differ greatly from one food to another. Thus if the food source contained a high proportion of fat, and had caloric content of 7·2 kcal/g dry weight (see Table 12.11) 1 ml of oxygen respired would be equivalent to only $4·6/7·2 \times 10^3$ g $= 0·65$ mg dry weight of food. On the other hand, if the food were mainly of protein and carbohydrate, with a caloric content of only 4·5 kcal/g dry weight, the dry weight equivalent of 1 ml of oxygen would be approximately 1·1 mg. Therefore, unless the food source and its chemical constitution are known, large errors of 50 per cent or more might be committed in the conversion of oxygen uptake into dry weight of food consumed.

Even the conversion of gas exchange to energy is based on two assumptions that may not always be true and are often overlooked.

First, it is assumed that all the energy released when oxygen is consumed is converted into heat or work. Should some of the energy released by the oxidation of metabolites be re-utilised to form high energy chemical bonds and the products so formed stored in the animal, the energy actually released as heat at the time will be less than the quantity calculated from the product of oxygen uptake and the normal oxy-calorific equivalent.

Secondly, if part of the energy were released through anaerobic processes, the oxygen uptake would give too low a value of energy loss. Little is known of the possible magnitude of such effects, and while anaerobic respiration would be inefficient and therefore unlikely to occur among animals living in fully aerobic environments, it is common among micro-organisms living in deoxygenated habitats, and therefore it is possible that some benthic metazoans inhabiting low oxygen environments may also display facultative anaerobiosis.

All laboratory methods of measuring respiration suffer from the defect that the animal is to a greater or lesser degree constrained in an unnatural situation during measurements. The respiration observed may in consequence be quite different from that which takes place in the natural environment, particularly in the case of active animals. In an attempt to correct this, Mann (1965) and Carefoot (1967b) found it necessary to double the observed respiration loss from laboratory experiments in order to balance the energy budget. This is an arbitrary procedure not to be generally recommended, but it indicates the present unsatisfactory state of means of measuring this large and important item in the energy flow equation. The errors are unlikely to reside in the methods of measuring oxygen uptake itself and, indeed, effort devoted to increasing the accuracy of respiration measurement in the laboratory is probably misdirected. All recognised methods suitable for the organism are likely to be sufficiently accurate. The choice of method should, therefore, rest mainly on the likelihood that the animal will be able to behave naturally in a respiration chamber.

The main effect of bringing animals into the laboratory is to alter their activity; activity changes may result in several-fold changes in metabolic rate (e.g. Newell and Northcroft, 1967). Thus Mann (1965) finds that when fish are captured there is an initial burst of activity followed by a fall, especially when starved, with peaks at dawn and dusk. Many marine organisms, such as mussels and barnacles, display 'metabolic economy' when kept in the laboratory without food.

Furthermore, respiration may vary diurnally, especially in those animals that display overt rhythms, while the illumination and water movement to which the animal is exposed can change respiratory rates significantly. Whether the animal is in air or in water, and whether it is stimulated by the presence of food odours can also profoundly alter its activity.

Even if, through exceptional co-operation on the part of the animal, these factors can be assessed in laboratory experiments, it is difficult to see how activity can be monitored in natural populations. To overcome such difficulties, Odum (1961) and Mishima and Odum (1963) have suggested a possible field method for determining respiratory loss. It is based on the possibility that the rate of loss of the more firmly bound fraction of radio-labelled zinc (Zn^{65}) is proportional to metabolic rate and will serve as an integrator of losses through respiration. Unfortunately, the usefulness of the method has not yet been established.

In laboratory experiments the animals are usually unstimulated and so maintained in a state of activity that is fairly constant and approaches that of 'basal metabolism'. Under these conditions, two variables influence uptake and should be taken into account in making predictions:

1   the effect of temperature
2   the effect of body weight.

If measurements are made on animals of various sizes over a range of temperature and the logarithm of rate of uptake of oxygen, q, or better, the logarithm of the rate of energy loss, Q, are plotted against the logarithm of the weight, w, at each temperature, a linear relation is usually found.

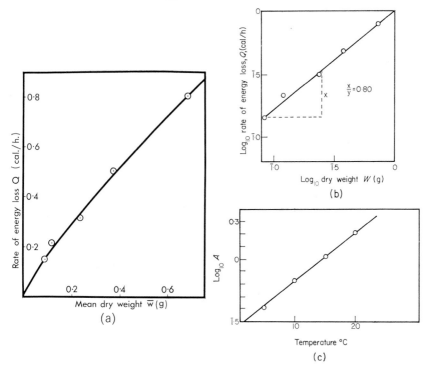

Figure 12.9(a). Respiratory energy loss, Q, as a function of dry weight, $\bar{w}$ (data from Table 12.9A).

(b) Logarithmic plot of energy loss on dry weight at 15°C to obtain the equation $Q = A\bar{w}^b$, $A = 1.05$, $b = 0.80$.

(c) Plot of $\log_{10}A$ against temperature θ for estimating A at any given temperature.

Table 12.9A gives an example of such data in which wet weight is converted to dry weight, and oxygen uptake to energy loss. Fig. 12.9(b) shows the fitting of the equation $Q = A\bar{w}^b$. The value of the constant A is dependent on temperature, but the exponent b is usually constant with a value of 0·7–0·8. The assessment of respiration loss is not very sensitive to small changes in b.

If $\log_{10}$ of A is plotted against temperature, θ, a straight line can usually be drawn; this helps in evaluating A at different temperatures. An example is given in Table 12.9B and Fig. 12.9c.

To apply such results to estimate the energy loss by respiration in a field population, the population must first be divided into n weight classes, and

Table 12.9. Computation of energy loss by respiration for a population.

A. *Data for oxygen uptake in relation to dry weight* $\theta = 15°C$.

$\bar{w}$ (dry wt.)$=0.15 \times \bar{w}'$ (wet wt.)

Q (cal)$=4.8 \times q$ (ml oxygen absorbed)

Mean wet wt. $\bar{w}'$ g	Mean oxygen uptake, q ml h^{-1}	Mean dry wt. $\bar{w}=0.15\,\bar{w}'$ g	Mean energy loss $Q=4.8\,q$ cal h^{-1}	$\log_{10}\bar{w}$	$\log_{10}Q$
0·56	0·029	0·084	0·140	$\bar{2}$·92	$\bar{1}$·15
0·79	0·045	0·119	0·216	$\bar{1}$·08	$\bar{1}$·33
1·58	0·066	0·236	0·316	$\bar{1}$·37	$\bar{1}$·50
2·50	0·105	0·375	0·504	$\bar{1}$·57	$\bar{1}$·70
4·50	0·166	0·675	0·798	$\bar{1}$·76	$\bar{1}$·90

Equation to line (Fig. 12.9a) $\log_{10}Q=\log_{10}A_\theta+b\log_{10}\bar{w}$

$\log_{10}A_\theta=0.02,\ b=0.8,\ \therefore Q=1.05\,\bar{w}^{0.8}$

B. *Data from similar experiments at* $\theta=20°$, $10°$ *and* $5°C$ *give*

$\theta\,(°C)$	$\log_{10}A$	b	
20	0·21	0·78	Values of b all$=0.80$ within
15	0·02	0·80	experimental error.
10	$\bar{1}$·85	0·81	Fig. 12.9c shows $\log_{10}A$ plotted
5	$\bar{1}$·61	0·79	against θ.

C. *Computation of losses during the period* 21.VI–31.VII.

Time $\triangle t=41$ days$=984$ h.

Temperature range$=15.6 - 17.8$, mean temperature $\bar{\theta}=16.5°C$.

$\log A$ for $\theta=16.5°C=0.07$ (Fig. 12.9c) $A=1.17$.

Population size distribution:

No. of size class	Size range (dry wt), g	Mean dry wt. $(\bar{w}_i)$ g	$\bar{w}_i^{0.8}$	Frequency of size class f_i m^{-2}	$f_i\bar{w}_i^{0.8}$
1	0·0–0·2	0·13	0·195	80	15·6
2	0·2–0·4	0·30	0·38	122	46·4
3	0·4–0·6	0·52	0·59	96	56·7
4	0·6+	0·78	0·81	12	9·7
				$\sum\limits_{0}^{4} f_i\bar{w}_i^{\,0.8}=$	128·4

$A_j\triangle t_j\sum\limits_{0}^{4} f_i\bar{w}_i^{0.8}=1.17\times984\times128.4=1.48\times10^5$ cal m$^{-2}=148$ kcal m^{-2}.

TABLE 12.9—*continued*

D. *Sum of respiration losses for the year* $R = \overset{m}{\underset{0}{\Sigma}} A_j \triangle t_j \left[\overset{n}{\underset{0}{\Sigma}} f_i \bar{w}_i^{0.8} \right]$

Dates of time interval $\triangle t$	$\triangle t$ (days)	$\triangle t$ (h)	Mean temperature $\bar{\theta}$ (°C)	$\log_{10} A$ (Fig. 12.9c)	A	$\overset{n}{\underset{0}{\Sigma}} f_i \bar{w}_i^{0.8}$	$\triangle t_j A_j \Sigma f_i \bar{w}_i^{0.8}$
21.VI–31.VII	41	984	16·5	0·07	1·17	128·4	148
1.VIII–19.IX	50	1,200	14·2	$\bar{1}$·97	0·93	116·6	129
20.IX–20.X	31	744	11·0	$\bar{1}$·86	0·72	115·3	62
21.X–30.XI	41	984	7·6	$\bar{1}$·73	0·54	107·2	57
1.XII–3.III	93	2,232	5·2	$\bar{1}$·64	0·44	98·2	96
4.III–10.IV	38	912	7·0	$\bar{1}$·705	0·51	90·6	42
11.IV–10.V	31	744	10·3	$\bar{1}$·835	0·68	152·3	77
11.V–20.VI	40	960	13·4	$\bar{1}$·92	0·83	138·0	110
Total 365		8,760				Total annual energy loss	721 kcal m^{-2}

the frequency f_i of each determined. Age classes or length classes can be substituted for weight classes if the mean weight $\bar{w}_i$ of each class can be found and if the range of weights in each class is not large. When the respiratory energy loss is required over a long period, such as a year, the summation must be divided into m separate periods during which there is no great change in temperature or population structure. For each such period of interval Δt_j the mean temperature $\bar{\theta}$ must be found and the value of A_j obtained by interpolation of $\log_{10} A$ on θ (using a graph such as Fig. 12.9c). For each size group within each period the values of f_i are each multiplied by $\bar{w}_i^b$ and summed as shown in Table 12.9C to obtain

$$\overset{n}{\underset{0}{\Sigma}} f_i \bar{w}_i^b$$

Then each summation must be multiplied by $A_j \Delta t_j$, appropriate to the temperature and time interval of the period, as shown in Table 12.9D. The same units of time in which A was determined (here A is expressed as cal h^{-1}g$^{-0.8}$) must be used for Δt (h). The resulting summation represents the estimate of annual energy loss by respiration.

$$R = \sum_{0}^{m} A_j \Delta t_j \left(\sum_{0}^{n} f_i \bar{w}_i^b \right)$$

Methods of measuring respiration in the laboratory are given in a later section.

Measurement of oxygen uptake in the field

Bottom deposits contain large numbers of smaller metazoa, protozoa and bacteria which together form an important factor in the benthic ecosystem. To enumerate and measure the respiratory activity of each species in turn would be impossible. Nor can the deposit be studied in the laboratory without disturbing its structure, and this in turn would change the diffusion gradients and oxygen levels throughout, profoundly altering those trophic changes that are diffusion limited. Moreover, the contribution of micro organisms to the energy flow of benthic deposits is likely to be considerably greater than that of the macro-fauna. *In situ* methods are therefore imperative.

Teal (1957) and Odum (1957a, b) have attempted such measurements by enclosing small areas of freshwater benthos in light and dark glass cylinders, funnels and bell jars and measuring changes in oxygen content of the water layers immediately above the bottom. Patmatmat (1966, 1968) inserted bell jars with plastic stirrers into marine deposits and sampled at intervals through vaccine type stoppers. The rate of oxygen uptake in the dark reported by Teal was equivalent to a loss of energy of the order of 20–50 kcal m^{-2} per month or an absorption of 4–10 mg m^{-2} h^{-1} of oxygen. Patmatmat obtained somewhat larger values of 25–30 mg oxygen m^{-2} h^{-1}. Such rates of uptake are sufficient to deplete of oxygen a layer of water 2 cm deep in about 4 hours. Hence measurable changes within a single tidal cycle are possible if only a few centimetres depth of water are enclosed in the chamber.

A more elegant method which overcomes the abnormally static conditions caused by enclosing the overlying water has been described by Patmatmat (1965). A perspex channel 100 cm long, 2 cm wide and 1 cm deep was placed over the substratum and oxygen levels measured at each end while a slow flow of seawater passed through the channel. The author claimed that the flow method agreed with the bell jar method, but the results were not sufficiently precise to allow a critical comparison of respiration rates with and without water flow.

In situ methods are not yet in a sufficiently advanced state to allow a standard method to be put forward, but efforts to develop such a method are urgently needed since it would have the potential of giving true measurements of benthos respiration under natural conditions.

The reservation made on p. 257 concerning the use, under inappropriate circumstances, of the oxy-calorific equivalent for aerobic conditions to convert oxygen uptake into energy loss, applies with special force to *in situ* measurements of benthic deposits. These deposits contain a high proportion of micro organisms living under conditions of depleted oxygenation. This whole subject requires much pioneer research work and is quite unsuited to any routine approach.

Laboratory methods for productivity measurements

Estimation of ash-free dry weight

Three main methods for removing water are available:

1   heating in an oven to about 100°C under atmospheric pressure,
2   drying *in vacuo* at lower temperatures up to 60°C,
3   freeze-drying.

When the sole objective of drying is to obtain a measure of the water content, and when the dry tissue is not needed for any other purpose, all three methods would give similar results, provided that sufficient time is allowed for complete drying. Larger organisms obviously require longer to dry to constant weight, and therefore a test should always be made to ascertain the minimum time for complete drying before a routine series of measurements is undertaken.

Freeze-drying is slow, requires special apparatus, and up to 5 per cent of the water in the tissue is very difficult to remove by this method. Oven heating at 100°C may cause losses of the volatile tissue components. Thus, if the temperature during the drying rises to 110°C a loss of volatile components of soft tissues of up to 10 per cent by weight in 48 hours may result (Giese, 1967). The disadvantage of gentle drying at room temperature is that the tissues may slowly autolyse.

Drying *in vacuo* at 60°C, a temperature which inactivates most enzymes yet does not cause serious loss through volatilisation, offers a good compromise and the dry material so obtained is usually suitable for bomb calorimetry. It is very important, in carrying out a seasonal survey, to ensure that every drying operation is carried out under identical conditions. Otherwise one set of samples may experience a greater loss of weight which may be erroneously interpreted as a seasonal effect, such as a change in condition factor.

When the objective of drying is to preserve material for further biochemical study, much more careful attention must be given to the choice of method. In general the gentlest method, freeze-drying, is to be recommended or vacuum desiccation of initially frozen tissue over sulphuric acid or calcium chloride in the cold. Some workers add 0·1 ml of 10 per cent trichloracetic acid solution to each gram wet weight of tissue prior to drying, in order to inactivate the enzymes. If gentle drying fails to remove all the water, a small aliquot of the partially dry tissue can be sacrificed for complete removal of water by a more vigorous method to ascertain the residual proportion of water by weight.

Dried materials awaiting further treatment are best stored sealed in a deep freeze or, if kept at room temperature, under continuous drying in a desiccator.

After drying, the ash content, consisting of such substances as sea-water salts, silica, calcium phosphate and carbonate, is determined by burning off the organic matter in a muffle furnace. Four to six hours at 500–600°C is recommended to ensure the complete destruction of all organic matter.

The main error in determining ash is caused by partial volatilisation of components of the inorganic fraction, notably loss of carbon dioxide from carbonates and chemically bound water from silicates. If the total ash weight or the calcium carbonate content of the ash is known to be small, these errors may be neglected. If the carbonate content is large and the ash weight constitutes a considerable fraction of the total dry weight, as in molluscs, barnacles, echinoderms etc. the loss of weight on ignition through removal of carbon dioxide could in theory rise to 44 per cent of the ash weight of the calcium carbonate present, resulting in a serious under-estimate of the ash. A different procedure in these cases must therefore be adopted.

Where it is practicable to remove the soft tissues from the shell without loss, as in bivalve molluscs and some gastropods, the dry organic weight of the body and of the shell can be measured separately. The former presents no difficulty. The dry ash-free weight of the shell can be found by decalcifying it in dilute hydrochloric acid, but the vigour of the effervescence may dissipate the delicate particles of shell tissue. To obviate this, calcium chelating agents in mildly acid media may be substituted for dilute acid; for example, a mixture of ethylene diamine tetracetic acid and sodium formate. The residual organic matter of the shell can be filtered off, dried and weighed on glass fibre filter paper, the tare weight of which has been previously determined.

Where the shell or skeleton cannot be mechanically separated from the tissues, for example where it is in the form of a number of small plates as in barnacles and echinoderms, it can often be separated by chemical cleaning with attendant destruction of the soft tissues. The whole animal, after being dried and weighed, is boiled in 10 per cent by weight aqueous caustic alkali for up to one hour, a procedure that destroys all the organic tissue except for a small amount of refractory material such as slips of chitin, threads of keratin etc. which are usually of negligible weight. The cleaned calcium carbonate plates or ossicles should then be well washed free of caustic alkali and of any loosely attached organic material, dried and weighed. This procedure may not remove all the organic matter from the interior of the shell, but the organic weight compared with that of the inorganic shell is usually negligible. Similar sources of error in measuring ash weight may be encountered in animals containing skeletons of hydrated silica which lose water at high temperature. This problem is discussed by Paine (1964).

When the calcium carbonate cannot be separated by either of the above methods, for example when measuring the ash weight of a mud or sand with a high proportion of shell, the dried material should first be weighed, then treated with hydrochloric acid until effervescence has completely ceased in order to remove carbonate, washed, dried and re-weighed to obtain the weight of carbonate removed. It can then be ashed at 600°C for 6 hours to obtain the remaining ash in the usual way. A small amount of organic material may be washed out in the removal of carbonate; therefore this procedure should be adopted only if necessary because of the large amount of carbonate present.

Measurement of biomass in terms of nitrogen content
Some authors have used nitrogen content as a measure of biomass (p. 200). The classical method of measurement of nitrogen is the Kjeldahl, in which the tissue is digested in concentrated sulphuric acid containing a catalyst; copper sulphate, selenium oxide and mercuric oxides are used. The operation is carried out by raising to boiling point or higher, in a sealed tube. After digestion, excess of strong alkali is added and the ammonia released is driven off either by passing steam through a condenser unit (Markham, 1942) or in a small Conway distillation cell at room temperature (Conway, 1947), and estimated by titration or other means. Details of methods are given in Barnes

(1959, pp. 148–150). Not all the organic nitrogen is converted to ammonia, but the substances that resist conversion are not usually present in large quantities in living tissues. Nevertheless, it is advisable to report figures so obtained as 'Kjeldahl nitrogen' rather than 'total nitrogen'. If only the nitrogen contained in the protein of the tissue is required, the sample should be treated first with trichloracetic acid to precipitate the protein while allowing most of the non-protein nitrogenous compounds to dissolve. The precipitate is then separated and used for Kjeldahl analysis. The protein: nitrogen ratio in most animal tissues is close to 6·25; hence the protein content of the sample can be approximated by multiplying the protein Kjeldahl nitrogen value by 6·25. Giese (1967) should be consulted for a critical review of methods.

Measurement of caloric content

The caloric content of a substance is defined as the energy released during complete combustion of one gram of the dry material. The caloric content of a dry tissue homogenate made from the whole animal is an important variable in energy flow studies which enables the biomass, expressed as dry weight, to be converted into biomass expressed as energy.

Lipids have a high energy content whereas proteins and carbohydrates have only about half that of lipids (Table 12.10). Consequently, organisms with considerable reserves in the form of fat have a high average caloric content; so also do those stages in the life history which store fat, such as the seeds, eggs and over-wintering adults. Seasonal changes in caloric content must be allowed for when converting dry weight into energy.

Few animals have an average caloric content outside the range 4·5 to 7·5 kcal g^{-1}, the majority lie between 5 and 6 kcal g^{-1} (Slobodkin and Richman, 1961). Examples of caloric contents of a number of organisms are given in Table 12.11. These values are all on a dry weight basis.

In fisheries work, some authorities have assumed a roughly constant value for caloric content. Winberg (1956) suggests a value of 1 kcal g^{-1} wet weight (including the skeleton) for fish, a figure supported by averaging the caloric contents listed by Spector (1956) for a variety of fish flesh. However, they range from 2·2 kcal g^{-1} for salmon to 0·7 kcal g^{-1} for flounder, indicating how far the estimate may be in error for a particular case. Calculation of the above on a dry weight basis gives rather more uniform values averaging 5 kcal g^{-1} dry weight in agreement with the range stated above. Nevertheless, it is clearly advisable to measure the caloric content for any species whose

TABLE 12.10. Average caloric content of biochemcal components (Brody, 1945).

Component	Caloric content kcal/g
Carbohydrate	4·1
Protein	5·65
Fat	9·45

TABLE 12.11. Caloric contents of various organisms in kcal/g ash-free dry weight (=cal/mg).

Material	Caloric content kcal/g	Reference
Millipore filter membrane	3·1	Comita and Schindler (1963)
Ensis minor (bivalve)	3·5	Slobodkin (1962)
Modiolus demissus (bivalve)	4·5	Kuenzler (1961)
Sthenelais articulata (polychaete)	4·7	Slobodkin (1962)
Pandorina sp (green alga)	4·9	Comita and Schindler (1963)
Microcystis sp (blue-green alga)	4·8	,,
Eupagurus bernhardus Zoea (hermit crab)	5·3	Pandian and Heinz-Schumann
Artemia salina nauplius (brine shrimp)	5·9	Paffenhofer (1967) (1967)
Crangon vulgaris egg, undeveloped (shrimp)	6·4	Pandian (1967)
Calanus finmarchicus and *C. hyperboreus* (copepods)	7·4	Slobodkin (1962)
Egg yolk, birds (various)	8·0	,,

productivity is being studied. A useful compendium of calorific contents has been prepared by Cummins (1967).

Direct measurement by calorimetry. Heats of combustion are measured in bomb calorimeters, made usually of stainless steel and filled with oxygen under pressure. A bomb calorimeter of the usual size employed for biological work will burn 1 g or less of material; the Parr Instrument Company manufacture such an instrument for energy flow studies and its operation is described in the Parr Manual (Parr Instrument Company, 1960). For some biological work a sufficient quantity of dry tissue is not easily available and micro-bomb calorimeters must be used instead. Their principle and operation is the same. The micro-bomb calorimeter designed by Phillipson (1964) has a capacity of 8 ml and takes samples of 5–10 mg (Fig. 12.10). The stainless

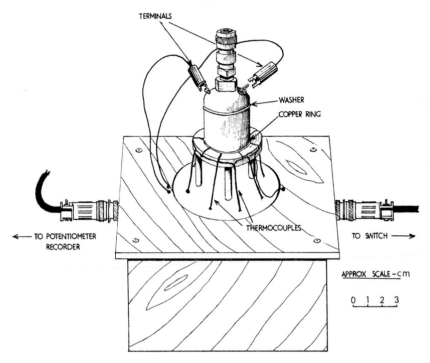

TERMINALS

WASHER

COPPER RING

THERMOCOUPLES

←— TO POTENTIOMETER
     RECORDER

TO SWITCH —→

APPROX SCALE – cm

0   1   2   3

Figure 12.10. Micro-bomb calorimeter.

steel bomb rests in good thermal contact with a copper ring provided with 8 electrically insulated thermocouple junctions. The bomb stands on an aluminium base which acts as the cold junction. The temperature changes resulting from each firing are registered on a recording potentiometer (Fig. 12.11a).

Material for combustion must be thoroughly dried and ground up to form a homogeneous powder which can be compacted into a small pellet by means of a press available for this purpose. The pellet is weighed and placed on the firing device, held by the fine platinum wire through which an electric charge is later passed to ignite the pellet. The platinum wire needs frequent replacement as it is liable to fuse during combustion. A small quantity of water is placed in the bomb which is flushed with oxygen from a cylinder. The bomb is then filled with oxygen under a pressure of 25–30 atmospheres; this operation raises its temperature and it must therefore be cooled before firing.

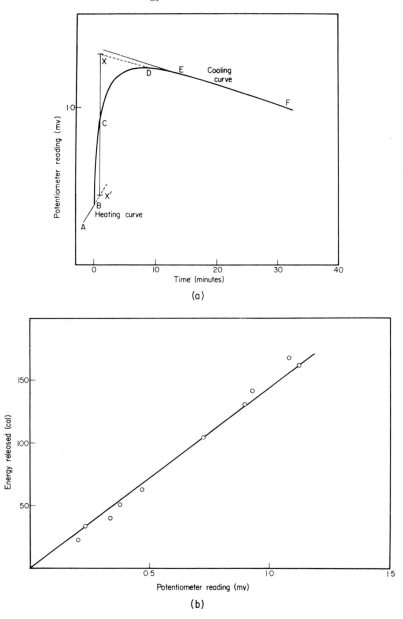

Figure 12.11. (a) Potentiometer recording obtained from micro-bomb calorimeter. (b) Calibration using benzoic acid.

It is most important that the specimen should burn completely and smoothly. If it burns too fast or too slowly some improvement can be achieved by compounding a known amount of benzoic acid of standard thermochemical quality into the pellet. If sputtering tends to occur, a firing chamber with a light lid may become necessary. Liquids such as oils can be burnt if contained in small inflammable capsules and small organisms can be dried and burned on Millipore filters. Obviously the capsules and filters must be calibrated beforehand for their caloric content. If the specimen is not fired by the discharge, the current passed through the platinum wire should be increased.

A successful firing results in a sudden change in the potential of the thermocouples which can be read with a sensitive potentiometer or, better, a continuous record made of the thermocouple potential (Fig. 12.11a). The latter allows a cooling curve correction to be applied. The potentiometer reading is calibrated by burning weighed pellets of benzoic acid, the caloric content of which is known to be of the order of 6320 kcal g^{-1}, the actual value for each batch being provided by the manufacturer (Fig. 12.11b). Addition of benzoic acid to the pellet or the calorific value of any Millipore filter or capsule must obviously be allowed for in the calculation. An example of results is given in Table 12.12.

Golley (1961) described small corrections for the heat generated by the acid produced and by the fuse wire but, according to Paine (1964), these corrections amount to less than 1 per cent of the heat measured and are negligible. When tissues or materials containing a considerable quantity of chalk or hydrated silica are burned, carbon dioxide and water may be lost. The dissociation is endothermic hence the caloric content of such material may be seriously under-estimated.

It is possible to attempt to weigh the ash after combustion but often the vigour of the reaction disperses the ash around the walls of the bomb and leads to incorrect measurements. It is therefore best to ignite another sample of the material separately by the method described on p. 263 to obtain the ash weight. If the inorganic material constituting the ash loses water or carbon dioxide on ignition and this is not allowed for, the apparent dry ash-free weight of the organic material will be over-estimated and the caloric content thereby further under-estimated. In some nudibranchs, errors from this cause and associated endothermic reactions can be as high as 50–60 per cent (Paine, 1966). Consequently, when the tissue or deposit contains large

TABLE 12.12. Estimation of caloric content by direct calorimetry.

A. *Calibration of micro-bomb calorimeter.*

I	II	III
Weight of benzoic acid pellet (mg)	Millivolts recorded on potentiometer after correcting for cooling	Calories liberated (1 mg≡6·319 cal) cal
3·52	0·202	22·2
5·34	0·233	33·7
6·29	0·337	39·7
8·10	0·379	51·2
9·96	0·469	62·9
16·45	0·724	104·0
20·64	0·896	130·4
22·34	0·930	141·1
25·62	1·118	161·9
26·50	1·080	167·5

Columns II and III are plotted in Fig. 12.11b, giving the relation
1 mv≡144 cal.

B. *Calculation of caloric content of molluscan eggs.*
Dry weight of eggs 23·18 mg
Ash weight (by separate experiment)=11·0% of dry weight
Ash free dry weight=20·64 mg
Millivolts recorded =0·88 mv (value of xx′ in Fig. 12.11a)

$$\text{Calories released per ash-free gram} = \frac{0{\cdot}88 \times 144}{20{\cdot}64} \times 1{,}000 = 6{,}130 \text{ cals/g}$$

quantities of inorganic material, the caloric content can be measured more reliably by the chemical methods below.

Chemical methods. The energy content of marine sediments and of faeces deposited by sediment feeders is likely to be of particular importance in benthos work. Dry sediments do not burn well and if large amounts of benzoic acid have to be added to ensure complete combustion the calorific values obtained will be based on a small difference between the heat evolved by the benzoic acid and sediment combined and that calculated for the benzoic acid alone. The error will therefore be considerable in comparison with the quantity that is being measured. Moreover, as described above, the presence of an excess of inorganic matter may lead to endothermic changes during burning which invalidate measurement of the heat of combustion.

An alternative to calorimetry is the use of an indirect chemical method. Two approaches are possible, the first to measure the total oxidisable matter in the sample and apply an appropriate oxy-calorific coefficient to convert oxygen demand into calories. Secondly, it is possible to analyse the biochemical components and multiply each by an appropriate caloric content.

Measurement of caloric content from total oxidisable organic matter. This method consists of treating the dried material with an oxidising agent, usually wet oxidation by dichromate, until the reaction is as complete as possible. The amount of oxidising agent remaining is then determined by back titration or spectrophotometry. There are three weaknesses in this method.

(a) not all the organic matter, especially the protein, is oxidised. Twenty to thirty per cent of the protein present may be able to resist oxidation by dichromate (and iodate) causing an under-estimate of biologically oxidisable material. Nearly all the methods based on the original Walkley and Black dichromate wet oxidation procedure therefore embody an arbitrary factor ranging from 1·3 to 1·8 to allow for complete oxidation. Since protein is the main source of error, it is more accurate to apply a correction based on the amount of protein nitrogen, which can be measured separately, rather than to apply a universal correction (see p. 265). The assumption that 80 per cent of this fraction is oxidised generally leads to results in good agreement with those obtained by direct calorimetry.

(b) Chlorides, ferrous salts and finely divided carbon in deposits (Southward, 1952) can act as reducing agents sometimes causing a serious over-estimate of the oxidisable matter.

The chloride error can be eliminated by washing the material with sodium sulphate solution or by the addition of silver sulphate. Sulphide and ferrous ions can be eliminated by aerating in the presence of dilute hydrochloric acid. Nothing can be done to prevent the oxidation of fine carbon deposits since these are, in fact, particles of oxidisable carbon. They will not be digested by the animal and should therefore appear in its faeces. Consequently, if this method is used to measure the absorption of energy by the animal the effect of oxidisable carbon in both food and faeces will tend to cancel out.

An interesting alternative approach to obtain the quantity of organic matter likely to be utilised by deposit feeders has been suggested by George (1964). The percentage of organic matter in the deposit digested by enzymes is measured in place of the organic matter oxidised chemically.

(c) The wet oxidation procedure estimates oxygen demand and must be converted to caloric content by an arbitrary factor.

As shown on p. 257, the energy of combustion per unit of oxygen consumed (oxy-calorific coefficient) is very similar for all the usual nutrients utilised by higher organisms. Hence the error caused by ignorance of the constitution of the organic constituents is not likely to be very serious.

Various forms of the dichromate method differing in detail have been adapted for marine work (Strickland and Parsons, 1965; Russell-Hunter *et al.*, 1968). Hughes (1970) has used an iodate oxidation method which avoids most of the errors mentioned in (a) and (b) above and has shown that the results are consistent with those obtained by direct calorimetry. The method of calculation of caloric content from a suitable wet oxidation method is given in Table 12.13.

Measurement of caloric content by analysis of biochemical components. It would be excessively time-consuming to analyse an organism or organic deposit into major biochemical constituents solely for the purpose of estimating caloric content. However, if the protein, carbohydrate and lipid fractions are required for some other purpose, for example in describing seasonal metabolic changes, the caloric content can be estimated from these results using the average values quoted by Brody (1945) and given in Table 12.10.

The estimate of the lipid present requires greater accuracy than that of the other two components because of its much higher energy content. The standard method in the past has been ether extraction by the Soxhlet procedure, but the lipid can be removed from ground homogenised dry tissue more completely by methanol-chloroform extraction in the cold. Some non-lipid material may also be extracted by such polar solvents. Ansell and Trevallion (1967) followed Bligh and Dyer's (1959) wet extraction procedure which is probably the most reliable method for molluscan tissues. The lipid extraction and evaporation should strictly be carried out under nitrogen to prevent oxidation, with a trace of anti-oxidant added as a further precaution (e.g. 2.6 di tert.-butyl 4-methyl phenol). The lipid extracted can be measured gravimetrically, or estimated by direct oxidation with dichromate. In the former

TABLE 12.13. Computation of caloric content by wet oxidation.

A sample weighing 226 mg which, by a previous ashing was known to contain 9·7% ash, was oxidised by potassium iodate in sulphuric acid. Free iodine produced by reduction was removed by boiling and bubbling air through the digest. The remaining iodate was estimated by addition of KI, and titration of liberated iodine with 0·1 N thiosulphate.

The titre difference between a blank and the sample enables the iodate reduced to be estimated:

3·567 mg iodate≡1 ml of 0·1 N thiosulphate≡0·6667 mg oxygen.

The observed difference in thiosulphate titre between experimental and blank for 1/20 aliquot was 20·25 ml.

Oxygen uptake by sample=20×20·25×0·6667 mg=270 mg.

Heat liberated by oxidation, using oxycalorific equivalent of 3·34 cal/mg oxygen= 270×3·34=902 calories.

We shall now assume that potassium iodate oxidises only 80% of protein present (Hughes, 1970).

Protein content (estimated as described in Table 12.14)=45% by weight (total wt. including ash).

Protein not oxidised=20% of 45%=9% by wt.=226×0·09 mg=20·34 mg.

Caloric content of protein=5·65 cal/mg.

Caloric content of unoxidised part of sample 20·34×5·65=115 cal.

Therefore, the total heat which would be liberated by complete oxidation would be 902+115=1,017 cal.

Dry ash free weight of sample=226×91·3/100 mg=0·205 g.

Therefore caloric content per ash free $g = \dfrac{1017}{0·205} = 4961$ cal/g.

case (Table 12.14A) the result must be multiplied by the assumed caloric content of lipid (9·45 cal g^{-1}, Table 12.10). In the latter case the caloric content of the lipid is obtained by multiplying the oxygen equivalent determined by dichromate oxidation by the oxy-calorific coefficient (3·34 cal mg^{-1} equivalent of oxygen absorbed) (Table 12.14B).

The estimation of protein and non-protein nitrogen is dealt with on p. 265.

Direct estimation of carbohydrate is difficult (see Giese, 1967) and, in any case, the sum of the weights of all three components, fat, protein, and carbohydrate, when separately determined is generally considerably less than the original dry ash-free weight. Therefore, in the estimation of caloric content, it is best to measure lipid, estimate protein as 6·25 × protein nitrogen, and assume that carbohydrate makes up the difference as shown in the calculations illustrated in Table 12.14. The approximation is justified because the caloric content of most organic materials including carbohydrates is similar, with the exception of fat (Table 12.10).

TABLE 12.14. Examples of calculation of caloric content from biochemical analysis.

A. 10·25 g dry tissue on extraction and evaporation gave 0·82 g lipid.

Therefore lipid content $= \dfrac{0·82}{10·25} = 8·0$ per cent.

1·07 g of dry tissue treated with T.C.A. and precipitate digested by Kjeldhal method, ammonia evolved titrated with 0·2 N HCl; Titre $= 26·1$ ml.
1 Equivalent HCl $\equiv 14$ g protein N.
  26·1 ml of 0·2 N HCl $\equiv 14 \times 0·2 \times 26·2 \times 10^{-3}$ g N
  $= 7·3 \times 10^{-2}$ g protein N.
This corresponds to $6·25 \times 7·3 \times 10^{-2}$ g protein
  $= 0·456$ g protein.
Protein content $= 45$ per cent.
'Carbohydrate content' by difference $= 47$ per cent.
Caloric content $= 0·08 \times 9·45 + 0·45 \times 56·5 + 0·47 \times 4·1$
  $= 0·76 + 2·54 + 1·93 = 5·23$ cal/g.

B. 10·25 g tissue extracted as above, but lipid estimated by dichromate oxidation.
  20 ml of a solution of 5·15 g/l potassium dichromate added; back titration showed 3·2 ml used up in oxidising lipid. 294 g of potassium dichromate yield 48 g oxygen.

Therefore oxygen equivalent of lipid $= 3·2 \times \dfrac{5·15}{1,000} \times \dfrac{48}{294} \times 1,000$ mg $= 2·69$ mg.

Caloric content of lipid fraction $= 2·69 \times \dfrac{3·34}{10·25} = 0·82$ cal/g

Per cent by wt. of lipid $= 0·82$ cal/g $\div$ caloric content assumed $= 0·82/9·45 = 8·7$ per cent.
Protein fraction $= 45$ per cent by weight (see Example 1).
'Carbohydrate' fraction $= 46·3$ per cent by weight (by difference).
Caloric content of tissue $= 0·82 + 2·54 + 0·463 \times 4·1 = 5·20$ cal/g.

Measurement of oxygen uptake in the laboratory

Oxygen uptake is measured either as millilitres of oxygen at n.t.p. or as milligrams of oxygen absorbed in unit time. The hour is the convenient unit of time for respiration experiments. Since volume measurements are made by the majority of respirometers, millilitres of oxygen at n.t.p. is the more widely employed unit. Volumes must of course be corrected to n.t.p. by taking the temperature, θ (°C) and barometric pressure, p (mm mercury), at the time of the experiment as well as the volume absorbed, V (ml).

$$\text{Volume at n.t.p.} = V \cdot \frac{273}{273+\theta} \cdot \frac{p}{760} \text{ ml}$$

Results obtained by chemical methods are more usually given as mg h^{-1} oxygen. It is useful to remember the conversion factor:

0·7 ml oxygen at n.t.p. = 1 mg oxygen by weight.

Numerous satisfactory methods exist for the measurement of oxygen uptake, the selection of method being mainly determined by the medium in which the animal is kept during measurement. Otherwise the choice is mainly a matter of convenience, scale, availability, and suitability of the method to the animal being studied.

For measurement with animals in water

If the animal is placed in water in a sealed vessel and the oxygen concentration measured initially and after a lapse of time, the amount taken up by the animal can be measured from the change in concentration. The concentration drop should not be excessive; for animals living in a normal aerobic environment the experimental oxygen tension should not be allowed to fall below 0·6 of the saturation level in air at the temperature of the experiment. If it should do so, respiration rate may be reduced or the animal's behaviour and consequent oxygen demand upset. Nor, however, should the concentration change be too small, since it must be large enough to be measured with reasonable accuracy. The medium should therefore be fully saturated, or better, slightly supersaturated with oxygen at the start of the experiment and fall ideally to about 80 per cent of saturation. In order to allow for the production or uptake of oxygen by micro-organisms in the water or on the surface of the vessel, the experiment should include a control vessel of exactly similar form and origin as the experimental vessel but without the animal. If the volume of the experimental vessel is V, and the concentration of oxygen in the water x_1 units ml^{-1} initially and x_2 units ml^{-1} finally, the uptake, q, is given by:

$$q = V(x_1 - x_2)$$

Alternatively, a known constant flow of water can be maintained over the animal with a bypass of approximately equal flow through an empty vessel identical with that containing the animal, so that the differences in oxygen levels between the inflow and outflow of each vessel will give the respiration attributable to the animal alone. If x_0 is the oxygen concentration at the inflow, x_1 at the exit of the experimental vessel, and x_2 at the exit of the control vessel, the flows being $(dV/dt)_1$ and $(dV/dt)_2$ respectively, then the oxygen uptake is given by the equation:

$$q = (x_0 - x_1)(dV/dt)_1 - (x_0 - x_2)(dV/dt)_2$$

The continuous flow method has the advantage of maintaining a fairly steady oxygen tension around the animal and more closely resembles natural conditions. Furthermore, oxygen tension can be continuously recorded by an appropriate piece of apparatus such as the galvanic oxygen electrode or a dropping mercury electrode, and if the amount of dead space within the apparatus is small, recorded changes in oxygen uptake can be related to observed changes in the animal's activity. Both the sealed vessel and the continuous flow method involve the measurement of dissolved oxygen with an accuracy of the order of ± 1 per cent of saturation by air.

The Winkler titration is a very reliable, though tedious, method. It is the method of choice for calibrating less reliable instruments. The oxygen present in a known volume of water is absorbed by a precipitate of manganous hydroxide in a special Winkler reagent bottle which has a bevelled ground glass stopper to prevent the inclusion of air bubbles when the sample is sealed off out of contact with air. When oxygen absorption is complete, acidification in the presence of iodide liberates two iodine atoms for every oxygen molecule originally present. The iodine is then titrated with thiosulphate. Details of methods recommended for sea water can be found in Jacobsen *et al.* (1950), Barnes (1959) and Strickland and Parsons (1965).

The presence of significant amounts of oxidising or reducing substances may invalidate the Winkler method, but in unpolluted areas and in the absence of concentrations of phytoplankton, the Winkler method determines the oxygen content of sea water satisfactorily. Modifications of the method for use in polluted water are described in Barnes (1959).

For subsampling purposes or when a large volume of water is not available, the micro-Winkler method is useful, the sample being collected out of contact with air by means of a syringe in which the reaction is carried out (Fox and Wingfield, 1938; Whitney, 1938).

When water is being transferred from an experimental vessel containing the animal to the Winkler reagent bottle, gaseous exchange with air must obviously be minimised. A clean glass siphon of narrow bore should be used to carry the water from the experimental vessel to the bottom of the Winkler bottle which should be allowed to overflow by 2 or 3 times its volume before being sealed. Siphons of plastic tubing are unsuitable, particularly if their bore is large, as they are not always fully wetted by water and may allow air bubbles to remain in the tube while the water is flowing through.

The Scholander micro-gasometric technique (Scholander *et al.*, 1955) is accurate, reliable, versatile and insensitive to pollutants in the water. The aqueous medium is drawn into an air-tight syringe and all gases dissolved in it are driven off by liberation of carbon dioxide bubbles. The liquid is then ejected, carbon dioxide absorbed in caustic alkali and the remaining bubble of oxygen and nitrogen transferred to a micro-gas analyser where the quantity of oxygen is determined by absorption in pyrogallol. The instrument blank needs to be measured using boiled gas-free water. The accuracy of oxygen determination is within 1–2 per cent of the oxygen present. The method is suitable for field or laboratory work and the gas analyser can be used to measure oxygen uptake by animals in air.

Polarographic methods for determining oxygen concentration are the most rapid and convenient, and allow continuous recording of oxygen tension, so that the course of oxygen uptake by an animal can be followed. The most reliable instrument of this class is the dropping mercury electrode; since the surface of the electrode is continually being renewed, it is not subject to drift and does not require frequent recalibration. However, the dropping mercury electrode is inconvenient; the diameter of the dropper and the temperature must be kept constant, the mercury must be cleaned from time to time, is toxic and is expensive, and the instrument is not suitable for use in the presence of animals. The instrument is however quite suitable for monitoring the oxygen level in the continuous flow type of apparatus.

More popular, and extremely convenient, are the various designs of galvanic oxygen electrodes in which the cathode consists of a noble metal separated from the liquid whose oxygen tension is to be measured by an oxygen diffusible membrane. The cathode, in contact with a very small amount of electrolyte, is held at a potential sufficient to reduce oxygen to water and hydrogen peroxide but not sufficiently low to cause the electrolysis of the water itself. If there is no oxygen outside the membrane, the small amount of oxygen in the electrolyte is quickly reduced and the current ceases to flow. If oxygen is present in the aqueous medium outside the membrane, it will diffuse through the membrane at a rate proportional to its concentration. Each electrochemical equivalent of oxygen passing through the membrane will allow one unit of current to pass through the electrode.

Many forms of such electrodes exist and suitable electrodes for physiological purposes are marketed by Beckman and other manufacturers. Some electrodes are easily poisoned and all such instruments are very liable to drift and therefore require regular calibration of the current in oxygen-free and in air-saturated water. They must be used in a thermostat bath at constant temperature (Beckman Instrument Incorp., 1964).

For very small organisms and pieces of tissue the Cartesian diver respirometer can be recommended. The tissue or organism, with a small quantity of air, is enclosed in a bulb with a short neck which floats in a pressure controlled chamber. As oxygen is absorbed, the volume of gas in the diver decreases thus reducing its buoyancy. To measure the amount absorbed, the outside pressure must be reduced sufficiently to expand the bubble and return the diver to its previous position. The amount of reduction in pressure is recorded. The method is extremely sensitive and the gas volumes used excessively small: Zeuthen (1943) quotes $0 \cdot 1$ μ litres.

A discussion of various forms of such apparatus, principles and computation is given in Glick (1961).

Measurement of oxygen uptake in air

Marine animals, such as mussels, barnacles, limpets and periwinkles, living intertidally, spend a significant period in air and can breathe air in a moist atmosphere. The standard constant temperature Barcroft and Warburg methods in which the volume or pressure change is measured as oxygen is absorbed are still in use, but calibration and computation are difficult and complicated (Dixon, 1951). Much more convenient equipment is now available incorporating a micrometer which inserts a stainless steel or plastic rod (Gilson, 1963) directly into the gas space so maintaining constant pressure. The volume change can thus be read directly.

Suitable micrometer devices in compensating chambers are marketed by Mark Company, Randolph, Mass., U.S.A. and multi-chamber Gilson type respirometers are marketed by W.G. Flaig and Sons, Broadstairs, Kent, England. A very conveniently assembled plastic apparatus for average sized marine organisms which can be used with this type of respirometer is described by Davies (1966).

The unique magnetic susceptibility of oxygen has led to the development of instruments with high sensitivity but these are not yet widely applied in biology.

Appendix 1

Working drawings of
Naturalist's rectangular dredge,
Anchor dredge, Agassiz trawl, Riley
push net and Butler corer

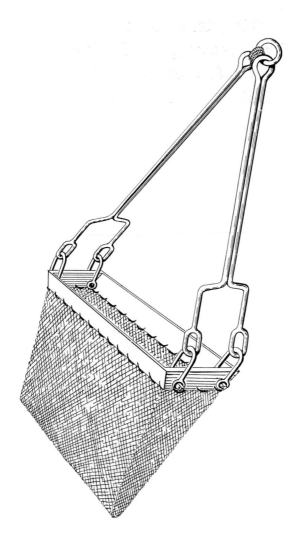

Fig. A.1. Naturalist's rectangular dredge, as supplied by the Marine Biological Laboratory, Plymouth, England. The table (facing page) gives a representative selection of sizes (in mm), but most dimensions are not critical and others may prove more suitable for particular purposes. Note that a metal ring is fitted to one towing arm only. The small holes along the dredge frame through which the net is seized to the frame should be about 5 mm diameter and be spaced at 50 mm intervals. The dredge is constructed of mild steel, with galvanized iron shackles. The size of the hole J should be such that the shackle pin is a loose fit.

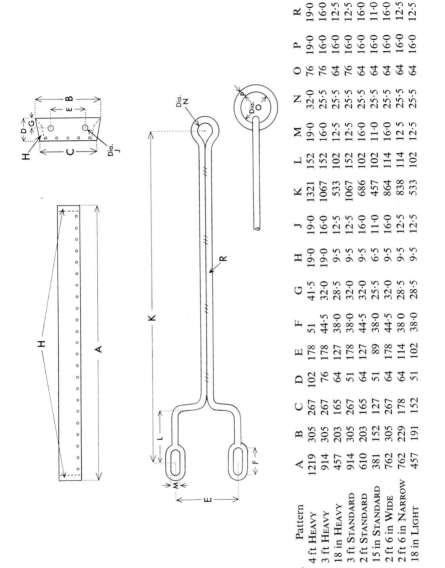

No.	Pattern	A	B	C	D	E	F	G	H	J	K	L	M	N	O	P	R
1	4 ft HEAVY	1219	305	267	102	178	51	41·5	19·0	19·0	1321	152	19·0	32·0	76	19·0	19·0
2	3 ft HEAVY	914	305	267	76	178	44·5	32·0	19·0	16·0	1067	152	16·0	25·5	76	16·0	16·0
3	18 in HEAVY	457	203	165	64	127	38·0	28·5	9·5	12·5	533	102	12·5	25·5	64	16·0	12·5
4	3 ft STANDARD	914	305	267	51	178	38·0	32·0	9·5	12·5	1067	152	12·5	25·5	76	16·0	12·5
5	2 ft STANDARD	610	203	165	64	127	44·5	32·0	9·5	16·0	686	102	16·0	25·5	64	16·0	16·0
6	15 in STANDARD	381	152	127	51	89	38·0	25·5	6·5	11·0	457	102	11·0	25·5	64	16·0	11·0
7	2 ft 6 in WIDE	762	305	267	64	178	44·5	32·0	9·5	16·0	864	114	16·0	25·5	64	16·0	16·0
8	2 ft 6 in NARROW	762	229	178	64	114	38 0	28·5	9·5	12·5	838	114	12 5	25·5	64	16·0	12·5
9	18 in LIGHT	457	191	152	51	102	38·0	28·5	9·5	12·5	533	102	12·5	25·5	64	16·0	12·5

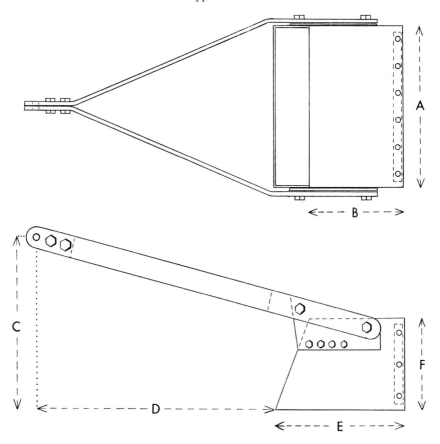

Fig. A.2. Anchor dredge, as supplied by the Marine Biological Association, Plymouth. For photograph see Fig. 6.7. The dredge is made up, of mild steel, in two sizes:

	Medium	Small
Wishbone towing arms	64 × 12·5 mm	51 × 6·5
Sheet for scoop	5	3
Dimensions A	457	350
B	279	203
C	490	384
D	724	457
E	381	279
F	260	184

The net (or a narrow canvas ring to which the net is laced, cf. Fig. 6.8) is attached by eyelets clamped between strips of metal bolted around the four sides of the scoop. These have bolts of about 10 mm diameter every 50 mm.

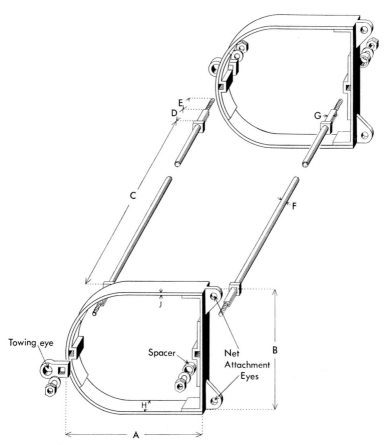

Fig. A.3. Agassiz trawl frame. The two cross-bars are made from solid mild steel round bar, ground to a square section at each end, on to which collars are welded to act as distance pieces. The extreme ends are threaded. The two bars are identical, a short length of tube on each end of the posterior (right hand) bar replacing the towing eye. The net is fitted to chains joining upper and lower attachment eyes respectively. One end of each chain is attached to the frame with twine to provide a weak link. The runners are constructed of mild steel, with either riveted or welded joints. Approximate dimensions for three sizes of trawl are:

	A	B	C	D	E	F	G	H	J
5 ft	610	480	1524	44	25	22	16	38	7
6 ft	660	560	1829	64	38	30	22	51	9·5
8 ft	660	560	2438	76	58	32	25	64	12·5

The Riley push-net

We would like to thank Mr J.D. Riley for the following description of his push-net, and for permission to reproduce Fig. 6.1.

In 1962 at the start of extensive survey work by staff of the Fisheries Laboratory, Lowestoft, in the Irish Sea for O-group flat-fish, the need was demonstrated for a specially designed net to sample populations in the shallow water of sandy bays; this led to the development of the 'Riley' push-net. Its design was made as similar as possible to the 2 m and 4 m beam trawls being used for the same survey work so that the catches of the two types of gear could be compared when fished at similar speeds.

Construction

The Frame (see Fig. A.4). The beam and uprights are made of a single piece of 2·54 cm (1 inch) outside diameter electric welded mild steel tube, with a wall thickness of 1·42 mm, bent on a slight curve into two right angles to give a distance between the inner side of the two limbs of 1·5 m.

The beam piece slots into a hole on each ski foot made of a 4 cm length of split metal tube welded on to the foot and fitted with two lugs which bear a tightening wing nut to

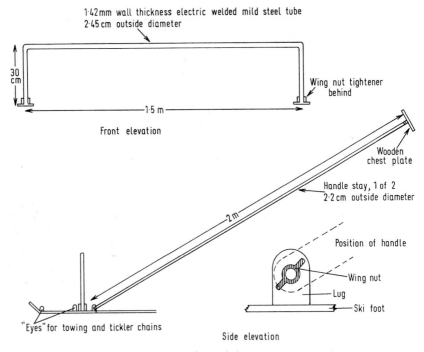

1·42mm wall thickness electric welded mild steel tube
2·45 cm outside diameter

30 cm

1·5 m

Front elevation

Wing nut tightener behind

Wooden chest plate

Handle stay, 1 of 2
2·2 cm outside diameter

2 m

Position of handle

Wing nut

Lug

Ski foot

"Eyes" for towing and tickler chains

Side elevation

Figure A.4

hold the uprights firmly. The correct positioning of the upright into the foot fixture is provided and maintained by a peg on the upright fitting into a V-shaped notch of the rim of the foot fixture.

The ski foot is fabricated from 3·2 mm thick ($^1/_8$ inch) sheet steel and measures 7·5 × 70 cm overall, with the leading edge bent up in a smooth curve so that the point is 6 cm above the base of the ski. The leading edge is fully rounded and the sharp edges are removed from the sides and trailing edge.

Each of the two handles which support the breast plate at their extremity is attached to the ski foot behind the upright fixture by an articulated joint consisting of a metal lug welded to the foot which bears a bolt pointing outwards from the net on which the hole in the lower end of the handle stay is secured by a brass wing nut and washers. The handle stays themselves are made of 2·2 cm outside diameter steel tube (wall thickness 1·42 mm), shaped at each end to bear a short length of solid steel inserted into the tube and welded on, through which at each end pass the fastening bolts. The breast plate of wood is mounted horizontally on a steel strip which bears similar lug and bolt fixtures to those of the ski foot.

On each ski foot are welded two eyes, made of cut chain links, one 6 cm in front of the upright fixture and the other immediately behind the curved leading edge of the ski. The former is to attach the tickler chain sets and the latter can be used to tow the net, with the handles removed, as a beam trawl.

All the steel tube pieces have their ends sealed by steel welds to prevent the entry of sea water. All metal parts of the frame are zinc sprayed, to prevent corrosion, and painted brown.

The design facilitates the easy dismantling of the push-net to allow it to be carried in a car, or to be ferried ashore from research vessels in a dinghy for shallow-water sampling.

The net (see Fig. A.5). The net is constructed of 210/9, 3-ply bonded nylon twine, dyed 'Cuprinol' green, with 156·6 rows/m (144 rows/yd). When fitted to the frame the top and sides are laced to the cross member and uprights, the lower edge is weighted with a PVC encased lead-line (weighing 12·4 kg/100 m) which acts additionally as a support to the leading edge of the net.

Rigging

A set of three tickler chains is attached to each 'eye' just in front of the upright by 3 cm shackles. The chain links are 38 mm long, 22 mm wide and 5 mm thick, and the weight of chain is approximately 470 g/metre. They are arranged so as to lie as in the figure. The number and correct disposition of the chains can influence the catches of young flatfish fourfold.

For very small flatfish (<2·0 cm overall length), or small crustacea, terylene knitted mesh fabric liners are fitted to the two legs of the net. These are in the form of bags, 100 cm long, 50 cm wide at the bottom and 60 cm wide at the open end, the edges of the open end being stitched in position inside each leg of the net.

Operation

The net was designed primarily for use on firm sand. Catches of most demersal organisms are considerably greater if the push netting is done at low water. In temperate latitudes

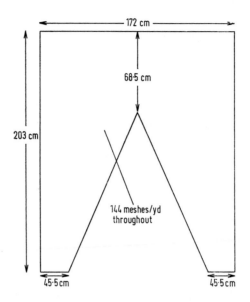

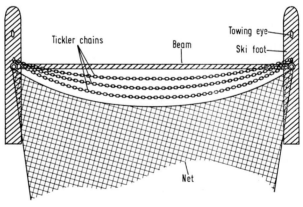

Figure A.5

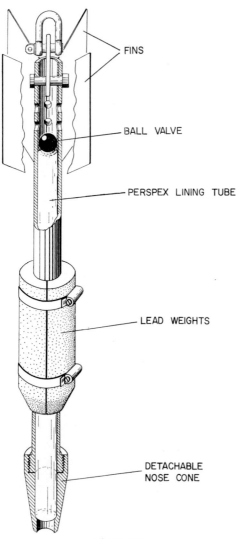

FINS

BALL VALVE

PERSPEX LINING TUBE

LEAD WEIGHTS

DETACHABLE
NOSE CONE

Figure A.6

waist-high waders are worn (see photograph) and this allows fishing in depths of water of 0·5 m even in a slight swell and breakers. When the net is used in moderate to severe breakers very few fish are caught and then only of species characteristic of the conditions, the more numerous other species moving off to slightly deeper water. The most efficient speed of fishing for small flatfish is 35 m/min, and in practice it has been found that this speed can be maintained over 10-minute periods, with a 20-minute period for sorting the catch, throughout a day.

The Butler corer

This simple corer, Fig. A.6, has been used by E.I. Butler and Miss S. Tibbits of the Marine Biological Laboratory, Plymouth, for sampling *soft estuarine muds*. It is made of brass, with a perspex lining tube. Its construction should be within the capabilities of most laboratory workshops.

Overall length, 70 cm;
Internal diameter of brass tube, 3·5 cm;
Internal diameter of perspex lining tube 2·5 cm, length 52·5 cm;
Weight 7 kg, plus 6 kg of lead weights.

Appendix 2

List of suppliers

This list does not claim to be comprehensive, and does not include manufacturers of such articles as ropes, nets, diving equipment, echo-sounders, radar etc. Its aim is to enable the less-easily obtainable types of gear to be located.

Alpine Geophysical Association Inc, Oak Street, Norwood, New Jersey 07648, U.S.A. Corers, dredges, pingers, meter wheels, cameras, transponders, precision depth recorder.

Benthos Inc, North Falmouth, Mass. 02556, U.S.A. van Veen grab, corers, dredges, weak links, pingers, cameras. Woods Hole type rapid sediment analyser.

Bergen-Nautik, Strandgt. 18, Bergen, Norway. Petersen grab, geological corer, wire strain gauge, meter wheels.

Franz Bergman K-G, Berliner Strasse 25, 1 Berlin 37 (Zehlendorf), Germany. Ekman-Birge grab.

G.H. Bloore Ltd, 480 Honeypot Lane, Stanmore, Middlesex, England. Plastic sheet (e.g. Vybak, Cobex) for labels.

Bridport-Gundry Ltd (Beetons Branch), Battery Green Road, Lowestoft, Suffolk, England. Beam trawl with jointed beam. Fishing nets and twines.

Endecotts (Test Sieves) Ltd, Lombard Road, Marden Factory Estate, London SW19. Test sieves, sieve shaker.

Foerst Mechanical Specialities Co, 2407N St Louis Avenue, Chicago, Ill. 60647, U.S.A. Ekman and Petersen grabs.

G.M. Mfg. and Instrument Corp, 2417 Third Avenue, New York, N.Y. 10451, U.S.A. Grabs, corers, dredges, weak links, pingers, meter wheels, deep-sea cameras.

Geodyne Division, 151 Bear Hill Road, Waltham, Mass. 02154, U.S.A. Pingers, deep-sea cameras, acoustic transponders.

Kay R. Grathwol, Dronningens Tvaergade 35, København K, Denmark. Glass storage jars with plastic snap-on lids.

The Hayward Company, 22–70 45th Street, Long Island City, New York 11105, U.S.A. Orange peel grab.

Hydro Products, P.O. Box 2528, San Diego, California 92112, U.S.A. Bouma box sampler, corers, Shipek sediment sampler, underwater cameras and T.V., pingers, underwater telephone system.

Hydro-Bios Apparatebau GmbH, 23 Kiel-Holtenau, W. Germany. Ekman-Birge and Lenz grabs, van Veen grab, rectangular dredge.

IBAK, Helmut Hunger, 2300 Kiel 14, Wehdenweg 122, W. Germany. Underwater cameras and T.V.

Kahl Scientific Instrument Corporation, P.O. Box 1166, El Cajon, California 92022, U.S.A. Mud snappers, orange peel grab, Emery grab, Ekman-Birge grab, Petersen grab, van Veen grab, Box sampler.

Kelvin Hughes, St Clare House, Minories, London EC3, England. Echo sounders, oblique sonar equipment, precision depth recorder, trawl warp tension meters, van Veen grab.

Laboratoire Océanographique, Charlottenlund, Bolbrovej 48, Rungsted Kyst, Denmark. Petersen and van Veen grabs, Knudsen sampler, meter wheels.

Friedrich Leutert, 3141 Erbstorf-Lueneburg, W. Germany. Reineck box sampler.

Marine Biological Association, The Laboratory, Citadel Hill, Plymouth, England. Dredges, anchor-dredge, Agassiz trawl.

Mecabolier, 57 Avenue de la République, 94 Villeneuve-le-Roi, France. Grab with toothed jaws, dredges, corers, meter wheels.

David Moir, 11/13 Broomhill Road, Aberdeen, AB1 6JA, Scotland. Smith-McIntyre grab.

R.W. Munro Ltd, Cline Road, Bounds Green, London N11, England. Meter wheels.

Norsemann (Cables and Extrusions) Ltd, Manningtree, Essex, England. Plastic-filled steel wire ropes, wire tension meter.

Ocean Research Equipment Inc, Falmouth, Mass. 02541, U.S.A. Acoustic pingers and transponders.

Plessey Co Ltd, Electronics Group, Ilford, Essex, England. Acoustic pingers and transponders. Underwater T.V.

Rigosha Co Ltd, 2 Kajicho 1-Chome Kandai Chiyoda-Ku, Tokyo, Japan. Smith-McIntyre grab, Ekman-Birge dredge, and other grabs, dredges, and oceanographic equipment.

Underwater and Marine Equipment Ltd, 18 Farnborough Road, Farnborough, Hants, England. Small corers, rock and pipe dredges, weak links, acoustic pingers, underwater cameras, transponders.

Appendix 3

Measurements at Sea

An interpretation of the International System of Units
(see Anderton and Bigg 1969).

Depth soundings should be made in metres (1 m=0·54681 fathom).

Distances at sea have traditionally been measured in sea miles or nautical miles, one sea mile being taken as equal to 1 minute of latitude at the latitude of the position, so allowing measurements from the scale of latitude at the edge of the chart. The International nautical mile has been defined as exactly 1,852 m, which differs slightly from the United Kingdom nautical mile of 6,080 feet (1853·18 m). It seems likely that nautical and sea miles will continue to be used for general navigational purposes, but where very precise measurements are required, these should be made in metres.

Speeds at sea are commonly expressed in knots (nautical miles/hour), but the International System proposes that these should be measured in metres/sec. (One International nautical mile/hour=0·514 m/sec.)

293

Bibliographies and References

BIBLIOGRAPHY OF
TAGGING AND MARKING TECHNIQUES

ABRAHAMSSON S.A.A. (1965) A method of marking crayfish *Astacus astacus* Linné in population studies. *Oikos*, **16**, pp. 228–231.

ANON. (1963) Ring-labelling of shrimps. *Priroda, Mosk.* **10**, p. 117.

BAILEY N.T.J. (1951) On estimating the size of mobile populations from recapture data. *Biometrika*, **38**, pp. 293–306.

BUTLER T.H. (1957) The tagging of the commercial crab in the Queen Charlotte Islands region. *Progr. Rep. Pacif. Cst Stns.* **109**, pp. 16–19.

CONOVER J.T. & PIERCE M.E. (1956) An adhesive for labelling animals exposed to sea-water for long periods. *Nature, Lond.* **178**, pp. 273–274.

CRONIN L.E. (1949) Comparison of methods of tagging the blue crab. *Ecology*, **30**, pp. 390–394.

DAWSON C.E. (1957) Studies on the marking of commercial shrimp with biological stains. *Spec. scient. Rep. Fish. U.S. Fish. Wildl. Serv.*, Fish. (231), 24 pp.

EDWARDS E. (1965) Observations on growth of the edible crab (*Cancer pagurus*). *Rapp. P.-v. Réun. Cons. perm. int. Explor. Mer*, **156**, pp. 62–70.

FORSTER G.R. (1967) The growth of *Haliotis tuberculata*. Results of tagging experiments in Guernsey, 1963–65. *J. mar. biol. Ass. U.K.* **47**, pp. 287–300.

GRAY G.W. Jr. (1964) Tag loss during ecdysis by the king crab *Paralithodes camtschatica* (Tilesius). *Trans. Am. Fish. Soc.* **93**, pp. 303–304.

GUNDERSEN K.R. (1963) Tagging experiments on *Cancer pagurus* in Norwegian waters. *Annls biol. Copenh.* **18** (1961), pp. 206–208.

HANCOCK D.A. & URQUHART A.E. (1959) Methods for marking whelks (*Buccinum undatum* L.). *J. Cons. perm. int. Explor. Mer*, **24**, pp. 494–496.

HANCOCK D.A. (1963) Marking experiments with the common whelk (*Buccinum undatum*). *I.C.N.A.F. Spec. Publ.* No. 4, pp. 176–187.

HANCOCK D.A. (1965) Yield assessment in the Norfolk fishery for crabs (*Cancer pagurus*). *Rapp. P.-v. Réun. Cons. perm. int. Explor. Mer*, **156**, pp. 81–94.

ICNAF (1963) North Atlantic Fish Marking Symposium, Woods Hole, Mass., May 1961. *I.C.N.A.F. Spec. Publ.* No. 4, 370 pp.

INTERNATIONAL COUNCIL FOR THE EXPLORATION OF THE SEA (1965) A guide to fish marks used by members of the International Council for the Exploration of the Sea, and by some non-participant countries (3rd ed.). *J. Cons. perm. int. Explor. Mer*, **30**, pp. 87–160.

JEFFERTS K.B., BERGMAN P.K. & FISCUS H.F. (1963) A coded wire identification system for macro-organisms. *Nature, Lond.* **198**, pp. 460–462.

KLAWE W.L. (1954) A method for marking marine worms. *Science,* **120** (3109), pp. 187–188.

MASON J. (1964) The Scottish crab-tagging experiments, 1960–61. *Rapp. P.-v. Rèun. Cons. perm. int. Explor. Mer,* **156**, pp. 71–80.

NEWMAN G.G. (1966) Movements of the South African Abalone *Haliotis midae. Invest. Rep. Div. Sea Fish. S. Afr.* **56**, 20 pp.

SINCLAIR M. (1963) Studies on the Paua, *Haliotis iris* Martyn in the Wellington district, 1945–46. *Zoology Publs Vict. Univ. Coll.* **35**, pp. 1–16.

THOMPSON J.M. (1962) The tagging and marking of marine animals in Australia. *Tech. Pap. Div. Fish. Oceanogr. C.S.I.R.O. Aust.* 13, 39 pp.

GENERAL BIBLIOGRAPHY

A selection of general works concerned with benthos and methods of sampling.

BARNES H. (1959) *Apparatus and methods of Oceanography. Part One: Chemical.* Allen and Unwin, London, 341 pp.

BARNES H. (1959) *Oceanography and Marine Biology. A book of Techniques.* Allen and Unwin, London, 218 pp.

DAVIS F.M. (1958) An account of the fishing gear of England and Wales (4th ed.). *Fish. Invest., Lond.,* Ser. 2, **21** (8), 165 pp.

FOWLER G.H. & ALLEN E.J. (1928) *Science of the Sea* (2nd ed.). Clarendon Press, Oxford, 502 pp.

HARDY A.C. (1959) *The Open Sea: Its Natural History. Part II. Fish and Fisheries* (New Naturalist Series, 37). Collins, London, 322 pp.

HOLME N.A. (1964) Methods of sampling the benthos. *Adv. mar. Biol.* **2**, pp. 171–260.

JONES N.S. (1950) Marine bottom communities. *Biol. Rev.* **25**, pp. 283–313.

LONGHURST A.R. (1964) A review of the present situation in benthic synecology (in English and French). *Bull. Inst. océanogr. Monaco,* **63** (1317), 54 pp.

McINTYRE A.D. (1969) Ecology of marine meiobenthos. *Biol. Rev.* **44**, pp. 245–290.

PÉRÈS J.M. (1961) *Océanographie Biologique et Biologie Marine. I. La Vie Benthique.* Presses Universitaires de France, Paris, 541 pp.

RUSSELL F.S. & YONGE C.M. (1963) *The Seas. Our knowledge of life in the Sea and how it is gained* (3rd ed.). Frederick Warne, London, 376 pp.

SCHLIEPER C. (1968) *Methoden der Meeresbiologischen Forschung.* VEB Gustav Fischer, Jena, 322 pp.

SHEPARD F.P. (1967) *Submarine Geology.* (2nd ed.). Harper International Edition, 557 pp.

SWEDMARK B. (1964) The interstitial fauna of marine sand. *Biol. Rev.* **39**, pp. 1–42.

THORSON G. (1957) Sampling the benthos. *Mem. geol. Soc Amer.* **67**, 1, pp. 61–73.

THORSON G. (1957) Bottom communities (Sublittoral or shallow shelf). *Mem. geol. Soc. Amer.* **67**, 1, pp. 461–534.

YONGE C.M. (1949) *The Sea Shore* (New Naturalist Series, 12). Collins, London, 311 pp.

ZENKEWITCH L. (1963) *Biology of the Seas of the U.S.S.R.* Allen and Unwin, London, 955 pp.

REFERENCES

ABEL E.F. (1959) Zur Kentniss der Beziehung der Fische zu Höhlen im Mittelmeer. Ergebn. Österr. Tyrrhenia-Exp. 1952, Teil XIV, *Pubbl. Staz. zool. Napoli,* 30 (Suppl.), pp. 519–528.

ABEL E.F. (1960) Zur Kentniss der Verhaltens und der Ökologie von Fischen an Korallenriffen bei Ghardaqa (Rotes Meer). *Z. Morph. Ökol. Tiere,* 48, pp. 430–503.

ABEL E.F. (1961) Über die Beziehung mariner Fische zu Hartbodenstrukturen, *Sber. öst. Akad. Wiss.* Abt. 1, 170, pp. 223–263.

ACKROYD T.N.W. (1964) *Laboratory Testing in Soil Engineering.* London, Soil Mechanics Ltd, 233 pp.

ADMIRALTY (1948) *Admiralty Manual of Hydrographic Surveying,* 2nd ed. Hydrographic Department, Admiralty, London, 572 pp.

ADMIRALTY (1954, 1966, 1967) *Manual of Navigation,* 1 (1967), 510 p.; 2 (1966), 306 p.; 3 (1954), 448 p. H.M. Stationery Office, London.

ADMIRALTY (1964) *Royal Navy Diving Manual,* BR 155 C. H. M. Stationery Office, London.

ALBERT, PRINCE OF MONACO (1932) Sur l'emploi des nasses pour des recherches zoologiques en eau profonde. *Result. Camp. scient. Prince Albert I,* 84, pp. 176–178.

ALEEM A.A. (1950a) Distribution and ecology of British marine littoral diatoms. *J. Ecol.* 38, pp. 75–106.

ALEEM A.A. (1950b) The diatom community inhabiting the mud-flats at Whitstable. *New Phytol.* 49, pp. 174–188.

ALEEM A.A. (1951) Contribution a l'étude de la flore de Diatomées marines de la Méditerranée. I. Diatomées des eaux profonde de Banyuls-sur-Mer. (Pyrénées-Orientales). *Vie Milieu* 2, pp. 44–49.

ALLEN D.M. & HUDSON J.H. (1970) A sled-mounted suction-sampler for benthic organisms. *Spec. Sci. Rep.—Fish.* 614, U.S. Fish, and *Wildl. Serv.,* 5 pp.

ALLEN K.R. (1950) The computation of production in fish populations. *N.Z. Sci. Rev.* 8, p. 89.

ALTMAN J.S. (1967) The behaviour of *Octopus vulgaris* Lam. in its natural habitat: a pilot study. *Underwater Ass. Rep.,* 1966–67, pp. 77–84.

ANDERSON R.O. (1959) A modified flotation technique for sorting bottom fauna samples. *Limnol. Oceanogr.* 4, pp. 223–225.

ANDERTON P. & BIGG P.H. (1969) *Changing to the metric system. Conversion factors, symbols, and definitions.* National Physical Laboratory. Publication SBN 11 480003 0. H.M. Stationery Office, London, 48 pp.

ANGEL H.H. & ANGEL M.V. (1967) Distribution pattern analysis in a marine benthic community. *Helgoländer wiss. Meeresunters.* 15, pp. 445–454.

ANSELL A.D. & TREVALLION A. (1967) Studies on *Tellina tenuis* da Costa I. Seasonal growth and biochemical cycle. *J. exp. mar. Biol. Ecol.* 1, pp. 220–235.

APOLLONIO S. (1965) Chlorophyll in Arctic sea ice. *Arctic,* 18, pp. 118–122.

BAARDSETH E. & HAUG A. (1953) Individual variation of some constituents in brown algae, and the reliability of analytical results. *Rep. Norw. Inst. Seaweed Res.* 2, 23 pp.

BACESCU M. (1957) Apucatorul-sonda pentru studiul cantitativ al organismelor de fund-un aparat mixt pentru colectarea simulana a macro-si microbentosulia. (La benne-sonde pour l'étude quantitative des organismes benthiques—un appareil mixte pour prelever à la fois le macro- et le micro-benthos.) *Bul Inst. Cerc. pisc.* 16, (2) pp. 69–82.

BACESCU M. (1965) Méthodes de la recherche du benthos en Mer Noire et importance des prélèvements directs en scaphandre autonome des échantillons de benthos pour d'études quantitatives. Méthodes quantitatives d'étude du Benthos et échelle dimen-sionelle des benthontes: *Colloque du Comité du Benthos* (Marseille, Nov. 1963) pp. 48–62. Comm. int. Explor. scient. Mer Méditerr. (Monaco), Paris.

BAGENAL M. (1955) A note on the relations of certain parameters following a logarithmic transformation. *J. mar. biol. Ass. U.K.* **34**, pp. 289–96.

BAIRD I.E. & WETZEL R.G. (1968) A method for the determination of zero thickness activity of ^{14}C labelled benthic diatoms in sand. *Limnol. Oceanogr.* **13**, pp. 379–382.

BAIRD R.H. (1955) A preliminary report on a new type of commercial escallop dredge. *J. Cons. perm. int. Explor. Mer.* **20**, pp. 290–294.

BAIRD R.H. (1958a) On the swimming behaviour of escallops (*Pecten maximus* L.). *Proc. malac. Soc. Lond.* **33**, pp. 67–71.

BAIRD R.H. (1958b) A preliminary account of a new half square metre bottom sampler. *I.C.E.S. Shellfish Committee* Paper No. 70.

BAIRD R.H. (1959) Factors affecting the efficiency of dredges, in Kristjonsson, H. (ed). *Modern Fishing Gear of the World,* pp. 222–224. Fishing News (Books) Ltd, London.

BAIRD R.H. & GIBSON F.A. (1956) Underwater observations on escallop (*Pecten maximus* L.) beds. *J. mar. biol. Ass. U.K.* **35**, pp. 555–562.

BALLANTINE W.J. (1961) A biologically-defined exposure scale for the comparative des-cription of rocky shores. *Field Studies* **1**, 3, 19 p.

BANDY O.L. (1965) The pinger as a deep-water grab control. *Undersea Technol.* **6**, p. 36.

BARNES H. (1952) The use of transformations in marine biological statistics. *J. Cons. perm. int. Explor. Mer*, **18**, pp. 61–71.

BARNES H. (1958) The future of underwater television, in Buzzati-Traverso A.A. (ed). *Perspectives in marine biology,* Part 1, pp. 105–116. Univ. Calif. Press, Berkeley.

BARNES H. (1959) *Apparatus and Methods of Oceanography. Part One: Chemical.* Allen & Unwin, London, 341 pp.

BARNES H. (1963) Underwater television. *Oceanography mar. Biol. Ann. Rev.* **1**, pp. 115–128.

BARNETT, P.R.O. (1969) A stabilising framework for the Knudsen bottom sampler. *Limnol. Oceanogr.* **14**, pp. 648–649.

BARNETT P.R.O. & HARDY B.L.S. (1967) A diver-operated quantitative bottom sampler for sand macrofaunas. *Helgoländer wiss. Meeresunters.* **15**, pp. 390–398.

BECKMAN INSTRUMENTS INCORP. (1964) *Instruction manuals PG IM 2, PG.TB.* 003. *for oxygen macro electrode* (32 pp.) and *Physiological gas analyser* (31 p.). Spinco Division, Palo Alto, California.

BELDERSON R.H., KENYON, N.H. & STRIDE A.H. (1970) 10-km wide views of Mediterranean deep sea floor. *Deep-Sea Res.* **17**, pp. 267–270.

BELDERSON R.H. & STRIDE A.H. (1966) Tidal current fashioning of a basal bed. *Mar. Geol.* **4**, pp. 237–257.

BELYAEV G.M. & SOKOLOVA M.N. (1960) On methods of quantitative investigation of deep-water benthos. (In Russian.) *Trudy Inst. Okeanol.* **39**, pp. 96–100.

VON BERTALANFFY L. (1934) Untersuchungen über die Gesetzlichkeit des Wachstums. I. Teil. *Arch. EntwMech. Org.* **131**, pp. 613–652.

BERTRAM C.R. (1966) The behaviour of Maltese fishes by day and night. *Symp. Underwater Ass. Malta,* 1965, pp. 39–41.

BEVERTON R.J.H. & HOLT S.J. (1957) On the dynamics of exploited fish populations. *Fishery Invest., Lond.* (2) **19**, 533 p.

BEYER F. (1958) A new bottom-living Trachymedusa from the Oslo Fjord. Description of the species, and a general discussion of the life conditions and fauna of the fjord deeps. *Nytt Mag. Zool.* **6**, pp. 121–143.

BIERI R. & TOKIOKA T. (1968) Dragonet 11, an opening-closing quantitative trawl for the study of micro-vertical distribution of zooplankton and the meio-epibenthos. *Publ. Seto mar. biol. Lab.* **15**, pp. 373–390.

BIGELOW H.W. (1964) Electronic positioning systems. *Under-sea Technol.* **5**, 4, pp. 24–28.

BIRKETT L. (1957) Flotation technique for sorting grab samples. *J. Cons. perm. int. Explor. Mer,* **22**, pp. 289–292.

BIRKETT L. (1958) A basis for comparing grabs. *J. Cons. perm. int. Explor. Mer,* **23**, pp. 202–207.

BLACKER R.W. & WOODHEAD P.M.J. (1965) A towed underwater camera. *J. mar. biol. Ass. U.K.* **45**, pp. 593–597.

BLIGH E.G. & DYER W.J. (1959) A rapid method of total lipid extraction and purification. *Can. J. Biochem. Physiol.* **37**, pp. 911–917.

BODEANU N. (1964) Contribution à l'étude quantitative du microphytobenthos du littoral Roumain de la Mer Noire. *Revue roum. Biol.* Ser. Zool. **9**, pp. 434–445.

BODEN B.P., KAMPA E.M. & SNODGRASS J.M. (1960) Underwater daylight measurements in the Bay of Biscay. *J. mar. biol. Ass. U.K.* **39**, pp. 227–238.

BOISSEAU J.-P. (1957) Technique pour l'étude quantitative de la faune interstitielle des sables. *C.r. Congr. Socs sav. Bordeaux,* 1957, pp. 117–119.

BOODA L.L. (1967) Underwater photography. *Undersea Technol.* **8**, 5, pp. 36–41.

BOOTH B. (1968) Navigation, in *The British Sub-Aqua Club Diving Manual,* p. 158–166. 6th ed. London, 424 pp.

BOSSANYI J. (1951) An apparatus for the collection of plankton in the immediate neighbourhood of the sea-bottom. *J. mar. biol. Ass. U.K.* **30**, pp. 265–270.

BOUMA, A.H. & MARSHALL N.F. (1964) A method for obtaining and analysing undisturbed oceanic sediment samples. *Mar. Geol.* **2**, pp. 81–99.

BOURNE N. (1967) Digging efficiency trials with a hydraulic clam rake. *Fish. Res. Bd Canada, Tech. Rept.* MS. 15, 23 pp.

BRESLAU L. (1965) Classification of sea-floor sediments with a shipborne acoustical system, in *Le Pétrole et la mer,* 1, 132, 9 pp. (*Coll. Repr. Woods Hole oceanogr. Instn.* No. 1678.)

BRESLAU, L.R., ZEIGLER, J.M. & OWEN D.M. (1962). A self-contained portable tape-recording system for use by SCUBA divers. *Bull. Inst. océanogr. Monaco,* **1235**, pp. 1–4.

BRETT C.E. (1964) A portable hydraulic diver operated dredge-sieve for sampling subtidal macrofauna. *J. mar. Res.* **22**, pp. 205–209.

BRIBA C. & REYS J.P. (1966) Modifications d'une benne 'orange peel' pour des prélèvements quantitatifs du benthos de substrats meubles. *Recl. Trav. stn mar. Endoume,* **41**, pp. 57, 117–121.

BRITISH SUB-AQUA CLUB (1968) *British Sub-Aqua Club Diving Manual.* Eaton Publications, London. 6th ed. 424 pp.

BROCK V.E. (1954) A preliminary report on a method of estimating reef fish populations. *J. Wildl. Mgmt* **18**, pp. 297–308.

BROCKMANN C. (1935) Diatomeen und Schlik im Jade-Gebiet. *Abh. Senckenb. naturforsch. Ges.* **430**, pp. 1–64.

BRODY S. (1945) *Bioenergetics and Growth.* Reinhold N.Y. 1023 pp.

BRUCE J.R. (1928) Physical factors on the sandy beach. Part 1. Tidal, climatic and edaphic. *J. mar. biol. Ass. U.K.* **15**, pp. 535–565.

BRUNDZA P. (1968) The many techniques in using camera lenses for underwater photography, in Proc. 4th nat. ISA Marine Sciences Instrumentation Symp. Florida, 22–26 Jan. 1968, Alt, F. (ed). *Marine Sciences Instrumentation,* 4, pp. 364–368, Plenium Press, New York.

BUCHANAN J.B. (1967) Dispersion and demography of some infaunal echinoderm populations. *Symp. zool. Soc. Lond.* **20**, pp. 1–11.

BUNT J.S. (1963) Diatoms of Antarctic sea-ice as agents of primary production. *Nature, Lond.* **199**, pp. 1255–1257.

BUNT J.S., OWENS O. VAN H. & HOCH G. (1966) Exploratory studies on the physiology and ecology of a psychrophilic marine diatom. *J. Phycol.* **2**, pp. 96–100.

BURNS R.E. (1966) Free-fall behaviour of small, light-weight gravity corers. *Mar. Geol.* **4**, pp. 1–9.

BUSH L.F. (1966) Distribution of sand fauna on beaches at Miami, Florida. *Bull. mar. Sci.* **16**, pp. 58–75.

BYBEE J.R. (1969) Effects of hydraulic pumping operations on the fauna of Tijuana Slough. *Calif. Fish Game,* **55**, pp. 213–220.

CABIOCH L. (1967) Résultats obtenus par l'emploi de la photographie sous-marine sur les fonds du large de Roscoff. *Helgoländer wiss. Meeresunters.* **15**, pp. 361–370.

CAREFOOT T.H. (1967a) Growth and nutrition of *Aplysia punctata* feeding on a variety of marine algae. *J. mar. biol. Ass. U.K.* **47**, pp. 565–589.

CAREFOOT T.H. (1967b) Growth and nutrition of three species of opisthobranch molluscs. *Comp. Biochem. Physiol.* **21**, pp. 627–652.

CAREY A.G. Jr. & HANCOCK D.R. (1965) An anchor-box dredge for deep-sea sampling. *Deep-Sea Res.* **12**, pp. 983–984.

CAREY A.G. Jr. & PAUL R.R. (1968) A modification of the Smith-McIntyre grab for simultaneous collection of sediment and bottom water. *Limnol. Oceanogr.* **13**, pp. 545–549.

CARLISLE D.B. (1961) Intertidal territory in fish. *Anim. Behav.* **9**, pp. 106–107.

CARPINE C., FREDJ G. & VAISSIÈRE R. (1965) Note préliminaire sur une méthode d'utilisation de la 'troika' sous-marine. Méthodes quantitatives d'étude du benthos et échelle dimensionelle des benthontes. *Colloque du Comité du Benthos* (Marseille, Nov. 1963), Comm. int. Explor. scient. Mer Méditerr. (Monaco), Paris.

CARRITT D.E. & KANWISHER J.W. (1959) An electrode system for measuring dissolved oxygen. *Analyt. Chem.* **31**, pp. 5–9.

CARROTHERS P.J.G. (1967) Automatic underwater photographic equipment for fisheries research. *Bull. Fish. Res. Bd Can.* 159, 34 pp.

CASSIE R.M. (1963) Microdistribution of plankton. *Oceanography mar. biol. Ann. Rev.* **1**, pp. 223–252.

CASTANGA M. (1967) A benthic sampling device for shallow water. *Limnol. Oceanogr.* **12**, pp. 357–359.

CASTENHOLZ R.W. (1963) An experimental study of the vertical distribution of littoral marine diatoms. *Limnol. Oceanogr.* **8**, pp. 450–462.

CHESTERMAN W.D., CLYNICK P.R. & STRIDE A.H. (1958) An acoustic aid to sea bed survey. *Acustica*, **8**, pp. 285–290. (*Coll. Repr. natn. Inst. Oceanogr.* No. 256.)

C.I.E.S.M.M. (1965) Méthodes quantitatives d'étude du benthos et echelle dimensionelle des benthontes. *Colloque du Comité du Benthos* (Marseille, Nov., 1963), Comm. int. Explor. scient. Mer Méditerr. (Monaco), Paris.

CLARK J.W. (1965) Methods and techniques for sea-floor tasks. *Ocean Science and Ocean Engineering* 1965, **1**, pp. 267–277. Mar. Techn. Soc. and Amer. Soc. Limnol. Oceanogr. Washington, D.C.

CLARK R.B. & MILNE A. (1955) The sublittoral fauna of two sandy bays on the Isle of Cumbrae, Firth of Clyde. *J. mar. biol. Ass. U.K.* **34**, pp. 161–180.

CLARKE G.L. & KELLY M.G. (1964) Variation in transparency and in bioluminescence on longitudinal transects in the western Indian Ocean. *Bull. Inst. océanogr. Monaco* 64 (1319), 20 pp.

CLARKE G.L. & WERTHEIM G.K. (1956) Measurements of illumination at great depths in the Atlantic Ocean by means of a new bathyphotometer. *Deep-Sea Res.* **3**, pp. 189–205.

CLARKE T.A., FLECHSIG A.O. & GRIGG R.W. (1967) Ecological studies during project Sealab 2. *Science, N.Y.* **157**, pp. 1381–1389.

COLMAN J.S. (1939) On the faunas inhabiting intertidal seaweeds. *J. mar. biol. Ass. U.K.* **24**, pp. 129–183.

COLMAN J.S. & SEGROVE F. (1955) The tidal plankton over Stoupe Beck sands, Robin Hood's Bay (Yorkshire, North Riding). *J. anim. ecol.* **24**, pp. 445–462.

COMITA W.G. & SCHINDLER D.W. (1963) Calorific values of microcrustacea. *Science, N.Y.* **140**, pp. 1394–1395.

CONOVER R.J. (1966) Assimilation of organic matter by zooplankton. *Limnol. Oceanogr.* **11**, pp. 338–345.

CONWAY E.J. (1947) *Microdiffusion Analysis and Volumetric Error.* (2nd ed.) Crosby Lockwood & Son Ltd, London, 357 pp.

COOPER L.H.N. (1961) Comparison between three methods of measuring underwater illumination in coastal waters. *J. mar. biol. Ass. U.K.* **41**, pp. 535–550.

COREY S. & CRAIB J.S. (1966) A new quantitative bottom sampler for microfauna. *J. Cons. perm. int. Explor. Mer,* **30**, pp. 346–353.

COUSTEAU J.Y. (1966) Working for weeks on the sea floor (Conshelf). *Natn. geogr. Mag.* **129**, pp. 498–537.

CRAIB J.S. (1965) A sampler for taking short undisturbed cores. *J. Cons. perm. int. Explor. Mer,* **30**, pp. 34–39.

CRAIG R.E. & LAWRIE R.G. (1962) An underwater light intensity meter. *Limnol. Oceanogr.* **7**, pp. 259–261.

CRAIG R.E. & PRIESTLEY R. (1963) Undersea photography in marine research. *Mar. Res.* 1963, No. 1. H.M.S.O., Edinburgh, 24 pp.

CREITZ G.I. & RICHARDS F.A. (1955) The estimation and characterization of plankton populations by pigment analysis. III. A note on the use of 'Millipore' membrane filters in the estimation of plankton pigments. *J. mar. Res.* **14**, pp. 211–216.

CRISP D.J. & DAVIES P.A. (1955) Observations *in vivo* on the breeding of *Elminius modestus* grown on glass slides. *J. mar. biol. Ass. U.K.* **34**, pp. 357–380.

CRISP D.J. & SOUTHWARD A.J. (1958) The distribution of intertidal organisms along the coasts of the English Channel. *J. mar. biol. Ass. U.K.* **37**, pp. 157–208.

CROSS E.R. (1954) *Underwater photography and television: a handbook of equipment and techniques.* Exposition Press, New York, 258 pp.

CUMMINS K.W. (1967) *Calorific equivalents for studies in ecological energetics.* Pymatuning Laboratory of Ecology, University of Pittsburg, Penn. 2nd ed. Oct. 1967, 52 pp.

CURRIE R.I. (1961) Scalar irradiance as a parameter in phytoplankton photosynthesis and a proposed method for its measurement. *Union Géod. Géophys. int., Monographie* 10, pp. 107–112.

CURRIE R. & DRAPER L. (1961) Time-integrated measurements of submarine irradiance. *Nature, Lond.* **191**, pp. 661–662.

CZIHAK G. & ZEI M. (1960) Photography, television, and the use of the bottom sampler, compared as methods for quantitative analyses of benthic populations. *Rapp. P.-v. Réun. Commn int. Explor. scient. Mer Méditerr.* **15**, pp. 81–83.

DAVIES P.S. (1966) A constant pressure respirometer for medium-sized animals. *Oikos,* **17**, pp. 108–112.

DAVIS C.C. (1963) On questions of production and productivity in ecology. *Arch. Hydrobiol.* **59**, pp. 145–161.

DAVIS F.M. (1925) Quantitative studies on the fauna of the sea bottom. No. 2. Results of the investigations in the southern North Sea, 1921–24. *Fish. Invest. Lond.* Ser. 2, **8** (4), 50 pp.

DAVIS F.M. (1958) An account of the fishing gear of England and Wales (4th ed.). *Fish. Invest. Lond.* Ser. 2, **21** (8), 165 pp.

DELAMARE-DEBOUTTEVILLE C. (1960) *Biologie des eaux souterraines littorales et continentales.* Hermann, Paris, 740 pp.

DICKIE L.M. (1955) Fluctuations in abundance of the giant scallop *Placopecten magellanicus* (Gmelin) in the Digby area of the Bay of Fundy. *J. Fish. Res. Bd Can.* **12**, pp. 797–857.

DILLON W.P. (1964) Flotation technique for separating fecal pellets and small marine organisms from sand. *Limnol. Oceanogr.* **9**, pp. 601–602.

DINGLE R.V. (1965) Sand waves in the North Sea mapped by continuous reflection profiling. *Mar. Geol.* **3**, pp. 391–400.

DIXON M. (1951) *Manometric methods as applied to the measurement of cell respiration and other processes.* (3rd ed.). Cambridge University Press, 165 pp.

DOBBS H.E. (1962) *Camera underwater.* Focal Press, London, 187 pp.

DOODSON A.T. & WARBURG H.D. (1941) *Admiralty Manual of Tides.* H.M. Stationery Office, London, 270 pp.

DOTY M.S. & OGURI M. (1957) Evidence for a photosynthetic daily periodicity. *Limnol. Oceanogr.* **2**, pp. 37–40.

DOTY M.S. & OGURI M. (1958) Selected features of the isotopic carbon primary productivity technique. *Rapp. P.-v. Réun. Cons. perm. int. Explor. Mer,* **144,** pp. 47–55.

DOTY M.S. & OGURI M. (1959) The carbon-fourteen technique for determining primary plankton productivity. *Pubbl. Staz. zool. Napoli,* **31** Suppl., pp. 70–94.

DOWDESWELL W.H. (1959) *Practical Animal Ecology.* Methuen, London, 316 pp.

DRACH P. (1948) Premières recherches en scaphandre autonome sur le peuplement des faciés rocheux de la zone littorale profonde. *C.r. hebd. Séanc. Acad. Sci. Paris,* **227,** pp. 1176–1178.

DRACH P. (1958) Perspectives in the study of benthic fauna of the continental shelf, in Buzzati-Traverso, A.A. (ed.). *Perspectives in Marine Biology,* pp. 34–36. Univ. Calif. Press, Berkeley.

DRAPER L. (1961) Self-contained integrating irradiance meter for use underwater. *J. scient. Instrum.* **38,** pp. 474–476.

DREW E.A. & LARKUM A.W.D. (1967) Photosynthesis and growth of *Udotea,* a green alga from deep water. *Underwater Ass. Rep.,* 1966–67, pp. 65–71.

DRISCOLL A.L. (1964) Relationship of mesh opening to faunal counts in a quantitative benthic study of Hadley Harbor. *Biol. Bull. mar. biol. Lab., Woods Hole,* **127,** p. 368

DUGAN J. (1965) Manned undersea stations. *Ocean Science and Ocean Engineering* 1965, **1,** pp. 652–656. Mar. Techn. Soc. and Amer. Limnol. Oceanogr. Soc., Washington, D.C.

DUNTLEY S.Q. (1963) Light in the sea. *J. opt. Soc. Am.* **53,** pp. 214–233.

DUNTLEY S.Q., UHL R.J., AUSTIN R.W., BOILEAU A.R. & TYLER J.E. (1955) An underwater photometer. *J. opt. Soc. Am.* **45,** p. 904 (A)

EATON J.W. & MOSS B. (1966) The estimation of numbers and pigment content in epipelic algal populations. *Limnol. Oceanogr.* **11,** pp. 584–595.

EBERT E.E. & TURNER C.H. (1962) The nesting behaviour, eggs and larvae of the bluespot goby. *Calif. Fish Game,* **48,** pp. 249–252.

EDGERTON H.E. (1963) Underwater photography, in M. N. Hill (ed.). *The sea. Ideas and observations on progress in the study of the seas,* **3,** pp. 473–479. Interscience Publishers, N.Y. and Lond.

EDGERTON H.E. (1967) The instruments of deep-sea photography, in Hersey, J.B. (ed.). *Deep sea photography,* pp. 47–54. Johns Hopkins Press, Baltimore.

EDGERTON H.E. & HOADLEY L.D. (1955) Cameras and lights for underwater use. *J. Soc. Motion Pict. Telev. Engrs,* **64,** pp. 345–350. (*Coll. Repr. Woods Hole oceanogr. Instn.* 1955, No. 817.)

EDGERTON H.E., PAYSON H., YULES J. & DILLION W. (1964) Sonar probing in Narragansett Bay. *Science, N.Y.* **146,** 3650, pp. 1459–1460.

ELLIS D.V. (1966) Aerial photography from helicopter as a technique for intertidal surveys. *Limnol. Oceanogr.* **11,** pp. 299–301.

ELLIS D.V. (1968) A series of computer programmes for summarising data from quantitative benthic investigations. *J. Fish. Res. Bd Can.* **25,** pp. 1737–1738.

ELLIS D.V. (1970) Ecologically significant species in coastal marine sediments of southern British Columbia. Syesis. (*In press.*)

EMERY K.O. (1960) *The sea off Southern California. A modern habitat of petroleum.* John Wiley & Sons, New York, 366 pp.

EMERY K.O. & DIETZ R.S. (1941) Gravity coring instruments and mechanics of sediment coring. *Bull. geol. Soc. Am.* **52,** pp. 1685–1714. (*Contr. Scripps Instn. Oceanogr.* 1941, No. 148.)

EMERY K.O., MERRILL A.S. & TRUMBULL J.V.A. (1965) Ecology and biology of the sea-floor as deduced from simultaneous photographs and samples. *Limnol. Oceanogr.* **10,** pp. 1–21.

EMIG C.C. & LIENHART R. (1967) Un nouveau moyen de récolte pour les substrats meubles infralittoraux: l'aspirateur sous-marin. *Recl Trav. Stn mar. Endoume,* **58,** pp. 115–120.

ERNST J. (1955) Sur la végetation sous-marine de la Manche d'après des observations en scaphandre autonome. *C.r. hebd. Séanc. Acad. Sci., Paris,* **241,** pp. 1066–1068.

EWING G.C. (1966) Space reconnaissance of the ocean: opportunities and limitations. *Ann. N.Y. Acad. Sci.* 140 art. 1, pp. 83–92. (*Coll. Repr. Woods Hole oceanogr. Instn,* 1967, No. 1740.)

EWING M., HAYES D.E. & THORNDIKE E.M. (1967) Corehead camera for measurement of currents and core orientation. *Deep-Sea Res.* **14,** pp. 253–258.

FAGER E.W. (1963) Communities of organisms, in M. N. Hill (ed.). *The Sea. Ideas and observations on progress in the study of the seas,* **2,** pp. 415–437. Interscience Publishers, N.Y. and Lond.

FAGER E.W. (1968) A sand-bottom epifaunal community of invertebrates in shallow water. *Limnol. Oceanogr.* **13,** pp. 448–464.

FAGER E.W., FLECHSIG A.O., FORD R.F., CLUTTER R.I. & GHELARDI R.J. (1966) Equipment for use in ecological studies using SCUBA. *Limnol. Oceanogr.* **11,** pp. 503–509.

FAHLEN L.A. (1967) Deck equipment layout on M/V 'Delaware' for surf clam survey. *Comml Fish. Rev.* **29,** 10, pp. 87–89.

FAO (1958) Annotated bibliography on fishing gear and methods. *Indo-Pacific Fisheries Council,* Spec. Publ. 4, FAO, Rome (unpaged).

FAO (1965) *FAO Catalogue of fishing gear designs.* FAO, Rome, 24 pp. + data sheets.

FENCHEL T. (1967) The ecology of marine microbenthos. I. The quantitative importance of ciliates as compared with metazoans in various types of sediments. *Ophelia,* **4,** pp. 121–137.

FENCHEL T. (1969) The ecology of marine microbenthos. IV. Structure and function of the benthic ecosystem, its chemical and physical factors and the micro-fauna communities with special reference to ciliated Protozoa. *Ophelia,* **6,** pp. 1–182.

FENCHEL T. & JANSSON B.D. (1966) On the vertical distribution of the microfauna in the sediments of a brackish water beach. *Ophelia,* **3** pp. 161–177.

FIELD J.G. & McFARLANE G. (1968) Numerical methods in marine ecology. 1. A quantitative 'similarity' analysis of rocky shore samples in False Bay, South Africa. *Zoologica Afr.* **3** pp. 119–137.

FINNISH IBP-PM GROUP (1969) Quantitative sampling equipment for the littoral benthos. *Int. Revue ges. Hydrobiol.* **54,** pp. 185–193.

FORSBER C. (1959) Quantitative sampling of sub-aquatic vegetation. *Oikos,* **10,** pp. 233–240.

FORSTER G.R. (1953) A new dredge for collecting burrowing animals. *J. mar. biol. Ass. U.K.* **32,** pp. 193–198.

FORSTER G.R. (1954) Preliminary notes on a survey of Stoke Point rocks with self-contained diving apparatus. *J. mar. biol. Ass. U.K.* **33,** pp. 341–344.

FORSTER G.R. (1959) The ecology of *Echinus esculentus* L. Quantitative distribution and rate of feeding. *J. mar. biol. Ass. U.K.* **38,** pp. 361–368.

FORSTER G.R. (1961) An underwater survey on the Lulworth Bank. *J. mar. biol. Ass. U.K.* **41**, pp. 157–160.

FOWLER G.H. & ALLEN E.J. (1928) *Science of the Sea.* Oxford 2nd ed. 502 pp.

FOWLER G.A. & KULM L.D. (1966) A multiple corer. *Limnol. Oceanogr.* **11**, pp. 630–633.

FOX H.M. & WINGFIELD C.A. (1938) A portable apparatus for the determination of oxygen dissolved in a small volume of water. *J. exp. Biol.* **15**, pp. 437–445.

FRAZER H.J. (1935) Experimental study of porosity and permeability of clastic sediments. *J. Geol.* **43**, pp. 910–1010.

FREIESLEBEN H.C. (1969) Position finding at sea. *Oceanogr. Mar. Biol. Ann. Rev.* 1968, **6**, pp. 47–81.

FROLANDER H.F. & PRATT I. (1962) A bottom skimmer. *Limnol. Oceanogr.* **7**, pp. 104–106.

GAARDER T. & GRAN H.H. (1927) Investigations of the production of plankton in the Oslo Fjord. *Rapp. P.-v. Réun. Cons. perm. int. Explor. Mer,* **42**, pp. 1–48.

GALLARDO V.A. (1965) Observations on the biting profiles of three 0·1 m² bottom samplers. *Ophelia,* **2**, pp. 319–322.

GEORGE J.D. (1964) Organic matter available to the polychaete *Cirriformia tentaculata* (Montagu) living in an intertidal mudflat. *Limnol. Oceanogr.* **9**, pp. 453–455.

GERKING S.D. (1955) Influence of rate of feeding on body composition and protein metabolism of Bluegill Sunfish. *Physiol. Ecol.* **28**, pp. 267–282.

GERKING S.D. (1957) A method of sampling the littoral macrofauna and its application. *Ecol.* **38**, pp. 217–226.

GIBSON R.N. (1967) The use of the anaesthetic quinaldine in fish ecology. *J. anim. Ecol.* **36**, pp. 295–301.

GIESE A.C. (1967) Some methods for study of the biochemical constitution of marine invertebrates. *Oceanogr. Mar. Biol. Ann. Rev.* **5**, pp. 159–186.

GILAT E. (1964) The macrobenthonic invertebrate communities on the Mediterranean continental shelf of Israel. *Bull. Inst. océanogr. Monaco,* **62** (1290), 46 pp.

GILBERT W.H. (1968) Distribution and dispersion patterns of the dwarf tellin clam, *Tellina agilis. Biol. Bull. mar. biol. Lab., Woods Hole,* **135**, pp. 419–420.

GILLESPIE D.M. & BROWN C.J.D. (1966) A quantitative sampler for macro-invertebrates associated with aquatic macrophytes. *Limnol. Oceanogr.* **11**, pp. 404–406.

GILSON W.E. (1963) Differential respirometer of simplified and improved design. *Science, N.Y.* **141**, pp. 531–532.

GLICK D. (1961) *Quantitative chemical techniques of histo and cytochemistry.* **1**, John Wiley & Son, N.Y. 470 pp.

GOLDMAN C.R. (1963) The measurement of primary productivity and limiting factors in freshwater with carbon-14, in Doty, M.S. (ed.). *Proceedings of the conference on primary productivity measurement, marine and freshwater, Univ. Hawaii,* 1961, pp. 103–115. U.S. Atomic Energy Commission TID–7633.

GOLLEY F.B. (1961) Energy values of ecological materials. *Ecology,* **42** (3), pp. 581–583.

GOLLEY F., ODUM H.T. & WILSON R.F. (1962) The structure and metabolism of a Puerto Rican red mangrove forest in May. *Ecology,* **43**, pp. 9–19.

GRIFFITHS J.C. (1967) *Scientific method in analysis of sediments.* New York, McGraw Hill Comp., Ch. 6–8, pp. 109–173.

GRØNTVED J. (1960) On the productivity of microbenthos and phytoplankton in some Danish fjords. *Meddr Danm. Fisk.-og Havunders.*, N.S. **3**, pp. 55–92.

GRØNTVED J. (1962) Preliminary report on productivity of microbenthos and phytoplankton in the Danish Wadden Sea. *Meddr Danm. Fisk.-og Havunders.*, N.S. **3**, pp. 347–378.

GUILLE A. (1965) Exploration en soucoupe plongeante Cousteau de l'entrée nord-est de la baie de Rosas (Espagne). *Bull. Inst. océanogr. Monaco*, **65**, (1357), pp. 1–12.

GULLAND J.A. (1966) Manual of sampling and statistical methods for fisheries biology. Part 1. Sampling Methods. *FAO Man. Fish. Sci.* 3, Foreword etc. 6pp.; Fasc. 1, 13 pp.; Fasc. 2, 16 pp.; Fasc. 3, 35 pp.; Fasc. 4, 20 pp.; Fasc. 5, 3 pp.

GUNTER G. (1957) Dredges and trawls. *Mem. geol. Soc. Amer.* **67**, 1, pp. 73–80.

HAMILTON A.L. (1969) A method of separating invertebrates from sediments using longwave ultra-violet light and fluorescent dyes. *J. Fish. Res. Bd Can.* **26**, pp. 1667–1672.

HARDING J.P. (1949) The use of probability paper for the graphical analysis of polymodal frequency distributions. *J. mar. biol. Ass. U.K.* **28**, pp. 141–153.

HARDY A.C. (1959) *The Open Sea: its Natural History. Part II. Fish and Fisheries* (New Naturalist Series, 37). Collins, London, 322 pp.

HARDY E. (1954) Local types of lobster and crab traps. *Wld Fishg*, **3**, pp. 354–358.

HARFORD J. (1968) Underwater lighting—a status report, in Alt, F. (ed.) in *Marine sciences instrumentation*, **4**, pp. 373–380. Proc. 4th nat. ISA Marine Sciences Instrumentation Symp. Florida, 22–26 Jan. 1968. Plenium Press, New York.

HARTMAN O. (1955) Quantitative survey of the benthos of San Pedro Basin, Southern California. Part I. Preliminary results. *Allan Hancock Pacif. Exped.* **19**, 185 pp.

HARTNOLL R.G. (1967) An investigation of the movement of the scallop, *Pecten maximus*, by diving. *Helgoländer wiss. Meeresunters.* **15**, pp. 523–533.

HASS H. (1948) Beitrag zur Kentniss der Reteporiden und einem Bericht über die dabei angewandte neue Methode für Untersuchungen auf dem Meeresgrund. *Zoologica Stuttg.* **37** (101), pp. 1–138.

HERSEY J.B. (1960) Acoustically monitored bottom coring. *Deep-Sea Res.* **6**, pp. 170–172.

HERSEY J.B. (ed.) (1967) Deep-sea photography. *Johns Hopkins oceanogr. Stud.* 3, 310 pp.

HESSLER R.R. & SANDERS H.L. (1967). Faunal diversity in the deep sea. *Deep-Sea Res.* **14**, pp. 65–78.

HEYWOOD J. & EDWARDS R.W. (1962) Some aspects of the ecology of *Potamopyrgus jenkinsi* Smith. *J. Anim. Ecol.* **31**, pp. 239–250.

HIATT R. & STRASBURG D. (1960) Ecological relationships of the fish fauna on coral reefs of the Marshall Islands. *Ecol. Monogr.* **30**, pp. 65–127.

HICKMAN M. (1969) Methods for determining the primary productivity of epipelic and epipsammic algal associations. *Limnol. Oceanogr.* **14**, 936 - 941.

HICKMAN M. & ROUND F.E. (1970) Primary production and standing crops of epipsammic and epipelic algae. *Br. phycol. J.* **5**, pp. 247–255.

HIGGINS R.P. (1964) Three new kinorhynchs from the North Carolina coast. *Bull. mar. Sci. Gulf Caribb.* **14**, pp. 479–493.

HIGH W.L. & LUSZ L.D. (1966) Underwater observations on fish in an off-bottom trawl. *J. Fish. Res. Bd Can.* **23**, pp. 153–154.

HOLD J. (1960) New diving sled for underwater photography. *Comml Fish. Rev.* **22**, 5, pp. 10–12.

HOLME N.A. (1949a) The fauna of sand and mud banks near the mouth of the Exe estuary. *J. mar. biol. Ass. U.K.* **28**, pp. 189–237.

HOLME N.A. (1949b) A new bottom-sampler. *J. mar. biol. Ass. U.K.* **28**, pp. 323–332.

HOLME N.A. (1950) Population-dispersion in *Tellina tenuis* da Costa. *J. mar. biol. Ass. U.K.* **29**, pp. 267–280.

HOLME N.A. (1953) The biomass of the bottom fauna in the English Channel off Plymouth. *J. mar. biol. Ass. U.K.* **32**, pp. 1–49.

HOLME N.A. (1959) A hopper for use when sieving bottom samples at sea. *J. mar. biol. Ass. U.K.* **38**, pp. 525–529.

HOLME N.A. (1964) Methods of sampling the benthos. *Adv. mar. biol.* **2**, pp. 171–260.

HOLMES R.W. (1957) Solar radiation, submarine daylight and photosynthesis. *Mem. geol. Soc. Amer.* **67**, 1, pp. 109–128.

HOLMES R.W. & SNODGRASS J.M. (1961) A multiple-detector irradiance meter and electronic depth-sensing unit for use in biological oceanography. *J. mar. Res.* **19**, pp. 40–56.

HOPKINS J.T. (1963) A study of the diatoms of the Ouse Estuary, Sussex. I. The movement of the mud-flat diatoms in response to some chemical and physical changes. *J. mar. biol. Ass. U.K.* **43**, pp. 653–663.

HOPKINS T.L. (1964) A survey of marine bottom samplers. *Prog. Oceanogr.* **2**, pp. 213–256.

HUGHES R.N. (1970) Appraisal of the iodate-sulphuric acid wet-oxidation procedure for the estimation of the caloric content of marine sediments. *J. Fish. Res. Bd Can. (In press.)*

HULINGS N.C. & GRAY J.S. (1971) A manual for the study of meiofauna. *Smithson. contr. Zool.* **78**. *(In press.)*

HUSE H.V. (1961) Hydraulic deck equipment for Research Vessels, in Traung J-O and Tujinami N. (eds.). *Research Vessel Design.* F.A.O., Rome.

HUTCHINSON G.E. (1967) *A Treatise on Limnology. Volume II. Introduction to Lake Biology and the Limnoplankton.* John Wiley & Sons, New York, 1115 pp.

ISAACS J.D. & SCHICK G.B. (1960) Deep-sea free instrument vehicle. *Deep-Sea Res.* **7**, pp. 61–67.

IVANOFF A. (1956) Etude de pénétration de la lumière dans la mer. *Annls Géophys.* **12**, pp. 32–44.

IVANOFF A. (1957) Un polarimètre sous-marin à cellule photo-électrique, premiers résultats obtenus. *Bull. Inf. Com. cent. Océanogr. Etude Côtes,* **9**, pp. 491–499.

IVANOFF A., JERLOV N. & WATERMAN T.H. (1961) A comparative study of irradiance, beam transmittance and scattering in the sea near Bermuda. *Limnol. Oceanogr.* **6**, pp. 129–148.

IVLEV V.S. (1934) Eine Mikromethode zur bestimming des Kaloriengehalts von Nahrstoffen. *Biochem. Z.* **275**, pp. 49–55.

IVLEV V.S. (1945) The biological productivity of waters. *Usp. sovrem. Biol.* **19**, pp. 98–120.

JACCARD P. (1912) The distribution of the flora in the alpine zone. *New Phytol.* **11**, pp. 37–50.

JACKSON J.B.C. (1968) Spatial and size-frequency distributions of two intertidal species. *Science, N.Y.* **161**, No. 3840, p. 479

JACOBSEN J.P., ROBINSON R.J. & THOMPSON T.G. (1950) A review of the determination of dissolved oxygen in sea water by the Winkler method. *Publs scient. Ass. Océanogr. phys.* **11**, 22 pp.

JERLOV N.G. (1951) Optical studies of ocean waters. *Rep. Swed. deep Sea Exped.* **3**, pp. 1–59.

JERLOV N.G. (ed.) (1961) Symposium on radiant energy in the Sea. *Union Géod. Géophys. int., Monographie*, **10**, 116 pp.

JERLOV N.G. (1963) Optical oceanography. *Oceanography mar. Biol. Ann. Rev.* **1**, pp. 89–114.

JERLOV N.G. (1965) The evolution of the instrumental technique in underwater optics. *Prog. Oceanogr.* **3**, pp. 149–154.

JERLOV N.G. (1968) *Optical oceanography.* 194 pp. Amsterdam: Elsevier.

JITTS H.R. (1963) The simulated *in situ* measurement of oceanic primary production. *Aust. J. mar. Freshwat. Res.* **14**, pp. 139–147.

JOHNSON N.G. & OLSSON H. (1943) On the standardisation of photo-electric elements by means of solar radiation. *Geogr. Annlr.* **25**, pp. 202–215.

JOHNSTON C.S. (1969) The ecological distribution and primary production of macrophytic marine algae in the Eastern Canaries. *Int. Revue ges. Hydrobiol.* **54**, pp. 473–490.

JOHNSTON C.S. & COOK J.P. (1968) A preliminary assessment of the techniques for measuring primary production in macrophytic marine algae. *Experientia*, **24**, pp. 1176–1177.

JOHNSTON C.S., MORRISON I.A. & MACLACHLAN K. (1969) A photographic method for recording the underwater distribution of marine benthic organisms. *J. Ecol.* **57**, pp. 453–459.

JÓNASSON P.M. (1955) The efficiency of sieving techniques for sampling freshwater bottom fauna. *Oikos*, **6**, pp. 183–207.

JONES N.S. (1950) Marine bottom communities. *Biol. Rev.* **25**, pp. 283–313.

JONES N.S. & KAIN J.M. (1964) The numbers of O-group plaice in Port Erin Bay in August 1963 observed by diving. *Rep. mar. biol. Stn Port Erin*, **76**, pp. 19–25.

JONES N.S. & KAIN J.M. (1967) Subtidal algal colonisation following the removal of *Echinus. Helgoländer wiss. Meeresunters.* **15**, pp. 460–466.

JONES N.S., KAIN J.M. & STRIDE A.H. (1965) The movement of sand waves on Warts Bank, Isle of Man. *Mar. Geol.* **3**, pp. 329–336.

JØRGENSEN C.B. (1962) Efficiency of growth in *Mytilus edulis* and two gastropod veligers. *Nature, Lond.* **170**, p. 714

JØRGENSEN C.B. (1966) *Biology of suspension feeding.* Pergamon Press, London, N.Y. 357 pp.

JOSEPH J. (1949) Uber die Messung das 'Vertikalen Extinktions-koeffizienten'. *Dt. hydrogr. Z.* **2**, pp. 255–267.

KAIN J.M. (1958) Observations on the littoral algae of the Isle of Wight. *J. mar. biol. Ass. U.K.* **37**, pp. 769–780.

KAIN J.M. (1960) Direct observations on some Manx sublittoral algae. *J. mar. biol. Ass. U.K.* **39**, pp. 609–630.

KAIN J.M. (1962) Aspects of the biology of *Laminaria hyperborea*. I. Vertical distribution. *J. mar. biol. Ass. U.K.* **42**, pp. 377–386.

KAIN J.M. (1963) Aspects of the biology of *Laminaria hyperborea*. II. Age, weight and length. *J. mar. biol. Ass. U.K.* **43**, pp. 129–151.

KALLE K. (1966) The problem of the Gelbstoff in the sea. *Oceanography mar. Biol. Ann. Rev.* **4**, pp. 91–104.

KANWISHER J. (1959) Polarographic oxygen electrode. *Limnol. Oceanogr.* **4**, pp. 210–217.

KEMP S., HARDY A.C. & MACKINTOSH N.A. (1929) Discovery Investigations. Objects, equipment and methods. *Discovery Rep.* **1**, pp. 141–232.

KEMPF M. (1962) Recherches d'écologie comparée sur *Paracentrotus lividus* (Lmk) et *Arbacia lixula* (L.). *Recl Trav. Stn mar. Endoume,* **39**, pp. 47–116.

KISSAM P. (1956) *Surveying.* 2nd ed. McGraw-Hill Book Co. Inc., N.Y., Toronto, London, 482 pp.

KNIGHT M. & PARKE M. (1950) A biological study of *Fucus vesiculosus* L. and *F. serratus* L. *J. mar. biol. Ass. U.K.* **29**, pp. 439–514.

KNIGHT-JONES E.W., NELSON SMITH A. & BAILEY J.H. (1967) Methods for transects across steep rocks and channels. *Underwater Ass. Rep.* 1966–67, pp. 107–111.

KNUDSEN M. (1927) A bottom sampler for hard bottom. *Medd. Komm. Havundersøg, Kbh,* Ser. Fisk. **8**, 3, 4 pp.

KOSLER A. (1968) Distributional patterns of the eulittoral fauna near the Isle of Hiddensee (Baltic Sea, Rugia). *Mar. Biol.* **1**, pp. 266–268.

KROGH A. & SPARCK R. (1936) On a new bottom sampler for investigation of the microfauna of the sea bottom. *K. danske Vidensk. Selsk. Skr.* **13**, pp. 1–12.

KRONENGOLD M. & LOWENSTEIN J.M. (1965) Cinematography from an underwater television camera. *Res. Film,* **5**, pp. 242–248.

KRUMBEIN W.C. & PETTIJOHN F.J. (1938) *Manual of sedimentary petrography.* Appleton-Century-Crofts Inc., New York, 549 pp.

KUENEN P.H. (1965) Geological conditions of sedimentation, in Riley, J.P. & Skirrow, G. (ed.). *Chemical Oceanography,* **2**, pp. 1–21. Academic Press, London.

KUENZLER E.J. (1961) Structure and energy flow of a mussel population in a Georgia salt marsh. *Limnol. Oceanogr.* **6**, pp. 191–204.

KULLENBERG B. (1951) On the shape and the length of the cable during a deep-sea trawling. *Swed. deep Sea Exped.* **2**, pp. 29–44.

KULLENBERG B. (1955) Deep-sea coring. *Rep. Swed. deep Sea Exped.* **4**, pp. 35–96.

KULLENBERG B. (1956) The technique of trawling, in Bruun, A.F. *et al.* (ed.). *The Galathea Deep Sea Expedition* 1950–1952, pp. 112–118, Allen and Unwin, London.

KUMPF H.E. & RANDALL H.A. (1961) Charting the marine environment of St. John, U.S. Virgin Islands. *Bull. mar. Sci. Gulf Caribb.* **11**, pp. 543–551.

KUZNETSOV S.I. (1956) Application of radioactive isotopes to the study of processes of photosynthesis and chemosynthesis in lakes. *Proc. Internat. Conf. Peaceful Uses of Atomic Energy,* **12**. Radioactive Isotopes and Ionizing Radiations in Agriculture Physiology and Biochemistry, pp. 363–376.

LABAN A., PÉRÈS J.-M. & PICARD J. (1963) La photographie sous-marine profonde et son exploitation scientifique. *Bull. Inst. océanogr. Monaco,* **60**, 1258, 32 pp.

LABOREL J. (1960) Contribution a l'étude directe des peuplements benthiques sciaphiles sur substrats rocheux en Méditerranée. *Recl Trav. Stn mar. Endoume,* **33**, pp. 117–173.

LABOREL J., PÉRÈS J.M., PICARD J. & VACELET J. (1961) Etude directe des fonds des parages de Marseille de 30 à 300 m avec la soucoupe plongeante Cousteau. *Bull. Inst. océanogr. Monaco,* **1206**, pp. 1–16.

LABOREL J. & VACELET J. (1959) Les grottes sous-marines obscures en Méditerranée. *C.r. hebd. Séanc. Acad. Sci., Paris,* **248**, pp. 2619–2621.

LARSSON B.A.S. (1968) Scuba-studies on vertical distribution of Swedish rocky-bottom echinoderms. A methodological study. *Ophelia,* **5,** pp. 137–156.

LASSIG J. (1965) An improvement to the van Veen bottom grab. *J. Cons. perm. int. Explor. Mer,* **29,** pp. 352–353.

LAUFF G.M., CUMMINS K.W., ERIKSEN C.H. & PARKER M. (1961) A method for sorting bottom fauna samples by elutriation. *Limnol. Oceanogr.* **6,** pp. 462–466.

LAUGHTON A.S. (1957) A new deep-sea underwater camera. *Deep-Sea Res.* **4,** pp. 120–125. (*Coll. Repr. natn. Instn Oceanogr.* **5,** No. 194.)

LAUGHTON A.S. (1963) Microtopography, in Hill, M.N. (ed.). *The Sea. Ideas and observations on progress in the study of the seas,* **3,** pp. 437–472. Inter-science Publishers, N.Y. and Lond.

LAUGHTON A.S. (1967) Dredging, in *International Dictionary of Geophysics,* pp. 261–262, Pergamon Press, Oxford.

LEDOYER M. (1966a) Ecologie de la faune vagile des biotopes Méditerranéens accessible en scaphandre autonome. I. Introduction. Données analytiques sur les biotopes de substrat dur. *Recl Trav. Stn mar. Endoume,* **56,** pp. 103–150.

LEDOYER M. (1966b) Ecologie de la faune vagile des biotopes Méditerranéens accessible en scaphandre autonome. II. Données analytiques sur les herbiers de Phanérogames. *Recl Trav. Stn mar. Endoume,* **57,** pp. 135–164.

LEDOYER M. (1966c) Ecologie de la faune vagile des biotopes Méditerranéens accessible en scaphandre autonome. III. Données analytiques sur les biotopes de substrat meuble. *Recl Trav. Stn mar. Endoume,* **57,** pp. 165–186.

LEIGHTON D.L., JONES L.G. & NORTH W.J. (1965) Ecological relationships between giant kelp and sea urchins in southern California. *Vth Int. Seaweed Symp.* pp. 141–154.

LENOBLE J. (1956) Etude de la pénétration de l'ultraviolet dans la mer. *Annls Géophys.* **12,** pp. 16–31.

LENOBLE J. (1958) Penetration du rayonment ultraviolet dans la mer. *Annls Inst. oceanogr., Monaco,* **34,** pp. 297–308.

LEWIS J.R. (1964) *The Ecology of Rocky Shores.* English Universities Press, London, 323 pp.

LIE U. & PAMATMAT U.U. (1965) Digging characteristics and sampling efficiency of the 0·1 m² van Veen grab. *Limnol. Oceanogr.* **10,** pp. 379–384.

LILLY S.J., SLOANE J.F., BASSINDALE R., EBLING F.J. & KITCHING J.A. (1953) The ecology of the Lough Ine rapids with special reference to water currents. IV. The sedentary fauna of sublittoral boulders. *J. an. Ecol.* **22,** pp. 87–122.

LIMBAUGH C. (1961) Cleaning symbiosis. *Scient. Am.* **205,** pp. 42–49.

LINDEMAN R.L. (1942) The trophic-dynamic aspect of ecology. *Ecology,* **23,** pp. 399–418.

LISITSIN A.I. & UDINTSEV G.B. (1955) A new type of grab. (In Russian.) *Trudy Vses Gidrobiol. Obsch.* **6,** pp. 217–222.

LITTLE F.J. Jr. & MULLINS B. (1964) Diving plate modification of Blake (beam) trawl for deep-sea sampling. *Limnol. Oceanogr.* **9,** pp. 148–150.

LONGHURST A.R. (1959) The sampling problem in benthic ecology. *Proc. N.Z. ecol. Soc.* **6,** pp. 8–12.

LORENZEN C.J. (1967) Determination of chlorophyll and pheo-pigments: spectrophotometric equations. *Limnol. Oceanogr.* **12,** pp. 343–346.

LUND J.W.G., KIPLING C. & LE CREN E.D. (1958) The inverted microscope method of estimating algal numbers and the statistical basis of estimations by counting. *Hydrobiologia*, **11**, pp. 143–170.

LUND J.W.G. & TALLING J.F. (1957) Botanical limnological methods with special reference to the algae. *Bot. Rev.* **23**, pp. 489–583.

LYDELL W.R.S. (1936) A new apparatus for separating insects and other arthropods from soil. *Ann. appl. Biol.* **23**, pp. 862–879.

LYMAN F.E. (1943) A pre-impoundment bottom fauna study of Watts Bar Reservoir area (Tennessee). *Trans. Am. Fish. Soc.* **72**, pp. 52–62.

MCALLISTER C.D., SHAH N. & STRICKLAND J.D.H. (1964) Marine phytoplankton photosynthesis as a function of light intensity: a comparison of methods. *J. Fish. Res. Bd Can.* **21**, pp. 159–181.

MCALLISTER R.F. (1957) Photography of submerged vertical structures. *Trans. Am. Geophys. Union*, **38**, pp. 314–319. (*Contr. Scripps Instn Oceanogr.*, 1957, No. 924.)

MCCANCE R.A. & MASTERS M. (1937) The chemical composition and the acid base balance of *Archidoris britannica*. *J. mar. biol. Ass. U.K.* **22**, pp 273–279.

MACFADYEN A. (1948) The meaning of productivity in biological systems. *J. Anim. Ecol.* **17**, pp. 75–80.

MACFADYEN A. (1963) *Animal ecology, aims and methods* (2nd ed.). London, Pitman, 344 pp.

MACGINITIE G.E. (1935) Ecological aspects of a California marine estuary. *Amer. Midl. Nat.* **16**, pp. 629–765.

MACGINITIE G.E. (1939) Littoral marine communities. *Amer. Midl. Nat.* **21**, pp. 28–55.

MACINNIS J.B. (1966) Living under the sea. *Scient. Am.* **214** (3), pp. 24–33.

MCINTYRE A.D. (1956) The use of trawl, grab and camera in estimating marine benthos. *J. mar. biol. Ass. U.K.* **35**, pp. 419–429.

MCINTYRE A.D. (1961) Quantitative differences in the fauna of boreal mud associations. *J. mar. biol. Ass. U.K.* **41**, pp. 599–616.

MCINTYRE A.D. (1964) Meiobenthos of sub-littoral muds. *J. mar. biol. Ass. U.K.* **44**, pp. 665–674.

MCINTYRE A.D. (1968) The meiofauna and microfauna of some tropical beaches. *J. Zool.* **156**, pp. 377–392.

MCINTYRE A.D. (1969) Ecology of marine meiobenthos. *Biol. Rev.* **44**, pp. 245–290.

MCINTYRE A.D. (ed.) (1970) Bibliography on methods of studying the marine benthos. *FAO Fish. tech. Pap.* **98**, 96 p.

MACNAE W. (1967) Zonation within mangroves associated with estuaries in North Queensland, in *Estuaries*, ed. Lauff, G.H. Publ. 83. American Assn Adv. Sci., Washington, D.C. 1967. pp. 432–441.

MACNAE W. (1968) A general account of the fauna and flora of mangrove swamps and forests in the Indo-West-Pacific region. *Adv. mar. Biol.* **6**, pp. 73–270.

MCNEELEY R.L. & PEREYRA W.T. (1961) A simple screening device for the separation of benthic samples at sea. *J. Cons. perm. int. Explor. Mer*, **26**, pp. 259–262.

MCPHAIL J.S. & MEDCOF J.C. (1962) Fishing efficiency trials with a hydraulic clam (*Mya*) rake—1961. *Manuscr. Rep. Ser. (Biol.) Fish. Res. Bd Can.* p. 724.

MACER T.C. (1967) A new bottom-plankton sampler. *J. Cons. perm. int. Explor. Mer,* **31,** pp. 158–163.

MANN K.H. (1965) Energy transformations by a population of fish in the River Thames. *J. Anim. Ecol.* **34,** pp. 253–275.

MARE M.F. (1942) A study of a marine benthic community with special reference to the micro-organisms. *J. mar. biol. Ass. U.K.* **25,** pp. 517–554.

MARGALEF R. (1949) A new limnological method for the investigation of thin-layered epilithic communities. *Hydrobiologia,* **1,** pp. 215–216.

MARKHAM R. (1942) A steam distillation apparatus suitable for micro-Kjeldahl analysis. *Biochem. J.* **36,** pp. 790–791.

MARSHALL S.M. & ORR A.P. (1961) On the biology of *Calanus finmarchicus.* XII. The phosphorus cycle: excretion, egg production, autolysis. *J. mar. biol. Ass. U.K.* **41** pp. 463–488.

MASSÉ H. (1967) Emploi d'une suceuse hydraulique transformée pour les prélèvements quantitatifs dans les substrats meubles infra-littoraux. *Helgoländer wiss. Meeresunters.* **15,** pp. 500–505.

MATTHEWS D.J. (1939) *Tables of the velocity of sound in pure water and in sea water.* 2nd ed. Hydrographic Dept., Admiralty, London. 52 pp

MEANS R.E. & PARCHER J.V. (1964) *Physical proportions of soils.* Constable, London, 464 pp.

MENZIES R.J. (1964) Improved techniques for benthic trawling at depths greater than 2,000 metres. *Antarct. Res. Ser.* **1,** pp. 93–109.

MENZIES R.J., SMITH L. & EMERY K.O. (1963) A combined underwater camera and bottom grab: a new tool for investigation of deep-sea benthos. *Int. Revue ges. Hydrobiol. Hydrogr.* **48,** pp. 529–545.

MILLS A.A. (1961) An external core retainer. *Deep-Sea Res.* **7,** p. 4

MISHIMA J. & ODUM E.P. (1963) Excretion rate of Zn^{65} by *Littorina irrorata* in relation to temperature and body size. *Limnol. Oceanogr.* **8,** pp. 39–44.

MITCHELL C.T. (1967) An inexpensive, self-contained underwater data recording camera. *Calif. Fish Game,* **53,** pp. 203–208.

MITSON R.B. (1963) Marine fish culture in Britain. V. An electronic device for counting the nauplii of *Artemia salina* L. *J. Cons. perm. int. Explor. Mer,* **28,** pp. 262–269.

MOORE H.B. (1931) The muds of the Clyde sea area. III. Chemical and physical conditions; rate and nature of sedimentation; and fauna. *J. mar. biol. Ass. U.K.* **17,** pp. 325–358.

MOORE H.B., DAVIES L.T., FRASER T.H., GORE R.H. & LOPEZ N.R. (1968) Some biomass figures from a tidal flat in Biscayne Bay, Florida. *Bull. mar. Sci.* **18,** pp. 261–279.

MOORE H.B. & NEILL R.G. (1930) An instrument for sampling marine muds. *J. mar. biol. Ass. U.K.* **16,** pp. 589–594.

MORGANS J.F.C. (1956) Notes on the analysis of shallow-water soft substrata. *J. Anim. Ecol.* **25,** pp. 367–387.

MORGANS J.F.C. (1957) The benthic ecology of False Bay. Part I. The biology of infratidal rocks observed by diving, related to that of intertidal rocks. *Trans. R. Soc. S. Afr.* **35,** pp. 387–442.

MORGANS J.F.C. (1962) The benthic ecology of False Bay. Part II. Soft and rocky bottoms observed by diving and sampled by dredging, and the recognition of grounds. *Trans. R. Soc. S. Afr.* **36,** pp. 287–334.

MORGANS J.F.C. (1965) A simple method for determining levels along seashore transects. *Tuakara,* **13,** pt. 3.

MORTENSEN T.H. (1925) An apparatus for catching the micro-fauna of the sea bottom. *Vidensk. Medd. dansk naturh. Foren. Kbh.* **80,** pp. 445–451.

MORTON J.E. (1954) The crevice faunas of the upper intertidal zone at Wembury. *J. mar. biol. Ass. U.K.* **33,** pp. 187–224.

MOSS B. (1967a) A note on the estimation of chlorophyll *a* in freshwater algal communities. *Limnol. Oceanogr.* **12,** pp. 340–342.

MOSS B. (1967b) A spectrophotometric method for the estimation of percentage degradation of chlorophylls to pheo-pigments in extracts of algae. *Limnol. Oceanogr.* **12,** pp. 335–340.

MOSS B. & ROUND F.E. (1967) Observations on standing crops of epipelic and epipsammic algal communities in Shear Water, Wilts. *Br. phycol. Bull.* **3,** pp. 241–248.

MOYSE J. & NELSON-SMITH A. (1963) Zonation of animals and plants on rocky shores around Dale, Pembrokeshire. *Field Studies,* **1,** 5, 31 pp.

MUNDEY G.R. (1968) Underwater photography. *Hydrospace,* **1** (2), pp. 36–42.

MURRAY J. & HJORT J. (1912) *The depths of the ocean.* MacMillan, London, 821 pp.

MURRAY J.W. (1966) A study of the seasonal changes of water mass of Christchurch Harbour, England. *J. mar. biol. Ass. U.K.* **46,** pp. 561–578.

MUUS B. (1964) A new quantitative sampler for the meiobenthos. *Ophelia,* **1,** pp. 209–216.

MYERS E.H. (1942) Rate at which Foraminifera are contributed to marine sediments. *J. sedim. Petrol.* **12,** pp. 92–95. (*Coll. Repr. Woods Hole oceanogr. Instn,* No. 314.)

NALWALK A.J., HERSEY J.B., REITZEL J.S. & EDGERTON H.E. (1962) Improved techniques of deep-sea rock dredging. *Deep-Sea Res.* **8,** pp. 301–302. (*Coll. Repr. Woods Hole oceanogr. Instn No.* 1216.)

NEUSHUL M. (1963) Studies on the giant kelp, *Macrocystis.* II. Reproduction. *Am. J. Bot.* **50,** pp. 354–359.

NEUSHUL M. & HAXO F.T. (1963) Studies on the giant kelp, *Macrocystis.* I. Growth of young plants. *Am. J. Bot.* **50,** pp. 349–353.

NEWELL R.C. & NORTHCROFT H.R. (1967) A re-interpretation of the effect of temperature on the metabolism of certain marine invertebrates. *J. Zool., Lond.* **151,** pp. 277–298.

NICHOLSON W.M., TOMSKY J.M. *et al.* (1968) Sealab III. *Undersea Technol.* **9,** 8, pp. 25–52.

NISHIMURA M. & HARA M. (1968) Utilisation de la télévision sous-marine au Japan. *Rev. Hydrogr. int.* **45,** pp. 125–134.

NORTH W.J. (1964) Experimental transplantation of the giant kelp, *Macrocystis pyrifera. IVth Int. Seaweed Symp.* pp. 248–254.

NORTON T.A. & BURROWS E.M. (1969) Studies on marine algae of the British Isles. 7. *Saccorhiza polyschides* (Lightf.) *Br. phycol. Bull.* **4,** pp. 19–53.

NYBELIN O. (1951) Introduction and station list. *Swed. deep Sea Exped.* **2,** pp. 1–28.

OCKELMANN K.W. (1964) An improved detritus-sledge for collecting meiobenthos. *Ophelia,* **1,** pp. 217–222.

O'CONNOR F.B. (1955) Extraction of enchytraeid worms from a coniferous forest soil. *Nature, Lond.* **175,** pp. 815–816.

ODUM E.P. (1959) *Fundamentals of Ecology.* (2nd ed.). Saunders, Philadelphia, 546 pp.

ODUM E.P. (1961) Excretion of radio-isotopes as indices of metabolic rates in nature: biological half-life of Zinc-65 in relation to temperature, food consumption, growth and reproduction in arthropods. *Biol. Bull. mar. biol. Lab., Woods Hole,* **121,** pp. 371–372.

ODUM E.P. & SMALLEY A.E. (1959) Comparison of population energy flow of an herbivorous and a deposit-feeding invertebrate in a saltmarsh ecosystem. *Proc. Nat. Acad. Sci.* **45,** pp. 617–622.

ODUM H.T. (1957a) Trophic structure and productivity of Silver Springs, Florida. *Ecol. Monogr.* **27,** pp. 55–112.

ODUM H.T. (1957b) Primary production measurements in eleven Florida springs and a marine turtle-grass community. *Limnol. Oceanogr.* **2,** pp. 85–97.

ODUM H.T., McCONNELL W. & ABBOTT W. (1958) The chlorophyll 'a' of communities. *Publs Inst. mar. Sci. Univ. Tex.* **5,** pp. 65–96.

ODUM H.T. & ODUM E.P. (1955) Trophic structure and productivity of a windward coral reef community on Eniwetok Atoll. *Ecol. Monogr.* **25,** pp. 291–320.

O'GOWER A.K. & WACASEY J.W. (1967). Animal communities associated with *Thalassia, Diplantheres* and sand beds in Biscayne Bay. I. Analyses of communities in relation to water movements. *Bull. Mar. Sci.* **17,** pp. 175–210.

OVERGAARD C. (1948) An apparatus for quantitative extraction of nematodes and rotifers from soil and moss. *Natura jutl.* **1,** pp. 271–277.

OWEN D.M. (1967) A multi-shot stereoscopic camera for close-up ocean-bottom photography, in Hersey, J.B. (ed.). Deep-sea photography, *Johns Hopkins oceanogr. Stud.* **3,** pp. 95–105.

OWEN D.M., SANDERS H.L. & HESSLER R.R. (1967) Bottom photography as a tool for estimating benthic populations, in Hersey, J.B. (ed.). Deep-sea photography, *Johns Hopkins oceanogr. Stud.* **3,** pp. 229–234.

PAFFENHÖFER G.-A. (1967) Caloric content of the larvae of the brine shrimp *Artemia salina. Helgoländer wiss. Meeresunters.,* **16,** pp. 130–135.

PAINE R.T. (1964) Ash and caloric determinations of sponge and opisthobranch tissues. *Ecology,* **45,** pp. 384–387.

PAINE R.T. (1965) Natural history, limiting factors and energetics of the opisthobranch *Navanax inermis. Ecology,* **46,** pp. 603–619.

PAINE R.T. (1966) Endothermy in bomb calorimetry. *Limnol. Oceanogr.* **11,** pp. 126–129.

PALMER J.D. & ROUND F.E. (1967) Persistent vertical-migration rhythms in benthic microflora. VI. The tidal and diurnal nature of the rhythm in the diatom, *Hantzschia virgata. Biol. Bull. mar. biol. Lab., Woods Hole,* **132,** pp. 44–55.

PAMATMAT M.M. (1965) A continuous-flow apparatus for measuring metabolism of benthic communities. *Limnol. Oceanogr.* **10,** pp. 486–489.

PAMATMAT M.M. (1966) *The ecology and metabolism of a benthic community on an intertidal sandflat (False Bay, San Juan Island, Washington).* Ph.D. Thesis, Univ. of Washington, 250 pp.

PAMATMAT M.M. (1968) Ecology and metabolism of a benthic community on an intertidal sandflat. *Int. Revue ges. Hydrobiol.* **53,** pp. 211–298. *(Contr. Dep. Oceanogr., Univ. Wash.* No. 427.)

PANDIAN T.J. (1967) Changes in chemical composition and caloric content of developing eggs of the shrimp *Crangon crangon*. *Helgoländer wiss. Meeresunters,* **16,** pp. 216–224.

PANDIAN T.J. & SCHUMANN K.-H. (1967) Chemical composition and caloric content of egg and zoea of the hermit crab *Eupagurus bernhardus*. *Helgoländer wiss. Meeresunters.* **16,** pp. 225–230.

PARDOE G.K.C. (1969) Earth resource satellites. *Sci. Jnl.* **5,** pp. 58–67.

PARKE M. (1948) Studies on British Laminariaceae. I. Growth in *Laminaria saccharina* (L.) Lamour. *J. mar. biol. Ass. U.K.* **27,** pp. 651–709

PARKER P.S. (1966) Ocean clam survey off U.S. Middle Atlantic Coast—1963. *Comml Fish. Rev.* **28,** 3, pp. 1–9.

PARKER P.S. (1967) Clam survey, Ocean City, Maryland to Cape Charles, Virginia. *Comml Fish. Rev.* **29,** 5, pp. 56–64.

PARKER R.H. (1965) A multi-environmental sensing system developed for *in situ* study of small scale variations in sublittoral habitats. *Ocean Science and Ocean Engineering* 1965, **2,** p. 780 Mar. Tech. Soc. and Amer. Soc. Limnol. Oceanogr., Washington, D.C.

PARR INSTRUMENT COMPANY (1960) *Oxygen bomb calorimetry and oxygen bomb combustion methods*. Manual No. 130, 430 Moline Illinois. Parr Inst. Co. 56 pp.

PARRISH B.B., HEMMINGS C.C., CHAPMAN C.J., MAIN J. & LYTHGOE J. (1964) Further observations by frogmen on the reactions of fish to the seine net. ICES, C.M. 1964, *Comparative Fishing Committee,* Doc. No. 134.

PARSONS T.R. (1963) A new method for the microdetermination of chlorophyll *c* in sea water. *J. mar. Res.* **21,** pp. 164–171.

PARSONS T.R. & STRICKLAND J.D.H. (1963) Discussion of spectrophotometric determination of marine-plant pigments, with revised equations for ascertaining chlorophylls and carotenoids. *J. mar. Res.* **21,** pp. 155–163.

PÉRÈS J.M. (1960a) La 'soucoupe plongeante' engin de prospection biologique sous-marine. *Deep-Sea Res.* 7, pp. 208–214.

PÉRÈS J.M. (1960b) Le bathyscaphe, instrument d'investigation biologique des mers profondes. *Recl Trav. Stn mar. Endoume,* **33,** pp. 17–24.

PÉRÈS J.M. (1966) Le rôle de la prospection sous-marine autonome dans les recherches de biologie marine et d'océanographie biologique. *Experientia,* **22,** pp. 417–424.

PÉRÈS J.M. & PICARD J. (1949) Notes sommaires sur le peuplement des grottes sous-marines de la région de Marseille. *C.r. somm. Séanc. Soc. Biogéogr.* **26,** pp. 42–46.

PHILLIPSON J. (1964) A miniature bomb calorimeter for small biological samples. *Oikos,* **15,** pp. 130–139.

PHILLIPSON J. (1966) *Ecological Energetics*. Arnold, London, 57 pp.

PICARD J. (1954) Notes de plongées sur le tombant est de l'Ile Maïre. *Recl Trav. Stn mar. Endoume,* **13,** pp. 77–82.

PLANTE M.R. (1966) Aperçu sur les peuplements de diatomées benthiques de quelques substrats meubles du Golfe de Marseille. *Recl Trav. Stn mar. Endoume,* **56,** pp. 83–101.

PLATT R.G. (1965a) Sealab II. *Geo-mar. Technol.* **1** (8), pp. 7–13.

PLATT R.G. (1965b) Men working—200 feet below. *Geo-mar. Technol.* **1** (9), pp. 13–14.

POMEROY L.R. (1959) Algal productivity in salt marshes of Georgia. *Limnol. Oceanogr.* **4,** pp. 386–397.

POMEROY L.R. (1960) Primary productivity of Boca Ciega Bay, Florida. *Bull. mar. Sci. Gulf Caribb.* **10,** pp. 1–10.

POMEROY L.R. (1963) Isotopic and other techniques for measuring benthic primary production, in Doty, M.S. (ed.). *Proceedings of the conference on primary productivity measurement, marine and freshwater, Univ. Hawaii* 1961, pp. 97–102. U.S. Atomic Energy Commission TID 7633.

POPHAM J.D. & ELLIS D.V. (1970) A technique for describing marine sediment faunas. *Limnol. Oceanogr.* (*In press*).

POULET G. (1962) *Connaissance et Technique de la Plongée.* Editions Denoël, Paris.

PRATJE O. & SCHÜLER F. (1952) Bodenkartierung des see-gebietes Hoofden (südliche Nordsee) mit Hilfe von Grundproben und Echogrammen. *Dt. hydrogr. Z.* **5,** pp. 189–195.

PULLEN E.J., MOCK C.R. & RINGO R.D. (1968) A net for sampling the intertidal zone of an estuary. *Limnol. Oceanogr.* **13,** pp. 200–202.

RANDALL J.E. (1962) Fish service stations. *Sea Frontiers,* **8,** pp. 40–47.

RANDALL J.E. (1963) An analysis of the fish populations of artificial and natural reefs in the Virgin Islands. *Caribb. J. Sci.* **3,** pp. 31–47.

RANDALL J.E. (1964) Contributions to the biology of the queen conch, *Strombus gigas. Bull. mar. Sci. Gulf Caribb.* **14,** pp. 246–295.

REEBURGH W.S. (1967) An improved interstitial water sampler. *Limnol. Oceanogr.* **12,** pp. 163–165.

REES C.B. (1940) A preliminary study of the ecology of a mud-flat. *J. mar. biol. Ass. U.K.* **24,** pp. 185–199.

REINECK H.E. (1958) Kastengreifer und Lotröhre 'Schnepfe', Gerate zur Entnahme ungestörter, orientierter Meeresgrundproben. *Senckenbergiana leth.* **39,** pp. 42–48, 54–56.

REINECK H.E. (1963) Der Kastengreifer. *Nat. und Mus., Frankfurt-a.-M.* **93,** 3, pp. 102–108.

REISH D.J. (1959) A discussion of the importance of screen size in washing quantitative marine bottom samples. *Ecology,* **40,** pp. 307–309.

RENAUD-DEBYSER J. (1957) Description d'un carrotier adapté aux prélèvements des sables de plage. *Revue Inst. fr. Pétrole,* **12,** pp. 501–502.

RENAUD-DEBYSER J. (1963) Recherches écologiques sur la faune interstitielle des sables. (Bassin d'Arcachon, Ile de Bimini, Bahamas) *Vie Milieu,* Suppl. **15,** 157 pp.

REYS J.-P. (1964) Les prélèvements quantitatifs du benthos de substrats meubles. *Terre Vie,* **1,** pp. 94–105.

REYS J.-P., TRUE M.A. & TRUE-SCHLENZ R. (1966) Un nouvel appareil de prélèvement quantitatif de substrats meubles. *Int. océanogr. Congr.* **2,** p. 350

REYSS D. (1964) Observations faites en soucoupe plongeante dans deux vallées sous-marines de la mer Catalane: le rech du Cap et le rech Lacaze-Duthiers. *Bull. Inst. océanogr. Monaco,* **1308,** pp. 1–8.

RICHARDS F.A. with THOMPSON T.G. (1952) The estimation and characterization of plankton populations by pigment analyses. II. A spectrophotometric method for the estimation of plankton pigments. *J. mar. Res.* **11,** pp. 156–172.

RICHARDS S.W. & RILEY G.A. (1967) The benthic epifauna of Long Island Sound. *Bull. Bingham oceanogr. Coll.* **19,** pp. 89–135.

RICKER W.E. (1958) Handbook of computations for biological statistics of fish populations. *Bull. Fish. Res. Bd Can.* **119**, 300 pp.

RICKER W.E. (1968) (ed.) *Methods for Assessment of Fish Production in Fresh Waters.* I.B.P. Handbook No. 3, Blackwell, Oxford and Edinburgh, 313 pp.

RIEDL R. (1954) Unterwasserfotografie in der Biologie. In Richter, H.U. *Unterwasserfotografie.* Halle/Saale.

RIEDL R. (1961) Etudes des fonds vaseux d l'Adriatique. Méthodes et résultats. *Recl Trav. Stn mar. Endoume,* **23**, pp. 161–169.

RIEDL R. (1963) Probleme und Methoden der Erforschung des litoralen Benthos. *Verh. dt. zool. Ges. in Wien* 1962. *Zool. Anz.* **26** (Suppl.), pp. 505–567.

RIEDL R. (1966) *Biologie der Meereshöhlen.* P. Parey, Hamburg, 636 pp.

RIEDL R. (1967) Die Tauchmethode, ihre Aufgaben und Leistungen bei der Erforschung des Litorals; eine kritische Untersuchung. *Helgoländer wiss. Meeresunters.* **15**, pp. 294–352.

RILEY J.D. & HOLFORD B.H. (1965) A sublittoral survey of Port Erin Bay, particularly as an environment for young plaice. *Rep. mar. biol. Stn Port Erin,* **77**, pp. 49–53.

ROUND F.E. (1953) An investigation of two benthic algal communities in Malham Tarn, Yorkshire. *J. Ecol.* **41**, pp. 174–197.

ROUND F.E. (1960) The diatom flora of a salt marsh on the River Dee. *New Phytol.* **59**, pp. 332–348.

ROUND F.E. (1965) The epipsammon; a relatively unknown freshwater algal association. *Br. phycol. Bull.* **2**, pp. 456–462.

ROUND F.E. (1966) Persistent, vertical-migration rhythms in benthic microflora. V. The effect of artificially imposed light and dark cycles. *Proc. Vth Internat. Seaweed Symposium, Halifax. August* 25–28, 1965. Pergamon Press, Oxford and New York, pp. 197–203.

ROUND F.E. & EATON J.W. (1966) Persistent vertical-migration rhythms in benthic microflora. III. The rhythm of the epipelic algae in a freshwater pond. *J. Ecol.* **54**, pp. 609–615.

ROUND F.E. & PALMER J.D. (1966) Persistent, vertical-migration rhythms in benthic microflora. II. Field and laboratory studies on diatoms from the banks of the River Avon. *J. mar. biol. Ass. U.K.* **46**, pp. 191–214.

RUSSELL-HUNTER W.D., MEADOWS R.T., APLEY M.L. & BURKY A.J. (1968) On the use of a 'wet oxidation' method for estimates of total organic carbon in mollusc growth studies. *Proc. Malacol. Soc. Lond.* **38**, pp. 1–11.

RYTHER J.H. (1956) Photosynthesis in the ocean as a function of light intensity. *Limnol. Oceanogr.* **1**, pp. 61–70.

RYTHER J.H. & VACCARO R.F. (1954) A comparison of oxygen and ^{14}C methods of measuring marine photosynthesis. *J. Cons. perm. int. Explor. Mer,* **20**, pp. 25–34.

SACHS P.L. (1964) A tension recorder for deep-sea dredging and coring. *J. mar. Res.* **22**, pp. 279–283.

SAND R.F. (1956) New diving sled. *Comml Fish. Rev.* **18**, 10, pp. 6–7.

SANDERS H.L. (1956) Oceanography of Long Island Sound, 1952–54. X. The biology of marine bottom communities. *Bull. Bingham oceanogr. Coll.* **15**, pp. 345–414.

SANDERS H.L. (1960) Benthic studies in Buzzards Bay. III. Structure of the soft-bottom community. *Limnol. Oceanogr.* **4**, pp. 138–153.

SANDERS H.L. (1968) Marine benthic diversity: a comparative study. *Am. Nat.* **102**, pp. 243–282.

SANDERS H.L., GOUDSMIT E.M., MILLS E.L. & HAMPSON G.E. (1962) A study of the intertidal fauna of Barnstable Harbor Massachusetts. *Limnol. Oceanogr.* **7**, pp. 63–79.

SANDERS H.L., HESSLER R.R. & HAMPSON G.R. (1965) An introduction to the study of deep-sea benthic faunal assemblages along the Gay Head-Bermuda transect. *Deep-Sea Res.* **12**, pp. 845–867.

SASAKI T. (1959) The use of light attraction for traps and setnets, in Kristjonsson, H. (ed.). *Modern Fishing Gear of the World*, pp. 556–558. Fishing News (Books) Ltd., London, 607 pp.

SASAKI T. (1964) On the instruments for measuring angular distributions of underwater daylight intensity, in J.E. Tyler (ed.). *Physical aspects of light in the sea*, pp. 19–21. Hawaii: University Press

SASAKI T., OKAMI N., WATANABE S. & OSHIBA G. (1955) Measurements of the angular distribution of submarine daylight. *J. scient. Res. Inst., Tokyo*, **49**, pp. 103–106.

SASAKI T., OSHIBA G. & KISHINO M. (1966) A 4 π-underwater irradiance meter. *J. oceanogr. Soc. Japan*, **22**, pp. 123–128.

SASAKI T., WATANABE S., OSHIBA G., OKAMI N. & KAJIHARA M. (1962) On the instrument for measuring angular distribution of underwater radiance. *Bull. Jap. Soc. scient. Fish.* **28**, pp. 489–496.

SAUBERER F. (1962) Emfehlungen für die Durchführung von Strahlungsmessungen an und in Gewässern. *Mitt int. Verein. theor. angew. Limnol.* **11**, 77 pp.

SCHENCK H. Jr. & KENDALL H. (1954) *Underwater photography*. Cornell Maritime Press, Cambridge, Maryland, 110 pp.

SCHINK D.R., KENT A. & FANNING J.P. (1966) A sea-bottom sampler that collects both water and sediment simultaneously. *J. Mar. Res.* **24**, pp. 365–373.

SCHLEE J. & WEBSTER J. (1967) A computer programme for grain-size data. *Sedimentology*, **8**, pp. 45–53.

SCHLIEPER C. (ed.) (1968) *Methoden der Meeresbiologischen Forschung*. Vels Gustav Fisher Verlag Jena, 322 pp.

SCHOLANDER P.F., VAN DAM L., CLAFF C.L. & KANWISHER J.W. (1955) Micro gasometric determination of dissolved oxygen and nitrogen. *Biol. Bull. mar. biol. Lab., Woods Hole*, **109**, pp. 328–334.

SCHWENKE VON H. (1965) Über die Anwendung des Unterwasserfernsehens in der Meeresbotanik. *Kieler Meeresforsch.* **21**, pp. 101–106.

SELLMER G.P. (1956) A method for the separation of small bivalve molluscs from sediments. *Ecology*, **37**, p. 206.

SHEPARD F.P. (1965a) Diving saucer descents into submarine canyons. *Trans. N.Y. Acad. Sci.* Ser. 2, **27**, pp. 292–297.

SHEPARD F.P. (1965b) Submarine canyons explored by Cousteau's diving saucer, in Whittard, W.F. and Bradshaw, R. (ed.). *Submarine Geology and Geophysics*, pp. 303–309.

Proc. 17th Symp. Colston Res. Soc., U. Bristol, April 5th–9th 1965. Butterworths, London.

SHEPARD F.P., CURRY J.R., INMAN D.L., MURRAY E.A., WINTERER E.L. & DILL R.F. (1964) Submarine geology by diving saucer. *Science, N.Y.* **145,** pp. 1042–1046.

SIEVER R. (1962) A squeezer for extracting interstitial water from modern sediments. *J. Sed. Petrol.* **32,** pp. 329–331.

SIGSBEE C.D. (1880) *Deep-sea sounding and dredging. A description and discussion of the methods and appliances used on board the coast and geodetic survey steamer, 'Blake'.* Washington, 221 pp.

SINCLAIR A.N. (1959) Observations on the behaviour of sea urchins. *Aust. Mus. Mag.* **13,** pp. 3–8.

SKARLATO O.A., GOLIKOV, A.N. & GRUZOV E.N. (1964) Die Tauchermethode bei hydrobiologischen Untersuchungen. *Okeanologiya,* **4,** pp. 707–719.

SLOBODKIN L.B. (1962) Energy in animal ecology. *Adv. ecol. Res.* **1,** pp. 69–101.

SLOBODKIN L.B. & RICHMAN S. (1961) Calories/gm in species of animals. *Nature, Lond.* **191,** p. 299

SMITH J.E. (1932) The shell gravel deposits, and the infauna of the Eddystone grounds. *J. mar. biol. Ass. U.K.* **18,** pp. 243–278.

SMITH W. & McINTYRE A.D. (1954) A spring-loaded bottom sampler. *J. mar. biol. Ass. U.K.* **33,** pp. 257–264.

SNODGRASS J.M. (1961) Some recent developments in oceanographic instrumentation. *Union Géod. Géophys. int. Monographie* 10, pp. 83–91.

SOKAL R.R. & SNEATH P.H.A. (1963) *Principles of numerical taxonomy.* Freeman, San Francisco, Calif. 359 pp.

SØRENSEN T. (1948) A method of stabilising groups of equivalent amplitude in plant sociology based on the similarity of species content and its application to analyses of the vegetation on the Danish Commons. *Biol. Skr.* **5.** pp. 1–34.

SOULE F.M. (1951) Physical oceanography of the Grand Banks region, the Labrador Sea and Davis Strait in 1949. *Bull. U.S. Cst Guard,* **35,** pp. 49–116. (*Coll. Repr. Woods Hole oceanogr. Instn.* No. 550.)

SOUTH G.R. & BURROWS E.M. (1967) Studies on marine algae of the British Isles 5. *Chorda filum* (L.) Stackh. *Br. phycol. Bull.* **3,** pp. 379–402.

SOUTHWARD A.J. (1952) Organic matter in littoral deposits. *Nature, Lond.* **169,** p. 888.

SOUTHWARD A.J. (1965) *Life on the sea-shore.* Heinemann, London, 153 pp.

SPECTOR W.S. (1956) *Handbook of biological data.* W.B. Saunders. Philadelphia and London.

SPIESS F.N. (1966) MPL participation in Sealab II. *Univ. Calif.* AD631, 38 pp.

STAMP L.D. (1958) The land use of Britain, in Yapp, W.B. & Watson, D.J. (ed.). *The Biological productivity of Britain.* Symposia of the Inst. of Biol. **7,** pp. 1–10.

STANDLEY M.L. & PARKER P.S. (1967) Development of a submersible pumping system for a hydraulic surf clam dredge. *Comml Fish. Rev.* **29,** 6, pp. 50–55.

STANTON L.W. (1968) Comparison of several films for underwater use, in Alt, F. (ed.). *Marine Sciences Instrumentation,* **4,** pp. 369–372. Proc. 4th nat. ISA Marine Sciences Instrumentation Symp. Florida, 22–26 Jan. 1968. Plenium Press, New York.

STARCK W.A. & SCHROEDER R.E. (1965) A coral reef at night. *Sea Frontiers,* **11,** pp. 66–79.

STEELE J.H. & BAIRD I.E. (1968) Production ecology of a sandy beach. *Limnol. Oceanogr.* **13**, pp. 14–25.

STEEMANN NIELSEN E. (1952) The use of radio-active carbon (C^{14}) for measuring organic production in the sea. *J. Cons. perm. int. Explor. Mer,* **18**, pp. 117–140.

STEEMANN NIELSEN E. (1960) Dark fixation of CO$_2$ and measurements of organic productivity. With remarks on chemo-synthesis. *Physiologia Pl.* **13**, pp. 348–357.

STEEMANN NIELSEN E. & AABYE JENSEN E. (1957) Primary oceanic production, the autotrophic production of organic matter in the oceans. *Galathea Rep.* **1**, pp. 49–136.

STEPHENS K. & STRICKLAND J.D.H. (1962) Use of a thermopile radiometer for measuring the attenuation of photosynthetically active radiation in the sea. *Limnol. Oceanogr.* **7**, pp. 485–487.

STEPHENS R.W.B. (1967) Kraken. *Geo-mar. Technol.* **3**, pp. 29–30.

STEPHENS W.M. (1967) Sophisticated underwater cameras to bring depths into sharp focus. *Oceanol. int.* **2**, pp. 37–40.

STEVEN G.A. (1952) *Nets. How to make, mend and preserve them.* Routledge & Kegan Paul, London, 128 pp.

STEVENSON R.A. (1967) Underwater television. *Oceanol. int.* **2** (7), pp. 30–35.

STRICKLAND J.D.H. (1958) Solar radiation penetrating the ocean. A review of requirements, data and methods of measurement, with particular reference to photosynthetic productivity. *J. Fish. Res. Bd Can.* **15**, pp. 453–493.

STRICKLAND J.D.H. (1960) Measuring the production of marine phytoplankton. *Bull. Fish. Res. Bd Can.* **122**, 172 pp.

STRICKLAND J.D.H. & PARSONS T.R. (1965) A manual of sea water analysis (2nd ed.). *Bull. Fish. Res. Bd Can.* **125**, 203 pp.

STRICKLAND J.D.H. & PARSONS T.R. (1968) A practical handbook of seawater analysis. *Bull. Fish. Res. Bd Can.* **167**, 311 pp.

STRIDE A.H. (1963) Current-swept sea floors near the southern half of Great Britain. *Q. Jl geol. Soc. Lond.* **119**, pp. 175–199. (*Coll. Repr. natn. Inst. Oceanogr.* No. 458.)

STUBBS A.R. (1963) Identification of patterns on asdic records. *Int. hydrogr. Rev.* **40**, pp. 53–68. (*Coll. Repr. natn. Inst. Oceanogr.* No. 461.)

TALBOT F.H. (1965) A description of the coral structure of Tutia Reef (Tanganyika Territory, East Africa), and its fish fauna. *Proc. zool. Soc. Lond.* **145**, pp. 431–470.

TALLING J.F. (1960) Comparative laboratory and field studies of photosynthesis by a marine planktonic diatom. *Limnol. Oceanogr.* **5**, pp. 62–77.

TALLING J.F. & DRIVER D. (1963) Some problems in the estimation of chlorophyll-A in phytoplankton, in Doty, M.S. (ed.). *Proceedings of the conference on primary productivity measurement, marine and freshwater, Univ. Hawaii, 1963,* pp. 142–146. U.S. Atomic Energy Commission TID-7633.

TAYLOR A.H. & KERR G.P. (1941) The distribution of energy in the visible spectrum of daylight. *J. opt. Soc. Am.* **31**, pp. 3–8.

TEAL J.M. (1957) Community metabolism in a temperate cold spring. *Ecol. Monogr.* **27**, pp. 283–302.

TEAL J.M. (1960) A technique for separating nematodes and small arthropods from marine muds. *Limnol. Oceanogr.* **5**, pp. 341–342.

TEAL J.M. (1962) Energy flow in the salt marsh ecosystem of Georgia. *Ecology*, **43**, pp. 614–624.

TERRELL M. (1965) *The Principles of Diving*. Stanley Paul, London, 240 pp.

THIENEMANN A. (1931) Der Produktionsbegriff in der Biologie. *Arch. Hydrobiol*. **22**, pp. 616–622.

THORNDIKE E.M. (1967) Physics of underwater photography, in Hersey, J.B. (ed.). Deepsea photography. *Johns Hopkins oceanogr. Stud.* **3**, pp. 43–45.

THORSON G. (1957a) Sampling the benthos. *Mem. geol. Soc. Amer.* **67**, 1, pp. 61–73.

THORSON G. (1957b) Bottom communities (sublittoral or shallow shelf). *Mem. geol. Soc. Amer.* **67**, 1, pp. 461–534.

TIMOFEEVA V.A. (1962) Spatial distribution of the degree of polarization of natural light in the sea. *Izv. Akad. Nauk. S.S.S.R., Ser. Geofiz.* **6**, pp. 1843–1851.

TRASK P.D. (ed.) (1955) *Recent marine sediments: a symposium*. Am. Ass. Petrol. Geol., Tulsa, Oklahoma. 736 pp. (1955 edition: Dover Publications, Inc., New York).

TRUE M.A., REYS J-P. & DELAUZE H. (1968) Progress in sampling the benthos: the benthic suction sampler. *Deep-Sea Res.* **15**, pp. 239–242.

TRUMBULL J.V.A. & EMERY K.O. (1967) Advantages of colour photography on the continental shelf, in Hersey, J.B. (ed.). Deep-sea photography. *Johns Hopkins oceanogr. Stud.* **3**, pp. 141–143.

TURNER C.H., EBERT E.E. & GIVEN R.R. (1965) Survey of the marine environment offshore of San Elijo Lagoon, San Diego County. *Calif. Fish Game*, **51**, pp. 81–112.

TURNER C.H., EBERT E.E. & GIVEN R.R. (1966) The marine environment in the vicinity of the Orange County sanitation district's ocean outfall. *Calif. Fish Game*, **52**, pp. 28–48.

TYDEMAN G.F. (1902) Description of the ship and appliances used for scientific exploration. *Siboga Exped.* **2**, 32 pp.

TYLER J.E. (1959) Natural water as a monochromator. *Limnol. Oceanogr.* **4**, pp. 102–105.

TYLER J.E. (1968) The Secchi disc. *Limnol. Oceanogr.* **13**, pp. 1–6.

TYLER J.E. & PREISENDORFER R.W. (1962) Transmission of energy within the sea. Light, in M.N. Hill (ed.). *The Sea. Ideas and observations on progress in the study of the seas*, **1**, pp. 397–451. Interscience, N.Y. and London.

TYLER J.E. & SMITH R.C. (1966) Submersible spectroradiometer. *J. opt. Soc. Am.* **56**, pp. 1390–1396.

UHLIG G. (1966) Untersuchungen zur Extraktion der vagilen Microfauna aus marinen Sedimenten. *Zool. Anz., Suppl.* **29**, pp. 151–157.

UHLIG G. (1968) Quantitative methods in the study of interstitial fauna. *Trans. Am. microsc. Soc.* **87**, pp. 226–232.

URSIN E. (1954) Efficiency of marine bottom samplers of the van Veen and Petersen types. *Meddr Danm. Fisk.-og Havunders.* **1** (7), pp. 3–7.

URSIN E. (1956) Efficiency of marine bottom samplers with special reference to the Knudsen sampler. *Meddr Danm. Fisk.-og Havunders.* **1** (14), pp. 3–6.

URSIN E. (1960) A quantitative investigation of the echinoderm fauna of the central North Sea. *Meddr Danm. Fisk-og. Havunders.* N.S. **2** (24), 204 pp.

U.S. NAVY (1963) U.S. Navy Diving Manual. Navy Department, Washington, D.C. 460 pp.

U.S. NAVY HYDROGRAPHIC OFFICE (1962) *American Practical Navigator. An epitome of Navigation. Originally by Nathaniel Bowditch, LL.D.* U.S. Navy Hydrographic Office, Washington, 1524 pp.

VACELET J. (1967) Quelques Eponges Pharétronides et 'Silico-Calcaires' de grottes sous-marines obscures. *Recl Trav. Stn mar. Endoume,* **58,** pp. 121–132.

VALENTINE J.W. (1966) Numerical analysis of marine molluscan ranges on the extratropical north-eastern Pacific Shelf. *Limnol. Oceanogr.* **11,** pp. 198–211.

VAN CLEVE R. & TING R.Y. (1962) Ecology and taxonomy, a new bottom sampling mechanism, in Research in Fisheries 1961, T.S.Y. Koo (ed.). *Contr. Univ. Wash. College (Sch.) Fish.* **139,** pp. 29–30.

VAN CLEVE R. & TING R.Y. (1963) Sampling of demersal animal populations, in Research in Fisheries 1962. *Contr. Univ. Wash. College (Sch.) Fish.* **147,** pp. 44–47.

VAN CLEVE R., TING R.Y. & KENT J.C. (1966) A new device for sampling marine demersal animals for ecological study. *Limnol. Oceanogr.* **11,** pp. 438–443.

VEVERS H.G. (1951) Photography of the sea floor. *J. mar. biol. Ass. U.K.* **30,** pp. 101–111.

VEVERS H.G. (1952) A photographic survey of certain areas of the sea floor near Plymouth. *J. mar. biol. Ass. U.K.* **31,** pp. 215–221.

VITIELLO P. (1968) Variations de la densité du microbenthos sur une aire restreinte. *Recl. Trav. Stn mar. Endoume,* **43** (59), pp. 261–270.

VON STOSCH H.-A. (1956) Die zentrischen Grunddiatomeen. Beiträge zur Floristik und Okologie einer Pflanzengesellschaft der Nordsee. *Helgoländer wiss. Meeresunters.* **5,** pp 273–291.

VYSKREBEZOV V.B. (1962) Observations on the work of fishing trawls in the Black Sea. The methods and results of underwater investigations. (R). *Trudy okeanogr. Kom.* 14. pp. 82–88.

EL WAKEEL S.K. & RILEY J.P. (1956) The determination of organic carbon in marine muds. *J. Cons. perm. int. Explor. Mer,* **22,** pp. 180–183.

WALFORD L.A. (1946) A new graphic method of describing the growth of animals. *Biol. Bull. mar. biol. Lab., Woods Hole,* **90,** pp. 141–147.

WALKER B. (1967) A diver-operated pneumatic core sampler. *Limnol. Oceanogr.* **12,** pp. 144–145.

WALKLEY A. & BLACK I.A. (1934) An examination of the Degtjareff method for determining soil organic matter, and a proposed modification of the chromic acid titration method. *Soil Sci.* **37,** pp. 29–38.

WALSH G.E. (1967) An ecological study of a Hawaiian mangrove swamp, in *Estuaries,* ed. Lauff, G.H. Publ. 83. American Assn Adv. Sci., Washington, D.C. 1967, pp. 420–431.

WANLESS H.R. (1969) *Sediments of Biscayne Bay: distribution and depositional history.* University of Miami Institute of Marine and Atmospheric Sciences. Technical Report, 69–2, 260 pp.

WARNER G.F (1969) The occurrence and distribution of crabs in a Jamaican mangrove swamp. *J. Anim. Ecol.* **38,** pp. 379–389.

WATERMAN T.H. (1955) Polarization of scattered sunlight in deep water. *Deep-Sea Res.* Suppl. 3, pp. 426–434.

WATKIN E.E. (1941) Observations on the night tidal migrant Crustacea of Kames Bay. *J. mar. biol. Ass. U.K.* **26,** pp. 81–96.

WEBB W.L. (1950) Biogeographic regions of Texas and Oklahoma. *Ecology,* **31,** pp. 426–433.

WEBB J.E. (1958) The ecology of Lagos Lagoon. V. Some physical properties of lagoon deposits. *Phil. Trans. R. Soc.* Ser. B, **241,** pp. 393–419.

WEBB J.E. (1969) Biologically significant properties of submerged marine sands. *Proc. R. Soc.,* B, **174,** pp. 355–402.

WELLS J.B.J. & CLARK M.E. (1965) The interstitial Crustacea of two beaches in Portugal. *Revta de Biol., Lisb.* **5,** pp. 87–108.

WESTLAKE D.F. (1963) Comparisons of plant productivity. *Biol. Rev.* **38,** pp. 385–425.

WESTLAKE D.F. (1965a) Some problems in the measurement of radiation under water: a review. *Photochem. & Photobiol.* **4,** pp. 849–868.

WESTLAKE D.F. (1965b) Theoretical aspects of the comparability of productivity data. *Memorie 1st. ital. Idrobiol.* **18** Suppl., pp. 313–322.

WETZEL R.G. (1963) Primary productivity of periphyton. *Nature, Lond.* **197,** pp. 1026–1027.

WETZEL R.G. (1964) A comparative study of the primary productivity of higher aquatic plants, periphyton and phytoplankton in a large, shallow lake. *Int. Revue ges. Hydrobiol.* **49,** pp. 1–61.

WHITE FISH AUTHORITY (1964, 1970) Warp load meters for stern trawlers. *Res. Dev. Bull. White Fish Auth.* No. 6, 4 pp. (1964); No. 39, 7 pp. (1970)

WHITNEY J.R. (1938) A syringe pipette method for the determination of oxygen in the field. *J. exp. Biol.* **15,** pp. 564–570.

WICKLUND R. (1964) Underwater night observations of marine animals. *Underwat. Natst. (U.S.),* **2,** pp. 19–31.

WICKSTEAD J. (1953) A new apparatus for the collection of bottom plankton. *J. mar. biol. Ass. U.K.* **32,** pp. 347–355.

WIENS H.J. (1962) *Atoll environment and ecology.* Yale U. Press, 532 pp.

WIESER W. (1952) Investigations on the microfauna inhabiting seaweeds on rocky coasts. IV. Studies on the vertical distribution of the fauna inhabiting seaweeds below the Plymouth laboratory. *J. mar. biol. Ass. U.K.* **31,** pp. 145–174.

WIESER W. (1960) Benthic studies in Buzzards Bay. II. The meiofauna. *Limnol. Oceanogr.* **5,** pp. 121–137. (*Coll. Repr. Woods Hole oceanogr. Instn.* No. 1054.)

WIGLEY R.L. (1967) Comparative efficiencies of van Veen and Smith-McIntyre grab samplers as revealed by motion pictures. *Ecology,* **48,** pp. 168–169.

WIGLEY R.L. & EMERY K.O. (1967) Benthic animals, particularly *Hyalinoecia* (Annelida) and *Ophiomusium* (Echinodermata), in sea-bottom photographs from the continental slope, in Hersey, J.B. (ed.). Deep-sea photography. *Johns Hopkins oceanogr. Stud.* **3,** pp. 235–249.

WILLEMOËS M. (1964) A ball stoppered quantitative sampler for the microbenthos. *Ophelia,* **1,** pp. 235–240.

WILLIAMS C.B. (1964) *Patterns in the balance of nature.* Academic Press, London and New York, 324 pp.

WILLIAMS J.S. (1968) Underwater 'toolsheds'. *Hydrospace,* **1,** pp. 22–23.

WILLIAMS R.B. (1963) Use of netting to collect mobile benthic algae. *Limnol. Oceanogr.* **8,** pp. 360–361.

WILSON W.D. (1960) Equation for the speed of sound in sea water. *J. acoust. Soc. Am.* **32**, p. 1357.

WINBERG G.G. (1956) Rate of metabolism and food requirements of fishes. (Translated from the Russian.) *Fish. Res. Bd Can. Translation serie.* 194, 202 pp., 1960.

WISCHHOEFER W. & JONES R. (1968) Submersible manipulator developments. *Undersea Technol.* **9**, 3, pp. 22–25, 43.

WOLFF T. (1961) Animal life from a single abyssal trawling. *Galathea Rep.* **5**, pp. 129–162.

WORLD FISHING (1967) High productivity dredging. *World Fishing,* **16**, 7, pp. 60–64.

YAPP W.B. (1958) Introduction. In W.B. Yapp and D.J. Watson (eds.). *The Biological Productivity of Britain.* Symp. Inst. Biol. No. 7. London.

YULES J.A. & EDGERTON H.E. (1964) Bottom sonar search techniques. *Undersea Technol.* **5**, 11, pp. 29–32.

ZENKEVICH L.A. (1930) A quantitative evaluation of the bottom fauna in the sea region about the Kanin peninsula. (In Russian, with English summary.) *Trudy morsk. nauch. Inst.* **4** (3), pp. 5–23.

ZENKEVICH L.A. (1963) *Biology of the Seas of the U.S.S.R.* (Transl. by S. Botcharskaya). George Allen & Unwin Ltd., London, 955 pp.

ZEUTHEN E. (1943) A cartesian diver micro–respirometer with a gas volume of 0·1 μl. *C. R. Trav. Lab. Carlsberg,* Sér. chim. **24**, pp. 479–518.

ZINN D.J. (1969) An inclinometer for measuring beach slopes. *Mar. Biol.* **2**, pp. 132–134.

Index

324